The MINARETS of CAIRO

The
MINARETS
of
CAIRO

Islamic Architecture from
the Arab Conquest to the
End of the Ottoman Empire

DORIS BEHRENS-ABOUSEIF

with contributions by
Nicholas Warner

Photographs by
Bernard O'Kane

I.B. TAURIS
LONDON · NEW YORK

Published in 2010 by I.B.Tauris & Co Ltd
6 Salem Road, London W2 4BU
175 Fifth Avenue, New York NY 10010
www.ibtauris.com

cau

ISBN 978 1 84885 539 7

A full CIP record for this book is available from
the British Library

Design and typesetting by E&P Design, Bath
Printed and bound in China by
Everbest Printing Co Ltd

Contents

Acknowledgements

It is my pleasure to thank colleagues and friends who have been generous with their assistance during the preparation of this book. Bernard O'Kane and J.M. Rogers have commented on the final draft of the text, offering convincing and pertinent suggestions. Husam al-Din Ismail has been extremely helpful on many occasions, in particular in regard to the documentation of this study. Istvan Ormos has promptly and graciously answered many queries. Muhammad Abu Jazia has contributed the elevation of the minaret of Abu 'l-'Abbas al-Harithi in Mahalla; Salman Salem Binladen with the photographs of the minaret of Qaytbay in Medina; and Geza Fehervari with the photographs of the minaret of Zayn al-'Abidin in Bahnasa. Muhammad Abul Amayem and Kristina Davies made valuable contributions to Nicholas Warner's work.

I am also very grateful to the staff of the Supreme Council for Antiquities (SCA) in Mahalla, Hanan Muhammad Qasim, Hasan al-Mansub Ibrahim and Sa'd al-Jundi for their kind support for my fieldwork and for their hospitality. The staff of the SCA in Cairo, particularly Magdi al-Ghandur, Mustafa Hasan, Mustafa Anwar, Hamdi 'Uthman and Iman Abdulfattah, should be also thanked for their assistance in Cairo. However, in spite of this invaluable help, it was not always possible to gain access to many of the buildings described in the text, which has meant that certain details of construction and decoration could not always be checked at close range. It is hoped that any errors will be rectified by future research.

Bernard O'Kane is the principal photographer of this book, other photographic contributions are indicated in the List of Illustrations; pictures taken by Nicholas Warner or myself are indicated by our respective initials.

Nicholas Warner has made all drawings of this book, with the exception of the minaret of al-Harithi in Mahalla. A number of different sources were used as a basis for the drawings, which are indicated in the list of illustrations with full references in the bibliography. Otherwise, the major source is the Comité de Conservation des Monuments de l'Art Arabe and its successor institution, the Supreme Council of Antiquities.

I would like to thank the Fondation Max van Berchem and the Alessandro Bruschettini Foundation for contributing to the costs of the illustrations and production of this book.

List of Illustrations

Map

NORTHERN CEMETERY

BIRKAT al-AZBAKIYYA

miles
0   0.6

0   1
km

BULAQ

RIVER NILE

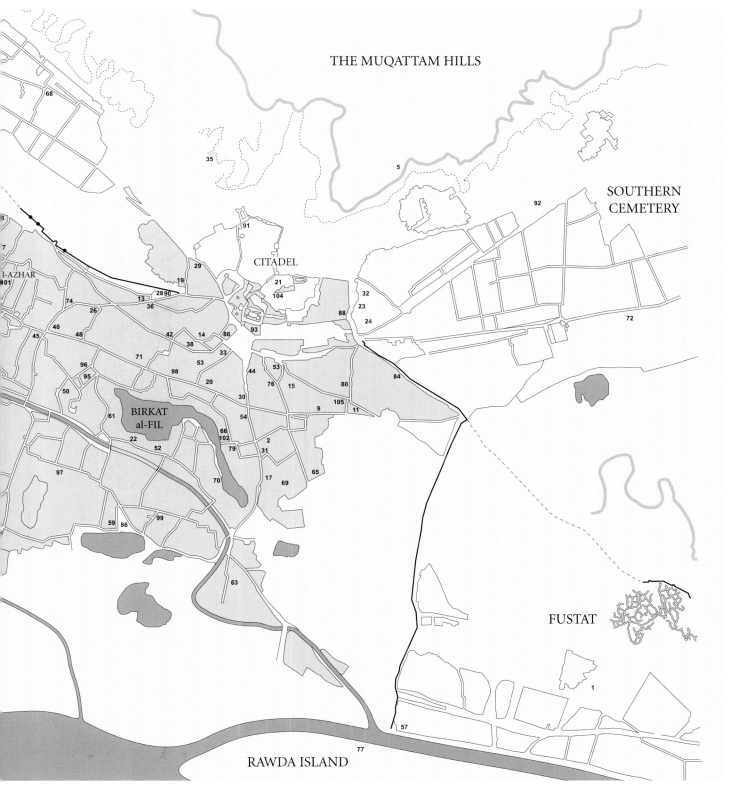

THE MUQATTAM HILLS

SOUTHERN
CEMETERY

CITADEL

l-AZHAR

BIRKAT
al-FIL

FUSTAT

RAWDA ISLAND

Map based on the Cairo map of the Description de l'Egypte showing the location of the minarets documented in this study (numbers refer to the entries of the minarets, pages 99 to 306)

© ADRIAN ROOTS

Preface

A significant number of Cairo's historic monuments were destroyed in the twentieth century. Others have suffered through neglect and inappropriate development. The historic minarets and domes, which once punctuated the skyline of the city, are being dwarfed and hidden by uncontrolled high-rise construction. More than two decades ago, in 1984, when I wrote a smaller book on this subject, it was already a matter of urgency to conduct a survey of the historic minarets of Cairo, before it became too late. At that time, the minaret of Emir Husayn was on the verge of collapse, and the Egyptian Antiquities Organisation had shored it up with scaffolding before there was time to make a good photograph of it; instead, I had to use an old photograph. Since then this minaret has disappeared altogether, along with the magnificent portal above which it stood. The minaret of Sidi Madyan is another structure that no longer stands. The double-headed minaret of Qanibay in the Nasiriyya quarter collapsed because of negligence and was entirely reconstructed. Other inadequate restorations have added their share of damage to the inheritance of the past. The aim of this book is to present a survey of the minarets of Cairo – a very specific and unique aspect of the monumental legacy of Islamic Egypt – in all their glory and variety before any more of them are lost.

Since I published *The Minarets of Cairo* in 1984, I have regretted that I did not include footnotes in the book. In subsequent years, the number of the historic minarets of Cairo has diminished while historical and art historical literature has increased and improved, as has my own knowledge. Considering the beauty of the subject, and its special significance for Cairo and Islamic art in general, I felt it necessary to treat the minarets in a more worthy manner, with a better production, an improved and more detailed text and more emphasis on the architectural technicalities of the minaret. The contribution of the architect Nicholas Warner in this project complements the new research with a documentation of the minarets as they appeared to European scholars and artists in the nineteenth century and with references to modern restoration works they have undergone. In addition to Chapter 8, he has made valuable architectural observations and amendments to the text.

Note to the Reader

This catalogue of the historic minarets of Cairo attempts to present all historically significant minarets that are extant as well as a number of minarets that have now disappeared but are documented in artistic works or photographs. The catalogue entries relating to these 'vanished' minarets are 'starred' to differentiate them from those still standing. The bases, or 'stubs', of many minarets in Cairo from the Mamluk period can still be seen attached to a variety of religious buildings; these are not included within the catalogue. Also excluded are a large number of Ottoman minarets that conform to a standard design of limited architectural interest.

The documentation of the individual minarets follows their chronological order of construction. Thus, for example, the Mamluk minarets added to the Fatimid mosque of al-Azhar do not appear in the discussion pertaining to the mosque, but are discussed individually in chronological order.

Almost all the buildings discussed are registered monuments, and their respective index numbers are given in the initial endnote for each entry. These numbers correspond to the numbers first assigned by the Comité de Conservation des Monuments de l'Art Arabe in their cumulative indices of the Islamic monuments of Cairo published in their Bulletins. These indices were later integrated into the 1950 Index of Muhammadan Monuments, published by the Survey of Egypt to accompany the two 1:5000 scale maps of the monuments of Cairo that remain a standard reference for architectural historians. The dates for the buildings in the catalogue do not

correspond to those of the Index, however, whenever subsequent scholarship proved otherwise. Primary sources, waqf documents and the chronology given by Michael Meinecke in his monograph on Mamluk architecture have been consulted for the dating. In some cases the date of construction of a minaret does not correspond to the foundation date of the rest of the building to which it is attached; the dates indicated in the list and individual minaret entries refer specifically to minarets. The bibliographic references in the entries of the individual minarets are relevant to the history of the minarets in particular, not to the monuments to which they are attached. The dates given in the text follow the Western calendar; the dual hijra-Western date is used only to document foundation and other specific dates according to the primary sources. References to drawings and images taken from libraries or copied from books are included in the list of illustrations and the bibliography.

Almost all the buildings discussed in the catalogue have been subject to restoration at one time or another in their history. The Comité de Conservation des Monuments de l'Art Arabe were particularly active in this regard. Substantial restorations have also taken place in more recent decades.

Regarding the epigraphy of the minarets, the verses of the Koran that have been read on the minarets are referred to in the minaret entries with the number of their Suras and verses. The full texts of these verses are quoted in Chapter 7 of this book, using the translation of M.A.S. Abdel Haleem. Rare Koranic inscriptions, as well as historical inscriptions, are translated within the respective entries with reference to their location on the minaret. Reading the inscriptions carved on medieval minarets is a difficult task because most of them show signs of erosion. The aim of this publication is therefore limited to identifying the Koranic text used, without checking every letter of each inscription. Missing or abbreviated words, or possible mistakes by the craftsmen carving the inscriptions, could not be recorded in this survey. The reading of the inscriptions is based on fieldwork, published material and the unpublished data of Bernard O'Kane et al.

As the elevations of the minarets presented in the catalogue are redrawn from a number of different sources, their scale is not uniform. In all drawings, the original elements of a structure are represented with a black line, while modern (late nineteenth- and twentieth-century) restorations are shown with a grey line. These restorations almost always occur at the top of the minarets. Conjectural reconstructions of missing upper sections where they have not been restored are similarly indicated with a grey line.

Stippling is used to indicate bichrome masonry. All minarets discussed in the general chapters 3 to 6 are visually documented under their resepctive entries in chapters 9 and 10.

A number of common Arabic words familiar to most readers, such as madrasa, imam, and muezzin, are not italicised, while other, less familiar, words appear in italics. Some important Arabic terms are explained in the glossary.

The designation of the building to which a minaret is attached is indicated in the title of the entry as 'mosque' meaning a Friday mosque, otherwise as 'madrasa' or 'khanqah', and in some cases as 'complex'. In the cases of minarets added to an earlier mosque or minarets having lost their original mosque, the title refers only to the minaret.

For the Arabic transliterations, I have avoided using diacritical signs in the text, except for the 'ayn ['] and the hamza [']. Otherwise the common system of transliteration applied in English academic literature has been used.

Introduction

Since the beginning of Egypt's recorded history, architecture has been a major expression of her civilisation. Two Egyptian architectural achievements were listed among the Seven Wonders of the ancient world – the Pyramids of Giza and the Lighthouse of Alexandria. The latter, a colossal tower, was still standing and in use in the early fourteenth century. Although heavily damaged and restored by that time, it was loaded with the memory of its long and almost legendary history: a memory that outlived its physical history by many centuries. Today, the fort of Sultan Qaytbay marks the place where it once stood. The sight of the Lighthouse of Alexandria and the Pyramids of Giza once signalled to medieval Egyptians the significance of the dialectic between architecture and immortality. A poem quoted by the medieval historian Maqrizi says:[1]

> *If kings wish their power to be remembered, they should speak the language of architecture.*
> *Do you not see how the pyramids remain while so many kings have vanished?*
> *Great monuments reveal the greatness of status.*

The 'language of architecture' was indeed also practised in Islamic Egypt.

The minaret emerged in Islamic architecture as an afterthought; it was not a feature that belonged to the earliest mosques. Although the Prophet Muhammad determined that the human voice, and not an instrument, should announce the times of prayer, no architectural expression of this decision is found in his mosque in Medina, built shortly after the Hijra (migration) there in AD 622. In those days Bilal, appointed by the Prophet as the first muezzin of Islam, used to climb to a high place to be heard, using an elevated structure for the call to prayer. This structure – said to be portable – was the forerunner of the minaret and had a liturgical parallel in the pulpit used by the Prophet and his successors to preach to the congregation gathered for the Friday sermon.[2]

The first minarets of Islam were not designed to be symbolic of the new religion. In Jerusalem, no minaret was constructed in the precinct of the Aqsa mosque and the entire *haram*, in spite of the strong symbolism of this site and its association with the Muslim conquest and the supremacy of the new religion. It was, rather, in Damascus that minarets grew from the corner towers of the precinct of the Roman temple, upon which the first mosque of the city stood. These provided the platforms for the call to prayer (*adhan*). We know that the Prophet's mosque in Medina, reconstructed slightly earlier by the same patron, the caliph al-Walid, was also equipped with four-corner minarets.[3] The rectangular shape of the towers in Damascus established a model for future minaret design in Syria, just as earlier on they may have inspired the design of church towers there.

The minaret is linked to a specific liturgical function, unlike that other characteristic superstructure found in Islamic architecture, the dome. Domes were one of many roofing methods used in mosques, and were not tied to a specific function. At the same time, they were associated with a variety of secular spaces. Functionally, the minaret had to be an elevated structure in order

FIG. 1

View of the old city of Cairo with minarets

to allow the muezzin to remind the townsfolk to fulfil their duty of prayer in their houses or in the mosque. In theory, the range of the human voice should dictate the optimal height of a minaret. However, in so far as architecture is an expression of power and the minaret a prominent external feature of the mosque, the design of the minaret naturally came to represent the status of its builder and the significance of the foundation to which it belonged. The construction of minarets marks the evolution of the mosque from a simple place of gathering and worship for the early community to a princely expression of piety, power and urban style.

Rectangular, circular, octagonal, hexagonal, faceted: Cairene minarets display all the profiles a tower can possibly have. Their forms have constantly evolved, creating a panoramic diversity along the skyline of the Egyptian capital. There are few, if any, other Islamic cities in the world today that could justify the dedication of a book merely to their minarets. The Egyptian minarets, however, embody a form of urban culture in their own right and as such provide a worthy subject to be explored.

Culture and Architecture of the Minaret in Cairo

FIG. 2

The muezzin performing

ONE

The Call to Prayer and the Muezzin

THE CALL TO PRAYER (ADHAN)[1]

The tradition of the *adhan* began in Medina one year after the Hijra, when the Muslim community was still in the process of being formed. Early Arab historians relate that after a period during which the wooden clapper (*naqus*) of the Christians had been in use, the Prophet Muhammad and his companions agreed to establish a call to prayer that would be distinct from that of the Christians and the Jews. It was then decided that the Muslim call to prayer should be performed by the human voice. Some believe that the *adhan*, which literally means 'announcement', was divinely revealed. The announcement of prayer is mentioned in the Koran in Sura 5: 58 and Sura 62: 9. A number of *hadith*s further emphasise the sanctity of the *adhan*. It is believed that during the call to prayer the doors of Heaven are open, and that God will not reject the prayers and invocations spoken at this moment. Bilal, a freed black slave of Abu Bakr, was the first and most prominent muezzin of the Prophet's time. He was called '*sayyid al-mu'adhdhinin*' or the 'lord of the muezzins', but he was not the only one. Another contemporary muezzin in Medina was Ibn Umm Maktum, and, as the muezzin for the shrine of Mecca, the Prophet appointed Abu Mahdhura, who was succeeded by his descendants. Bilal continued to perform the call to prayer during the lifetime of the Prophet and the caliphate of Abu Bakr and he also accompanied 'Umar in his conquest of Damascus, where he performed the first *adhan*. Known for his beautiful voice, Bilal's status is often cited by Muslim scholars who defend the practice of music in Islam.

Within Sunnism there are, as always in religious practice, divergent opinions regarding certain aspects of the call to prayer and related subjects. These are recorded in manuals of jurisprudence for each of the four *madhhab*s, or orthodox rites (Maliki, Hanbali, Hanafi and Shafi'i). The differences in the form of the call to prayer between the four Sunni rites are, however, slight, and usually concern the pattern of repetition of phrases and the emphasis of certain passages over others. Some puritanical theologians, including the Hanbalis, reject the melodious performance of the call to prayer, as they reject the melodic recitation of the Koran and the gilding of its manuscripts. The Hanafis approve of the *taghanni* or melodic rendition of the call to prayer. The differences between the Sunni and the Shi'i call to prayer are, however, more pronounced, and bear witness to deeper doctrinal division. Puritans of all schools advocated that ritual matters should be dealt with exactly in the same manner as in the Prophet's time or in the early days of the Muslim community. This period was viewed as the 'ideal' age of Islam and all departures from common practice were considered to be unwelcome innovations or *bid'a*. This attitude, however, has never prevailed in Islamic culture. Although the minaret, like the mihrab, the *minbar* and the decoration of mosques, did not exist in the Prophet's time, the qualitative and quantitative expansion of Islam resulted in a corresponding cultural elaboration of this architectural element.

Although the call to prayer is a form of worship in and of itself, and should be performed before the obligatory five daily prayers, it has a different status from the actual prayer ritual. The call to prayer is *sunna*, that is, it is recommended, not obligatory (*fard*). Of the four orthodox rites, it is only the Hanbali which claims that the call to prayer is a *fard kifaya* – obligatory for the Muslim community as a whole but not for each individual, meaning that the community has the duty to assign someone to perform it.

The traditional Sunni *adhan* consists of seven phrases, of which phrase one is called the *takbir* (performing 'Allah is Great'), phrases two and three are called the *shahada* (testimony of faith), and phrases four and five are called *tathwib* (asking for God's *thawab* or favour):

1. *Allahu Akbar* ('Allah is the almighty'), intoned four times.
2. *Ashhadu alla ilaha illa'llah* ('I testify that there is no deity other than God'), intoned twice.
3. *Ashhadu anna Muhammadan rasul Allah* ('I testify that Muhammad is the Messenger of God'), intoned twice.
4. *Hayya 'ala 'l-salat* ('Come to prayer'), intoned twice.
5. *Hayya 'ala 'l-falah* ('Come to salvation'), intoned twice.
6. *Allahu Akbar* ('God is almighty') intoned twice.
7. *La ilaha illa'llah* ('There is no deity other than God'), intoned once.

In addition to these seven phrases, there are two further phrases added to the end of the morning call to prayer. These are:

8. *Al-salat khayr min al-nawm* ('Prayer is better than sleep'), intoned twice between the fifth and sixth phrases.
9. *Al-salat wa'l-salam 'alayka ya rasul Allah* ('Benediction and Peace upon you, O Messenger of God'), intoned once at the end of the morning prayer by the Hanafis.

Though primarily a call to prayer, historically the *adhan* also had important political associations:

FIG. 3

Musical notation of the adhan

EDWARD W. LANE

additional phrases varied with regimes. Bilal used to add to the conclusion of the *adhan* the phrase *al-salat wa'l-salam 'alayka ya rasul Allah wa rahmat Allah wa barakatuh* or 'Benediction and peace on you, O Messenger of God, and the mercy of God and his blessing'. After the Prophet's death, he addressed the benediction to Abu Bakr, the first caliph, as *khalifat rasul Allah* or 'successor of the Messenger of God'. 'Umar and each caliph after him was addressed as *amir al-mu'minin* or 'commander of the faithful'. The Umayyad caliphs used to add to the *adhan* a tribute to the caliph and his main officials, a custom that was abolished by the Abbasids. The Fatimids maintained the tribute to the caliph after the dawn *adhan*. Salah al-Din replaced the tribute to the caliph with a tribute to the Prophet, *al-salam 'alayka ya rasul Allah* or 'Peace on you, O Messenger of God'. This practice continued henceforth into the early Mamluk period.

The Shi'i *adhan* includes the phrase *hayy 'ala khayr al-'amal* or 'Come to the best of works' inserted between the fifth and the sixth phrases. This phrase became emblematic of Shi'i rule. When the Fatimids, who followed Isma'ili Shi'i doctrine, conquered Egypt, they modified the *adhan* accordingly. The first time the Shi'i *adhan* was announced in Egypt was on the 8th of Jumada I 359/970 when Jawhar al-Siqilli, the Fatimid general, went to the Friday prayer at the mosque of Ibn Tulun. On the following Friday, the same formula was pronounced at the 'Amr mosque, and other mosques later followed suit.

In 1009–10 the Fatimid caliph al-Hakim abolished the phrase 'Come to the best of works', and replaced it with *al-salat khayr min al-nawm* or 'prayer is better than sleep'. The original Shi'i call to prayer was, however, reinstated in 1012 by al-Hakim himself. In 524/1130 the Fatimid vizir Abu 'Ali, the grandson of Badr al-Jamali and a fanatical adherent of the Imami or Twelver Shi'i doctrine rather than the Isma 'ili doctrine espoused by the Fatimids, introduced a similar, short-lived change he ordered that the phrase 'Come to the best of works' should be omitted from the call to prayer altogether. Two years later Abu 'Ali was murdered, and the Isma'ili *adhan* was reinstated in Egypt.

After Salah al-Din had overthrown the Fatimids, he restored the Sunni call to prayer according to the Shafi'i rite, as Nur al-Din al-Zanki had previously done in Syria. Although Mecca was attached politically to Egypt, the Shi'i Zaydiyya sect of South Arabia were still very influential there so that the use of the Shi'i call to prayer continued in the holy city until 702/1302. At this point, the Emir Burulji, who was sent to Mecca as the Commander of the Pilgrimage by the Mamluk sultan al-Nasir Muhammad, forbade this practice and reintroduced the Sunni call to prayer there.

In the Mamluk period the tribute to the Prophet included in the dawn call to prayer was sometimes repeated in the Thursday evening call to prayer as well. This occurred in 760/1359 by order of the *muhtasib*, or market inspector, of Cairo. Three decades later, in 791/1389, during the reign of Sultan Hajji, a Sufi, having seen the Prophet in a dream, suggested to the *muhtasib* the addition of the same phrase to every call to prayer. His suggestion was adopted. The historian Maqrizi severely criticised this innovation with the argument that it was a *bid'a*, or a heretical innovation, introduced moreover by an ignorant market inspector with a long record of corruption. Eventually the classical *adhan* without this final clause was restored, and ever since the formula has remained unchanged in Egypt.

In addition to performing the call to prayer, the muezzin also had other duties. He had to carry out the *tabligh*, the repetition of the *takbir* (*Allahu akbar* – the first phrase of the *adhan*) pronounced by the imam during prayer for the benefit of those who were too far back in the mosque to hear it. Both the *tabligh* and a second *adhan*, called *iqama* and performed within the mosque, usually took place on the *dikka*, a raised platform located some distance in front of the mihrab. In large Mamluk mosques these *dikka*s stand in the prayer hall, and are built of stone or marble and supported by columns. Endowment deeds describe this structure as the *dikkat al-mu'adhdhinin* (bench of the muezzins). At the mosque of al-Nasir Muhammad in the Citadel, however, the *dikka* takes the form of a stone balcony located above the entrance, and is reached by a door off the staircase of the minaret. In later, smaller, covered mosques, the *dikka* was similarly set in the wall opposite the mihrab and reached by an inner staircase, but was made of timber. The mosque of Ibn Tulun originally had a fountain in the centre of its courtyard under a domed canopy on columns from where the second call to prayer was given. This was later supplemented by a more traditional *dikka* platform raised on marble columns within the main prayer hall.

Maqrizi reports that Ibn Tulun introduced the *takbir* and *tasbih*, or recitations of *Allahu akbar* and *subhan Allah*, and other invocations and recitations to be performed by the muezzins from minarets during the night. The historian adds that this custom still prevailed in his own day (the early fifteenth century). Ibn al-Hajj, a thirteenth-century scholar of the Maliki rite, wrote a long list of customs practised at that time by the muezzins in Egypt that he considered should be prohibited as heretical innovations. This list provides a useful guide to practices that were then current. They included the muezzin's standing at the mosque door to perform additional calls to prayer, the addition of Koranic recitations to the dawn call to prayer, and nocturnal recitations. Ibn al-Hajj also rejected the employment of muezzins at funerals to perform eulogies for the deceased and to walk in the cortège reciting *takbir*s, that is, chanting *Allahu akbar*. Moreover, he condemned the performance of the call to prayer in concert by more than one muezzin. However, his puritanical Maliki views were far from being implemented in Cairo. Royal mosques in the Mamluk period employed a number of muezzins, who, working in shifts, would perform the royal call to prayer, or *adhan sultani*, in chorus.[2] The mosque of Sultan al-Nasir Muhammad at the Citadel, had eighteen muezzins.[3] The funerary complex of Sultan al-Ghawri employed sixteen muezzins, as indicated in the endowment deed. The mosque of Sultan Hasan was supposed to have had forty-eight muezzins to perform in two shifts of six muezzins for each of the originally planned four minarets. As only two minarets were eventually built, the number of employed muezzins may have been half this number if not less, as the endowment of the mosque was subsequently reduced after the sultan's death. Such large numbers were not unusual: Ibn Battuta relates that there were seventy muezzins appointed to the Great Mosque of Damascus.[4] Royal palaces also had muezzins: a practice begun in Egypt by Ibn Tulun, who employed twelve Koran readers at his palace to perform the call to prayer within the palace and recite doxologies afterwards.[5] The Fatimid imam-caliphs also appointed muezzins to recite the *adhan* at the different gates of their palace.[6]

Egypt has cultivated a particularly musical and captivating call to prayer (in parallel with its melodic tradition of Koranic recitation), which is the most admired and widely imitated throughout the Muslim world. Pious Muslims often stop what they are doing when they hear the *adhan* and repeat the phrase 'God is almighty'. The characteristic Egyptian melody for the call to prayer is rendered in the musical mode *maqam rast* and was first transcribed by the British Orientalist Edward Lane in the nineteenth century (fig. 3).[7] Evliya Çelebi, who was himself an occasional muezzin,[8] reports that the dawn *adhan* performed at the Citadel, the residence of the Ottoman governor, was in the mode *maqam sika*.[9] Lane wrote 'there is a simple and solemn melody in their chants which is very striking, particularly in the stillness of the night'. Khumarawayh, Ibn Tulun's son, who led an otherwise licentious lifestyle, would order his singers and musicians to interrupt their own performances during the call to prayer, at which point he would put his wine glass on the floor and listen.[10] Another ruler described as debauched, the young Mamluk sultan al-Muzaffar Hajji (r. 1346–7), showed less reverence to the call to prayer when he ordered the muezzins to stop their performance while his homing pigeons were flying in order not to disturb them![11]

THE MUEZZIN

The first muezzin of Egypt was Abu Muslim al-Muradi, a companion of the Prophet.[12] 'Amr Ibn al-'As, the conqueror and first Muslim governor of Egypt, appointed together with Abu Muslim nine other muezzins for the day and night shifts at the mosque of 'Amr in Fustat. Later on, Abu Muslim's brother, Sharhabil, became the chief muezzin at the mosque and was the first to perform the call to prayer from a minaret, which at the time of his brother did not exist. Today, although minarets continue to be an integral feature of mosque architecture, the

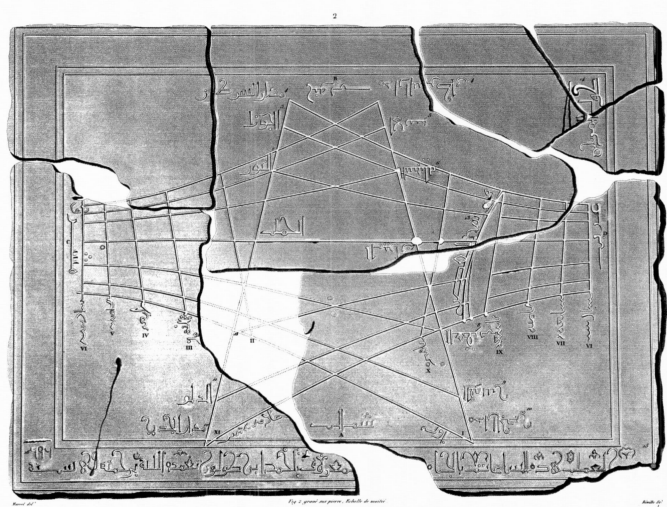

INSCRIPTION ET CADRAN KOUFIQUES DE LA MOSQUÉE DE TOULOUN.

FIG. 4

A now vanished sundial at the mosque of Ibn Tulun

DESCRIPTION DE L'ÉGYPTE

importance of the muezzin has greatly diminished. The call to prayer is transmitted by the muezzin through loudspeakers from inside the mosque or is even pre-recorded. When performing the call to prayer within the mosque the muezzin is supposed to face Mecca, then turn to the right and to the left. On the minaret, he was supposed to turn to all sides.

According to Islamic law, a muezzin must be an adult male who is pious, trustworthy, educated in law and theology and familiar enough with elementary astronomy to enable him to know the phases of the moon and the planets. He should be capable of calculating the times of prayer, which are established according to the sun's position, at dawn (*fajr*), noon (*zuhr*), in the afternoon (*'asr*), at sunset (*maghrib*) and in the evening (*'isha*). The stringent qualifications for a muezzin may not have always been enforced, for there exists an old tradition, which Ibn Hanbal rejected, of keeping cocks to wake up worshippers for the dawn prayer.[13] In this context, the historian Suyuti tells an interesting anecdote about cocks being kept on the roof of the mosque of Ibn Tulun to wake the timekeepers (*muwaqqit, miqati*) and muezzins in the morning. When the Mamluk sultan Lajin refurbished the mosque and set up a new endowment there for teaching and various other services, he found that the endowment deed that had been drafted included a fund for the maintenance of cocks on the mosque's roof. He is reported to have exclaimed: 'Stop this! Don't let people make fun of us!'[14]

The Hanafi rite permits women to perform the call to prayer on condition that their voice does not arouse sexual desire.[15] The Imami or Twelver Shi'a doctrine, however, takes a more flexible attitude, allowing both juvenile males and adult women (especially for a female audience) to perform the call to prayer.[16] Bilal and Ibn Umm Maktum were selected by the Prophet for the beauty of their voices. The latter, indeed, had been chosen for the task from among twenty competitors. Beauty of voice is therefore seen to be a requirement for a muezzin, and this attribute is also stipulated in the endowment or *waqf* deeds of mosques. His voice should be far-reaching and yet sound without strain. Chronicles and biographical encyclopaedias have given special acknowledgement to muezzins gifted with a particularly fine voice.

As mentioned, The muezzin often also served as the timekeeper (*muwaqqit, miqati*) for a mosque, which implies that he had some knowledge of astronomy. Important mosques usually had their own timekeeper, who was appointed especially to calculate the times of prayer using sundials and astrolabes. The timekeeper of al-Azhar in the nineteenth century had six sundials at his disposal, and it was usually from al-Azhar's minarets that the first call for each of the daily prayers would be given, followed by all the other mosques of the city.[17] In earlier times at Fustat, this timekeeping function was fulfilled by the mosque of 'Amr.[18] Sundials were either separately carved on slabs of marble that were attached to the side of one wall of a mosque (such as that of the mosque of Ibn Tulun, now lost) or directly inscribed on the minarets themselves, such as on the minarets of the mosques of Manjaq and Bashtak. In some cases, the muezzin who served as timekeeper in a mosque that employed a number of muezzins was appointed chief muezzin (*ra'is al-mu'adhinin*). A man called Ahmad Ibn Muhammad al-Baktimuri, who died in 1398, is mentioned as chief muezzin and timekeeper.[19] It is not clear what the exact responsibility of the chief muezzin was; by analogy with the roles of the chief physician and chief architect at the Mamluk court, he may have been in charge of training muezzins and admitting new candidates to the profession.

In addition to calling the *adhan* from the minaret, the muezzin would also have delivered a second call, called the *iqama*, from inside the mosque just before prayer. His employment may have extended further to the recitation of religious poetry and liturgical chanting. During the month of Ramadan, the muezzin was also in charge of extinguishing the lantern at the summit of the minaret to announce the beginning of the day and the period of fasting, and lighting it again at nightfall.

Raised up on his minaret, the muezzin stood in the delicate position of overlooking people's homes, and thus their private lives. Until the nineteenth century, mosques in Cairo, along with markets, fell under the supervision of the *muhtasib*, who was also in charge of moral behaviour in the city. According to the *muhtasib* manuals, only one muezzin was allowed to ascend the minaret, and then only at times of prayer. He was also required to take an oath, before performing his duties, not to look into neighbouring houses.[20] Historians relate that the market inspector of Kufa, not satisfied with this oath, ordered the muezzins to ascend minarets with blindfolds. Ibn al-Hajj, writing with reference to Cairo, expressed similar concern and recommended that minarets should not be built higher than the surrounding dwellings, and even that they should not be erected at all in the vicinity of houses.[21] He also rejected the employment of young unmarried muezzins.[22] Blindness being a widespread affliction in the past, the career of muezzin provided a suitable employment opportunity for blind men. High moral standards were expected in the muezzin's personal life. It is recorded that a muezzin of the madrasa of Sultan Barsbay at the 'Anbariyyin was severely punished by God for his addiction to liquor, which had often led him to call the *adhan* while drunk. During one drunken slumber, he dreamed that Sultan Barsbay was beating him on the feet with a whip. When he awoke, he saw and felt the evidence of this punishment on his body and, despite his prayers for forgiveness, he remained disabled until his death.[23]

Historically, there has been a scholarly debate regarding whether muezzins should be remunerated for their services or should work on a voluntary basis. Imam Shafi'i, for one, preferred the latter.[24] Eventually consensus had it that muezzins were entitled to regular payment.[25] The four muezzins appointed to the Prophet's mosque at Medina by 'Uthman, the third Caliph, were the first to receive salaries. *Waqf* documents always indicate the muezzin's salary. Its relation to the stipends of the students and Sufis, or the salaries of other staff members, varied greatly between mosques. Generally,

the salary was additional to the stipend or salary the muezzin received for another function he may have held in the same mosque. A muezzin could also have a second profession in the neighbourhood of the mosque to which he was attached. However, because punctuality was mandatory, it is specified that he should not work as a muezzin in more than one mosque at the same time. Apart from wages, some endowment deeds include the provision of woollen caps for the muezzins to keep their heads warm in winter during the performance of the call to prayer. One remarkable muezzin was Abu 'l-Raddad (d. 892), who was employed at the mosque of 'Amr in Fustat but was also in charge of designing the inner decoration of the Nilometer on the island of Rawda, ordered by the Abbasid caliph al-Mutawakkil in 861. In a rare and detailed account, Abu 'l-Raddad describes how he selected the Koranic inscriptions and planned their layout in conjunction with the decoration.[26] Abu 'l-Raddad must also have been in charge of watching and registering the rise of the Nile during the flood, because all subsequent men who assumed this task were called Ibn Abu 'l-Raddad.

An interesting Egyptian muezzin was Muhammad al-N-sh-bi or N-sh-ni,[27] who between the years 1480 and 1506 spent much of his time on the minaret of the funerary complex of Sultan Qaytbay, in the great cemetery that lies immediately to the east of Cairo. Here, he carved the stone door-jambs and inner walls of the minaret's shaft with numerous inscriptions containing Koranic texts, Sufi maxims and pious invocations, which he signed and dated. One of these simply reads: 'Death must be'.

FIG. 5

Balcony for the call to prayer at the mosque/zawiya of ʿAbd al-Rahman Katkhuda

TWO

Functions and Use of the Minaret

The variety of uses that minarets were put to is indicated by the three terms in Arabic that are commonly used to designate the minaret. The first is *mi'dhana*, which indicates its function as the place from where the *adhan* is given. The second is *sawma'a*, which occurs mainly in North African and Muslim Spanish terminology. This word is also used to designate the hermitage of a Christian monk, and means 'silo' in modern Arabic. The third term, *manar* or *manara*, was widely used in Egypt in medieval sources, documents and inscriptions. Literally meaning 'a place from which light (*nur*) or fire (*nar*) is emitted', it was also a word used to designate a lighthouse or a watchtower. This may go back to the tradition of pre-Islamic towers and in particular to the famous Lighthouse of Alexandria, erected by Alexander the Great's Ptolemaic successor Philadelphus II. Maqrizi even refers to ancient Egyptian obelisks as *manar* because of the electrum coating their tips, which reflected the sun's rays.[1]

In the Fatimid period, the term *manara* described, besides the minaret, an illumination device that people used to parade on festive occasions. Such *manara*s have been mentioned in the description of the imam-caliph's palace in the centre of Cairo, where they were stored alongside ceremonial tents.[2] Maqrizi reports that an oratory in the cemetery, the *masjid* of the 'Azim al-Dawla, had in front of it 'a high copper Greek *manara* with branches' (*manara rumiyya nahas dhat al-sawa'id*). This object was so tall that the branches of a tree standing nearby had to be cut to make room for it. The description would seem to apply to a monumental branched candelabrum. Elsewhere in his text, Maqrizi mentions a portable copper Greek *manara* with branches to hold candles that was used during the Fatimid illumination festivals held in the month of Rajab.

Manar was also a word that was employed symbolically: 'to raise the *manar* of Islam' meant to promote the triumph of the faith. An inscription of the Ayyubid period on the minaret at the shrine of al-Husayn states that it was built 'to please God and to raise the *manar* of Islam' (*taqarruban ila 'llah wa raf'an li manar al-islam*).[3] The phrase was also used of persons: 'may God raise his *manar*' means 'may God succour him'. A sixteenth-century shadow play entitled *al-Manar* provides an interesting confluence of the symbolic and physical roles of the Lighthouse of Alexandria, represented as a fort that Muslim soldiers had to defend against Christian raids.[4] A shadow-puppet related to this play, and datable to the later eighteenth century, shows the Lighthouse as a three-tiered structure being defended from attack. Such symbolic meanings for the term *manar* imply recognition of functions beyond the merely practical, as the historian Ibn Khaldun suggests in a eulogy he wrote for the Mamluk sultans: 'they erected mosques for prayer and *adhan* … Minarets were raised for redemption and prayer and for the promulgation of the tenets of faith.'[5]

The minaret is essentially a herald of worship. Of the five pillars of Islam, it is closely associated, apart from prayer itself, with the five daily proclamations, within the call to prayer, of the *shahada* or the duty of witnessing that 'there is no deity but God and that Muhammad is the prophet of God'. As this proclamation is quintessential to the faith of Islam it confers a sacral significance on the minaret, which functions as the transmitter between the community in and around the mosque and God.

Reaching to the sky of the medieval city to broadcast the call to prayer, minarets add a spiritual dimension to the urban topography. The cumulative effect of the numberless minarets in Cairo diffusing their *adhan* in chorus, five times a day, must have had a powerful impact on the city. A French consul in Cairo in the early eighteenth century, de Maillet, reckoned that with an average of two muezzins per mosque – Cairo having approximately 300 mosques – the call to prayer in the city resonated from a chorus of 600 voices. This figure was doubled on festive occasions, when the number of muezzins was increased to four per mosque, making a total of 1,200 voices rising from the minarets of Cairo. Monsieur de Maillet was not very pleased by the magnitude of the *adhan*, especially when it coincided with the time of his sleep![6] Also, visually, the minaret contributed to the urban aesthetic of density that is specific to Cairo, where mosques ranged 'wall to wall and minaret to minaret', as noted in the seventeenth century by the Ottoman traveller Evliya Çelebi.[7] The cluster of minarets of the sultans al-Salih Najm al-Din, al-Zahir Baybars,[8] al-Mansur Qalawun, al-Nasir Muhammad and al-Zahir Barquq that marked the heart of the old city along the Bayn al-Qasrayn Street is a remarkable and unparalleled urban phenomenon that could not have been merely motivated by the necessity to summon people to prayer. This could be fulfilled by simpler means; the small balcony projecting from the façade of the small mosque (*zawiya*) founded by Emir 'Abd al-Rahman Katkhuda in 1729 at Mughrabilin Street, which must have been dedicated to the call to prayer, shows that a tower was not always indispensable to that end, in particular when the street already included a number of religious buildings with minarets (figs 5–6).

On festive occasions, the minaret became an urban jewel. Besides the Ramadan lamp that signalled the time of fasting, mentioned above, minarets used to be, and still are, extensively decorated with lights during the holy month and on other religious occasions such

as the *mawlid al-nabi*, or Birthday of the Prophet. Endowment deeds and chronicles frequently mention the use of wooden brackets fixed on the uppermost sections of minarets for the purpose of hanging lamps. Some examples of these brackets can still be seen today attached to the stone or plastered brick bulbs that often crown a minaret (fig. 30). Other, non-religious but significant, occasions were also celebrated by artificial illumination. When the construction of the minaret of Barquq at al-Azhar was completed in 1397, its shaft was covered with lights to celebrate the occasion.[9] The historian Jabarti also describes how, after the final departure of the French in 1801 from Cairo, 'for seven consecutive nights the minarets were lit up'.[10] In medieval Cairo miniature minarets were made for festive occasions to emit light and fireworks. The chronicler Ibn Iyas mentions a light festival hosted by Sultan al-Ghawri on the Nile's shore with fireworks and illuminations. The naphtha used for the celebration was borne in fifty 'citadels' and sixty 'minarets' (*mi'dhana*) in a procession accompanied by the music of drums, pipes and cymbals, to be lit in front of the sultan's palace on the island of Rawda.[11]

European visitors in the Mamluk period were struck by the appearance of the minarets at night during Ramadan, and, again, by the cumulative effect of their lights: 'When the sun goes down,' wrote the German pilgrim Bernhardt von Breydenbach,[12] who saw Cairo in the late fifteenth century during the reign of Sultan Qaytbay, 'they light many lamps on the towers of their mosques … While watching this spectacle we were struck by the sight of towers sparkling with light, each of them lit with numerous lamps at three levels. Thanks to those lights, the city has the splendour of day.' Another traveller of the same period, the Franciscan Friar Felix Fabri, was even more specific in his comments when he wrote:

An amazing multitude of lamps was burning on top of the towers, so that the city seemed to be on fire; there was also a crowd of priests shouting on the towers. It was like this every night during the month of fasting. The lamps are hung with wooden sticks and lifted with wheels. They carry a small cover so that the wind does not extinguish the flame. Some minarets have forty or sixty lamps and some twenty,

FIG. 6

The mosque/zawiya of ʿAbd al-Rahman Katkhuda

according to the endowment made to the mosque. In any case, there are enough lamps on the minarets to give light to the whole quarter during the night. Sometimes at night, I would climb the roof of a house and I would shudder at the ardent fire of the lamps. A Christian with some experience said that no Christian king would ever be able to afford so much money as the fortune spent alone on the oil of the city.[13]

During the month of Ramadan, the minaret assumed a significant practical role, with the presence of a lantern at its top that was lit at the time of fast-breaking at dusk and extinguished at dawn to signal that the time of fasting was to commence. This custom was practised throughout the Muslim world, also within the shrine of Mecca.[14] Today electric lamps fulfil this function.

The use of an elevated structure adds a public, and hence a political, dimension to the proclamation of faith. At least since the reign of Ibn Tulun, if not earlier, the Lighthouse of Alexandria, the symbol of the city and the first thing seen by mariners sailing towards Egypt, was equipped with an oratory at its summit. This oratory constituted an effective signal to travellers that they were approaching Muslim territory. Minarets were also used to broadcast major public events. The nineteenth-century historian 'Ali Mubarak records that when an important religious figure died, the muezzins of al-Azhar as well as of the other mosques announced his death by performing funerary prayers from the minarets.[15] The minaret was also used to communicate political statements, of both a negative and positive nature. The foundation deed of the Ottoman emir Ibrahim Agha refers to an endowment made on the Mamluk mosque of Qijmas al-Ishaqi to the effect that every morning the muezzins would perform prayers from the minaret for the well-being of the Ottoman sultan, his soldiers, those dwelling in the quarter and for Ibrahim Agha himself.[16] On the negative side, the Syrian historian Ibn Tulun, writing at the end of the Mamluk period, mentions a group of angry men shouting the *takbir*, that is to say calls of '*Allahu akbar*' from the minarets of the Great Mosque of Damascus in protest against the authorities. This also happened in cases where a public official oppressed the innocent, a man was unjustly beaten, or when there was a shortage of sugar in the markets.[17] In Cairo during the late eighteenth century, Jabarti reports similar protests as having taken place at the minarets of the Azhar mosque.[18]

A scholar of the French Expedition to Egypt at the close of the eighteenth century once described the minaret as the bell-tower of the Muslims, 'le clocher des Mohametans',[19] which is not a totally unsuitable parallel. By announcing the time of prayer, the muezzin also effectively announces the time of day. In an age before the clock was a common commodity, people often regulated their affairs and made their appointments according to the prayer schedule, after or before one of the *adhan*s. Thus, while indicating the moment of prayer for those who pray in their homes and calling those in the street to come and pray in the mosque, the minaret also came to fulfil the function of a speaking clock that could be heard by all.

The early minaret in many Islamic countries clearly borrowed architectural forms as well as functions from its pre-Islamic predecessors. According to Qalqashandi the great minaret of the Umayyad mosque in Damascus had been one link in a chain of towers connecting Mesopotamia, Syria and Egypt with a system of fire signals to give the alarm in case of a Mongol attack.[20]

Outside urban centres, minarets functioned as watchtowers, as has been suggested for the Upper Egyptian Fatimid period minarets.[21] The remarkable height of some Egyptian provincial minarets cannot be justified by their urban environment, but must derive from their use as lighthouses and watchtowers. Nineteenth-century views and photographs of the Nile valley depict such minarets as being close to major routes along the river.

Because of its elevated position near the sky, the finial of the minaret, together with that of the dome, came to have many symbolic and legendary associations. Some finials were described as rotating with the wind. The Lighthouse of Alexandria, for example, is described in ancient texts as having copper statues at its summit, one of which would roar to warn of approaching enemies, and another representing a man pointing with his finger to the sun and following its movement.[22] A mounted lancer at the top of the dome of the Abbasid caliph's palace in Baghdad was also reported to have been able to rotate towards the direction of approaching enemies. The minaret of the mosque of Ibn Tulun was crowned by a finial in the form of a boat, which seems to have been used as a bird feeder, copying a similar finial that crowned the dome of the tomb of Imam Shafi'i. With reference to the latter, Edward Lane recorded a belief that its movements provided good or bad omens.[23] The same belief is mentioned in connection with the crescent surmounting the shrine dome of Shaykh Ibrahim al-Dasuqi,[24] which provided auguries by its movements.

The Egyptians added a sportive note to the function of their minarets, using them as a platform for various acrobatic feats. In the Fatimid period, the caliph al-Mustansir (1036–94) used to pass by the mosque of Ibn Tulun each year in a procession from Qahira to Fustat on the day of the great festival of the Opening of the Canal to celebrate the Nile flood. As the caliph passed in front of the mosque of Ibn Tulun, an acrobat dressed in the costume of a cavalier greeted him from the summit of the minaret. The acrobat then slid down a rope stretched between the finial and the street while performing pirouettes until he landed at the caliph's feet.[25] In the year 1426, a man described by Maqrizi as a 'converted European in a soldier dress' gave a stunning performance using one of the major minarets of Cairo. He danced on a rope stretched between the summit of the northern minaret of Sultan Hasan and the Ashrafiyya palace in the Citadel. The sultan al-Ashraf Barsbay attended the spectacle and a huge crowd gathered in the city to watch what Maqrizi describes as 'one of those extraordinary events that cannot be believed unless witnessed'.[26] Afterwards, the sultan bestowed a robe of honour on the acrobat and encouraged his emirs to reward him, which they did generously. Al-Sayrafi who reported the same episode, describes the man as a Circassian Mamluk named Yashbak, who had spent some time in Cyprus before he migrated that year to Egypt and converted to Islam.[27] Shortly afterwards, an Egyptian began to imitate these feats. He first practised on a rope stretched between two palm trees and gradually improved until he was able to dance on a rope stretched between the minarets of the funerary complexes of Qalawun and Barquq. He announced his act and gathered a large crowd to watch his spectacle of pirouettes and tricks. After this exercise, he repeated the performance of his predecessor between the minaret of Sultan Hasan and the Ashrafiyya palace, with yet more boldness. He used a second rope to climb up to the main one which was stretched taut, and slid down from the minaret to the roof of Sultan Hasan's mausoleum,

from where he climbed on top of the dome. This took place on a day so stormy that the trees were almost uprooted, the birds could not fly and people could hardly walk on the streets. The acrobat appeared 'as if he were of air'. The sultan watched the spectacle from the Citadel. Maqrizi, who dedicates two full pages to this event, was fascinated by the man's skill, and praised his passion and courage to achieve this on his own without the help of a teacher, thus accomplishing what no one else could do.[28] The same author also describes at length a similar spectacle that occurred only one month later. This time, a Persian merchant strung a rope between the two minarets of the mosque of Sultan Hasan to perform his show. He not only walked along the rope but also straddled it, dangling his feet while shooting arrows from a bow he was carrying. He performed a number of bold acrobatics, which included putting his foot in his mouth and sliding in and out of a ring in a variety of postures. He finally knelt on the rope in a gesture of kissing the ground before the sultan, who was watching from the Citadel.[29] Such spectacles shed an interesting light on the complex role of the minaret in urban life, which clearly provided a backdrop for performances of both a profane and a sacred nature.

THREE

Evolution of the Minaret

THE POLITICS OF STYLE

After its integration into the Muslim Empire, Egypt followed the imperial capitals established by the Umayyads and later the Abbasids in the eighth and ninth centuries, at Damascus, Baghdad and Samarra. The first minarets of Fustat were built at the four corners of the mosque of 'Amr Ibn al-'As, similar to the arrangement of the Umayyad mosque of Damascus that made use of the Roman corner towers as minarets.[1] They were not towers, however, but small structures projecting from the roof. The mosque of Ibn Tulun and its minaret echoed Abbasid imperial prototypes at Samarra. With the foundation of Qahira as the capital and residence of the Shi'i Fatimid caliphs, Egypt became an imperial centre in its own right. Royal patronage fashioned an architectural identity where local traditions were merged with other Islamic and Mediterranean cultures. Although their palaces have vanished, the Fatimids bequeathed a legacy of unparalleled military and religious architecture that had a lasting impact upon Egypt. This included decisive contributions to the design of minarets. The Sunni Ayyubid sultans, whose rule corresponded to the age of the Crusades, not only produced outstanding feats of civil engineering such as the colossal Citadel of Cairo with its extended fortifications and the gigantic dam of Giza; they also constructed remarkable religious monuments such as the mausoleum of Imam Shafi'i and the twin madrasas of al-Salih Najm al-din Ayyub, the latter crowned by an exquisite minaret.

These Ayyubid constructions, which reflected a historical period of threat and transition, continued to serve their strategic and pious purposes for centuries. The Mamluk sultans, who put an end to the Crusades, bestowed regal brilliance on their capital, which they associated with mausoleums for themselves. They attached their mausoleums to mosques, madrasas and Sufi institutions, coupling their funerary domes with minarets over the entire skyline of Cairo. The multiplication of commemorative sanctuaries required distinctive architectural and decorative variations to mark their individuality. The minaret and the mausoleum dome in this period became individual representations of their patrons, and symbols of their status. When the Mamluks were overthrown by the Ottomans, and Cairo's status was reduced to that of a capital of an Ottoman province, the minaret lost much of its previous significance.

The stylistic evolution of the pre-modern minaret in Cairo can only be traced from a relatively late date. This is because, from the first five centuries of Egypt's Islamic history, only the minarets of the mosques of Ibn Tulun, al-Hakim, al-Juyushi and Abu 'l-Ghadanfar survived. The minaret of Ibn Tulun, whether one accepts its present form as original or the result of a later restoration, is singular in its design and, therefore, can hardly be integrated within an Egyptian evolutionary line of development. The original minarets of the mosque of al-Hakim were concealed shortly after they were built and their impact on subsequent constructions would have been limited. Although many of their features remained unique, the southern minaret of

FIG. 7 *(page 20)*

Minarets in the cemetery, from left to right: the 'Southern' minaret, the minarets of Qawsun and the Sultaniyya mausoleum

al-Hakim shares some basic features with other Upper Egyptian minarets of the Fatimid period. The line of development that leads to the classical minaret of the Mamluk period seems to begin, rather, with the Fatimid minaret of the mosque of al-Juyushi. Until the Ottoman period, this architectural evolution seems to have been relatively unaffected stylistically by changes in political regimes, whether by the overthrow of the Shi'i Fatimid caliphate by the strict Sunni sultanate of the Ayyubid dynasty, or the seizure of power by the Mamluks from their Ayyubid predecessors. The Ayyubids built their domes according to Fatimid Cairene tradition, while increasing their scale, and the Mamluks built upon the architectural legacy of the Ayyubids.

The expertise of builders and craftsmen developed and elaborated form and style from inherited regional traditions, not from abstract ideas. The patrons who defined the use and content of these architectural forms, however, also played a significant role in the stimulation of architectural developments and innovation. The tradition of the patrons' personal involvement in the design of their monuments is well documented in Islamic history, religious and monumental patronage forming a significant element of the competence and duty of a Muslim ruler. This role naturally had a decisive impact on the history of architecture. Ibn Tulun's Samarran origin explains the style of his minaret. The eccentric character of the caliph al-Hakim is reflected in the equally eccentric history of the minarets of his mosque. The memorial and funerary intent of the religious architecture of the Mamluks is connected with their system of non-hereditary succession, and their obsession with building contributed to the variety and evolution of patterns. The Mamluk minaret acquired its distinctive features through a gradual evolution over more than two and a half centuries of uninterrupted and intensive building activity. This evolution came to an abrupt end with the Ottoman conquest of Egypt in 1517.

There is no architectural development in the history of Cairo that can be so closely linked to political change as the almost universal replacement of the Mamluk multiple-tiered minaret with the pencil-shaped shaft following the Ottoman conquest. The political symbolism of the minaret in Ottoman culture may be related to the fact that in the course of their conquest of Christian territories in south-east Europe, the Ottomans commonly turned churches into mosques. There, the addition of a minaret to a pre-existing structure provided the only visible symbol of a new Islamic and, at the same time, Ottoman identity. The Ottoman minaret, erected for the first time in Cairo at the mosque of Sulayman Pasha in 1528, advertised the change of regime in the Citadel, which continued to be the centre of government. After the conquest, Sultan Selim is reported to have transferred a number of Egyptian artisans and scholars to Istanbul, at the same time as sending Ottoman craftsmen to Cairo.[2] Not much of the latter's work is identifiable today, but it would seem probable that these craftsmen would have been responsible for introducing the Ottoman style of architecture to local masons. Although there is no evidence that the Ottoman authorities issued explicit regulations to subject the minaret in Cairo to their prevailing style, the political significance of this change is obvious and is not undermined by the few examples of Mamluk-style minarets that were built during their rule. These include the minaret of the madrasa of the first Ottoman governor of Egypt, the Mamluk emir Khayrbak, whose construction most likely predated the conquest, and the minaret of the seventeenth-century mosque of al-Burdayni. However, the adoption of the Ottoman minaret occurred only in Cairo: the Mamluk style of building minarets was perpetuated in the Egyptian provinces until modern times. Furthermore, the Ottoman stylistic regulation of the minaret in Cairo does not seem to have been the case in Syria: Sultan Selim's own mosque attached to the mausoleum of Ibn 'Arabi in Damascus has a Mamluk-style minaret with an Ottoman cap.

Following the Ottoman conquest, the design of Cairo's minarets remained static for almost three centuries, until the reign of Muhammad 'Ali. He introduced a visual transformation in the Egyptian capital, and brought the Turkish baroque mode to Cairo. Such a dramatic change must also have been implemented with the help of foreign craftsmen. The absence of any reference to local traditions in the architectural style of Muhammad 'Ali's reign was premeditated and politically motivated: he actively rejected the neo-Mamluk designs for mosques presented by his French architect, Pascal Coste. The imported style favoured by Muhammad ʿAli, however, was itself rejected at the end of the nineteenth century, when the reign of the Khedive ʿAbbas Hilmi saw the Mamluk style revived as the approved national style.

From this briefly charted evolution, it appears that the 'politics of style' was a relatively late development in Cairo's architectural tradition. An equally late phenomenon was the linguistic differentiation of periods. In his description of the monuments of Cairo, the seventeenth-century Ottoman traveller Evliya Çelebi was the first to make a stylistic distinction between 'Turkish' and 'old' buildings. This kind of stylistic distinction was unknown to earlier Mamluk historians and not even used by ʿAli Mubarak, the late nineteenth-century polymath, in his description of Cairo's architectural heritage.

For our study of the history and architecture of the Cairene minaret, the relative absence of physical data for the early period of construction requires a reliance on historical sources. The significance of the Mamluk period, both in terms of its length and the number of minarets it produced, imposes a distinction between this period and all others. The minarets of the Ottoman period obviously form a category of their own. This kind of periodisation does not make sense for the history of minarets in the provinces, however, where the Mamluk style was consistently maintained through the Ottoman period. It is also important to note that the stylistic evolution of the minaret was not intimately tied to that of the mosque. The mosques of the sultans al-Nasir Muhammad and al-Ghawri, from the early fourteenth and early sixteenth century respectively, for example, have conventional plans but unusual minarets.

THE FIRST MINARETS

Before the Fatimid foundation of Qahira in the second half of the tenth century AD, each of the preceding urban centres had a single congregational, or Friday, mosque (*jamiʿ*). Thus, the mosque of ʿAmr at Fustat (641–2), the Abbasid mosque at ʿAskar (783–4) and the Tulunid mosque at Qataʾiʿ (876–9), each served

a separate community. Each, moreover, had at least one minaret. In the case of the mosque of ʿAmr the minarets, totalling four, were additions, while that of Ibn Tulun has been planned from the outset. Little information is available regarding the minaret of the mosque of ʿAskar.

The historians Kindi (d. 870) and Ibn ʿAbd al-Hakam (870–1), our earliest sources on Egypt's Islamic history, report that the Umayyad governor of Egypt, Maslama ibn Mukhallad (667–82), after he enlarged and decorated the mosque of ʿAmr in Fustat, added four minarets at its corners and ordered at the same time that all mosques (*masajid*) of the city should also have minarets (*manar*) attached to them, whose *adhan* should follow the principal one performed from the mosque of ʿAmr.[3] The night *adhan*, however, should be performed by all muezzins at the same time. This information, which has not been given due attention before, is most significant because it implies that already at that time non-congregational mosques were equipped with minarets, which does not seem to have been common in other early Muslim cities. The spread of minarets in the city beyond the congregational mosque is confirmed by the Christian historian Abu Salih, who wrote in the thirteenth century, that in the early period of the Arab conquest (without specifying exactly when), the Arabs transformed monastic towers (*sawamiʿ*) into minarets for the call to prayer.[4] It is very likely that the proliferation of minarets at such an early date was an Egyptian peculiarity initiated by Maslama, and that it was a response to the large number of pre-existing Christian *sawamiʿ*. Such an articulate attitude by Maslama towards Christian religious symbols is confirmed by another source[5] reporting that he ordered the *naqus* (the wooden clapper used by the Christians) not to be used during the night *adhan*, adding that the night *adhan* was characterised by its high resonance (*dawiyy shadid*) as it was performed simultaneously from all mosques.

The practice initiated by Maslama ibn Mukhallad in the seventh century was maintained in subsequent periods. The fifteenth-century historian al-Zahiri wrote that minarets in Cairo could be found attached to Sufi monasteries and oratories (*khanqahs* and *zawiyas*), colleges (*madrasas*), and mausoleums.[6] This was also the case in the provinces: the emir Aytimish, for

FIG. 8

Elevation parallels, from left to right: The minarets of Ibn Tulun, al-Hakim (north), al-Juyushi, al-Salih Najm al-Din, Qalawun, Sanjar, al-Muzaffar Baybars, al-Nasir Muhammad (west), Bashtak, Qawsun, 'Southern' minaret

FIG. 8 *(continued)*

Aqsunqur, Manjaq, Shaykhu (khanqah), Sarghitmish, Sultaniyya, Asanbugha, Mu'ayyad, Emir Husayn, Qijmas al-Ishaqi, Qaytbay (Azhar), Qaytbay (Rawda), Ghawri, Ghawri (Azhar), Khayrbak

example, built a *zawiya* in a village with a spectacular minaret sixty cubits – almost thirty metres – in height.⁷ In 872–3 Ibn Tulun built a mosque equipped with a minaret (*manara*) on the Muqattam Hills at the site of a pre-Islamic lighthouse known as *tannur fir'awn* or 'Pharaoh's Furnace'.⁸ Similarly, the oratory (*mashhad*) of the vizier of the Fatimid imam-caliph al-Mu'izz, Badr al-Jamali, known as al-Juyushi, and also constructed on the Muqattam in 1087, was endowed with a minaret whose significance in such a remote location may have been strategic rather than religious (although the building is a conspicuous religious landmark that can be seen from afar). The minaret of Abu 'l-Ghadanfar (1157), attached to a saint's mausoleum,⁹ confirms that the Fatimids also built minarets within the city, other than those attached to Friday mosques. According to Maqrizi, other Fatimid mosques (*masjids*) in the cemeteries had minarets, such as the *masjid* al-Rahma and the *masjid* al-Waziriyya.¹⁰ Even cave oratories dug into the Muqattam Hills, like that cave referred to as al-'Arid,¹¹ were equipped with minarets that were presumably constructed as free-standing towers outside their entrances. Abu Salih, who wrote in the thirteenth century, reported that the caliph al-Hakim, in the course of his persecution of the Christians, added a mihrab and a tall minaret to a Christian monastery in the quarter called Harat Zuwayla.¹²

The Fatimids were the first to establish multiple Friday mosques within the city, some of which were of modest scale. In Qahira, the first mosque known as al-Azhar had a single minaret that was built above the portal. The second mosque, begun by the imam-caliph al-'Aziz and completed by his son al-Hakim, had two minarets. It is therefore unlikely that the Friday mosque called al-Aqmar, built by the vizier al-Ma'mun al-Bata'ihi, would not have had one.¹³ We know that the Friday mosques of the imam-caliph al-Zahir (no longer extant) and the vizier al-Salih Tala'i' both lost their minarets during the great earth-quake of 1303 which also damaged the minarets of the mosque of al-Hakim.¹⁴ Other mosques on the periphery of the city and now destroyed, are also known to have had minarets such as the Friday mosque of al-Qarafa¹⁵ (the southern cemetery of Fustat), the mosque of al-Rashida and the mosque at the port of al-Maqs.

Following the precepts of the Shafi'i school, the Ayyubids restricted the number of congregational mosques in urban settlements. Salah al-Din (r. 1171–93) assigned the Friday sermon (*khutba*) in Cairo only to the mosque of al-Hakim and that of Fustat to the mosque of 'Amr. He also founded a new congregational mosque on the island of Rawda, which must have been treated as an independent urban entity.¹⁶ However, this restriction of the number of Friday mosques, which was not maintained throughout the entire Ayyubid period,¹⁷ seems to have resulted in no corresponding reduction in the number of minarets then being constructed. We do not know whether Salah al-Din's madrasa near the tomb of Imam Shafi'i in the southern cemetery was equipped with a minaret; his *khanqah* in the centre of Qahira is reported to have acquired a minaret in the late fourteenth century, sponsored by the Sufi scholar Ahmad ibn Muhammad al-Ansari (d.1391), while he was its imam.¹⁸ However, the minaret stub at the shrine of al-Husayn, and the extant minaret of the madrasa of al-Salih Najm al-Din indicate that the Ayyubids followed Fatimid custom in attaching minarets to structures that were not Friday mosques.¹⁹ The Ayyubid madrasa al-Fakhriyya founded in 1228–9 had a minaret, which collapsed in 1455.²⁰ Moving into the early Mamluk period, the madrasa of al-Zahir Baybars at Bayn al-Qasrayn, which has not survived, had a three-storeyed minaret when Evliya Çelebi saw it in the seventeenth century. This is very likely to have been original.²¹

The peculiarity of attaching minarets to madrasas in Egypt can be understood with reference to other regional examples. Neither the famous Mustansiriyya madrasa in Baghdad nor Ayyubid madrasas in Syria had minarets. Ottoman madrasas were also built without minarets. In Cairo, too, the Ottoman madrasas of Sulayman Pasha and Sultan Mahmud I diverge from local tradition by their lack of a minaret.²² This was also the case for Sufi oratories and monasteries (*zawiya*s, *khanqah*s and *takiyya*s).

Besides great sanctuaries such as the mosques of 'Amr and al-Azhar, which acquired their additional minarets over time, the mosques in Cairo that possessed multiple minarets were almost exclusively founded by monarchs. After the construction of the mosque of

al-Hakim, with its pair of minarets, it is likely that the
next mosque to have originally had multiple minarets
was that of Sultan al-Zahir Baybars. The mosques of
the sultans al-Nasir Muhammad and al-Nasir Faraj ibn
Barquq had two minarets each, which were identical
in design in the latter case. The mosque of al-Mu'ayyad
Shaykh, built shortly after the mosque of al-Nasir Faraj,
also had a matched pair of minarets, as well as a third
minaret that disappeared. Sultan Hasan's scheme of
four minarets for his mosque-madrasa was exceptional
and remained unrealised. Unlike the Ottomans, who
systematically and exclusively associated multiple
minarets with royal foundations, the Mamluks seem
to have been more flexible in their approach to this
architectural question. This is indicated by the mosque
of the emir Qawsun, today demolished but originally
built with two minarets.[23] The minarets of Shaykhu,
which appear as matched twin towers facing one
another across a street, belonged to two different
buildings erected at different times. It cannot be
excluded that there were more mosques with
multiple minarets that have not survived.

THE LIGHTHOUSE OF ALEXANDRIA AND THE MINARET

At the beginning of the last century the German
scholar Hermann Thiersch developed a theory
regarding the origins of the minaret in Egypt, which
he presented in a brilliant and detailed study.[24] He
argued that the typical Cairene minaret built in three
storeys that were sequentially a square, an octagon and
a circle in plan, was related to the ancient Lighthouse
of Alexandria, one of the famous Seven Wonders of
the World. The lighthouse was erected by Alexander
the Great's second successor, Ptolemy Philadelphus
(283–246 BC). According to all accounts, the majority
of which were compiled by Muslim historians, the
lighthouse also had a tripartite configuration. On
the basis of descriptions in Arabic, Greek, Latin and
other European languages, Thiersch made a series of
reconstructions of the lighthouse at various stages of
its history and drew a direct parallel with the Mamluk
minarets of Cairo. His theory found some favour until

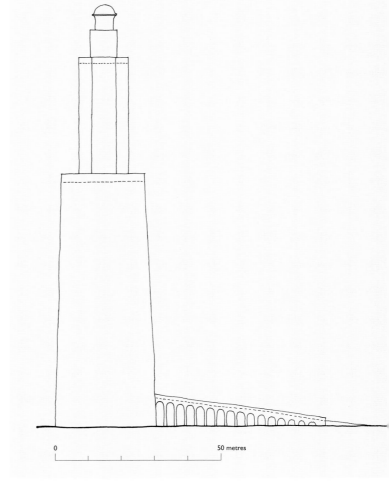

FIG. 9

*A reconstruction of the Lighthouse of Alexandria as it
was in the twelfth–thirteenth centuries*

it was rebuffed by the arguments of K.A.C. Creswell, the noted historian of Islamic architecture. According to Creswell, the Cairene minaret, built in three storeys of different sections, appeared no earlier than the fourteenth century, by which time the Lighthouse of Alexandria was already dilapidated. The square/octagonal/circular sections of the Cairene minaret, he explained, had evolved gradually from the minaret of al-Juyushi to the minaret of Qawsun without reference to the Lighthouse of Alexandria.[25]

Thiersch's theory is, however, still worthy of consideration. One of his arguments was based on another lighthouse, at Taposiris Magna, situated some twenty kilometres west of Alexandria and still standing today. Attributed to the Greek period, this lighthouse shows the same arrangement as that of Alexandria: a square base, growing into an octagon and probably ending in a circular section. It was depicted in the *Description de l'Egypte*,[26] and also published in a photograph by Thiersch. There may well have been in Egypt an ancient tradition of building towers in three storeys, each with a different section, which survived into the Middle Ages. This argument is supported by the general fact that the minarets found in various parts of the Muslim world usually adopt the shape of regional pre-Islamic towers. In Iran, for example, the first minarets resemble watchtowers to such a degree that it is sometimes impossible to differentiate between the two; in Syria, the minaret developed a rectangular form like church towers, and in Iraq, as late as the ninth century, the minarets of Samarra adopted the idea of the external staircase/ramp of ancient Mesopotamian temples. It would be natural, therefore, for local building traditions and local solutions to the structural problems posed by the construction of towers to have persisted in Egypt.

No visitor to medieval Egypt failed to mention the Lighthouse of Alexandria, which continued in operation until the reign of al-Nasir Muhammad (r. 1294–5, 1299–1309, 1309–40). The traveller Ibn Battuta described it as he saw it on his journey from North Africa to China 1326. noting on his return in 1348 that it had ceased to function and that al-Nasir Muhammad, who had intended to build a new one, had died before realising his plan.[27] Even if the lighthouse had lost its original configuration by

that time, it was a famous monument which remained well known. 'Abd al-Latif al-Baghdadi wrote in the early thirteenth century: 'It is needless to describe it since everyone knows its appearance'.[28] Maqrizi, who rarely dwelt on physical descriptions of buildings, compiled a detailed description of the lighthouse, using material from Mas'udi and other historians and travellers. Ibn Iyas wrote that the architect of Sultan al-Ghawri, Mu'allim Hasan ibn al-Sayyad, made for his master a three-dimensional plaster representation of the city of Alexandria, which showed the city with its walls and gates and also the lighthouse 'which used to be there'.[29] The cultural memory of the lighthouse appears to have thus persisted so strongly that it continued to be represented as a landmark of the city centuries after it had disappeared from view.

The lighthouse described in Arabic sources, however, was not exactly the one erected by Alexander's successor. According to some of these sources the caliph al-Walid (705–15) had ordered the demolition of its upper structure in search of a treasure, which the Byzantines made him believe was hidden inside. Whether this was true or not is difficult to tell, but it means that the lighthouse had already lost its original shape by the early Islamic period, maintaining only the monumental rectangular section. The original octagonal and circular structures, which might have been topped by a statue, were never described in Arabic sources in any trustworthy terms. We do not know how the lighthouse looked before Ibn Tulun reconstructed the upper sections in brick, instead of the original stone masonry, in the form of an octagonal shaft carrying a circular domed top. Subsequent Muslim rulers more or less regularly restored the lighthouse to keep it functioning as a watchtower and at the same time to guide ships with fire signals into the harbour of Alexandria (fig. 9). By the thirteenth century, however, the lighthouse had decayed so much that it could no longer be restored in its original, though reinterpreted, three-storeyed composition. It finally collapsed during the first half of the following century. Thus, with the exception of its monumental base, the Lighthouse of Alexandria in the Islamic period was an Islamic, and more precisely an Egyptian, structure. In consistence with the general absence of historicism in the medieval approach to restoration, it can be assumed that the reconstructions that took place at the lighthouse were executed in their respective contemporary styles. This means that each time the upper structure was restored it must have resembled contemporary minarets. This is how Thiersch reconstructed the appearance of the lighthouse at the various stages of its restoration.

VARIETY AND INNOVATION

Whatever its origins, the characteristic feature of the Cairene, and for that matter Egyptian, minaret is the variation in plan of its successive storeys. Even the minaret of Ibn Tulun differs from its Samarran prototype in one important feature: its section changes from square into circular towards the top. The use of dual sections, rectangular and circular, also characterises the Fatimid minarets of Upper Egypt, as well as the southern minaret of the mosque of al-Hakim. The latter minaret was built at a time when the lighthouse was still functioning and develops from a square shaft to an octagonal one: the missing top, later replaced by a Mamluk construction, was probably circular.

According to Creswell, the minaret of the oratory of al-Juyushi, built in 1085 by the Fatimid vizier Badr al-Jamali, forms the basic prototype of the 'classic' Cairene minaret, which consists of three storeys, successively square, octagonal and circular in section. Al-Juyushi's minaret has a rectangular shaft carrying a second, narrower rectangular storey with a domed structure, or cupola, on top. In the next stage of development, following Creswell's thesis, the rectangular base of the cupola became octagonal and the cupola was adorned with ribs, as can be seen at the later Fatimid minaret of Abu 'l-Ghadanfar (1157). The upper storeys became increasingly elongated at the expense of the square base, as demonstrated at the Ayyubid minaret of Sultan al-Salih Najm al Din (1250), ultimately culminating in a minaret with three distinct tiers that were successively square, octagonal and circular in plan.[30] The earliest example of this final stage of development is the minaret of the madrasa of Sanjar al-Jawli, built in 1304. The minaret of the *khanqah* of Qawsun (1336–7) in the Suyuti cemetery,

built entirely in stone in 1336–7, represents the artistic climax of this style.

Creswell's demonstration of this evolution was principally aimed at destroying the theory connecting the shape of the classic Cairene minaret with that of the Lighthouse of Alexandria by showing that the minaret took centuries to acquire its final form. His argument is valid if one starts the sequence of evolution with al-Juyushi and ignores the earlier south minaret of al-Hakim, which has exactly the arrangement Creswell claims to be the culmination of the entire sequence. This minaret, which may have been already built by al-Hakim's father in the last decade of the tenth century, has a square shaft, above which stands an octagonal section. Although the original top is missing one may safely assume that this was circular and that it had a domical top similar in form to its successors at the shrines of al-Juyushi and Abu 'l-Ghadanfar. The early use of domes to crown structures (other than tombs) of different scales is widely attested: Ibn Tulun is reported to have built a dome on top of the Lighthouse of Alexandria when he reconstructed it, and al-Hakim himself commissioned a wooden *minbar* for his mosque surmounted by a small domed structure at its top.[31]

THE EARLY MAMLUK STYLE

The minaret of the madrasa of al-Salih Najm al-Din Ayyub, the only Ayyubid minaret to have survived entirely, can be considered as the ancestor of the early Mamluk minaret. This is is consistent with the general continuity of Ayyubid artistic and other traditions under their Mamluk successors. Its architecture was, however, refined while being translated in stone. At the very same moment that the minaret with a rectangular-octagonal shaft and circular top reached its apogee in the masterly construction of Qawsun's minaret, a new architectural development ended this evolution. The builders turned to another model by replacing the square first storey with an octagonal one, thus creating a smoother transition to the second cylindrical section that was not there in the rectangular-cylindrical profile. The earliest extant examples of this form are the minarets at the mosques of Bashtak and Aqbugha. The octagonal first storey eventually became a standard feature of minarets, often combined with a cylindrical second storey. From there the evolution led to the minaret with an octagonal plan at all levels with receding tiers, including a pavilion with a bulb at the summit. The minaret at the mosque of al-Maridani provides the earliest extant example of this type.

Parallel to the rectangular-octagonal and octagonal models, the rectangular-circular composition displayed at the minarets of al-Muzaffar Baybars al-Jashnakir and the eastern minaret of the mosque of al-Nasir Muhammad reappeared on some minarets of the first half of the fifteenth century. This is the case at the mosques of Faraj ibn Barquq, Barsbay, and Qanibay al-Sharkasi, all built in the early fifteenth century. The origin of this combination seems to go back to an earlier, late thirteenth-century, type represented by the minarets of the madrasa of Fatima Khatun and the mosque of al-Baqli, though their second storeys are octagonal and hexagonal respectively rather than circular, they recede from the first storey without a transition. The handsome minaret attached to the funerary *khanqah* of the emir Tankizbugha follows the same pattern of a two-storeyed shaft, which stands out as an archaism among contemporary minarets. The entirely circular shaft was another oddity of the fourteenth century displayed by the western minaret of the mosque of al-Nasir Muhammad at the Citadel and at the mosques of Aqsunqur and Jamal al-Din Mahmud (al-Kurdi).

The stylistic development of the form of the minaret in Cairo cannot be separated from the materials with which it was made. As far as construction is concerned, the use of stone, rather than fired brick, seems to have taken place gradually and with some trepidation. More than a century elapsed between the Fatimid brick construction of the minaret of Abu 'l-Ghadanfar and the early Mamluk hybrid stone and brick minaret of the madrasa of Fatima Khatun and the stone minaret of the complex of Qalawun. Slightly later, Sultan Lajin added a stone octagonal structure with a ribbed helmet to the minaret of Ibn Tulun. However, even by the beginning of the fourteenth century the stone minaret had not yet established itself as the constructional norm: the minarets of the madrasa of al-Nasir Muhammad at Bayn al-Qasrayn and the *khanqah* of al-Muzaffar Baybars, although attached to royal monuments, are both brick structures. The minaret of the complex of Sanjar al-Jawli combines a stone first storey with a brick upper structure. This irregular pattern of materials demonstrates that the builders of Qalawun's reign were particularly bold and unconventional.

Following the construction of al-Nasir Muhammad's minarets at his mosque in the Citadel in 1318, the supremacy of stone masonry in minaret architecture was finally confirmed. With few exceptions, this supremacy was maintained until the end of the Mamluk period and continued under Ottoman rule. Whereas Iranian or Anatolian models can be said to have influenced the design of the western minaret of al-Nasir Muhammad, with its cylindrical and tapering profile, local patterns (evident in the minarets of Fatima Khatun and al-Baqli) affected the form of the northern minaret, with its rectangular-circular shaft. Shafts made of brick could never achieve the slenderness of their stone counterparts. The shift to stone manifest in the construction of the minarets of al-Nasir resulted in considerable changes in proportion, profile and decoration. It also resulted in the replacement of the domed upper structure, called the mabkhara, with a pavilion supporting a bulb, which is a more slender and airy structure. The earlier form of upper structure in the shape of an octagonal shaft crowned with a ribbed cupola was named mabkhara or 'incense-burner' by Creswell, going back to a nineteenth-century term, and has been used ever since by art historians to describe this style.[32] The mabkhara at Qawsun's minaret already has larger openings than all its antecedents, anticipating the octagonal pavilion with the bulb that characterised the Mamluk minarets of the following period. The latest example of the mabkhara design can be seen at the minaret of the funerary *khanqah* of Tankizbugha built in 1362 on the edge of the northern cemetery. The earliest surviving octagonal pavilion is found at the minaret of al-Maridani: the minaret of Aqbugha, which was designed by the same architect, might have had a similar top but this disappeared in the nineteenth century.

THE LATER MAMLUK STYLE

Despite occasional variations in design, the majority of later Mamluk builders continued to favour the cylindrical/octagonal shaft for their minarets. Although stone masonry replaced brick construction in minaret architecture, some brick minarets were still erected during the fifteenth century. Their style does not go back to the earlier tradition of thirteenth- and fourteenth-century brick minarets, however; rather, they adopt the forms of contemporary stone constructions. This is the case with the minarets of the mosques of Mahmud al-Ustadar (al-Kurdi), Janibak al-Ashrafi, al-Khatiri, al-Alaya and Khayrbak. There is a further remarkable development during the reign of Sultan Jaqmaq. Both of his minarets – which attached to his madrasa and the vanished minaret of his mosque at Dayr al-Nahas – were built of stone but decorated in stucco, including their muqarnas. The use of exterior stucco decoration on stone seems to be exclusive to these minarets and to an undated minaret, which may have been sponsored by Sultan Jaqmaq that was added to the mosque of Arghun.

The long reign of al-Ashraf Qaytbay (r. 1468–96) was a period of intense building activity. As was the case with Sultan al-Nasir Muhammad, Qaytbay ruled long enough to achieve architectural patronage on a wide scale, which brought about a renaissance of all the arts. Architectural decoration, and in particular carved masonry, reached an unprecedented quality under Qaytbay. Unlike the reign of al-Nasir Muhammad, however, no significant innovation or experimentation took place in the architectural design of the minaret and no contribution of foreign craftsmen can be detected during this period; forms were standardised and perfected without disturbing components whose place was already fixed. The minaret of Qaytbay's time is a stone construction with an octagonal first storey, a circular carved middle section, and a third storey composed of slender stone columns carrying a bulb. The lavish carving of niches, panels and colonettes, including also the base of the minaret, which had already been introduced at the minaret of Sultan Inal (1451), where elaborate mouldings and fine muqarnas highlight all points of architectural transition, were maintained and refined.

The reign of Sultan al-Ghawri introduced a last, but bold, innovation in Mamluk minaret architecture. Fully rectangular shafts appeared for the first time and a mutation also occurred at the top for the first and last time since the construction of the mosque of al-Maridani. The quadruple-headed minaret of al-Ghawri's funerary complex was the culmination of an evolution that seems to have begun in the later years of the fifteenth century. The mosque of Sultan Janbalat that once stood near the gate of Bab al-Nasr had, according to Jabarti, a double-headed minaret. Janbalat ruled for only one year, 1500–1. This mosque, which was also remarkable for its two large stone domes, specifically mentioned by Jabarti and praised by Evliya Çelebi, was demolished by Bonaparte's soldiers three centuries later.[33] However, Janbalat's minaret was probably not the first with a double bulb. The brick minaret of Shaykh Abu 'l-'Abbas al-Ghamri in the town of Mit Ghamr in the Delta, built in 1499, has a double bulb, suggesting that this design might have been used in Cairo even earlier on minarets that have not survived.[34] The chronicler Ibn Kathir describes the north-east minaret of Sultan Hasan's mosque, which collapsed in the seventeenth century, as having a shaft carrying a double upper structure.[35] If this information, unconfirmed by other sources, is true, such a design might have been more common than has been hitherto assumed. The double bulb appears on two minarets built by Qanibay Qara and the minaret of al-Ghawri at al-Azhar; this composition was doubled at the minaret of al-Ghawri's funerary complex, which was built with four bulbs covered with blue ceramic tiles. Rather than being supported on columns, these bulbs stood on elongated masonry bases pierced with arched openings. This device was revived two and a half centuries later at the minaret of Abu 'l-Dhahab with a fifth bulb added between the initial four.

THE OTTOMAN MINARET

A major contribution of the Mamluks to the architecture of the minaret was to treat it as sculpture as much as architecture. The frequent comparison of the minaret with a doll (*arus*)[36] reflects this aesthetic concern.[37]

FIG. 11

The minaret of Masih Pasha

FIG. 10

The reconstructed seventeenth-century minaret at the mosque of Sultan Hasan

Mamluk patrons and architects created the silhouettes of their minarets with a sense of urban perspective and a taste for variety. The sheer multitude of minarets built in Cairo during the Mamluk period remains striking. Equally striking is the contrast between the richness of the patterns displayed in the architecture of Mamluk minarets and the repetitiveness of the minarets built in Cairo between the Ottoman conquest in 1517 and the late eighteenth century. With few exceptions, the architectural and aesthetic qualities of the minarets built under Ottoman rule remained mediocre. It is obvious that the Mamluk-style minarets were costly and time-consuming to build whereas pencil-shaped shafts with only one balcony for the muezzin and a conical top were relatively simple constructions.

Restoration work on Mamluk minarets in the Ottoman period, such as the minaret reconstructed in the seventeenth century at the mosque of Sultan Hasan, attests to a decline in the quality of masonry at that time. Ottoman rule could not completely prevent the revival of the Mamluk style of minaret. Four Mamluk-revival minarets can be attributed without any doubt to the Ottoman period. These structures are too distant from each other chronologically and seem to express the individual choice and inclination of their respective patrons rather than an architectural trend. The first was the minaret of Shaykh al-Burdayni built in 1629, which follows the style of the minarets of the Qaytbay period without the octagonal pavilion. It was followed a century later by the minaret al-Kurdi built in 1732, and a half century later, in 1774, by the minaret of the mosque of Abu 'l-Dhahab, which was almost a copy of the minaret of al-Ghawri nearby. The last occurrence is the minaret of Hasan Pasha Tahir built in 1809, which also returns to the tradition of fifteenth-century minaret architecture. All these minarets precede the Mamluk revival of the late nineteenth century that took place under European influence and continues to the present day. However, it cannot be excluded that more minarets were built in the Mamluk style during the Ottoman period, as the problematic case of the minaret of al-Ruway'i demonstrates.[38] As long as no evidence is available to support its dating, its attribution remains open to speculation.

It is interesting to note that when the minaret of a Mamluk mosque had to be replaced in the Ottoman

period, the reconstruction was often carried out with a certain degree of faithfulness to the original style, or at least with this intention. This is demonstrated by the reconstructed northern minaret of the mosque of Sultan Hasan and the minaret of the mosque of Ulmas (figs 10 and 11). This approach to restoration is noteworthy and it was unprecedented. Until then restorers had worked in the style of their own period; an example would be Sultan Lajin's mabkhara at the top of the minaret of Ibn Tulun or Baybars al-Jashnakir's work on the minarets of al-Hakim. In their reconstructions of Mamluk minarets, however, the builders of the Ottoman period frequently eliminated the octagonal pavilion and set the bulb immediately above the second storey, giving the whole structure a rather truncated and disproportioned appearance. In other cases, as shown by nineteenth-century photographs predating the restorations undertaken by the Comité, the restorations of the Ottoman period replaced missing tops of minarets by a cylinder surmounted by a conical cap.

Specimens of this type of restoration can be seen at the minarets of Aytimish al-Bajasi, Janibay, and Barsbay in the cemetery.

It is not until the nineteenth century that the Ottoman minaret in Cairo acquired metropolitan features. The mosque of Muhammad 'Ali was the first to display a remarkable improvement upon the pencil-shaped profile of the Turkish minaret. These minarets are more slender than their Ottoman counterparts and have elongated conical caps. The same development can be seen at the minarets of the mosque of Sulayman Agha al-Silahdar, the shrine of Fatima al-Nabawiyya (now rebuilt) (fig. 40),[39] and the shrine of al-Husayn. These minarets represent the last vestiges of Ottoman influence on Cairene architecture. At the close of the nineteenth century, hand in hand with the formation of a modern Egyptian national identity, the design of minarets reverted to Mamluk tradition, as in the case of the royal mosque of al-Rifa'i, thereby celebrating a revival of Cairo's remote golden age of the Mamluk sultans.

FIG. 12

View of minarets from the Ottoman period, from left to right: the minaret of the mosque of Mahmud Pasha, the reconstructed minaret at the mosque of Sultan Hasan, the minarets of the mosque of al-Rifa'i, and the minaret of the mosque of Ahmad Kathuda al-'Azaban

FIG. 13

The minarets of the mosques of Emir Sarghitmish (left) and Ibn Tulun

FOUR

Placement

The practical prerequisite for any minaret's location vis-à-vis the building to which it was attached and the neighbourhood it served was, in principle, the optimal broadcast of the call to prayer. To achieve this, the muezzin Bilal used to stand at the entrance of the Prophet's mosque. It is also mentioned that he stood on a cylindrical structure (*ustuwan*, which also means column) located in a house nearby.[1] Once it became an architectural element in its own right, the minaret was fashioned to herald the mosque to which it was attached, and at the same time, to enhance its presence on the street. It formed part of the design of the façade, in terms of mass rather than as decoration, however. Unlike other regional traditions, the positioning of the minaret in Cairo was not always dependent on the position of the main portal or principal axis of the building. Although it generally stood near the entrance, its positioning was more flexible.

The first minarets in Egypt, at the mosque of ʿAmr in Fustat, were located at the four corners of the mosque. This arrangement allowed the call to prayer to be heard on all sides of the city. Despite these early precedents, the design of four-corner minarets remained the exception rather than the rule for the positioning of minarets in Cairo. Later minarets, by contrast, stood axially positioned opposite the mihrab, though that of Ibn Tulun was built slightly off the axis. Fatimid minarets also seem, in general, to have been located axially at, or directly above, the main portal. An exception to this is minarets at the mosque of al-Aziz/al-Hakim, which project from the corners of the façade wall – a layout that emulates the Great Mosque in the first Fatimid capital, Mahdiyya in North Africa. In the particular case of al-Hakim's mosque this layout may be explained by the fact that the mosque was erected outside the city walls before Badr al-Jamali rebuilt them and included the mosque within their confines. If the mosque's architect had erected a single minaret over the entrance at the centre of the western wall, as was common then, it would have been too distant from the city and the primary congregation of the mosque. The arrangement of two minarets flanking the principal entry façade placed the south-west minaret near the first city wall erected by Jawhar al-Siqilli, within reach of the eyes and ears of the city's inhabitants. The north-western minaret at the other end of the façade, could have been used as a watchtower overlooking the caravan route connecting Cairo to Syria and beyond. The mosque of the southern cemetery, al-Qarafa, built by Taghrid, the widow of the caliph al-Muʿizz, in 976–7, followed the model of the mosque of al-Azhar which probably had its minaret located above the main portal.[2] This is also the case with the mosque of al-Juyushi on the Muqattam Hills. The minaret of the mosque of al-Salih Talaʾiʿ, which was demolished by the earthquake of 1303, also stood above the main entrance, judging from the minaret that replaced it before it was demolished during the reconstruction of the mosque in the 1920s.[3] Regarding the mosque of al-Aqmar, it is not possible to determine the location of the original minaret, but the present minaret, a late fourteenth-century addition, also stands near the entrance, as was common in the Mamluk period.

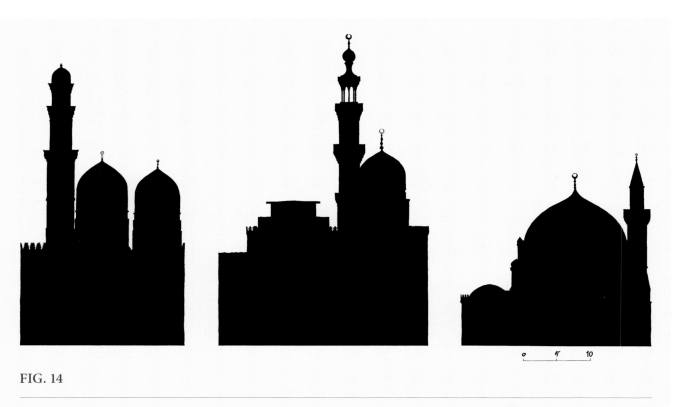

FIG. 14

Silhouettes of the mosques (from left to right) of Sanjar al-Jawli, Qijmas al-Ishaqi and Sinan Pasha

Like their Fatimid predecessors, the Ayyubids also favoured centrality. At the shrine of al-Husayn, the minaret stands directly above the principal doorway to the mausoleum, and at the madrasa of al-Salih Najm al-Din it is located above the entrance to the street which runs between the two sections of the complex, and is centred on the main façade looking onto Bayn al-Qasrayn. Some early Mamluk minarets – such as those at al-Zahir Baybars' mosque, al-Nasir Muhammad's madrasa, al-Muzaffar Baybars' *khanqah*, Emir Husayn's mosque and Shaykhu's mosque and *khanqah* – followed this pattern and were built above the entrances of their respective buildings. This position, however, subsequently lost favour and the minarets were built instead over one of the door-jambs rather than directly over the portal vault. This change might be explained by the builders' preference for supporting the minaret with a solid mass of masonry instead of a vault, a preference that may have developed in tandem with the growing use of stone rather than

brick for minaret construction and a greater familiarity with the demands of statics. Aesthetic or urban considerations may also have played a role in the separation of the minaret from the portal.

In mosques where the main façade and entrance corresponded to the Mecca-oriented (*qibla*) wall, the minaret was also commonly placed at the façade/*qibla* side of the mosque. This is the case with the complexes of sultans Qalawun, al-Nasir Muhammad, Barsbay and al-Ghawri, all of which are located on the west side of the Bayn al-Qasrayn. If the *qibla* wall of the mosque did not correspond to the main façade and entrance, however, it was rare for the minarets to be attached to this side. Exceptions to the rule can be seen in the case of the two Mamluk minarets added to the mosque of Ibn Tulun and that added to the mosque of al-Hakim (all since disappeared). These minarets were intended to serve those dwelling to the rear of these large mosques, who would have been too far away to hear the call to prayer delivered from minarets attached to the façade. Similarly, the reason why the mosque of al-Nasir Muhammad at the Citadel has an additional minaret on the north-east corner of the prayer-hall was the presence of the military and administrative quarters on this side of the building, as opposed to the sultan's palace that was served by the minaret on the entrance façade.

The practical concern for the audibility of the call to prayer, however, was not the only factor in the positioning of the minaret. Another consideration was clearly uppermost at the mosque of al-Azhar, where a cluster of no fewer than four minarets was constructed at different periods immediately adjacent to the main entrance within a radius of fifteen metres. This was clearly an assertion of 'demonstrable piety' by patrons wishing to associate themselves with the most important religious centre of the city, and had little to do with the audibility of the call to prayer.

While the positioning of early minarets was defined by axis and symmetry, the street perspective became the decisive factor that affected location in the Mamluk period. If not standing at the entrance to the building, Mamluk minarets could project from any part of the façade, separated from the entrance to be better appreciated at a distance. In many cases, the mosque itself, following the alignment of a winding street, lay hidden from the view of passers-by until the last moment of approach. From the perspective of someone descending from the Citadel along Tabbana Street, the minarets of the mosques of Aqsunqur and Khayrbak dominate the approach, attracting and holding attention long before their façades come into view. It is no wonder that these two minarets were particular favourites in nineteenth-century pictures and photographs of Cairo. In some cases, the placement of minarets was a grand, bold, urban gesture. The twin minarets built by the emir Shaykhu at his mosque and *khanqah* directly face each other across Saliba Street and form a spectacular composition. At the mosque of Sultan Hasan, the visual impact on the Citadel, the residence of the sultans, and the Rumayla Square, a major venue of public gatherings, suggested the unusual positioning of a pair of minarets flanking the mausoleum dome on this side. Visual impact also played a role in the positioning of the twin minarets intended for the portal; which is set askew to the façade alignment,

turning towards the Citadel and the square.

Particular attention was paid to the positioning of minarets along the central north–south axis of the city. To a viewer coming from the Bab al-Futuh and arriving at the Bayn al-Qasrayn, the massive minaret of Qalawun at the northernmost tip of his royal funerary complex-cum-hospital dominates the main avenue. In this case the minaret was attached to the mausoleum rather than to the madrasa built to the south of the passage that separates the two structures. This allowed the builder to create the close juxtaposition of minaret and dome that came to assume great importance in Mamluk architectural aesthetics. Further to the south, the minaret of the madrasa of al-Ghawri projects from the southern corner of the façade so as to be seen as soon as one crosses the threshold of the Bab Zuwayla into the city. This effectively creates an illusion that the mosque is closer than it really is. In the case of al-Ghawri's complex, the minaret faced the enormous dome of the founder's mausoleum (now vanished) on the other side of the street, so that taken together the two elements effectively 'framed' the street and claimed the urban landscape as their own. The minarets of Sultan al-Mu'ayyad, with their exceptional location above the flanking towers of the Bab Zuwayla (which greatly increased their overall elevation), announce the mosque outside the city walls, from where it cannot be seen. This applies not only to the axial view of the minarets from the south, but also to oblique views from the Darb al-Ahmar to the east and Taht al-Rab' Street to the west. A third minaret once stood at the mosque's western entrance to serve those living within the walls.[4] By placing his minarets directly above the Bab Zuwayla, al-Mu'ayyad claimed for himself the most privileged access to Cairo, the spine or *qasaba* of Cairo itself.

Even in apparently 'extra-urban' settings, the placement of the minaret was still given careful consideration. At the funerary mosque of Qawsun and the mausoleum of al-Sultaniyya in the southern cemetery, the minaret occupied the north-western corner of each building, offering an impressive perspective to the viewer approaching from the Rumayla Square or the eastern gate of the Citadel (fig. 7). The position of the twin minarets on the west façade of the *khanqah* of al-Nasir Faraj ibn Barquq in the northern cemetery is unique. The minarets are separated from both the two entrances and the twin domes of the building, which relates not only to the north–south route that ran past the building on this side but also to the more distant city lying to the west. Indeed, when the architecture of the cemeteries acquired urban features, the minarets followed the rules of the city. This trend can be detected as early as the thirteenth century in the case of the minaret of Fatima Khatun, which was placed near the portal, following the road alignment that diverges from the axis of the madrasa itself. The awkward location of the minaret of Sultan Inal in the northern cemetery is to be explained by the history of the complex. The minaret and the mausoleum belonged to an earlier stage of construction before the mosque was inserted between them.

Since the Fatimid period and in particular since the foundation of the Aqmar mosque in 1125, many medieval mosques in Cairo were built with their façades aligned to the street and their interiors differently aligned to Mecca. Normally the base of the minaret or the dome follows the façade rather than the inner alignment. A few minarets, however, stand at an angle to the street-aligned façade, following this internal orientation to the *qibla*. This is the case with the minarets of the madrasas of al-Nasir Muhammad, Barsbay, and the mosques of Jaqmaq and Mughulbay Taz. When a building had more than one façade, the minaret was often set at one corner, as at the mosques of Aslam al-Silahdar, Arghunshah, Umm al-Sultan Sha'ban and Qaytbay at Qal'at al-Kabsh. At the mosque of Qanibay al-Sharkasi, although the portal is in the northern façade that once overlooked the hippodrome, the minaret was built on the south-west corner of the mosque, overlooking a side street, where its call could be heard in the more densely populated area.

From this brief survey it can be seen that there was no fixed rule for the positioning of minarets in Mamluk architecture. The location of each minaret was dependent on a combination of simple functional requirements and the imperatives of designing within an often tightly compressed urban context. The portal, the dome and the minaret were the three key components in any religious structure. As the latter two are located on the same level, the felicitous

juxtaposition of the minaret with the mausoleum dome assumed great architectural importance, giving the building a distinctive silhouette. Once the funerary dome became an integral element of religious architecture, the respective positions and proportions of minaret and dome were coordinated to achieve an optimal visual effect. Even in cases where the minaret did not stand near the dome, as in the *khanqah* of Tankizbugha on the slope of the Muqattam Hills, the minaret and the dome were designed to form a harmonious composition, since this monument once stood isolated against a bare hillside when seen from the city. Within the dense fabric of the city, the minaret and dome were usually placed directly adjacent to each other. In the more spacious cemetery areas, however, the elevations of funerary monuments were stretched out, unfolding on more than one façade, and the dome and the minaret were separated and balanced against one another. In cemetery contexts, even when the size of the mosque was reduced and the open courtyard eliminated entirely, as in the funerary complexes of the sultans Barsbay, Qaytbay and Emir Qurqumas, the minaret was distanced from the dome.

The harmonious integration of the minaret into a monumental façade was a matter of primary concern in the history of Cairene architecture. In Ottoman tradition, however, the positioning of the minaret was a less flexible matter; the reason lies in the general layout of the Ottoman mosque, which emphasises symmetrical freestanding domed spaces rather than individual and elaborate street façades where the position of the minaret was optional. Traditionally, the minaret of the Turkish Ottoman mosque stands on a corner of the mosque connected to the courtyard, notto the portal. At the mosque of Sulayman Pasha in the Citadel of Cairo, the minaret stands on a bulky buttress placed next to the portal in an awkward manner that was not common to either Mamluk or Ottoman imperial architecture. In mosques with a Mamluk layout, like the mosques of Mahmud Pasha and al-Burdayni, the minaret was integrated into the façade in the Mamluk style. The minarets of the mosque of Muhammad 'Ali are beautifully incorporated into the building in a manner that can compete with the imperial mosques of Istanbul.

FIG. 15

The complex of Sultan al-Ghawri in the nineteenth century

GIRAULT DE PRANGEY

FIG. 16

The base of the dome and minaret of the mosque of Emir Qanibay al-Muhammadi

FIVE

Construction and Materials

By the nature of their construction, minarets were more fragile than other architectural elements. Besides the damage caused by earthquakes, lightning strikes are also recorded, for example, at the minaret of Sultan Qaytbay at the holy city of Medina,[1] at one of the minarets at the mosque of 'Amr and at the original minaret of the mosque of Emir Husayn.[2] The collapse of any minaret was, unsurprisingly, considered to be a major disaster in the city. The collapse of a minaret at the portal of the madrasa of Sultan Hasan whilst under construction, which allegedly killed two hundred children, was viewed as an omen that foretold the sultan's assassination a month later.[3] The reason for this failure is unknown as there is a considerable mass of supporting masonry on either side of the doorway that would have been used as the minaret buttress. During the construction of al-Mu'ayyad's mosque in the early fifteenth century, a deficiency was noticed in the structure of one of the minarets which led to its demolition and rebuilding. According to the poets who celebrated the rebuilt tower, the evil eye was to blame.[4] When the minaret of the madrasa al-Fakhriyya collapsed in 1445 destroying an adjoining apartment building and killing many people, the then Sultan Jaqmaq's anger was extreme. He severely punished the deputy Shafi'i judge (qadi) and supervisor of the foundation, who happened to be the great historian Ibn Hajar. Only the intercession of an emir prevented Ibn Hajar's being whipped but it could not prevent his fall from grace: he was sacked and compelled to compensate the victims' families. Later, the sultan personally inspected the reconstruction

works.[5] Even the fall of one of the wooden brackets used for hanging lanterns from a minaret at the Citadel was an evil omen for Sultan Qaytbay, who indeed suffered a fall from his horse the following day.[6]

Only two signatures of builders in Mamluk Cairo have survived to this day, one of which is associated with the construction of a pair of minarets. The first builder's signature is found on the portal of the Emir Qawsun's (later Yashbak's) palace (1337–9) and the second on the twin minarets of the mosque of al-Mu'ayyad Shaykh that stand above the Bab Zuwayla. The signature on Qawsun's portal does not specify the exact work done by the craftsman who signed his name,[7] whereas the signature of the mu'allim al-Qazzaz that is inscribed on both of al-Mu'ayyad's minarets explicitly states that he was the one who built them. Textual sources also provide us with the name of another master-builder, the mu'allim Ibn al-Suyufi, who constructed the minarets of Aqbugha at al-Azhar and the minaret of the mosque of al-Maridani in 1339–40.[8]

Minarets and domes represent the two most challenging feats of masonry construction seen in the monumental architecture of the city. We still know too little about the organisation of labour in medieval Cairo, but it seems that the builders worked in a highly specialised way. The fact that some architectural elements, such as the transitional zones, or certain decorative patterns such as chevrons, appeared on minarets decades before they were applied to domes suggests that two distinct and specialised groups of masons were at work on each of the two types of construction. With the exception of the minarets at the mosques

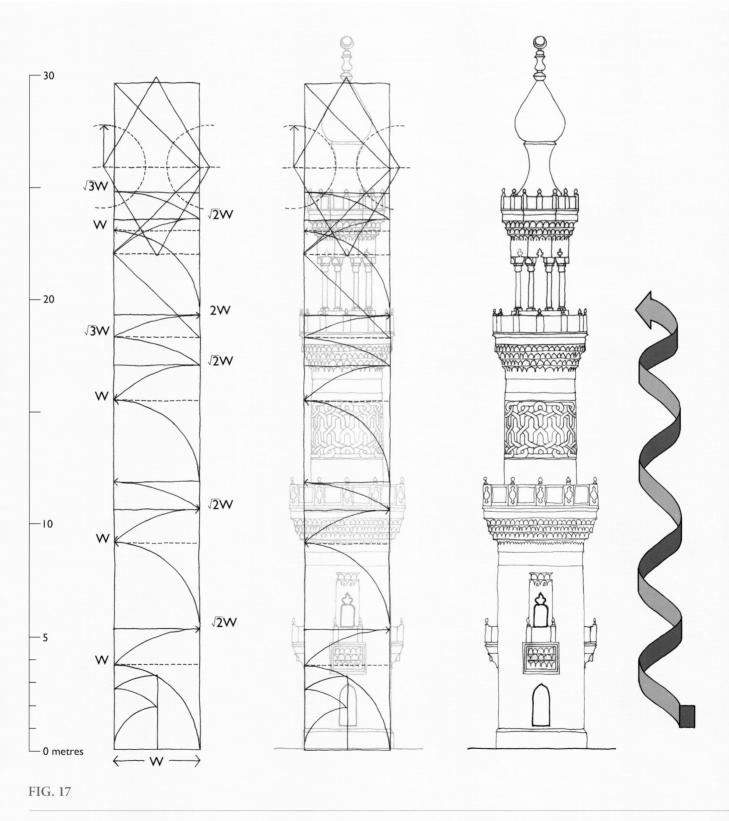

FIG. 17

Minaret of the complex of Sultan Faraj ibn Barquq showing system of proportioning and sectional properties

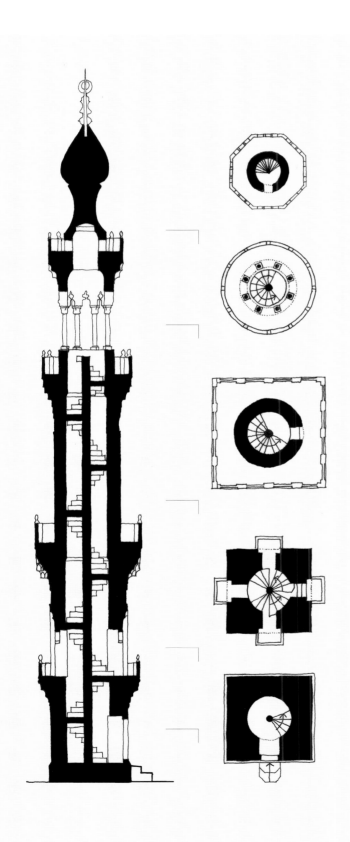

of Ibn Tulun and al-Hakim, the minaret's design was generally planned upwards from the level of the roof of the building to which it was attached, without much visual connection to the façade below. This is due to the fact that the minaret was normally erected on a rectangular buttress concealed behind the façade wall. That is not to say that the positioning of the minaret in relation to the façade was random: there were often good structural or compositional reasons for this particularly in relation to other architectural elements such as the monumental portal and dome (see Chapter Four). Sometimes, the base of the minaret was expressed structurally on the façade in the form of a salient, as with the madrasa of Sultan Hasan, where the buttresses protrude as circular corner towers. Despite this structural expression of the thrust of the minarets to the ground, they still stand on square bases above the roof of the building, and there is a pronounced break between the lower and the upper structures: it looks as if the minarets and the buttresses below them were designed and built by different teams of craftsmen who had little interaction with each other. By contrast, one of the only examples of an integrated design of salient and minaret stands nearby: the Ottoman mosque of Mahmud Pasha (1568).

The structural disjunction between façade and minaret also finds its corresponding expression in the decoration of the minaret, which often follows a separate logic. The muqarnas cornices and crenellation that crown the façades of most monumental buildings in Cairo also serve to reinforce this separation. These elements create a strong horizontal line at roof level, with the crenels running in front of the base of the minaret. Another type of disjunction can be noticed at the mosque of Qanibay al-Muhammadi (fig. 16) where the minaret and the dome rise at different levels.

Due to the fact that the vast majority of minarets in Cairo have had their upper structures rebuilt at some point in their history, it is hard to provide definitive measurements of their overall heights. However, even a cursory study of the elevations of medieval buildings that have minarets attached to them shows that there was a relatively constant ratio between the height of the minaret and that of the building below it of two to one, with only minor variations. This ratio was already employed at the

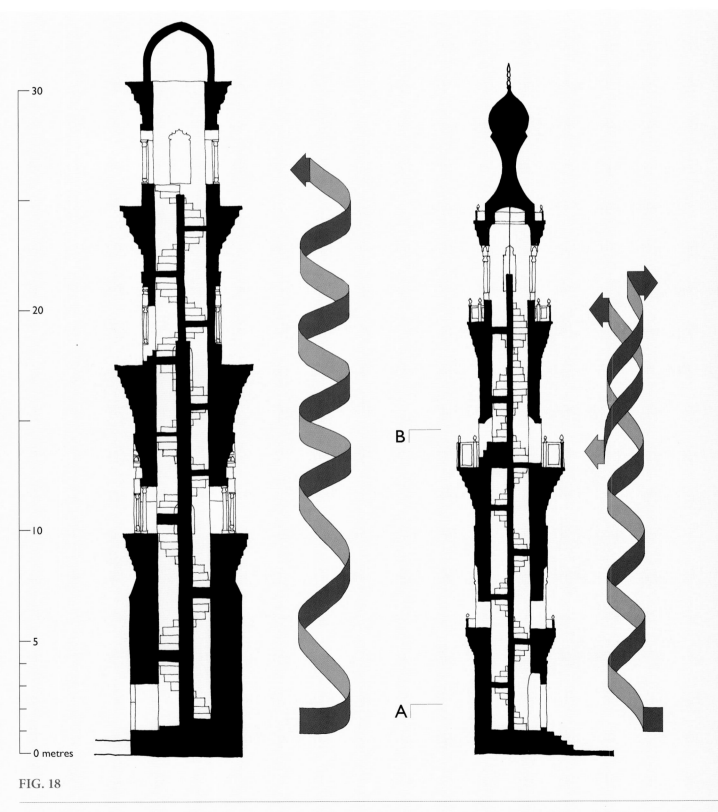

FIG. 18

Section through the minaret of Emir Qawsun showing differences in staircase pitch between tiers (left) and section through the minaret of Qaytbay at the Azhar mosque showing the double-helix staircase in the upper tier (right)

Plan B

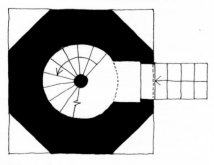

Plan A

0   5 metres

madrasa of al-Salih Najm al-Din Ayyub, which is one of the two earliest extant minarets to retain an original configuration. It cannot be excluded that the Fatimids also followed this rule: the minaret of the oratory of al-Juyushi exceeds this ratio by the height of its cupola. In any case, the same rule of thumb is apparent well beyond the Mamluk period: the minarets of the mosque of Muhammad 'Ali, for example, also demonstrate the same ratio. The rule seems not to have been applied when a minaret was added to an earlier building. In such cases the proportions might vary, as for example at the Azhar mosque where the later minarets of Qaytbay and al-Ghawri are more than twice the height of the mosque.

Most minarets have their staircases accessible from an entrance at roof level that is entirely separate in its vertical axis from the staircase leading to the roof from the interior of the building. This was not always the case historically, however, and certainly does not hold true for the provincial minarets. When minarets were added to the mosque of 'Amr they were initially reached by an external staircase, perhaps a kind of ladder. It was only later that staircases to the roof were introduced within the mosque. In the case of the mosque of Ibn Tulun, the staircase is entirely external and forms an integral part of its spiral design, which was inspired by Iraqi prototypes. The Fatimid minarets of the mosque of al-Hakim were built as independent tower structures with their staircases commencing at ground level within the shaft. This is also the case with the minaret of Abu 'l-Ghadanfar. When minarets were built directly above the vault of a portal they obviously could only be entered from the roof, as at the oratory of al-Juyushi, the shrine of al-Husayn, the complex of al-Salih Najm al-Din Ayyub, or the twin minarets of the complex of Shaykhu. In the subsequent evolution of the slender stone Mamluk minaret, a substantial buttress was usually constructed beneath it, either articulated on or concealed within the façade. The minaret of the mosque of Manjaq al-Silahdar – a freestanding structure with the entire staircase from ground level to apex being within the shaft – is exceptional in the Mamluk period, and this design is most likely the outcome of topographic considerations that are no longer apparent today. Even the minaret of the madrasa of Qaraquja al-Hasani, which is located outside and opposite the mosque on a side street, has no lower staircase: it is reached from the roof of the mosque by a wooden bridge. Likewise, the minaret of the funerary complex of the emir Azdumur, which is not attached to the main façade but stands near a side entrance, is accessible from the mosque through a passage carried by an arch.

The position of the minaret relative to the rest of the building, its structural composition and the design of its staircase were interrelated factors. Early minarets, often built directly above an entrance portal, were lighter brick structures. Examples of this type are the minaret of the mosque of al-Juyushi, the shrine of al-Husayn, the madrasas of al-Salih Najm al-Din and al-Nasir Muhammad and the *khanqah* of Baybars al-Jashnakir. In brick minarets, the structure is actually composed of a timber frame infilled with brick. This would have given the minaret a much greater elasticity in the event of an earthquake, and the capacity to deform quite considerably without collapsing. The helmet, or mabkhara, that crowns the superstructure of this minaret appears to have been constructed out of woven timber laths with a gypsum-plaster fill and final coat of lime render giving the desired profile. The brick minarets of the provincial city of al-Mahalla al-Kubra are constructed in a similar fashion.

The shaft of rectangular brick minarets, formed by a hollow masonry box, contains no further masonry within it to support the staircase. This is made of timber and attached directly to the walls of the rectangular shaft; it only becomes a spiral at the upper level. The weight of brick minarets could also be supported directly by the roof of the building, such as that of Baybars al-Jashnakir's *khanqah*, or even by the vault of a passage, as in the case of the madrasas of al-Salih Najm al-Din and al-Nasir Muhammad. The minaret of the Zawiyat al-Hunud stands above a room, while the minaret of Khayrbak is located above a stone vaulted room.

Stone minarets, especially when they were designed to be slender, usually required a solid base of masonry that extended from the ground to the roof of the building. By preference, this base was not weakened by the introduction of a staircase. This solid base is not always easily recognisable in plan, owing to the considerable skill with which it was incorporated

FIG. 19

View of the staircase of the minaret of Emir Bashtak

into the masonry of the walls defining the entrance or façade of the building. Stone minarets were only occasionally placed directly over stone-vaulted entrance corridors, as with those of the mosque and *khanqah* of Shaykhu. The staircase of stone minarets is spiral and winds around a central column of masonry that is formed of superimposed blocks that include each tread. The stone minaret of Sultan Qalawun, though built on a rectangular plan, also has a circular spiral staircase within it. K.A.C. Creswell suggested that this design was favoured because it was better adapted to tie the outer skin to the inner core.[9] The choice was more likely to have been made because of the ease of fabricating a regular shape of stone tread that included the central newel and was bonded into the masonry of the external skin. The northern minaret of the mosque of al-Nasir Muhammad in the Citadel has an unusual feature in this regard – an octagonal spiral stone staircase within an externally square shaft.

Four minarets in Cairo contain a double-helix spiral staircase in their upper sections. This consists of two parallel stairways with independent entrances, arranged so as to allow two persons to ascend/descend simultaneously without encountering one another. These are the minarets of sultans Qaytbay and al-Ghawri at al-Azhar (fig. 8), and those attached to the mosque of Azbak al-Yusufi and the funerary complex of Khayrbak. These minarets all fall late within the evolution of the Mamluk minaret and, with the exception of the last named, all are built of stone. Double-helix staircases were used in Seljuk minarets.[10] The Ghurid minaret of Jam is also a prominent example of this architectural feature. The tallest three-gallery minaret at the Üç Serefeli mosque in Edirne, built in 1447, half a century earlier than the minaret of Qaytbay at al-Azhar, has three separate spiral staircases. This was imitated later by the architect Sinan in the two northern minarets of the Selimiye mosque in the same city, which is equipped with four minarets.[11] The double staircase in Cairene minarets may be indeed of Anatolian origin, the builder in charge of Qaytbay's renovations at the Azhar mosque, Ibn Rustam, being an Ottoman from Bursa.[12] However, the double-helix staircase was already known to Cairene builders; the largest and most famous structure to possess a double-helix staircase/ramp is the 'Bir Yusuf', the eighty-metre-

FIG.20

View of the staircase of the minaret of the mosque of Emir Azbak al-Yusufi

FIG. 21

Detail of the south minaret of the mosque of al-Hakim

deep rock-cut well built by Salah al-Din in the Citadel. In the case of the minaret, the double-helix staircase must have been intended to fulfil a structural function, since it strengthens the shaft by doubling the number of points of contact between the central newel of the staircase and the outer wall of masonry. This would have created a stiffer structure, which may have been thought by the builders to have more resistance to the lateral forces exerted by seismic action. Similar reasoning may have determined another variation in the design of the spiral stone staircase: the diminution of the height of the risers in the staircase resulting in the creation of a tighter spiral. This can be seen in the case of the minaret of Qawsun in the southern cemetery, where the spiral of the staircase becomes tighter in

the second storey than in the rest of the shaft. The fact that the double-helix staircase was a comparatively late arrival in the evolution of the minaret in Cairo, and one that was not universally adopted, suggests that whatever structural advantages may have been conferred by the design, the complexity of construction that it demanded outweighed these considerations.

The Ottoman minaret presented fewer structural challenges than its Mamluk counterpart. This was partly a matter of scale: with the exception of the minarets of the mosque of Muhammad 'Ali, few Ottoman period minarets matched or surpassed the scale of their Mamluk antecedents. The upper section of an Ottoman minaret was a hollow construction without a staircase, and was much lighter and easier

FIG. 22

View of the interior of the bulb of the minaret at the khanqah *of Emir Shaykhu*

to build. Indeed, many Ottoman minarets had their caps built of timber lath and simply plastered to achieve the desired profile.

As is the case with other architectural elements, spoils were used in the construction of the minarets, either stone from Ancient Egyptian monuments or timber from earlier Islamic buildings. The casings around the minarets of al-Hakim that were added by al-Muzaffar Baybars, for example, contain blocks inscribed with hieroglyphs, and the timber staircase of the minaret of al-Salih Najm al-Din Ayyub was partly made of Fatimid carved planks. In Cairo, the stone that was used for masonry was generally quarried locally from the soft limestone of the Muqattam Hills immediately to the east of the city.

The stonemasonry of minarets above roof level was invariably ashlar, both internally and externally, and it is likely that some finishing and carving of blocks was carried out *in situ* although the majority would have been prefabricated off-site. Palm logs were used for the framing of brick minarets, and other types of locally available timber were used for smaller elements such as internal stairs, balustrades, and brackets. The construction of larger minarets must have demanded large quantities of timber for external scaffolding, although the staircase internal to the structure would have assisted in access during building work. Lath and plaster upper-level constructions were common: the plaster used for this and for renders was invariably lime-based.

FIG. 23

Modern finials on sale at Bayn al-Qasrayn

SIX

Architecture and Decoration

THE FINIAL

Cairo's domes and minarets are, as elsewhere in the Muslim world, usually surmounted by finials. These are mostly made of beaten brass or copper alloy sheet, forming a hollow construction. The finials are said to be oriented with their flat sides facing the direction of Mecca. They are most often made up of multiple superimposed elements such as globes or discs, and are topped with a crescent symbolising the lunar calendar upon which Islamic chronology is based. The crescent was not a traditional Islamic religious symbol, equivalent to the cross of the Christians; rather, its use was irregular and often purely ornamental.[1] It appeared in secular contexts as, for example, on the excursion boats used on Fatimid feast days.[2]

Another, much more unusual, kind of finial took the shape of a boat with a curving prow and stern. Only a single example of this form survives today, at the top of the dome of the mausoleum of Imam Shafi'i. The minaret of the mosque of Ibn Tulun likewise used to carry a boat-shaped finial from the time of its original construction until the nineteenth century. This boat, said to have been found in an Ancient Egyptian cache,[3] was torn down by a heavy storm in 1694,[4] and must eventually have been replaced by the finial that was illustrated by Robert Hay and Prisse d'Avennes in the mid-nineteenth century. A brass finial from the dome of the mausoleum of Barquq in the desert, now in the Islamic Museum of Cairo, carried below the usual crescent a boat-shaped object made of brass

with openings like those of a lamp.[5] The boats of Ibn Tulun and Imam Shafi'i bear a striking resemblance to a certain type of medieval oil lamp: the fact that the Ayyubid Sultan al-Malik al-Kamil ordered the boat of Ibn Tulun to be lit during mid-Sha'ban suggests that this similarity was not completely accidental.[6] A finial element that was once above one of the domes of Sultan Faraj Ibn Barquq's domes combines shapes of both a boat and a lamp.[7]

Boats appear elsewhere in related contexts: some provincial shrines used until modern times to possess a boat, which on a saint's anniversary would be decorated and carried on wheels in procession. A small boat used to hang in the shrine of Sidi Sarya at the Citadel, founded in the Fatimid period and rebuilt in the early sixteenth century. A similar boat used to be suspended on the outside of the Bab Zuwayla, and a further example can still be found in the shrine of Athar al-Nabi. In Egypt the symbol of the boat may have had a special significance: the use of boats in the procession of the saint, Abu 'l-Hajjaj, in Luxor has been considered to be a survival of the Ancient Egyptian practice of parading the barque of Amun at the time of the Opet festival. The talismanic role of the boat was not only restricted to Egypt: it is common to many cultures. In this context the historian Ibn Tulun provides some information, which, although from the early sixteenth century, may shed some light on the matter. When the Ottomans conquered Damascus, they hoisted their banner over the roof of the Umayyad mosque. It was red and plain and attached to a pole with a gilded silver crescent at its top, looking like

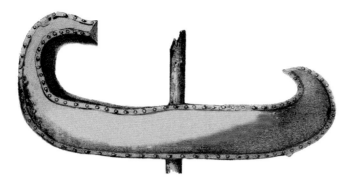

FIG. 24

Boat finial of the minaret of Ibn Tulun
PRISSE D'AVENNES

FIG. 25

Boat finial at the mausoleum of Imam Shafi'i
THE MOSQUES OF EGYPT

FIG. 26

Finial element from the khanqah *of Sultan Faraj ibn Barquq*

what the historian calls a *sanawbara,* meaning pine cone. The Mamluk banner it replaced was made of yellow silk adorned with embroidery and tassels, and attached to a pole with a golden crescent. From a distance this looked like the 'Prophet's slipper' and, in the view of the historian Ibn Tulun, was more pleasing.[8] Although the term *sanawbara* may refer to a conical finial on the banner, it is used elsewhere by the same author to describe a kind of lamp lit on special occasions at the top of the dome of the Umayyad mosque. The banner finial in the shape of a lamp or a slipper may have resembled the boat of Imam Shafi'i, a flat-shaped crescent with one end higher than the other.[9] The finials of Ibn Tulun's minaret and Imam Shafi'i's dome were, furthermore, said to have rotated. Maqrizi denied a popular belief that the boat of Ibn Tulun rotated with the sun, adding that the movement followed the wind.

One final, unique form of finial adorns the minaret of the funerary complex of the Mamluk saint Hasan Sadaqa (Sunqur al-Sa'di). This is a substitution made by the Mevlevi dervish order that came to occupy and extend the complex in the nineteenth century. As an emblem of their order, the Mevlevis placed above the minaret a finial shaped in the likeness of the tall woollen hats characteristic of their order.

THE UPPER STRUCTURE: THE MABKHARA, THE BULB AND THE CONE

The shift from brick to stone masonry construction had an impact on both the shape and the decoration of minarets in Cairo. The shafts became slender, inspiring a new design for the top of the structure that replaced the domed brick pavilion, called the mabkhara, with a more delicate superstructure formed by a ring of stone piers crowned with muqarnas supporting a pear-shaped stone bulb.

In Arabic the term mabkhara means 'incense-burner'. Its association with the domed structure or helmet at the top of early minarets is modern; it is not used either in the medieval chronicles or in *waqf* documents of either the Mamluk or the Ottoman period. Rather, medieval

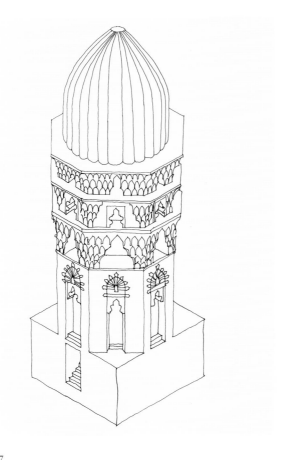

FIG. 27

Drawing of a mabkhara

sources indiscriminately use the term *khudha*, of Persian origin, meaning helmet or head-gear, for the upper structure of a minaret no matter in what style. According to Stanley Lane-Poole, who wrote in the first decade of the twentieth century, the term mabkhara was popularly used at his time to describe this kind of minaret top because of its peculiar shape.[10] K.A.C. Creswell adopted this term to describe the minaret upper structure composed of a domed pavilion. However, no incense-burner of this shape is known. Although *waqf* documents regularly refer to the suspension of lamps at the summit of minarets and the use of incense inside mosques, as was common practice from the earliest days of Islam, they do not mention incense being dispersed from minarets.[11] Neither do literary sources refer to such a practice, which would have been an extravagance and a waste

of a valuable material, and unlikely to have been perceived from the street below. Although the recent conservation work undertaken at the minaret of the madrasa of Salih Najm al-Din Ayyub has revealed that the inner surface of the mabkhara was heavily encrusted with a resinous residue, the use of the minaret as incense-burner cannot be confirmed.[12]

As an architectural term, mabkhara was adopted by Creswell to designate the ribbed helmet supported by an open circular or octagonal structure, such as those adorning the minarets of Abu 'l-Ghadanfar, the Zawiyat al-Hunud, Ibn Tulun, al-Hakim, al-Muzaffar Baybars, Sanjar al-Jawli, Sunqur al-Sa'di, Qawsun and Tankizbugha. The shape of the mabkhara is also found on the curious stone finials that form the corner elements of crenellated parapets around the interior courtyards of some mosques such as the mosques of al-Nasir Muhammad at the Citadel and the emirs Maridani and Shaykhu (fig. 28). The mabkhara pattern was abandoned during the fourteenth century in favour of a more slender structure composed of an octagonal pavilion crowned by a bulb set above a ring of muqarnas.[13] This became the characteristic top of late Mamluk minarets. Occasionally, the bulb itself was decorated around its neck with an inscription band, as seen on the minarets of Shaykhu.

The latest surviving example of the old variety of mabkhara is that of the mausoleum of Tankizbugha built in 1362 in the southern cemetery. The earliest extant octagonal pavilion is found on the minaret of the mosque of al-Maridani, dated 1340; the minaret of Aqbugha designed by the same architect lost its original top a long time ago. A variant of the octagonal pavilion had, in fact, been used earlier at the brick minarets of Fatima Khatun (1284) and al-Baqli (1297), the latter being hexagonal in plan. The upper structures of the two stone minarets of the mosque of al-Nasir Muhammad at the Citadel, dating to 1318, represent a further variation. These are closed cylindrical structures carrying ribbed bulbs, which are clad in glazed tiles. The experiment with tiled decoration, seen today as a unique feature at the minarets of the mosque of al-Nasir Muhammad, was repeated at the mosque of Qawsun (1330), which has been almost entirely replaced by a modern construction. The form of the upper structures of both minarets of al-Nasir

necks in a similar manner to bulbs. In this context, the description of
al-Hakim's pulpit as having a dome carried by an open pavilion extends the formal similarity of these two types of structure back to an earlier period.[15] At the same time, it can be observed that in Ottoman architecture, too, the conical cap of minarets is also commonly found on contemporary pulpits. Apart from the inference that both the top of the pulpit and the top of the minaret have a formal relationship, it is difficult to deduce more from this case of direct architectural parallelism.

In the late Mamluk period, the device of a paired bulb was introduced to form the top of minarets, followed by the quadruple bulb at the minaret of al-Ghawri's funerary complex where each bulb rested on its own rectangular pavilion. The slender pavilion carrying a pear-shaped bulb was not, however, a very sturdy construction; most of the minaret tops in Cairo have either been reconstructed completely or now lack their original pavilions altogether. In the Ottoman period the upper pavilions of many Mamluk minarets were often consolidated by walling up the spaces between their piers. All the newly built minarets of that period lacked the open pavilion altogether, even when they were constructed in the Mamluk style, as in the case of the minarets of the madrasa of Sultan Hasan and the mosque of Ulmas. The restorations undertaken by the Comité in the late nineteenth and early twentieth centuries further altered the appearance of the pavilion owing to the use of slender marble columns instead of the original limestone piers with engaged carved columns, which can be seen at the minarets of Asanbugha and Qaytbay at Qal'at al-Kabsh. The Comité also seem to have adopted a standard model of pavilion in their reconstructions, exemplified by their restorations of the minarets of al-Mu'ayyad Shaykh at the gate of Bab Zuwayla. This arbitrary and careless attitude to restoration was criticised even at the time.[16]

The pavilion crowned with a bulb is generally taller than it might appear from the street. This is revealed by the structure that once surmounted a Mamluk minaret, and is now displayed in the open-air museum of the Citadel (fig. 31). It consists of eight marble columns, some with cusped arches above them. Another detached pavilion, perhaps belonging to the minaret

FIG. 28

Decorative mabkhara at the mosque of Sultan al-Nasir Muhammad

Muhammad was reproduced at the minaret of the mosque of Emir Bashtak in a simpler version, without ribs or tiles. There, a circular shaft pierced with four openings and crowned with a bulb seems to be the intermediary stage that led the builder to the bolder design of the more airy octagonal pavilion crowned with pear-shaped bulb.

The pear-shaped bulb, used on later minarets, is a hollow structure and bears a close resemblance to the top of pulpits (minbar) of the same period (fig. 22).[14] These bulbs were usually made of wood, but in some cases of marble or limestone. Some of the stone examples, such as the pulpit of Sultan al-Nasir Faraj ibn Barquq, added by Sultan Qaytbay, in his complex in the northern cemetery, are inscribed around their

FIG. 30

The bulb of the minaret of Emir Bashtak with brackets for lamps

of the madrasa of Tatar al-Hijaziyya, stood about six metres high and was made of mismatched spoliated column shafts and capitals.[17] In some cases, stone piers with engaged pilaster-like columns rather than freestanding columns provided the structure of the pavilion. On the minarets of the mosque and *khanqah* of Shaykhu and at the minaret of Sultan Qaytbay at the mosque of al-Azhar, the top pavilion consists of a cylindrical structure pierced with four arched openings rather than on eight individual columns or piers.

With the exception of the minaret of the mosque of Jamal al-Din Mahmud (known as Mahmud al-Kurdi), surviving brick minarets of the fifteenth century are crowned by bulbs without pavilions. It is difficult to

tell whether this was the original design intention for these minarets, or whether this is due to the collapse of the pavilion and a rebuild of the bulb on its own to reduce the risk of structural failure. Some of the late Mamluk minarets made of brick have their bulbs made of timber lath and plaster, as is the case at the minarets of Jaqmaq and Khayrbak. The minaret of Badr al-Din al-Wana'i, although it is built in stone, also has a wooden bulb, which might be part of a later restoration. The use of lightweight elements in this location on a minaret would have conferred structural advantages, and was a feature of construction commonly adopted by builders in the Ottoman period. Ottoman minarets typically end with a plain cylindrical or

FIG. 31

An octagonal pavilion without its bulb

multi-faceted top that is capped by a cone. In the best-quality minarets of the nineteenth century, the angle of the cone is steeply pitched to accentuate the slenderness and overall height of the minaret. The tops of minarets in Alexandria and the northern Delta region, all of which date to the Ottoman period, also have bulbs, but of a very distinctive design. They are composed of a narrow cylindrical shaft with a collar at its top, above which sits the bulb. All these elements are ribbed, and made of plastered brick. Regardless of the period or style of minaret, the uppermost part of the mabkhara or bulb or cone was the location preferred for attaching wooden lamp brackets, most of which disappeared in the course of restoration.

THE DECORATED SHAFT

The earliest surviving minarets to receive an elaborate decorative treatment, which effectively extended to ground level, are those of the mosque of al-Hakim. Their remarkable horizontal carved banding, with geometric or epigraphic content, had no impact, however, on the decorative treatments of later minarets, perhaps because they were concealed behind the walls of the rectangular salients added to their exteriors soon after construction. After these unique cases, the decorative programme of the minaret typically began at roof level. This characteristic of Cairene minarets may suggest that the craftsmen who worked on the superstructure of minarets were specialists who were not necessarily involved in the construction of other parts of the same building.

Ever since the construction of the minarets of al-Hakim, two types of carved decoration have been applied to the stone shafts of Cairene minarets. These are raised linear mouldings that emphasise architectural form and a combination of geometric and arabesque ornament that infills intervening spaces. The minarets of al-Nasir Muhammad, both at his mosque in the Citadel and at his funerary complex in the Bayn al-Qasrayn, are the earliest to exhibit an overall treatment of the surface of the shafts themselves. In the case of the latter, this is accomplished by carved stucco using a variety of geometric and arabesque

FIG. 32

The Burmali minaret in Amasya, early thirteenth century

patterning framing epigraphic cartouches. Such decoration is a unique survival among the minarets of Cairo. In the case of al-Nasir's western minaret at the Citadel, which is made of stone, the decoration consists of finely carved chevrons in high relief. The minarets of Bashtak, Qawsun, Aqsunqur, Baybak al-Aydumuri, and the so-called 'Southern' minaret, all exhibit high-quality stone carving of a similar type.

A different, but related, form of carving dating to the same period may have been present on the minarets erected by a Tabrizi craftsman in Cairo. As these have not survived, we must rely on textual evidence for an impression of what they looked like. When the Mamluk emir Aytamish al-Ashrafi was sent to Tabriz on a diplomatic mission in 1322, he admired the mosque of 'Alishah there and recruited its builder, who remained anonymous, to work in Egypt. Aytamish wrote a description of the mosque of 'Alishah, later copied by the chronicler al-'Ayni, in which the term *halazawn* is used to define the appearance of its minarets. Medieval dictionaries explain the term *halazawn* as designating a snail rather than a shape, but the word has commonly been used until the present day to mean a spiral. Al-'Ayni also described the minaret erected by the same Tabrizi builder for the mosque of Aytamish in the village of Fishat al-Manara,[18] formerly called Fishat Salim, near Tanta, as having a *halazawn* interior.[19] The term *halazawn* is problematic here. All stone minarets in Cairo have a spiral staircase, as was already the case with the minarets of the mosque of al-Hakim, so there was no point in emphasising this feature as something special imported from Tabriz. The minarets of the mosque of 'Alishah are likely to have been cylindrical, as was traditional for Iranian minarets. The term *halazawn* appears once again slightly later in the context of another minaret. In his obituaries of the year 743/1343, Ibn Taghribirdi mentions that the emir Sayf al-Din Tashtimur, also known as Hummus Akhdar ('Green Chickpea'), built a mosque in the northern cemetery with a spiral minaret, *al-mi'dhana al-halazawn*.[22] Neither the mosque nor the minaret has survived; only a mausoleum dome dated to 735/1334 stands on the site today. In another text, Ibn Taghribirdi describes the same minaret as being very beautiful and of accomplished craftsmanship (*fi ghayat al-husn wa*

fi jawdat al-'amal) without referring to the *halazawn* feature.[22] It is unlikely that these *halazawn* minarets had an external staircase like that of the minaret of Ibn Tulun, and it is more probable that this historian was referring to a form of spiral decoration, which was common on Iranian and Anatolian minarets.[22] The Ilkhanid minarets at the portal of the Great Mosque of Ashtarjan (1305–6) in Iran, for example, were decorated with spiral 'corkscrew' bands of glazed bricks, in alternating blue and white.[23] The view of the Sultaniyya complex with Öljeytü's mausoleum (1303–7) depicted by the Ottoman artist Matrakçi Nasuh (*c.*1537) shows a pair of minarets with this kind of bichrome banding extending to the level of the first projecting balcony.[24] In Amasya, a Seljuk minaret (1237–44), called Burmali meaning 'spiral', displays this pattern in carved stone (fig. 32). The same corkscrew-like spiral also adorns other Anatolian minarets including the south-western minaret of the Üç Serefeli mosque in Edirne (1435).[25] It is likely that the Tabrizi builder, or the workshop he established in Cairo, was also responsible for the *halazawn* minarets of Aytamish and Tashtimur. Although the historians do not mention it, the minarets may have been decorated with tiles, as were the minarets of al-Nasir Muhammad and Qawsun. The latter are attributed by both al-'Ayni and Maqrizi to the Tabrizi craftsman although neither of them refers to tiling, which was mentioned later by Evliya Çelebi.[26] Interestingly, carved spiral ribbed decoration can be seen today in Cairo on the masonry domes of Uljay al-Yusufi (1373) and Aytamish al-Bajasi (1383–4).[27] As much of the decorative vocabulary of the masonry dome is derived from minarets, it may be that such spiral ribbing was also copied from examples seen on minarets that have now disappeared.

Carving was not the only medium of decoration employed in the mid-fourteenth century, however. A large number of contemporary and slightly later minarets reveal a different decorative concept based on inlaid, usually bichrome, stonework (figs 33 and 37). The earliest specimen of this style of decoration is found on the minaret of Aqbugha at al-Azhar (1339), built by the *mu'allim* Ibn al-Suyufi; the latest is at the minaret of Uljay al-Yusufi (1373). It was not until the late 1360s, with the construction of the minarets of Umm al-Sultan Sha'ban and Asanbugha, that carving

FIG. 33

The octagonal section at the minaret of Emir Aqbugha at the Azhar mosque

definitively replaced inlaid stone decoration as the standard method of decorating minaret shafts. The rectangular minarets of the early sixteenth century, however, bear no carving on their shafts, but instead have recesses framed with inlaid stonework.

Carved relief decoration was more suitable to challenge the sand and dust of Cairo, which tends to obscure flat surface treatments, and to allow decoration to be clearly picked out by harsh light casting strong shadows. The middle section, more than any other part of the minaret, was the place where decorators tended to concentrate their creativity, while the design of the octagonal and upper sections remained basically the same. The carved patterns varied across minarets, with very few repetitions. A favourite design, however, was a row of interlocked x-shaped crosses, which also appeared on carved masonry domes. The first occurrence of this pattern is on the minaret of Asanbugha. Some carved patterns were combined with a three-dimensional shaft profile. The shaft was not only carved with a zigzag pattern, but its profile was zigzagged, having the plan of a multi-pointed star, which accentuated the light and shadow contrast of the decoration. This device was used in stucco on the brick minaret of al-Khatiri in Bulaq,[28] no longer extant, and at the minaret of al-ʿAlaya, also in Bulaq. It was used in stone on the minaret added in 1462 to the mosque of Emir Husayn, also no longer standing. The minaret of Sultan Inal in the eastern cemetery has a similar zigzagged surface executed in stone. At the adjacent minaret of Qurqumas, the profile of the middle section of the shaft is zigzagged but the carved pattern is different, displaying diamond-shaped lozenges.

In the decade between the mid-1440s and mid-1450s there seems to have been a crisis in the craft of stone carving. The minarets of the mosques of Taghribirdi, the rebuilt minaret at the mosque of Arghun, the minarets at the madrasa of Sultan Jaqmaq and his vanished mosque at Dayr al-Nahhas, and the reconstructed minaret at the mosque of Emir Husayn all have stone shafts with carved stucco decoration; plastered stone remained, however, a rare occurrence in Mamluk exterior decoration. Plastered timber lath was also used in the construction of minaret shafts, as is revealed in an archival photograph of the minaret of Qadi Yahya at Habbaniyya showing the

now demolished second storey that was of cylindrical shape made of this material.[29] It cannot be excluded that this technique was applied to other minarets as well. With the construction of the minaret of Sultan Inal came a revival of carved masonry and a decade later the reign of Qaytbay introduced a second golden age for carved stone decoration.

In the last quarter of the fifteenth century, the decoration of minarets became less architecturally orientated. Designs were no longer adapted to the shape of the surface they decorated, as mouldings or arches, but were general patterns that were not specific to minarets, or even to architecture, but applicable to any medium. One is inclined to believe that such forms of decoration were produced in those pattern workshops in the market, *suq al-rassamin*, which Maqrizi mentions as specialised in creating designs.[30] There also seems to have been a mass production of rectangular carved panels with standard decoration that could be inserted indiscriminately on the base of minarets or on façade walls, to fill empty spaces. Such panels appear on the base of the minaret of Sultan Inal and henceforth on most subsequent minarets. The carved decoration in the middle section of the minarets of Qaytbay in the cemetery and Qalʿat al-Kabsh, Yashbak, Timraz and Janim al-Bahlawan looks as if it was copied from a pattern book rather than being a bespoke design for a cylindrical architectural structure.

In the early sixteenth century, the rectangular shafts of the minarets of al-Ghawri and Qanibay Qara were not carved (excepting their muqarnas); their decoration consisted rather of inlaid and striped masonry. Glazed tiles were also introduced as a coloured element in the decoration of the monumental minarets of al-Ghawri at al-Azhar and his funerary mosque. Perhaps it is from this time that the minarets of Cairo and the buildings to which they were attached began to be subjected to a relentless decorative treatment of bichrome painted stripes (or chequerboard) that soon covered all architectural surfaces, whether they were carved or not.

Because the evolution of masonry minarets preceded that of masonry domes, decorative patterns carved on minarets were often subsequently transferred to domes: the zigzag pattern carved on many masonry domes, for example, had been used earlier on the minarets of al-Nasir Muhammad, Umm al-Sultan Shaʿban, Qanibay

FIG. 34

The octagonal section of the minaret of Sultan Qaytbay at al-Azhar

FIG. 35

The base and transitional zone of the minaret of Emir Bashtak

al-Muhammadi and al-Mu'ayyad. The interlace motif carved on the minaret of Asanbugha was later used on the domes of Umm al-Ashraf in the southern cemetery[31] and Taghribirdi. The diamond-shaped motif on the minarets of Qadi Yahya at Bulaq and Qaytbay at Qal'at al-Kabsh were subsequently applied to the mausoleum domes of Qurqumas and 'Usfur. Projecting, spiky, muqarnas elements, the earliest of which is seen crowning the minaret of Qawsun, were later adopted at the dome of Tankizbugha in the southern cemetery.[32] Indeed, the architecture of stone domes itself, as has been demonstrated by Christel Kessler,[33] was influenced by techniques first applied on the masonry mabkharas of minarets.

THE TRANSITIONAL ZONE

Minarets with a rectangular shaft have no articulated base. Minarets with an octagonal or cylindrical shaft were not set directly on the roof, however, but above a rectangular base. As with the architecture of the dome, the base of the minaret, moving from the square to the octagonal or circular shaft, was for aesthetic reasons articulated with a zone of transition. Initially, the corners of the base were simply chamfered to form triangles pointing downwards at each corner. Another device was the use of pyramidal supports set at the corners instead of triangles. The transitional zones of the two minarets of the complex of Shaykhu (1349 and 1355) at Saliba Street display both devices: the minaret of the mosque has pyramidal facets and that of the *khanqah* has downward-pointing triangles. The earliest known minaret with an elaborate transitional zone is that of Bashtak (1336); the triangles here were carved to display an undulating profile. This bears a certain stylistic resemblance to the volutes used at the base of domes in Renaissance and Baroque architecture.

The minaret of the complex of Sultan Inal (1451) is the earliest extant minaret to display a network of mouldings running along and segmenting the transitional zone into rectangles alternating with corner triangles. The moulding is composed of two parallel bands that intersect to form loops. This device articulates the transitional zone and sets it apart from the rectangular base below. The transitional zone was initially below the octagonal section, and visibly separated from it. In a later development, however, the transitional zone was integrated into the first storey, with its corner triangles inserted between the four miniature balconies that correspond to staircase windows pierced in four of the eight keel-arched niches of the octagonal section. The earliest shaft to display this feature is that of the minaret of Timraz al-Ahmadi; it was also adopted on the minarets of the Qaytbay period mosques of Janim al-Bahlawan, Abu Bakr ibn Muzhir, Qijmas al-Ishaqi and Khushqadam al-Ahmadi, but not on the minarets of the mosques of Qurqumas and Khayrbak.

On early brick domes, the transitional zone consisted of steps between the square and the octagonal base of the dome. The development of masonry domes, however, led to the adoption of transitional zones similar to those already applied on minarets. The domes of Barquq's mausoleum, for example, are thus adorned with an undulating transitional zone similar to that of Bashtak's minaret built half a century earlier. Later domes were further adorned with a moulding at their base similar to the type of moulding commonly applied to the base of minarets. Further transitional zones between the individual tiers of a minaret were executed for the most part with stepped muqarnas corbels or cornices, and occasionally with horizontal or vertical flutes as on the minarets of Shaykhu and Manjaq.

MUQARNAS, BALCONIES, WINDOWS AND INSCRIPTIONS

The muqarnas is one decorative element that has accompanied the development of the Cairene minaret for all of its history, starting with the Fatimid period. The term is used to describe a series of faceted geo-metrically designed connecting niches and arcades that create a subtle interplay of light and shade on the surface of a building. There is a plastered brick muqarnas cornice crowning the square shaft of al-Juyushi's minaret and another one below its cupola. These are the earliest occurrences of muqarnas in the architecture of Cairo, if not Egypt. Later, muqarnas

executed in stone became a standard device at the top of each storey of a minaret, used to elaborate the transition between sections of differing diameters where a balcony was located. A truly remarkable feature of Cairene Mamluk minarets was that no single pattern of muqarnas was ever used twice on the same shaft: each storey was treated differently. Commencing in the period of Sultan Qaytbay, individual units of muqarnas were connected by pierced miniature screens. One of the most unusual patterns can be seen on the

FIG. 36

Drawing of the balustrades of the minaret of Emir Qawsun

minaret of the mosque of 'Ali al-'Imari, which has
pineapple-like pendants at the end of one tier of
muqarnas. Besides the minaret, the portal vault and
the transitional zone of domes provided the other
major loci for muqarnas decoration on any Mamluk
building. The Ottoman conquest had a negative impact
on the art of muqarnas carving. With the absence
of royal mausoleum domes, the disappearance of
muqarnas portal vaults, which already in the fifteenth
century were being partially replaced by groin vaults,
and the limitation of the number of minaret balconies
to one, stonemasons had little opportunity to practise
their carving skills. The resulting decline is apparent
in the reconstructed minarets of the madrasa of Sultan
Hasan and the mosque of Ulmas. In the eighteenth
century a revival of muqarnas carving took place
under the patronage of the Janissary commander 'Abd
al-Rahman Katkhuda.[34] Although his minarets remain
conventional, their balconies display fine muqarnas
work, often elaborately pierced in the style created in
the period of Sultan Qaytbay.

The balconies of minarets, which appear as rings
around the shaft at the top of the first and second
storeys, were for the use of the muezzin to stand and
broadcast his call to prayer on all sides. On early
minarets, the balcony was a timber structure, with
a handrail that was tied back above head height to
the main shaft. Brick minarets always had timber
handrails, for the sake of lightness of structure. With
the evolution of masonry minarets in the Mamluk
period, however, balconies acquired handrails of
carved and/or pierced stone. These stone handrails
may have had their origins in the magnificent carved
stone screens at the funerary complex of Sanjar
al-Jawli. The designs used in such handrails could
be both geometric and arabesque, or an alternating
combination of the two. Today, due to the extensive
restoration work carried out on many minarets, it is
often difficult to be sure as to the original appearance
of these stone-carved handrails. As in the case of
the bulbs at the top of minarets, it seems that in the
course of modern restorations, many missing handrails were replaced with new models of a standardised
design. The newly discovered foundation deed of
al-Ghawri's minaret at al-Azhar[35] indicates that it
was originally designed to have wooden not stone

FIG. 37

Detail of masonry at the minaret of the khanqah *of*
Emir Shaykhu

handrails on the balconies, as the restorers assumed. Such a detailed description of a minaret is, however, rare to find in foundation documents. Very often, the minaret is missing altogether from the description of the building, perhaps because it was usually the last structure to be completed, sometimes even postdating the compilation of the deed.

Ancillary to the balconies that circle the shaft at the top of the first and second storeys of the typical Mamluk minaret are graceful miniature projecting balconies that are only seen attached to the octagonal first storey. These balconies are not designed for anyone to stand on, being too small, but are connected with windows that light the staircase of the minaret and provide an integral decorative element. They were usually given handrails, sometimes made of pierced stone, as found on the larger balconies.

A different type of miniature balcony projects from the façade of the small eighteenth-century oratory or *zawiya* founded by 'Abd al-Rahman Katkhuda in the Mugharbilin quarter of Cairo (figs 5 and 6). As the building was too small to warrant a minaret, a miniature balcony for the muezzin to deliver the call to prayer was placed directly above the main portal, projecting out on a muqarnas corbel.

Miniature balconies containing windows were frequently framed within keel-arched niches with radiating hoods. Keel-arched niches were another major feature to appear consistently in the decoration of minarets. They adorn the rectangular section of the minaret of al-Salih Najm al-Din Ayyub, and they became a standard element in the octagonal section of later stone minarets. Ever since the construction of the minaret of Qalawun, such niches have been traditionally flanked by colonettes. The later development of this element included clusters of three colonettes, rather than singles, which might all receive individual decorative treatments.

Inscriptions are also an important component in the decorative schema of many Mamluk minarets. Their content is generally Koranic, and is discussed in detail in the following chapter. The inscriptions most often took the form of continuous bands, of different widths and carved to different depths, running around the shaft of the minaret, but are also occasionally found in cartouches, as at the minaret of the madrasa of

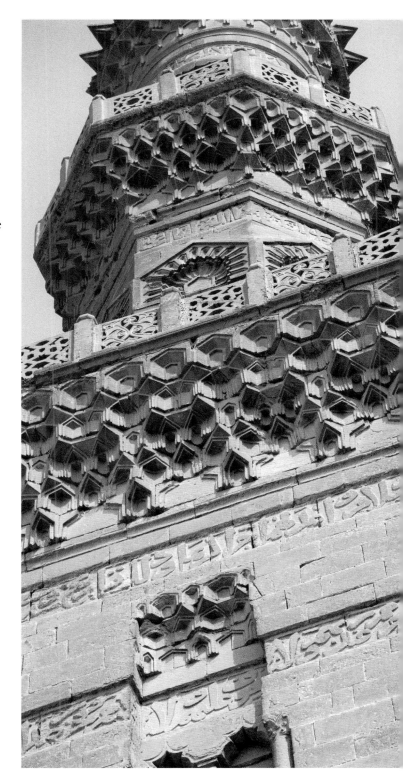

FIG. 38

View of the muqarnas at the minaret of Emir Qawsun

FIG. 39

The minarets of Mahmud Pasha (left) and Muhammad 'Ali Pasha

al-Nasir Muhammad in the Bayn al-Qasrayn. They could be placed at almost any height on the minaret, even on the bulb where they would be almost impossible to read, except from another minaret of equivalent height standing nearby. The style of the script employed in the overwhelming majority of inscriptions on minarets is *thuluth*.

THE OTTOMAN TRANSFORMATION

Compared with their Mamluk predecessors, the Ottoman-style minarets of Cairo can be described as either 'impoverished' or 'limited' in terms of their architectural expression and decoration. The shaft of the typical minaret is either wholly circular, or so heavily faceted as to appear circular. With the exception of the minarets of Sulayman Pasha and Shahin al-Khalwati, the shaft is usually decorated with vertical mouldings, executed in carved stone or plaster, running along the edge of each facet. The former has a decorative 'collar' of shallow carved fleur-de-lis at the base of the shaft. Apart from the two early minarets of Sulayman Pasha, at his mosques at the Citadel and at Bulaq, Ottoman minarets have only a single balcony located above a projecting muqarnas cornice. The transitional zone is normally carved with a series of pyramidal patterns rising to the shaft from a base whose top is mostly set below the level of the roof. The shaft is constructed of stone either in its entirety or up to the level of the balcony, with the upper structure being fabricated of lath and plaster, as seen on the minaret of Sinan Pasha in Bulaq. Like their Turkish prototypes, the Ottoman minarets of Cairo were not inscribed: only the minaret of al-Burdayni, built in the Mamluk style, has an inscription. In the nineteenth century, the tops of minarets such as those of the mosques of Sulayman Agha al-Silahdar, Muhammad 'Ali, the shrines of Fatima al-Nabawiyya (second quarter of the nineteenth century), and al-Husayn became elongated. In the case of the first two examples, the lower section of the shaft came to resemble more closely an oversized column with an identifiable base and a capital supporting the balcony.

FIG. 40

The vanished late Ottoman minaret of the mosque of Fatima al-Nabawiyya

FIG. 41

Inscription band at the minaret of the mosque of Emir Azbak al-Yusufi

SEVEN

Epigraphy

With the exception of the lavishly inscribed minaret shafts of the mosque of Caliph al-Hakim, dating from the Fatimid period, and the minaret of Shaykh al-Burdayni, dating from the Ottoman period, all extant minarets in Cairo that bear inscriptions date to the Mamluk period. Although not all Mamluk minarets bear inscriptions, the royal minarets are mostly inscribed. Epigraphic bands must have been costly and time-consuming to design and produce. It is perhaps unsurprising, therefore, that provincial minarets were not inscribed.

The first minarets to be built in Egypt, attached to the mosque of ʿAmr in Fustat in 673, are reported to have displayed the name of their founder, the Umayyad governor of Egypt, Maslama ibn Mukhallad, on an inscription placed in an unknown location.[1] The original pair of minarets of the mosque of al-Hakim, later concealed behind monumental masonry salients, are, unlike the façade of the mosque, adorned with elaborate inscription bands that include several Koranic texts, the founder's name and the foundation date.[2] These are the earliest extant minarets in Cairo to bear inscriptions.

Generally, minarets did not bear foundation inscriptions since the founder's name and date were more usually placed on a more visible part of the building such as the portal or main façade. However, the minarets that were added to pre-existing religious buildings, as was the case with other additional structures, were often inscribed with the names of their sponsors to document their contribution. This was particularly true when the addition or restoration

was carried out at a highly venerated shrine or important mosque. In a mosque of the status of al-Azhar, for example, such inscriptions also had a great propagandistic value and enhanced the sponsor's image. The three minarets added to the mosque of al-Azhar by Aqbugha, Qaytbay and al-Ghawri bear no Koranic texts, but each has a foundation inscription.[3] The minaret at the shrine of al-Husayn added during the Ayyubid period bears the name of its sponsor,[4] as does that added to the shrine of Imam al-Layth by Emir Yashbak min Mahdi.[5] An inscription panel in the name of Emir Yalbugha al-Salimi refers to the minaret and pulpit he added to the Aqmar mosque.[6] An inscription on the minaret of Sultan Qalawun was added by his son al-Nasir Muhammad to commemorate his reconstruction of the upper storey, which had collapsed during the earthquake of 1303.[7] On that same occasion, the Emir Baybars al-Jashnakir restored the upper structures of the minarets of al-Hakim and inscribed his name on one of them.[8] Besides these cases of inscriptions documenting additional constructions or restorations, two minarets constructed *ex novo*, at the mosques of the emirs Bashtak and Azbak al-Yusufi, bear independent foundation texts.

Apart from these relatively few historical texts, the vast majority of inscriptions applied to Cairene minarets were Koranic. In general, the repertoire of verses employed was limited, varying little from the minarets of al-Hakim to those of the reign of Qaytbay. They are usually texts praising Allah as the Creator of Heaven and Earth and summoning believers to devote themselves to Him rather than material rewards.

FIG. 42

Inscription band at the minaret of Emir Bashtak

Another group of texts refer to the Heavens and Earth, the passage of the hours, and the transitions from night to day, and darkness to light. These seem to be particularly appropriate given the role the minaret played in announcing the times of prayer according to the position of the sun. The often-inscribed Sura 3:190–1 explains the transition from night to day as a sign from God to His believers. The Sura of the Light (24:35–6), which compares the light of God with the light of an oil lamp, is usually inscribed on the upper part of the minaret close to where such lamps were suspended from wooden brackets. Also the verse of the Sura of the Throne (2:255) occurs in upper sections. In cases where minarets combine a foundation text and a Koranic inscription, as the minarets of Aqbugha at al-Azhar and Azbak al-Yusufi, the historical inscription seems to have been given more importance, as it is placed lower than the other and can, therefore, be read more easily.

Not all Koranic inscriptions were used in all historical periods. Although some of the Koranic inscriptions of the minarets of al-Hakim, for example,

were frequently repeated on the minarets of the Mamluk period, such as the Sura of the Light, others never appeared again. Sura 11:73 offers a demonstration of this as it includes the words 'people of the house', interpreted by Shi'a believers as referring to their patron, the Prophet's son-in-law and caliph 'Ali, thus enlisting the support of the Koran to reinforce their claim for a dynastic caliphate. Sunni Muslims, however, would never have endorsed such an interpretation.

In exceptional cases an inscribed text seems to express a personal experience of the patron, as at the minaret of Qadi 'Abd al-Basit. This inscription refers to the commandment of pilgrimage, and by the same token to the mosque's sponsor who was in charge of the organisation of the production of the Kaaba curtain (*nazir al-kiswa*) that was dispatched yearly from Cairo to Mecca. The inscriptions found on the minaret of Shaykh Abu 'l-'Ila are another special case. These express the mystic character of the founder and the community of his mosque. The inscription of the minaret of Princess Tatar, uniquely in Mamluk minaret epigraphy, seems to refer to a specific event in the life of the patroness.

Opinions differ as to whether architectural epigraphy was really intended to be read or whether it served as mere decoration.[9] Both interpretations are probably valid, depending on time and place. Minaret inscriptions usually begin on the right side to the onlooker from the street. This would allow a literate person, after identifying the first words of the inscribed Koranic text, to recall the remainder of the passage from memory even if it was out of sight on the rear side of the minaret. In a few cases, the *basmala* or opening formula ('in the name of God, the Lord of Mercy, the Giver of Mercy') begins on the opposite side; this occurs when the rear side of the building faced a more densely populated area, as was the case with the minarets of Sanjar, Bashtak and Qaraquja. Longer citations tend to start on an upper band and continue downwards, as on the northern minaret of al-Hakim and the minaret of the mosque of Shaykh Abu 'l-'Ila. On the minaret of Qawsun, however, this order is reversed, with the text running from the lower to the upper band, which may be interpreted as an attempt to make the beginning of the citation more legible to those on the ground. As a further aid to their legibility, inscriptions were frequently painted in blue and gold. As long as the buildings were well maintained, their inscriptions would have been more visible than they appear today. They were also less remote to the eye of a man on horseback than they were to a viewer on foot. It should be added, however, that horse riding was in principle, yet not always in practice, reserved for the ruling aristocracy and their close clientele. Even when inscriptions were not legible, they still had a meaning. The mere presence of Koranic texts, the literal word of God, bestowed upon them a sense of sacredness and offered a protection against evil. Such inscriptions can, furthermore, be interpreted as a written form of recitation, a religious ritual designed to gain God's blessing. The presence of the word of God was in itself a form of visual piety performed by the patron, who disseminated it for the onlooker to respond to with his pious gaze.

A distinction should be made here between early and late epigraphy. An interesting document in this connection is the biography of Abu 'l-Raddad, the craftsman who carved the inscriptions on the Nilometer on Rawda Island in 861. He stated that he painted the letters in blue on a gold ground 'so that the text would be more visible'.[10] The inscriptions on the Nilometer are legible even today, in fact, without their gold and blue. Several other examples of early Cairene inscriptions likewise demonstrate, by their legibility, that they were intended to be read, like the monumental inscription bands on the original minarets of al-Hakim. Early Mamluk minarets bear deeply carved inscriptions that are quite legible, like those of Qalawun, al-Nasir Muhammad and Sanjar al-Jawli. In the late Mamluk period inscriptions were more frequently applied to minarets, but at the same time they became more difficult to read owing to the small size of the lettering and the depth of their carving. Although the reign of Qaytbay was a golden age for stone carving, the inscriptions of this period were executed with less care and depth than contemporary architectural ornament. It seems that by this time epigraphy had been abandoned to the decorator, who fitted the inscription bands into the compositional scheme without giving priority to their legibility or seeking originality in their content. Importance was placed on the grace of the slender shafts of the minarets

of this period, which would have been disturbed by large and heavy inscriptions intended to be read.

At the upper tier level on the minaret of Qaytbay at his funerary complex in the northern cemetery is a partially completed inscription that exists as lettering scratched into the surface of a dedicated horizontal band. Other minarets display completely empty horizontal bands of the kind that would normally be inscribed. Examples of this phenomenon are found on the minarets of the mosques of Sarghitmish, Manjaq, Sultan Sha'ban's mother, her husband Uljay al-Yusufi, Taghribirdi, Qaytbay at Qal'at al-Kabsh and Khushqadam al-Ahmadi, as well as on the second storey added in the fifteenth century to the minaret of the madrasa of al-Nasir Muhammad. The absence of inscriptions on the minaret of Sultan Hasan is not surprising since the whole complex was not completed: even the courtyard of the mosque displays an uninscribed band along its four walls. The minaret of the funerary complex of Sultan al-Ghawri has no inscriptions on the first and second storeys although space for them is available; however, inscriptions were included on the two tiled upper storeys, as can be seen on Coste's drawing: today these have disappeared (fig, 215 and 216). The two rectangular minarets of Qanibay were uninscribed although the design of the decoration would have allowed the addition of epigraphic bands. The frequent presence of uninscribed bands on minarets suggests that the monuments were not planned to the last detail from the outset. Unlike more regular forms of decoration, which were a matter of routine for the experienced mason, monumental inscriptions required the involvement of two individuals: an epigraphist to provide a design that fitted the available space and a carver or decorator capable of implementing it. This meant an increased cost for epigraphic undertakings, and may ultimately have led the patron to do without them. Inscriptions must have been one of the last elements to be added to a minaret. This is confirmed by the case of the minaret of Abu 'l-'Ila, where rectangular panels were obviously added as an afterthought to contain the conclusion of a text for which no room was left in the allotted inscription bands. The fact that this inscription begins at the top of the minaret indicates that epigraphic carving began after the completion of the entire structure and proceeded downwards, perhaps in tandem with the final dismantling of the scaffolding.

KORANIC VERSES ON MINARETS IN CAIRO, LISTED IN NUMERICAL ORDER[11]

1:1 'In the name of God, the Lord of Mercy, the Giver of Mercy.' This verse is called *basmala*.

2:73 'We said "Strike the [body] with a part of [the cow]": thus God brings the dead to life and shows His signs so that you may understand.'

2:164 'In the creation of heavens and earth; in the alternation of night and day; in the ships that sail the seas with goods for people; in the water which God sends down from the sky to give life to the earth when it has been barren, scattering all kinds of creatures over it; in the changing of the winds and clouds that run their appointed courses between the sky and earth: There are signs in all of these for those who use their minds.'

2:255 'God: There is no God but Him, the Ever Living, the Ever Watchful. Neither slumber nor sleep overtakes Him. All that is in the heavens and in the earth belongs to Him. Who is there that can intercede with Him except Him by His leave? He knows what is before them and what is behind them. But they do not comprehend any of His knowledge except what He wills. His throne extends over the heavens and the earth; it does not weary Him to preserve them both. He is the Most High, the Tremendous.'

2:262 'Those who spend their wealth in God's cause, and who do not follow their spending with reminders of their benevolence or hurtful words, will have their rewards with their Lord: no fear for them, nor will they grieve.'

2:277 'Those who believe, do good deeds, keep up the prayer, and pay the prescribed alms will have their reward with their Lord: no fear for them, nor will they grieve.'

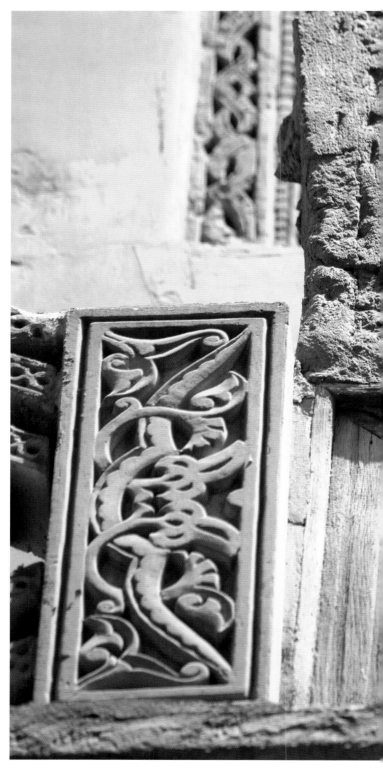

FIG. 43

Foundation inscription of the Ayyubid minaret at the shrine of al-Husayn

2:285 'The Messenger believes in what has been sent down to him from his Lord, as do the faithful. They all believe in God, His angels, His scriptures, and His messengers. "We make no distinction between any of His messengers" they say, "We hear and obey. Grant us Your forgiveness, our Lord. To You we all return!"'

3:18 'God bears witness that there is no god but Him, as do the angels and those who have knowledge He upholds justice. There is no god but Him, the Almighty, the All Wise.'

3:190–1 'There truly are signs of the creation of the heavens and earth, and in the alternation of night and day, for those with understanding, who remember God standing, sitting, and lying down, who reflect on all this without purpose – You are far above that! – so protect us from the torment of Fire.'

5:16 '…God guides to the ways of peace those who follow what pleases Him, bringing them from darkness out into light by, His will, and guiding them to a straight path.'

5:55 'Your true allies are God, His Messenger, and the believers – those who keep up the prayer, pay the prescribed alms, and bow down in worship.'

7:52 'We have brought people a Scripture – We have explained it on the basis of true knowledge – as guidance and mercy for those who believe.'

7:54 'Your Lord is God, who created the heavens and the earth in six Days then established Himself on the throne; He makes the night cover the day in swift pursuit; He created the sun, moon and stars to subservient to His command; all creation and command belong to Him Exalted be God, Lord of all worlds!'

9:3 'On the day of the Great Pilgrimage [there will be] a proclamation from God and His Messenger to all people: "God and His Messenger are released from [treaty] obligations to the idolaters. It will be better for you [idolaters] if you repent; know that you cannot escape God if you turn away [Prophet], warn those who ignore [God] that they will have a painful punishment."'

9:18 'The only ones who should tend God's places of worship are those who believe in God and the Last Day, who keep up the prayer, who pay the prescribed alms, and who fear no one but God: such people may hope to be among the rightly guided.'

9:107 'Then there are those who built a mosque – in an attempt to cause harm, disbelief, and disunity among the believers – as an outpost for those who fought God and His Messenger before: they swear, our intentions were nothing but good, but God bears witness that they are liars.'

9:128 'A Messenger has come to you from among yourselves. Your suffering distresses him: he is deeply concerned for you and full of kindness and mercy towards the believers.'

11:73 'They said "Are you astonished at what God ordains?" The grace of God and His blessings be upon you, people of this house.'

17:80 [fragment] 'Say, My Lord, make me go in truthfully, and come out truthfully.'

18:108–9 'There they will remain, never wishing to leave. Say [Prophet]. "If the whole ocean were ink for writing the words of my Lord, it would run dry before those words were exhausted", even if We were to add another ocean to it.'

22:27–9 'Proclaim the pilgrimage to all people. They will come to you on foot on every kind of swift mount, emerging from every deep mountain pass to attain benefits and celebrate God's name, on specified days, over the livestock He has provided for them – feed yourselves and the poor and unfortunate – so let the pilgrims perform their acts of cleansing, fulfil their vows, and circle around the Ancient House.'

22:41 'Those who, when We establish them in the land, keep up the prayer, pay the prescribed alms, command what is right, and forbid what is wrong: God controls the outcome of all events.'

24:26–8 'Corrupt women are for corrupt men: good women are for good men and good men are for good women. The good are innocent of what has been said against them; they will have forgiveness and a generous provision.'

24:35–8 'God is the Light of heavens and earth. His Light is like this: there is a niche, and in it a lamp, the lamp inside a glass, a glass like a glittering star, fuelled from a blessed olive tree from neither east nor west, whose oil almost gives light even when no fire touches it – light upon light – God guides whoever He will to His light, God draws such comparisons for people; God has full knowledge of everything – shining out in houses of worship. God has ordained that they be raised high and that His name be remembered in them, with men in them celebrating His glory morning and evening: men who are not distracted, either by commerce or profit, from remembering God, keeping up the prayer, and paying the prescribed alms , fearing a day when hearts and eyes will turn over. God will reward such people according to the best of their actions, and He will give them more of His bounty: God provided limitlessly for anyone He will.'

33:41–6 'Believers, remember God often and glorify Him morning and evening: it is He, who blesses you, as do His angels, in order to lead you out of the depths of darkness, into the light, He is ever merciful towards the believers – when they meet Him they will be greeted with "Peace" – and He has prepared generous reward for them. Prophet, We have sent you a witness, as a bearer of good news and warning as one who calls people to God by His leave, as a light-giving lamp.'

33:56 'God and His angels bless the Prophet – so, you who believe, bless him too and give him greetings of peace.'

36:13 'Give them the example of the people to whom town messengers came. We sent two messengers but they rejected both. Then We reinforced them with a third. They said "Truly, we are messengers to you."'
39:73 'Those who were mindful of their Lord will be led in throngs to the Garden. When they arrive, they will find its gates wide open, and its keepers will say to them "Peace be upon you. You have been good. Come in: you are here to stay."'

41:30–2 'As for those who say 'our Lord is God', and take the straight path towards Him, the angels come down to them and say "Have no fear or grief, but rejoice in the good news of Paradise, which you have been promised." We are your allies in this world and in the world to come, where you will have everything you desire and ask for as a welcoming gift from the Most Forgiving, Most Merciful One.'

48:1–2 'In the name of God, the Lord of Mercy, of the Giver of Mercy. Truly We have opened up a path to clear triumph for you [Prophet], so that God may forgive you.'

55:1–7 'It is the Lord of Mercy who taught the Koran. He created man and taught him to communicate. The sun and the moon follow their calculated courses; the plants and trees submit to His designs; He has raised up the sky. He has set the balance.'

57:9 'It is He who has sent clear revelations to His Servant, so that He may bring you from the depth of darkness into light; God is truly kind and merciful to you.'

62:9–10 'Believers! When the call to prayer is made on the day of congregation, hurry towards the reminder of God and leave off your trading – that is better for you, if only you knew – then when the prayer has ended, disperse in the land and seek out God's bounty. Remember God often so that you may prosper.'

FIG. 44

F.H. Coventry, Le Caire, *Egyptian railway promotional poster, 1935, colour lithograph*

The Minaret Depicted

by Nicholas Warner

A THOUSAND MINARETS

One of Cairo's epithets, whose origin is now shrouded in mystery, is 'The City of a Thousand Minarets'. Most European visitors to the city were quick to notice this profusion, and to comment on the power of the religion symbolised by the minaret. An excellent visual impression of the density of minarets within the city, and one that parallels these rich verbal descriptions, is conveyed by the first surviving large-scale European bird's-eye view of Cairo, printed in Venice in 1549 in the workshop of Matteo Pagano (fig. 46).[1] This view goes beyond earlier European representations in which minarets appear as campaniles of Italian inspiration, or even as obelisks. Here we find the minarets of the city shown with multiple stages, patterned shafts, balustrades, ribbed caps, wooden brackets for hanging lamps, and crescent-shaped finials. All the shafts are shown as square in plan, except for a putative representation of the minaret of the mosque of Ibn Tulun, which is shown as circular. The majority, but not all, of the mosques that are named on the view as such (*gema*) have minarets attached to them. A similar attention to detail can be perceived in a watercolour view of Cairo, the *Nova et Exacta Cayri Aegyptiorum Chorographia* by Brocardo, dating to 1556. Neither the view by Pagano nor that by Brocardo contains anything that resembles an Ottoman-style minaret, which is unsurprising given that the impetus for their construction was relatively slow in developing. For Ottoman-style minarets, we must look to some of the representations of Cairo found in the many surviving manuscripts of the *Kitab-i Bahriye* which was first compiled by the Turkish admiral and cartographer Piri Reis in the 1520s. While certain of the manuscripts show the city's mosques with Mamluk-style tiered minarets, others portray them with the 'pencil' minarets characteristic of Ottoman architecture (to the exclusion of all other forms). This bias, which was clearly not a reflection of reality, was extended to the treatment of domes, shown in the classic Ottoman form, and even houses, shown with pitched roofs rather than the flat roofs universally employed in Egypt.

TAXONOMY

The printed view of Cairo presented by Pagano and the manuscript versions of the *Kitab-i Bahriye* continued to be recycled for centuries. This largely impressionistic image of the city was changed only at the end of the eighteenth century, with the advent of the Napoleonic expedition to Egypt. In 1798, a small team of French surveyors used the minarets of Cairo for a different representational purpose. This was the first detailed plan ever drawn of the city, subsequently printed as a large copperplate engraving in the *Description de l'Égypte*. Without the use of many minarets as key points for the triangulation of the survey, their task would have been much harder. A total of thirty-four minarets, most of which still stand today, were climbed during this process (fig. 45). Although minarets can be

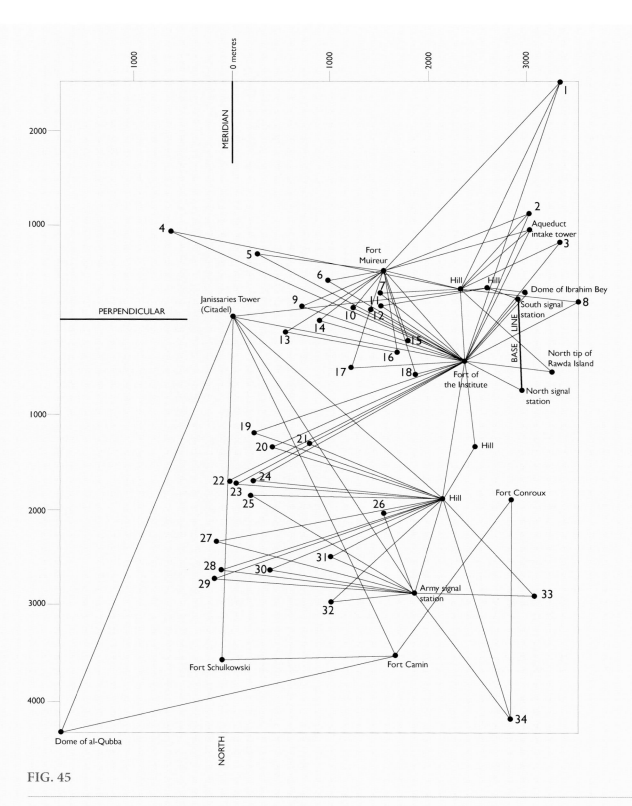

FIG. 45

Plan showing minarets used as triangulation points in the creation of the map of Cairo by the surveyors of the French Expedition in 1798, after the Canvas trigonométrique du Kaire, *scale 1: 25,000*

KEY

1. South minaret of Old Cairo
2. North minaret of Old Cairo
3. Minaret at the centre of Rawda Island [Qaytbay?] (77)
4. Mosque of al-Juyushi (5)
5. Mosque of Messih Pasha
6. Mosque of Saiyyida Sakina
7. Mosque of Qanim al-Tajir
8. North minaret on Rawda Island
9. Mosque of Kushqadam (76)
10. Mosque of Ibn Tulun (2)
11. Mosque of Qaytbay, Qal'at al-Kabsh (69)
12. Mosque of Sanjar al-Jawli (17)
13. Mosque of Sultan Hasan (33)
14. Khanqah/Mosque of Shaykhu (30)
15. Mosque of al-Geneyd [?]
16. Mosque of al-Kurdi (40)
17. Mosque of Qaraquja al-Hasani (53)
18. Mosque of Amir Akhur [Qanbibay Qara?] (86)
19. Mosque of Qijmas al-Ishaqi (74)
20. Mosque of Mu'ayyad Shaykh (45)
21. Maristan [?]
22. Mosque of al-Azhar (al-Ghawri?] (89)
23. Mosque of Abu'l-Dhahab (101)
24. Mosque of al-Ghawri (85)
25. Mosque of al-Ashraf Barsbay (47)
26. Mosque of Kihyeh [Uthman Katkhuda?]
27. Mosque of al-Ashraf [?]
28. South minaret of mosque of al-Hakim (4)
29. North minaret of mosque of al-Hakim (4)
30. Mosque of al-Sharawi
31. Mosque of al-Sharaybi
32. Mosque of al-Salmeh[?]
33. South minaret of Bulaq
34. North minaret of Bulaq

Fort Schulkowski: the minaret of the mosque of al-Zahir Baybars (10)

Numbers in parentheses relate to catalogue numbers

FIG. 46

Detail from Matteo Pagano, La Vera Descrizione del Caiero, *woodcut in 21 sheets*

FIG. 47 *(overleaf)*

Louis François Cassas, Cairene Minarets, *1785, pencil on paper*

FIG. 48

Pascal Coste, Parallèle des minarets des principales mosquées du Kaire, *1835, pen and watercolour on paper*
ARCHITECTURE ARABE, PL.XXXVII

seen in many of the general views of Cairo and
its suburbs, the record provided by the *Description*
is relatively sparse when it comes to more detailed
images. Only the minarets of the mosques of Ibn Tulun
(with its boat finial), al-Hakim, Fatima Khatun (with an
intact top), al-Nasir Muhammad in the Citadel, Sultan
Hasan,and Sinan Pasha are represented.[2] The ruined
base of the minaret above the principal entrance to the
mosque of al-Zahir Baybars is also recorded.[3] In the case
of Sultan Hasan, attention is drawn to the pronounced
bichrome *ablaq* masonry of the shafts. Outside Cairo,
we find small views of the minarets of the principal
mosques of Esna and Assiut, and Bani Suwayf.[4]

The earliest known documentary depiction of
Cairene minarets slightly predates the work of the
Description. It was made by the French architect Louis
François Cassas during his visit to Egypt in 1985, and
is an elegant pencil study (fig. 47). The drawing clearly
shows the minarets of the mosque of al-Hakim, although
the other examples shown are less identifiable suggesting
that the drawing contains an amalgam of different
sites. The study was never elaborated, however, in any
engraving or painting. A more precise approach to
recording minarets was adopted by another French
architect, Pascal Coste, who was hired by Muhammad
'Ali in the 1820s. In his *Monuments de l'Art Arabe*,
printed in 1839, Coste presents a group of minarets in
descending order of size.[6] They are Sultan Hasan, the
madrasa of al-Ghawri (showing its original blue-tiled
final tier), Qalawun, al-Mu'ayyad, al-Ghawri's minaret
at al-Azhar, al-Nasir Faraj ibn Barquq, the funerary
complex of Qaytbay, Muhammad Bey Abu 'l Dhahab
(also shown with its original top), Ibn Tulun, an
unknown Ottoman minaret, and a late minaret of the
mosque of 'Amr. Coste's carefully measured elevations
appeared as line engravings in his publication, but rare
coloured versions of his work, including a manuscript
copy, survive (fig. 48).[7] The idea of presenting what Coste
called a 'Parallel of Minarets' was one that was to
resurface later, and also led to the creation of additional
architectural taxonomies such as one for domes.

Other French artists were to follow Coste's example
during the course of the nineteenth century. Prominent
among them was Emile Prisse d'Avennes who published
his encyclopaedia of the Arab art of Cairo, with many
colour plates, after spending the year 1858 in the city

FIG. 50

Prisse d'Avennes, detailed elevation of the minaret of the madrasa of al-Nasir Muhammad at Bayn al-Qasrayn, 1869–77, chromolithograph

L'ART ARABE, VOL.1, PL.VII

FIG. 49

Jules Bourgoin, detail of composite plan of the minaret of Aqsunqur, 1892, copper engraving

PRÉCIS DE L'ART ARABE, PL. VII

collecting his material.[8] Perhaps endowed with a better sense of art historical development and variation than his predecessor, Prisse included many views and details of minarets in his work. Among them are: a general view of the courtyard at al-Azhar, the minaret of al-Muzaffar Baybars (al-Jashnakir), the minaret of the madrasa of al-Nasir Muhammad (fig. 50), the funerary complex of Qaytbay, the minaret of the madrasa of Qaytbay at Qal'at al-Kabsh (including details of the muqarnas and balustrades), the minaret of al-Sultaniyya, the minaret of the mosque of Qanim al-Tajir (al-Qalmi, now demolished), the minaret of Qanibay al-Rammah at al-Nasiriyya (now rebuilt), the minaret of the mosque of al-Burdayni, the minaret of the madrasa of al-Ghawri, and the minaret of Khayrbak. He also provides an elevation of the Bab Zuwayla in which the original pavilions are clearly discernible prior to their collapse and rebuilding by the Comité. Apart from their documentary value, these images manage to combine exactitude with a nuanced painterly quality. This may be partly due to

the fact that, when compiling his work, Prisse d'Avennes relied upon the earlier efforts of the daguerrotypist and artist Joseph Philibert Girault de Prangey, who visited Cairo in the 1840s. At that time, de Prangey created perhaps the earliest photographic images of the architecture of the city, which he then reworked in the form of watercolour and pen and ink studies.[9] Girault de Prangey's name is visible on many of the plates of Prisse's *Art Arabe*.

Jules Bourgoin was another French architect who made a particular study of the architecture of Cairo, including minarets, in his survey. His 1892 *Précis* of Arab art contains a large number of line drawings of minarets that focused especially on the details of their stonework such as muqarnas. The buildings thus presented have the quality of anatomical specimens, but include the minarets of al-Nasir Muhammad in the Citadel, Aqsunqur and the 'Southern Minaret' in the southern cemetery.[10] Uniquely, Bourgoin also provides comparisons with Mamluk minarets in Damascus.[11] The representations of Bourgoin are also remarkable from a technical point of view. An example of this is his combination, in a single planimetric drawing, of elements from all the different levels of the minaret of Aqsunqur including the underside of each muqarnas tier (fig. 49).

ARTISTRY

Minarets, though not specifically those of Cairo, have appeared as key elements in European paintings since at least the late fifteenth century.[12] The increasing ease of travel to Egypt and the East in the nineteenth century, however, ensured that the image of the minaret became inextricably linked with developing narratives of Orientalism and Romanticism. It would be tedious to list all the many Orientalist artists who included examples of the minarets of Cairo in their drawings and paintings. Some examples, however, will underscore the importance of the minaret, above all other architectural forms, in creating an instant impression of the East. The strong visual attraction of the form of the minaret was well expressed by the Scottish artist David Roberts, who visited Egypt in the

FIG. 51

David Roberts, Minaret of the Mosque of al-Ghamree, *1846, oil on canvas*

1840s. He writes: 'The narrow streets, thus overhung by the houses on either side, are darkened but cooled by the exclusion of the sun's rays, yet those objects of beauty, the minarets of the mosques, frequently burst upon the observer as they rise above the buildings, and strikingly characterise the architecture of Cairo.'

Roberts recorded numerous urban scenes in Cairo, and is renowned for his creation of a romantic oriental topography – perhaps a reflection of his training in theatrical set design.[13] His representations of the city often include minarets as compositional foci, but have been criticised as lacking in veracity. This criticism is sustained when one looks, for example, at a view he

produced of the al-Darb al-Ahmar quarter seen from the rubbish mounds to the east.[14] Here, the minaret of Aqsunqur has been moved to the north-east corner of the mosque, and an 'invented' portal positioned so as to lead directly into the domed space in front of the mosque's mihrab. This was undoubtedly done for pictorial reasons, but at the same time the rendering of the minaret appears accurate when judged alongside other contemporary images of its original state with four storeys. Another example of Roberts' method of working, however, that may refine this assessment, is his view of the minaret of the al-Ghamri mosque, which has since been demolished. This view of the minaret, therefore, has an added documentary value as the only surviving image of the structure. The same view survives in three versions: a watercolour drawing made on site in 1839 (Nottingham, City Museum & Art Gallery), a lithograph published in 1842–9 in *Egypt and the Holy Land,*[15] and an oil painting made in 1846 (Royal Holloway College, University of London). Of the three images, the direct correspondence between the architectural composition of the sketch and the lithograph suggests a good degree of faithfulness to reality. The street is extremely narrow, which only serves to emphasise the astonishing verticality of the minaret seen from below. Only the arrangement of human figures in the street is at variance. In his presentation oil painting, however, Roberts took more artistic licence, while maintaining the minaret in all its detail). The street has been widened to give a more open perspective, which allows a fabricated façade of the mosque, complete with crenellations, to be introduced along with more turned wooden screen (*mashrabiyya*) on a house façade. More striking is the picturesque but implausible insertion of a wooden bridge that spans the street and collides with the façade of the mosque (fig. 51).

Although Roberts has often been criticised for celebrating romance over verisimilitude, his depictions of Cairo's architecture, especially where individual buildings survive that can be directly compared with his representations of them, are generally remarkably accurate. As a group, they emphasise the fact that all the architecture of the city was boldly 'striped' with red and white over-painted horizontal bands. This seems to have been an accentuation, in some cases, of existing

FIG. 52

Albert Goodwin, An Arabian Night, *1876, oil on canvas*

FIG. 53

Robertson and Beato, the Bab Zuwayla and minarets of al-Mu'ayyad Shaykh seen from the east, c.1857

bi-chromatic *ablaq* masonry, but more usually seems to have been applied to the façades of all religious buildings (including their minarets), regardless of period. The over-painting was also often used to accentuate architectural detail such as muqarnas or inscriptions.

The English artist Albert Goodwin chose to represent the minarets of Cairo by night. His *An Arabian Night* (1876) is painted in the Bayn al-Qasrayn looking south towards the minarets of the mosques of Sultans Barquq and Qalawun (fig. 52). It is a scene lit by the moon, rather than by artificial light blazing from the tops of the minarets, and is animated in the foreground by that often-used standby of Orientalist painters: a wedding procession. The architectural

detail is rendered, however, with great accuracy. Given the prominence of the *Arabian Nights* as almost required reading at the time for anyone travelling to the East, and the common equation of Cairo with the setting for the tales, it is perhaps surprising that so few attempts were made to portray the nocturnal city.

Another artist who created some of the most striking Orientalist images of the nineteenth century was the Frenchman Jean-Léon Gérôme.[16] For Gérôme, the architecture of Cairo served primarily as the frame for his ethnographic subjects, and this is reflected in the titles of his works. *Prayer on the Roof Tops* (1865), *The Muezzin* (in three versions, one being a night scene), and *The Call of the Muezzin to Prayer* (1880) all include realistic detailing of specific monuments and minarets, but their primary focus is human. The last of this group presents a *capriccio* of the city appearing from on high, with the dome and minaret of the complex of Khayrbak simultaneously seen in the foreground and in the distance: a triumph in the economy of recycling and manipulating imagery.[17] Gérôme's views certainly made good use of photography, a discipline that was soon to radically transform the diffusion of Orientalist imagery in the West.

PHOTOGRAPHY

The rapid development of photography in the latter half of the nineteenth century not only had an impact on the work of topographic artists such as Gérôme, who were quick to avail themselves of this resource. It also enabled the creation of a vast corpus of images of the city, which in the case of Cairo had a strong commercial appeal. The new medium favoured static subjects such as buildings, which in Egypt at least were well lit by strong sunlight. As with artists, there were many photographers who worked in Cairo or had their studios there; and it is superfluous to name them all here.[18] A close study of the numerous multi-part panoramic photographs taken from high vantage points overlooking Cairo (by photographers such as Francis Frith, Pascal Sebah and the Zangakis) is particularly revealing of many minarets that have today disappeared or been materially altered in their appearance. Street-

significance of photography in an ever-changing landscape. In time, this documentary value became apparent to organisations such as the Comité de Conservation des Monuments de l'Art Arabe, who assembled their own archive of images of historic buildings. Over the period 1882–1926 some 13,000 negatives (mostly on glass plates) were taken.[19] Particularly valuable are those photographs that show buildings before and during major restoration projects. There are numerous examples of this, but one is presented here: the image of the Fatimid mosque of al-Salih Tala'i' under reconstruction (fig. 54). Here, and only here, do we find a clear image of the minaret of the mosque that was a later addition to it, and that was removed during the course of the project. Photographic recording was also a key element in the work of Cairo's greatest architectural historian, K.A.C. Creswell (1879–1974), who assembled a personal archive of over four thousand negatives relating to Cairo alone.[20] From this corpus he selected a number to illustrate his own evolutionary chronological sequence for the construction of the Ayyubid and early Bahri Mamluk minarets of Cairo, commencing with the minaret of the mosque of al-Husayn (1237), and ending with the minaret of the complex of Sunqur al-Sa'di (1315).[21]

BRANDING

Beginning with the Paris Universal Exposition in 1867, facsimiles of building types found in Oriental cities from Marrakesh to Isfahan were constructed at the world fairs that presented a myriad of foreign cultures to European and American audiences. The Paris exposition included Moroccan, Tunisian, Egyptian and Turkish 'quarters', the latter boasting a replica of a mosque with Ottoman-style minaret among other structures. The Cairene minaret, however, was not represented until the Universal Exposition of 1873, held in Vienna. The 'Egyptian pavilion' took the form of a structure whose linearity was emphasised by the use of painted horizontal stripes (*ablaq*), and verticality expressed through the re-creation of two minarets and a dome (fig. 55). One of these minarets and the dome appear to have been directly derived from

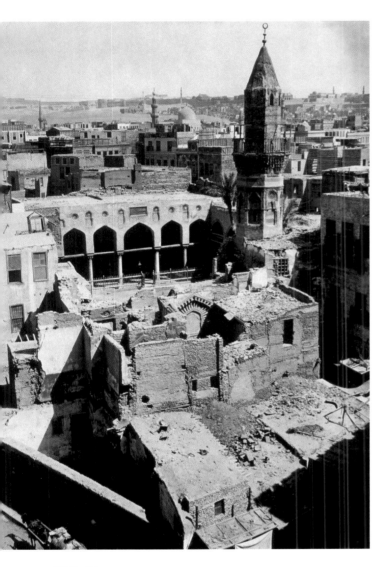

FIG. 54

K.A.C. Creswell, the mosque of al-Salih Tala'i' under restoration showing the minaret before demolition, before 1919

based photography often included minarets, for the same visual reasons that appealed to artists. One example by the photographers Robertson and Beato, who visited Cairo in the 1850s, shows the minarets of the mosque of al-Mu'ayyad atop the Bab Zuwayla prior to the replacement of their upper structures and the clearance from the gateway of later structures (fig. 53).

Such images demonstrate the purely documentary

FIG. 55

The Egyptian pavilion in the Universal Exposition of Vienna 1873, woodcut

the funerary complex of Sultan al-Ashraf Qaytbay in the northern cemetery of Cairo, while the other was inspired by minarets with a square base.[22] The pavilion was also intended to serve as the temporary residence of the Khedive Isma'il when he visited the exhibition, and had no religious content: even the minarets are referred to as 'towers' in texts accompanying the exhibit.[23] The 1889 Paris Exposition had an entire street from Cairo recreated by its promoter Delort de Gleon, a Frenchman who had long lived in Egypt. The street contained twenty-five houses built from recycled architectural fragments (such as *mashrabiyya*) and a scaled-down copy of the same complex of Qaytbay that had appeared in the Vienna exhibition. De Gleon justified his choice by declaring this to be the 'most gracious monument' of Cairo,[24] but at the same time filled its interior with a café and dance-hall. Another

facsimile of a Cairo street (including a copy of the minaret of Abu Bakr ibn Muzhir, which was attached to a replica of Qaytbay's funerary mosque) was made for the World's Columbian Exposition of 1893, held in Chicago.[25] In this case, the minaret was also supplied with muezzins to provide additional verisimilitude.

These re-creations of Cairo's architecture abroad, though significant in the history of Orientalism, were ephemeral. For more permanent constructions that attempted to capture the character, and emulate the glory, of the Mamluk heritage of the city we must look to the examples of a number of royal mosques dating to the late nineteenth and early twentieth centuries. The mosques of al-Rifa'i, Sayyida Zaynab, Sayyida 'A'isha, and Sayyida Nafisa all show an overwhelming preference for a Mamluk architectural vocabulary that extended to their minarets. It was only later that the Ministry of Waqf (Pious Endowments), which was responsible for the construction of all new mosques in Egypt, adopted more 'reductive' designs that departed from strict historical prototypes, sometimes built by foreign architects such as Mario Rossi. This stylistic development can be witnessed in the ambitious bilingual Arabic and English publication by the Ministry of Waqf in 1949, of the two-volume *Mosques of Egypt*, which includes both ancient and modern examples of the type. In this publication, we also find the last great photographic 'sequence of minarets' (fig. 56), arranged chronologically (probably again by Creswell, who was an advisor to the publication).

Currency often provides a valuable key to cultural perception and national branding. As anyone who has handled Egyptian banknotes will be aware, their design traditionally portrays Ancient Egyptian objects or buildings on one side, and perspectives of Islamic monuments on the reverse. The latter images are dominated by their minarets, which invariably provide

the focus of the composition. The chosen monuments are: the mosque of Sayyida 'A'isha (twenty-five piastres), the Azhar mosque (fifty piastres), the mosque of Qaytbay in the northern cemetery (one pound), the mosque of Ibn Tulun (five pounds), the mosque of al-Rifa'i (ten pounds), the mosque of Muhammad 'Ali (twenty pounds), the mosque of Qijmas (fifty pounds), the mosque of Qanibay al-Rammah (one hundred pounds) and the mosque of Sultan Hasan (two hundred pounds).

Pride in national architectural heritage, as well as a certain competitive element inherited from the world fairs, also influenced the design of advertisements in the first half of the twentieth century. This is particularly apparent in the many posters advertising the joys of travel to North Africa by boat, train or plane. One example of this is to be seen in the adoption in 1935 by the Egyptian State Railway Company of graphics that use three abstracted minarets (including one of al-Mu'ayyad's over the Bab Zuwayla) and a dome in a colour-lithograph poster (fig. 44).[26]

FIG. 56

Photographic sequence of minarets
THE MOSQUES OF EGYPT

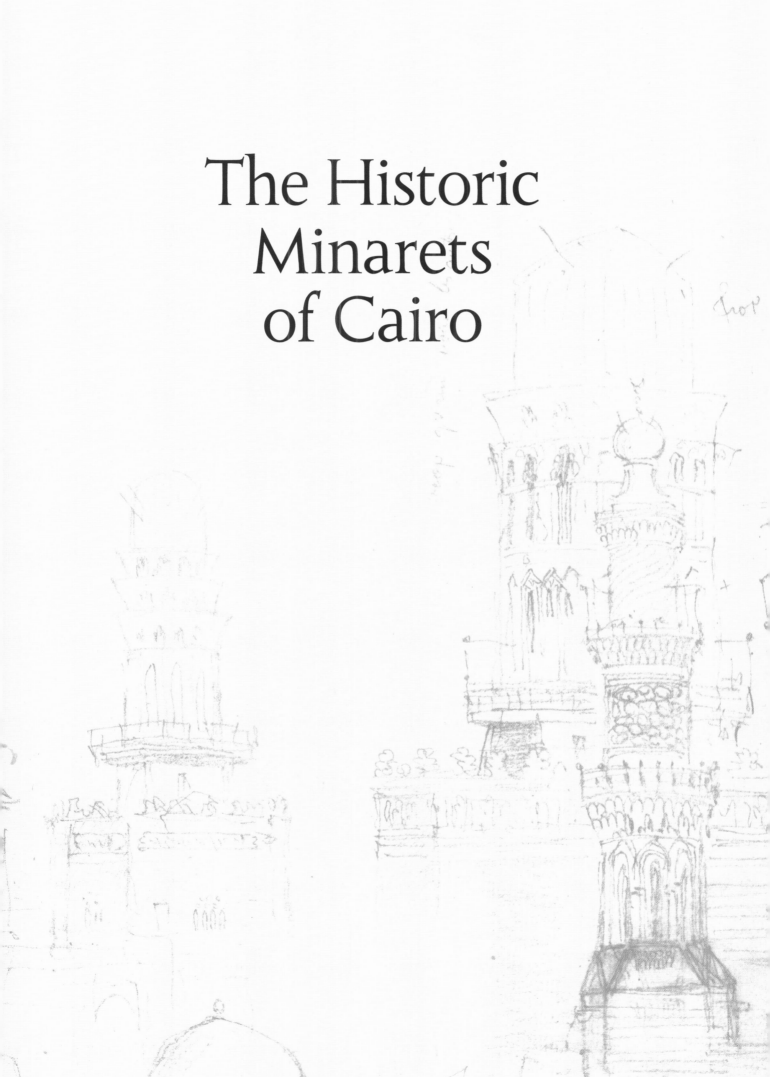

The Historic
Minarets
of Cairo

NINE

Early History and Formation of the Minaret in Cairo

EARLY HISTORY

1. THE MOSQUE OF ʿAMR IBN AL-ʿAS (641–2)

The first minarets of Egypt belonged to its first mosque, built by the conquering General ʿAmr Ibn al-ʿAs in his nascent capital of Fustat.[1] They were not however built at the same time as the mosque itself (641–2), but more than thirty years later in 53/673, when the governor of Egypt Maslama Ibn Mukhallad asked the Umayyad caliph in Damascus, Muʿawiya, for permission to enlarge the mosque. According to another version mentioned by Maqrizi, it was Muʿawiya who ordered the governor to attach minarets to the corner of the mosque. Eventually, Maslama erected a minaret at each of the four corners of the building and inscribed his name on them. The addition of these minarets coincided with the earliest enlargement of the mosque on the western side, when it was also whitewashed and decorated for the first time. Maslama also ordered the addition of minarets (*manar*) to all other mosques of

FIG. 58

The mosque of ʿAmr ibn al-ʿAs

Fustat and that their muezzins follow the *adhan* of the mosque of ʿAmr.[2] The idea of placing minarets at the corner of the mosque has been attributed to the use of the corner towers of the Roman temple, where the first mosque of Damascus was built, as a platform for the call to prayer. However, Maslama's governorship predated the reign of al-Walid I (705–15) and the foundation of his glorious and monumental mosque (712) that was yet to occupy the entire area within the temple walls; the earlier Umayyad mosque of Damascus, prior to this foundation, had been a smaller building that shared the temple area with a church. At that time the corner towers of the temple did not coincide with the corners of the mosque, unlike the

FIG. 57 *(facing page)*

The minaret of the mosque of Ibn Tulun, view from the external courtyard

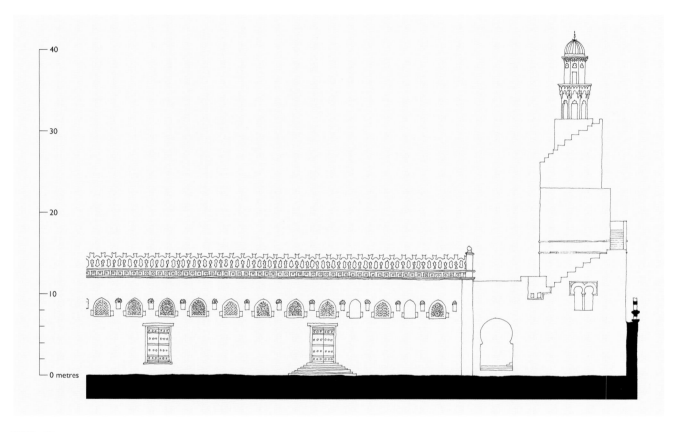

FIG. 59

The minaret of the mosque of Ibn Tulun, north–south elevation through the external courtyard

case of the mosque at Fustat. Furthermore, unlike the monumental towers of the Roman temple, minarets of the mosque of 'Amr must have been small projections from the roof. They were initially ascended by means of external staircases that were later on transferred to the interior. This suggests that the early mosque of 'Amr was a simple construction without a staircase to the roof. Maslama's towers were short-lived and must have been replaced several times in the following period while the design of four corner minarets was maintained; an arrangement that remained unique in Egypt. In 79/698–9 the mosque was enlarged by order of the Umayyad governor 'Abd al-'Aziz ibn Marawan.

When, in 92–3/710–12, the entire mosque was pulled down by the then governor of Egypt, Qurra Ibn Shurayk, the reconstruction must have been accompanied by four new minarets at the corners of the new building. Another radical reconstruction took place during the

reign of the Abbasid caliph al-Ma'mun in 212/827, by order of the Abbasid governor 'Abd Allah Ibn Tahir. At this date, the mosque was doubled in size, which must have entailed yet another reconstruction of the four minarets.

Further work was carried out at the mosque during the Fatimid period. In Rajab 358/969, the prayer hall on the *qibla* side was enlarged. This means that the two minarets at the northern and southern corners must have been replaced, unless they were not attached to the walls, in which case they might have remained but no longer at the corners, which is unlikely. As was the case with major sanctuaries that had multiple minarets, such as the Umayyad mosque of Damascus and the Prophet's mosque in Medina, the Fatimids gave names to the minarets of the mosque of 'Amr. The one at the southern corner of the prayer hall, or south-eastern corner of the mosque, was called 'Arafa, which is a proper name; with the addition of a dot above the ʿayn, the word could also be read as *ghurfa,* meaning 'an elevated room'. The tower at the northern corner of the prayer hall, or the north-eastern corner of the mosque, was called al-Kabira, 'the Big One'. The north-western one was called al-Mustajadda, 'the Recent One,' and the south-western minaret was known as al-Jadida, 'the New One'.

The Fatimids also added in 445/1053, during the reign of al-Mustansir and the vizierate of al-Yazuri, a fifth minaret to the mosque. It is reported to have been in the north-west wall between the Jadida and the Mustajadda minarets, which would be on or near the axis of the mosque. It was called either al-Saʿida, which would mean the Felicitous, or, according to Ibn Muyassar al-Saʿidiyya, meaning 'of Saʿid', which would be an attribution to an unidentified proper name. Ibn al-Muyassar attributed the three western minarets to the Fatimid vizier al-Afdal Shahinshah, which would date them sometime between 1094 and 1121. Having been a great patron of architecture, al-Afdal is likely to have rebuilt the three minarets. By then, the youngest of the minarets, the Saʿida/Saʿidiyya, would have already been more than a century old. In 536/1141, one of the minarets was struck by a lightning and collapsed.[3]

As their names indicate, the five minarets were not all built at thee same time and were of different sizes. In the Mamluk period one of the minarets was renamed al-Manzara, meaning 'the Loggia'. This was probably the minaret called al-Kabira, under which a loggia (*manzara*) had been built by Salah al-Din.

The mosque having already five minarets prior to the Mamluk period, no new minaret is reported to have been erected by the Mamluks. Although the mosque was severely damaged by the earthquake of 1303, and was eventually heavily restored by Emir Salar, no reference to any Mamluk work on the minarets is made in either Ibn Duqmaq's or Maqrizi's accounts of this or subsequent restorations. It is very likely, however, that, considering the religious significance of the first mosque of Egypt, the Mamluks would have regularly restored and perhaps reconstructed the existing minarets. During the reign of Sultan Barquq, the head of the merchants, Burhan al-Din Ibrahim al-Mahalli, demolished and rebuilt the entire prayer hall, but we have no mention of any alteration to the

minarets. When Evliya Çelebi was in Egypt (1672–80), he saw four minarets at the corners, which he described as built in 'the old style'.[4]

The two unremarkable brick minarets that survive today at the mosque of ʿAmr, one near the main entrance and the other at the south-eastern corner, were added by Murad Bey in 1800 when he reconstructed the mosque. The southern one has an octagonal first storey with recesses but no decoration.

2. THE MOSQUE OF IBN TULUN (879)

The oldest mosque in Egypt to survive in its original form is the mosque of Ahmad Ibn Tulun, erected in 263–5/879 in Qataʾiʿ, the new capital he built for himself to the north-east of Fustat.[5] The second congregational mosque in Egypt, after that of ʿAmr at Fustat, had been the mosque of ʿAskar, the Abbasid foundation that lay between Fustat and Qataʾiʿ, but this building disappeared centuries ago and no information regarding its architecture is available.

DESCRIPTION (fig. 57)

The minaret of the mosque of Ibn Tulun is perhaps the most exotic construction in medieval Cairene architecture. It is the only existing minaret in Egypt with a staircase outside the shaft, and for this reason, legends and theories were spun around it. According to one such legend, the design of a spiral staircase was Ibn Tulun's own invention. He was reported to have amused himself during a conversation by idly rolling a piece of parchment around his finger. When a bystander sought to embarrass him by asking the meaning of this game, he was not at a loss, but promptly replied that he had been planning the design of the minaret of his new mosque. Of course we know from stylistic evidence that both the minaret and the mosque were built on the pattern of the Great Mosque at Samarra, the temporary Abbasid capital and Ibn Tulun's own place of origin. The minaret of Ibn Tulun, however, is built of stone, unlike the Samarra brick prototypes. Moreover, rather than following the

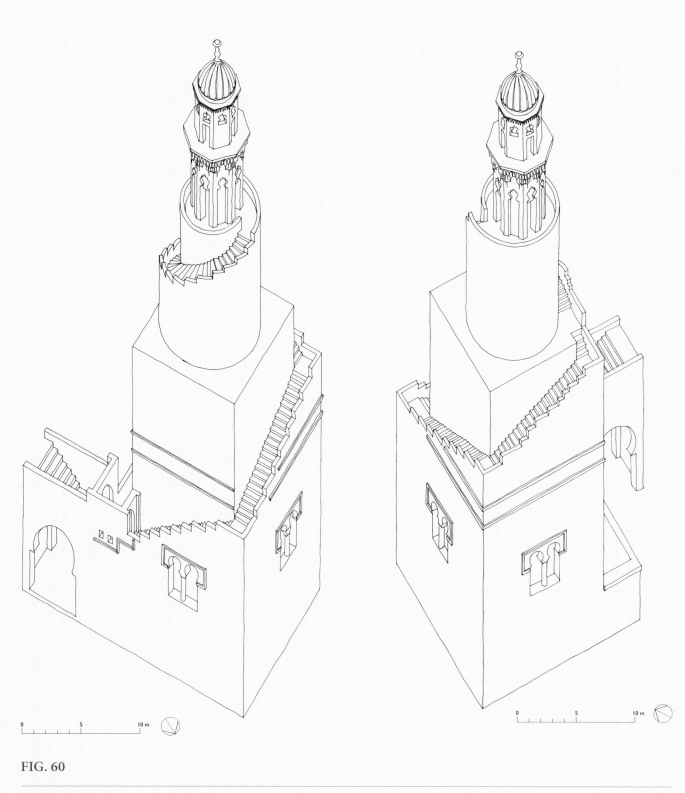

FIG. 60

The minaret of Ibn Tulun: axonometric projections

Samarran minarets' continuously conical section, its shaft begins as a square before developing into a circle. The square section of the shaft is ornamented with pairs of blind horseshoe arches on all its sides. A bridge connects the minaret to the roof of the mosque, supported by stone corbels of West Islamic style. This stylistic connection to the Maghrib may be due to the presence of a Maghribi community in this area since the reign of Salah al-Din.[6] A Maghribi quarter continued to exist near the mosque well into the Ottoman period.[7]

The superstructure of the minaret is built in the early Mamluk style, with an octagonal section and a ribbed cupola. This is the earliest extant mabkhara made of stone. The eight facets of its lower part, crowned with a muqarnas cornice, have alternate blind and open arches. The upper domed structure is pierced on each facet with a lobed arch and has engaged colonettes at the eight corners. A second muqarnas cornice underlines the base of the stone cap.

Until the nineteenth century, a copper boat served as the finial attached to the mabkhara. The sacral significance of the boat in Egypt goes back to ancient history. Medieval literary sources associate the boat of this minaret with a treasure that Ibn Tulun allegedly found on the site of a mosque called 'Pharaoh's Furnace' on the Muqattam Hills, which he used to finance the construction of his mosque.[8] Although this story has a strong legendary element it is interesting because it associates the boat with the pharaonic past. Interpreting the function of the boat, Evliya Çelebi in the seventeenth century wrote that it had the talismanic function of protecting the city against the dangers of catastrophic Nile floods. He also records that an Ottoman emir, excited by the outside staircase of the minaret, amused himself by riding a horse to its top![9]

Although the present minaret is today the only minaret serving the mosque, this was not always the case. In the first half of the fourteenth century the *qadi* Karim al-Din al-Kabir, who oversaw the administration of the mosque, added a plastered brick minaret to each corner of the prayer hall. Their function must have been to address the inhabitants of the quarter located on these two sides of the building who were too far away from the surviving north-west minaret to hear the call to prayer from there. One of this pair of Mamluk

minarets survived into the beginning of this century but had to be removed for reasons of structural stability. Judging from archival photographs and drawings, it had the unusual combination of two circular storeys: a plain circular first storey with a flared cornice over a projecting curved moulding and a circular second tier with a muqarnas cornice. The bulb was placed directly above this cornice line. Assuming the pair to this minaret was of a similar design, the mosque would have had a very distinctive silhouette from the rear for much of its later history.

DATING

Since the minaret bears no inscriptions, its dating must derive from material and stylistic considerations as well as textual sources. Creswell and other scholars attribute the whole of the present minaret to the restoration work done in 1296 by Sultan Lajin. It is reported that Lajin, while he was still an emir, had to hide away from his persecutors who were chasing him for being involved in the assassination of Sultan al-Ashraf Khalil. He sought refuge in the abandoned mosque of Ibn Tulun and its minaret. He eventually vowed that if ever given the opportunity, he would restore the mosque, which at that time was in bad condition. Lajin became sultan and fulfilled his vow. He erected the domed ablution fountain we see today in the courtyard, redecorated the existing mihrab with painted wood and an inscription executed in glass mosaics, and added a wooden dome in the ceiling immediately in front of the mihrab. He also added a second mihrab to one of the piers of the prayer hall. The bridge connecting the minaret with the mosque and the construction of the octagonal domed mabkhara surmounting the minaret were also his contribution. Most of all, he enlarged the endowment (*waqf*) of the mosque to add a teaching curriculum that also included medical studies.

The arguments of Creswell and others for attributing the entire minaret to Sultan Lajin may be summarised as follows: the minaret is built in stone while the rest of the mosque is built in brick; the minaret stands off the main axis of the mosque, unlike its Samarran prototypes; the shaft is decorated with blind horseshoe arches and the bridge connecting the minaret with the mosque also has horseshoe arches and corbels of Western Islamic style that have to be later than the date of foundation; and finally, the junction of the bridge and the wall of the mosque blocks a window in the wall of the mosque, indicating that this element must have been added later. Various theories may be advanced, however, to counter the evidence for the minaret being a construction of Lajin. The fact that the minaret was built in stone while the rest of the mosque is built in brick does not, in itself, preclude the minaret being contemporary with the mosque. Egypt, unlike Mesopotamia, has an ancient tradition of stone architecture, and though the design follows a Mesopotamian pattern, the building of the mosque must have been executed by local craftsmen, who may have chosen stone rather than brick for this freestanding element of the complex. The Nilometer of Rawda, ordered by the Abbasid caliph al-Mutawakkil, was built slightly earlier in stone and attests to the masonry skills of that period.

A major argument that suggests that the original minaret was made of stone is the testimony of al-Muqaddasi, a trustworthy eyewitness, who came to Egypt in the tenth century and reported that the minaret of Ibn Tulun had an outside staircase and that it was made of stone.[10] There is no reason to believe that the structure seen by Muqaddasi was a Fatimid reconstruction. According to the common patterns of restoration and reconstruction in medieval architecture, a reconstruction would have been in the contemporary style, without the external staircase. Had Lajin built the entire minaret, he would have built it as a Mamluk tower. The ablution fountain in the courtyard and the dome over the mihrab, as well as the upper structure of the minaret, were obviously built in the Mamluk style. Lajin, who was fulfilling a vow, had every reason to emphasise and document his own contribution. The sources, cited by Maqrizi, that list Lajin's several restorations, fail to mention any reconstruction of the minaret, which would be odd in the case of such a prominent and unique structure. As noted earlier, minarets added to pre-existing buildings were usually inscribed with foundation inscriptions, to acknowledge the sponsor's contribution; this is not the case with the minaret of the mosque of Ibn Tulun.

FIG. 61

The minaret of Ibn Tulun, view from the central courtyard

Finally, the horseshoe arches and the bridge, which doubtless belong to the period of Lajin, do not necessarily date the entire structure. Neither the horseshoe arches nor the bridge have structural implications for the minaret itself; they both could well be part of a later embellishment that included a new stone dressing. The new stone dressing may also explain the absence of a break in the bond between the minaret and the additions pointed out by Creswell. Most probably, the original minaret, as in the case of the Samarra prototypes, was not connected to the mosque. An anecdote told by the traveller Nasir-i Khusraw, who came to Egypt in the early eleventh century, would seem to confirm this idea: the Fatimid caliph al-Hakim bi Amr Allah bought the mosque from Ibn Tulun's heirs, who appeared one day unannounced at the site and began demolishing the minaret.[11] The astonished al-Hakim summoned and questioned them about their doing. They replied that they had sold the mosque, but not the minaret, so that al-Hakim was obliged to pay them an additional sum of money to obtain the minaret as well. This anecdote recalls the well-known story 'mismar juha', according to which Juha, after having sold his house, returned every day to a particular place where he had kept all sorts of things hanging from a nail in the wall. These daily incursions disturbed the new owners, who protested. Juha countered their protests by saying that while he had sold the house he had never agreed to sell the nail along with it. Nasir-i Khusraw's anecdote may be explained by the unusual position of the minaret outside the mosque as a freestanding structure that is not obviously connected with the rest of the building.

Another anecdote related by Maqrizi seems to confirm the continuity of the configuration of Ibn Tulun's minaret from its foundation to Lajin's time. He wrote that the architect of the mosque, a Christian who had previously built Ibn Tulun's aqueduct, had been jailed for some reason. Upon learning that Ibn Tulun intended to build a grand mosque, the architect offered to design it for him. Ibn Tulun agreed and released him with the commission. On the Friday of the inauguration, as he prepared to pray, Ibn Tulun heard a voice calling him from the top of the minaret near the copper boat finial. It was the architect, asking for his salary and his freedom! Ibn Tulun gave the man 10,000 dinars, a robe of honour, and freedom for the rest of his life. This anecdote associates the boat with the original minaret and it shows at the same time that the tradition of a boat-shaped finial at this minaret has been maintained until the nineteenth century, as attested in engravings of the period. The fact that the boat-shaped finial of the minaret of Ibn Tulun was maintained by Lajin suggests that the summit of the minaret had remained in place until Lajin rebuilt the top and returned the finial. The story also implies that the original structure never reached such an advanced state of dilapidation that would require it to be replaced with a completely new structure. In fact, being a massive construction, like its Samarran prototypes which significantly outlasted their mosques, the minaret would have eroded rather than collapsed, unless it

FIG. 62

Fifteenth-century minaret at the mosque of Ibn Tulun, no longer extant

was deliberately demolished. Had this been the case, it is likely that the incident would have been reported. We know that Ibn Tulun restored the summit of the Ptolemaic lighthouse of Alexandria and added a wooden domed structure at its summit. The top of his minaret might likewise have been a light timber structure that Lajin replaced with masonry. It is hard to imagine how Lajin could have hidden of all places within a minaret that had no inner shaft, as the historians relate. The only convenient place to hide would be inside the upper structure, which was probably domed. This would have had the advantage of allowing the hunted emir to watch for approaching danger. The reconstruction of the summit of the minaret would thus have had a particular significance for Sultan Lajin.

FIG. 63

The minarets of Sultan Qaytbay (left), Emir Aqbugha and Sultan al Ghawri at the Azhar mosque

Had the architect placed the minaret along the mosque's axis, he would have had to give up the symmetry of the multiple entrances into the building. The original plan with symmetrical entrances in the walls of the mosque matching the alignment of the doorways in the outer wall of the external courtyard, or *ziyada*, allowed a central and axial entrance through both of the two walls opposite the mihrab. If the minaret had been positioned axially, it would have blocked the axial entrances of the *ziyada* and the mosque. In Samarra, the two spiral minarets stand directly in front of the axial entrances to their respective mosques, but the *ziyada*s in these cases were so much wider than at the mosque of Ibn Tulun that the minarets did not impede access through these entrances.

3. THE AZHAR MOSQUE (970–2)

The mosque known since Fatimid times as al-Azhar[12] has been a major institution for religious studies in Egypt since its foundation by the imam-caliph al-Muʿizz li-Din Allah as the Friday mosque of the Fatimid capital Qahira in 359–61/970–2. After the Ayyubids deprived it of the status of Friday mosque it regained prestige during the Mamluk sultanate, when its endowments were regularly enlarged, and its architecture was expanded and elaborated. The Ottomans continued to promote al-Azhar after their conquest of Egypt in 1517, making it the major teaching institution of Islamic studies in Egypt.

No minaret of the Fatimid period has survived at al-Azhar. During the reign of Sultan al-Zahir Baybars (1260–77), consensus had it that the existing minaret was too low and an upper structure was added to it. Even this extended minaret was felt to be inadequate by Sultan Barquq: in 1397 he decided to pull it down and replace it. Maqrizi informs us that in order to support the new minaret a vault was constructed at the northern entrance, with stones taken from the madrasa of al-Ashraf Khalil near the Citadel, which Barquq had demolished. Maqrizi probably meant the madrasa of al-Ashraf Shaʿban; Khalil's madrasa, of which no trace survives, was not near the Citadel but

near the madrasa of Fatima Khatun in the cemetery of Sayyida Nafisa; elsewhere he refers to Barquq's demolition of Shaʿban's madrasa. This information and the absence of al-Azhar's minaret in the list of minarets damaged by the earthquake of 1303 and subsequently restored, suggests that the original minaret must have been a relatively light structure built of brick. It also suggests that the original minaret was above the entrance. Barquq saw the completion of his minaret at al-Azhar, but not its collapse some twenty years later. Sultan al-Muʾayyad Shaykh rebuilt it, but this minaret also had to be demolished soon after its completion in 1423 due to a structural deficiency.

Today the Azhar mosque has three Mamluk minarets and two Ottoman ones.[13] The earliest belongs to the adjacent madrasa of the Emir Aqbugha (1339), and the two others were attached to the mosque itself by the sultans Qaytbay in 1495 and al-Ghawri in 1511. We do not know whether the two other Mamluk madrasas of the mosque, the Taybarsiyya and the Jawhariyya, had minarets of their own. The *waqf* deed of al-Ghawri's minaret, suggests that it replaced an earlier one, perhaps that of the Emir Taybars, in the same position. The tradition of adding minarets to the mosque continued into the Ottoman period. In 1754, the Janissary emir ʿAbd al-Rahman Katkhuda, who restored a large number of Cairene monuments, carried out substantial additions and restorations to al-Azhar including three new minarets. One of them stands on the rear or south-east side of the mosque, attached to the founder's mausoleum; another is located behind the *qibla* wall and is associated with a secondary entrance (the 'Soup Gate', or *Bab al-Shurba*) to the mosque from the residential quarter behind. The third minaret was erected near the main entrance but is no longer there: it can be seen in archival photographs. Although the design of the portals ʿAbd al-Rahman Katkhuda reconstructed at Azhar is flamboyant and reflects the innovations in architectural decoration introduced by this patron, his extant minarets are both unpretentious conventional constructions, notable only for differences in the patterns of muqarnas used to define the tiers of the different storeys.

Because of the centrality and significance of al-Azhar, in particular in the Ottoman period, its minarets served occasionally as platforms for public

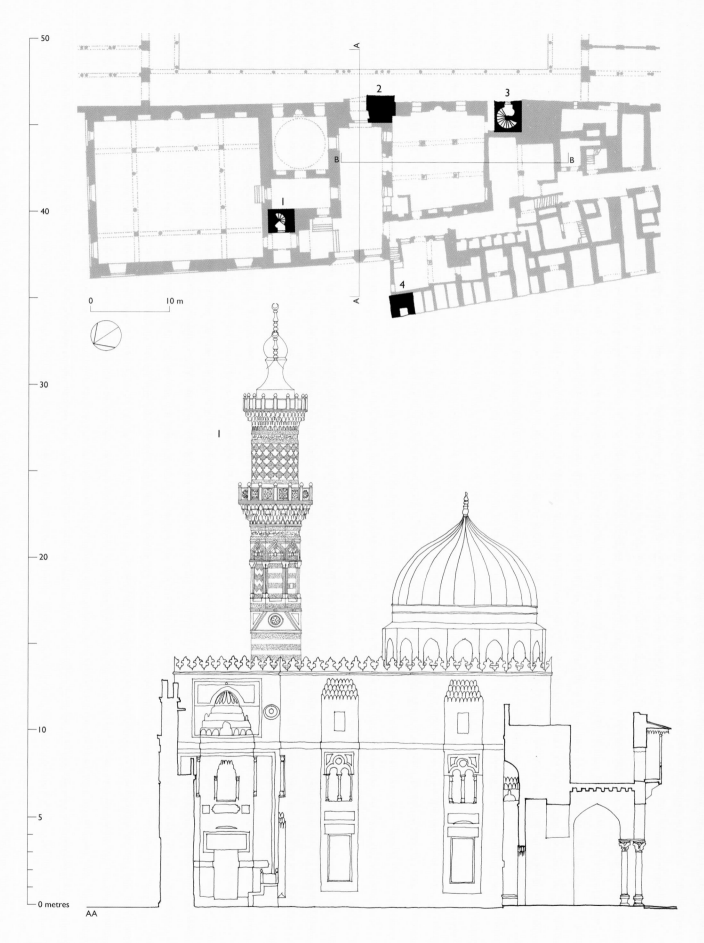

FIG. 64

Plan of the entrance to the Azhar mosque prior to 1896 showing positions of the minarets of:
1. Aqbugha; 2. Qaytbay; 3. al-Ghawri;
4. 'Abd al-Rahman Katkhuda (demolished), and sectional elevations of surviving minarets

BB

statements. In 1571, for example, one of the governors of Egypt, Iskandar Sharkas, who turned out to be a tyrant and despot of such proportions that the Ottoman Sultan himself felt obliged to recall him to Istanbul, was publicly cursed from there.[14] In 1785, when the beggars who normally received their daily bread from the pious foundations of al-Azhar found this charity suddenly cut off, they closed the doors of the mosque (thereby preventing prayer), climbed the minarets and broadcast the injustice to the city. They repeated their demonstrations several times until a promise to restore their bread supply was eventually fulfilled. Hearing about the success of this method of protest, groups from the popular quarter of Husayniyya marched to al-Azhar in the same year, armed with sticks and beating drums, and likewise climbed the minarets to make their demands heard.[15] Even Napoleon made use of al-Azhar to garner publicity when, having conquered the city of al-'Arish in Sinai, he celebrated his triumph by raising two flags captured from the enemy over the double-headed minaret of al-Ghawri. Cannons were fired to enhance the festivities. Later, after the conquest of Jaffa, he restricted his victory proclamation to hanging captured banners at the doors of the mosque.[16]

4. THE MOSQUE OF CALIPH AL-HAKIM BI AMR ALLAH (990–1010)

CHRONOLOGY AND ATTRIBUTION

The two minarets at the mosque of the caliph al-Hakim are the earliest extant minarets in the Fatimid precinct of Qahira.[17] Among the four extant minarets of the Fatimid period, these are the only ones built by a royal patron. This is perhaps the simplest statement that can be made about these structures, which are multilayered constructions with a complex architectural development that is not yet fully understood.

The mosque was founded in Ramadan 380/November–December 990 by the caliph al-'Aziz, al-Hakim's father, under the supervision of his grand vizier Ya'qub Ibn Kilis. Al-'Aziz led the inaugural prayer and held

the sermon in the mosque in Ramadan of the following year 381/November 991 and he continued to pray there on Fridays until his death.[18] It seems that although the mosque, which was called al-Jami' al-Anwar or the Brightly Illuminated Mosque, was in regular use it was not completed by al-'Aziz. Al-Hakim, who came to power in 386/996, ordered its completion in Sha'ban 392/June 1002. The southern minaret is inscribed with his name and the date Rajab 393/May 1003, suggesting that the mosque had remained for eleven years after its inauguration without complete minarets. A foundation inscription at the portal assigns the building to al-Hakim without any mention of al-'Aziz. In fact, no inscription in the name of al-Aziz survives elsewhere on the mosque. Eleven months elapsed between the time al-Hakim gave the order to finish the building and the inscribed date of completion.

According to Maqrizi, in Safar 401/September 1010 al-Hakim added the rectangular masonry structures to the exterior of the minarets he had completed seven years earlier. He performed his inaugural prayer in the mosque as late as Ramadan 403/1013, and established its endowment or *waqf* in the following year, 404/1014. Between the date of the completion of the portal and the minarets, and the inauguration of the mosque, ten years had elapsed. Maqrizi's Fatimid chronicle, *Itti'az al-Hunafa'*, regularly reports the caliph's Friday prayers. Unlike his father who prayed there several times, al-Hakim is not reported to have visited the mosque prior to its second inauguration in 1013. The fact that he endowed the mosque as late as 1014 strongly suggests that it has not been in use between the date of his father's death and the date of his own inaugural prayers. We know from Mamluk architectural practice that it was usual to start the construction of a mosque with the prayer hall, setting the orientation of the building. The prayer hall would be in use immediately after its construction, before the rest of the mosque was completed. Nevertheless, it seems strange that a royal mosque could stand for so many years without a minaret, and that it could take so many years to complete, apparently without compelling reasons.

This is not the only unusual feature about this mosque and its minarets. The fact that the original towers were partly concealed at a later date behind the walls of monumental masonry we see today is

FIG. 65

View of the northern minaret of the mosque of the caliph al-Hakim near the gate of Bab al-Futuh

enigmatic to say the least. The shape of these austere rectangular tapering towers, unparalleled in Islamic architecture, adds to the mystery. A close look at the chronology of the stages of construction and the inaugural sermons held at the mosque suggests that the original minarets had already been designed and probably even built during the reign of al-'Aziz, and that al-Hakim either completed them or merely

inscribed them with his name and a new date. He subsequently abandoned the mosque until 1003 when he returned to it with the decision to build the rectangular towers around the minarets and, finally, to re-inaugurate the mosque together with a new or re-established endowment. The architect of this later construction, or al-Hakim himself, was apparently reluctant to demolish the original minarets, which

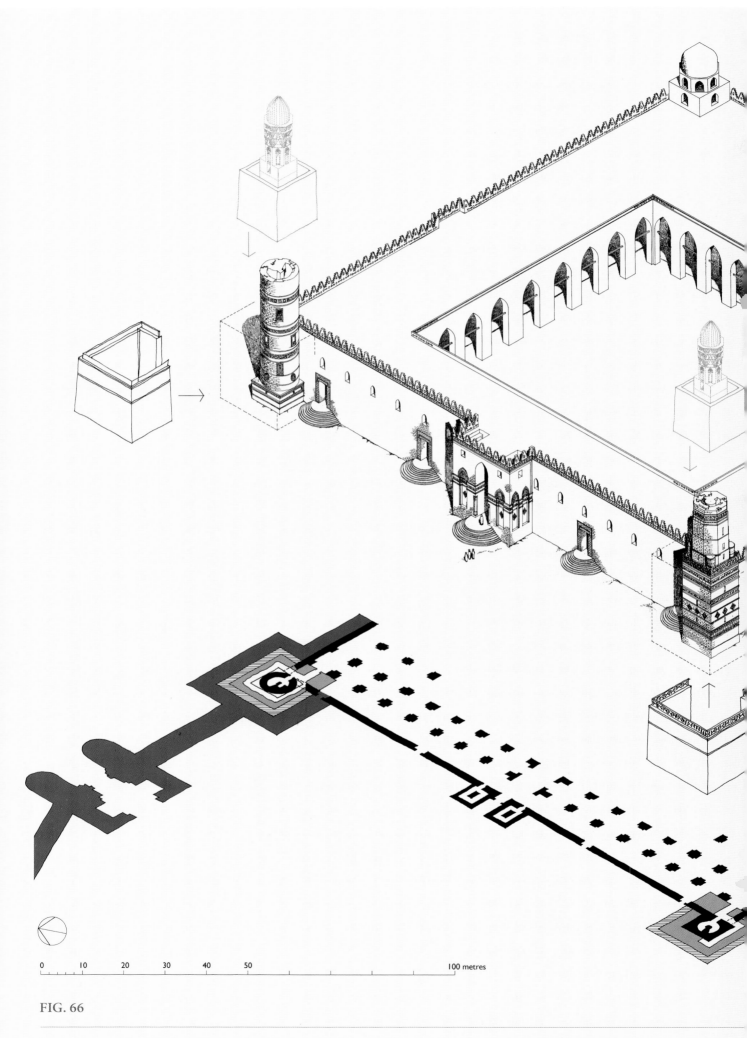

FIG. 66

The mosque of the caliph al-Hakim: isometric projection and plan showing sequential construction of minarets

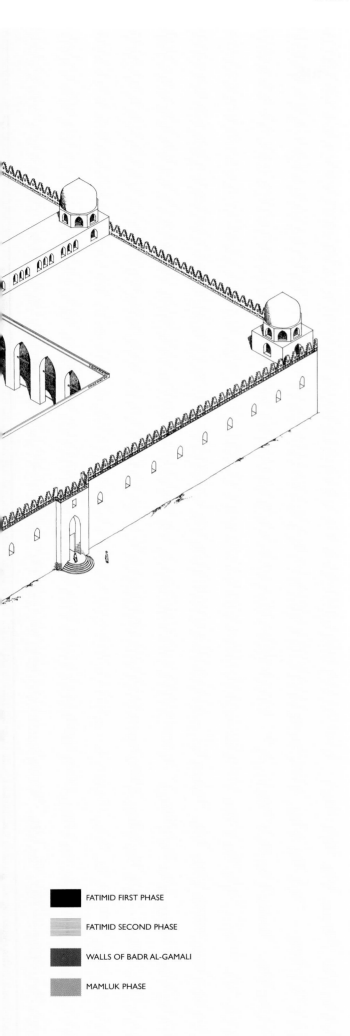

FATIMID FIRST PHASE

FATIMID SECOND PHASE

WALLS OF BADR AL-GAMALI

MAMLUK PHASE

were masterpieces of stonework. Instead, whether for aesthetic or practical reasons, the original structures were simply preserved within new masonry walls that were built three metres away from the face of the original shafts, leaving a void between the old and the new structures. The height of these walls corresponded to the height of the perimeter wall of the mosque, and a crenellation ran around them at this level. The walls were later extended vertically, set back from the crenellations, by the Mamluk emir Baybars al-Jashnakir in an early fourteenth-century remodelling that included the addition of new mabkharas on top of the original minarets. Perhaps there was a structural motivation for the creation of these upper enclosure walls by Baybars, as they brace the inner structure with flying buttresses. The external rectangular towers added by al-Hakim can hardly be described as minarets: their main purpose seems rather to have been the partial disguise of the earlier shafts. Nor were they built for structural reasons, as the original minarets did not require buttresses. It seems most likely that al-Hakim built the cubes because he disliked the appearance of his father's minarets, or at least their inscriptions, which were concentrated at the lower levels.

It should be pointed out in this connection that this mosque had never been al-Hakim's principal foundation. His main mosque, founded on the site of a pre-existing church, was in the quarter of Rashida at Fustat. Its foundation date was either Rabiʿ I 392/January–February 1002, as indicated in Maqrizi's *Ittiʿaz* (slightly before he ordered the completion of his father's mosque in Shaʿban of the same year), or the following year in Safar 393/December–January 1002–3, according to different sources cited by Maqrizi and other authors.[19] After the mosque of Rashida was completed and furnished in Ramadan 395/June 1005, al-Hakim rode there to celebrate the feast of ʿid al-fitr with special pomp, accompanied by a cortège that included six horses in bejewelled trappings, six elephants and five giraffes.[20] No such elaborate ceremony was recorded for the inauguration of the mosque begun by his father. The mosque of Rashida was also subject to the caliph's whimsical temperament; although it was initially made of brick, it was pulled down in Safar 401/September–October 1010 and

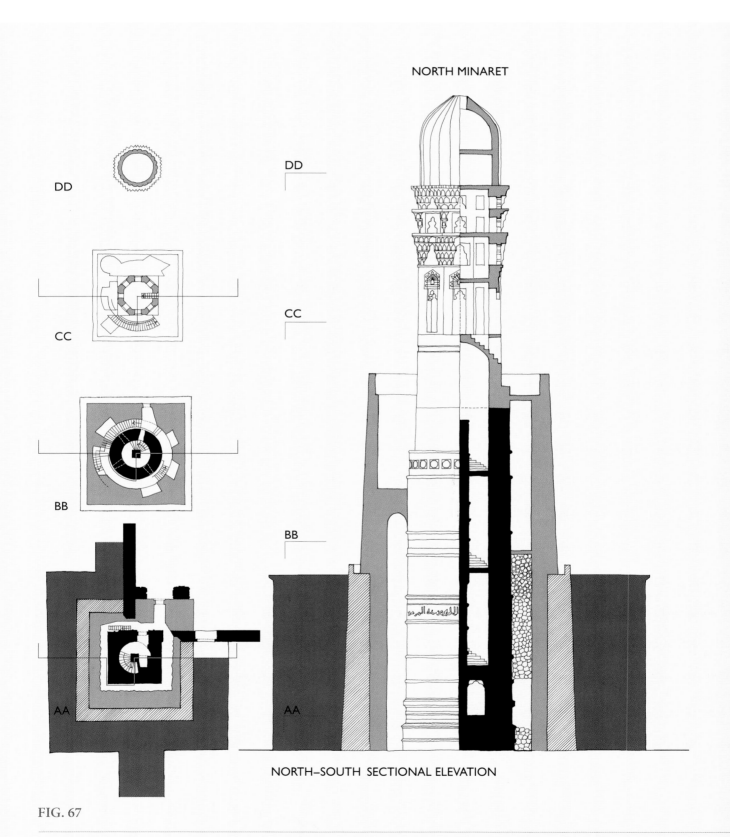

NORTH MINARET

DD

CC

BB

DD

CC

BB

AA

AA

NORTH–SOUTH SECTIONAL ELEVATION

FIG. 67

The mosque of the caliph al-Hakim, plans and sectional elevations of the northern (left) and southern (right) minarets

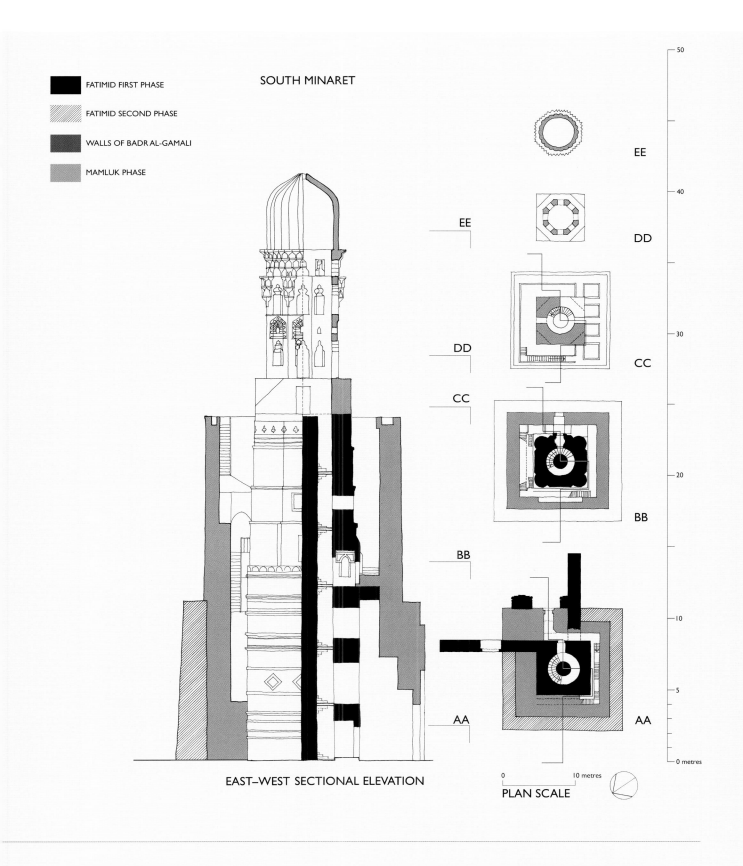

SOUTH MINARET

FATIMID FIRST PHASE

FATIMID SECOND PHASE

WALLS OF BADR AL-GAMALI

MAMLUK PHASE

EE

DD

CC

BB

AA

EAST–WEST SECTIONAL ELEVATION

PLAN SCALE

0   10 metres

0 metres

rebuilt on a larger scale in stone. Al-Hakim performed a second inaugural prayer there in Ramadan 403/March–April 1013; on this occasion he arrived without pomp and devoted much attention to the petitions brought to him by the gathered populace.[21] A direct chronological parallel can thus be seen between the al-Anwar mosque and the mosque of Rashida; al-Hakim founded the Rashida mosque at the same time as he 'completed' his father's mosque and he rebuilt it at the same time as he transformed his father's minarets.

A CHANGE OF HEART

The founder of the mosque, most likely al-'Aziz but perhaps also al-Hakim, obviously attached great significance to its minarets which were designed as the most spectacular elements of the building. This is evident from their dimensions, their asymmetrical design, the richness and variety of their decoration and the excellence of their calligraphic inscriptions. If they had not been already erected by al-'Aziz, as al-Hakim's inscription states, they would have taken an unusually long time to build. The sources provide no explanation for this. The austerity of the later twin cubes that we see today masking the original minarets, which contrasts so strikingly with the opulence of the inner structures, suggests that this opulence was the very reason for their concealment. Although the inscriptions refer only to al-Hakim, it is more likely that he appropriated his father's mosque. The absence in the inscriptions of any reference to his father as the founder, who began the mosque, is suspicious. In any case, the construction of the cubes points to a radical change of heart during the period when the mosque was taking shape.

It has been argued that the configuration of the two initial, different-looking minarets was a reference to the minarets at the Holy mosques of Mecca and Medina, at that time under Fatimid rule, and that al-Hakim's change of mind came as a response to his loss of control of the Holy Cities.[22] This view assumes that the Cairene viewer of that time was as visually minded as we are today to make such parallels and, moreover, to conceptualise them. The most problematic aspect of this speculation is its association of

FIG. 68

Northern minaret of the mosque of the caliph al-Hakim

architectural forms and styles with political ideas, a concept for which there is no evidence in medieval Egypt before the Ottoman conquest. The stylistic evolution of the Cairene minaret between the Fatimid and the Ayyubid periods provides the best evidence against such conceptualisation.

Medieval sources portray al-Hakim as an enigma. He remains the most controversial and incomprehensible figure of Egypt's Islamic history. He inherited the throne at a young age and soon became an eccentric and cruel tyrant, whose regime of terror kept his subjects in a permanent state of fear. His rule was particularly difficult to bear for the entire population mainly because he assumed the task of the *muhtasib* or market inspector, who was in charge of implementing moral behaviour in the city. He thus issued a long series of regulations regarding social, political and religious conduct, many of which were often abruptly revoked. Soon after his accession, he began to roam alone at night through the streets of Cairo, which had to be kept lit and decorated all night with their markets open and busy. The prohibition of certain kinds of food, the killing of all dogs in the city and the destruction of all vine plantations in the country provide a rebarbative picture of the caliph. And yet his foundation of the *dar al-hikma* or House of Wisdom, an academy and library for religious and secular sciences, and his generous donations in the later period of his reign convey the image of an enlightened patron with a social conscience.

Although al-Hakim's character cannot provide direct answers to the questions raised by the history of his minarets, one may discern in the confusing history of his reign a development that could shed light on his change of mind regarding the minarets of his father's mosque. At the beginning of his reign, al-Hakim was much inclined to excess in his personal regalia and ceremonial appearance: he wore lavish clothes and a bejewelled turban, even a crown.[23] This attitude changed around 403/1013 when he turned towards asceticism, which he maintained until his mysterious disappearance. After this point, he used to ride on a donkey like a commoner, wearing a plain black woollen garment, his hair hanging down on his shoulders, wandering through the desert and the hills to watch the stars. He abandoned all regal pomp and

FIG. 69

Southern minaret of the mosque of the caliph al-Hakim

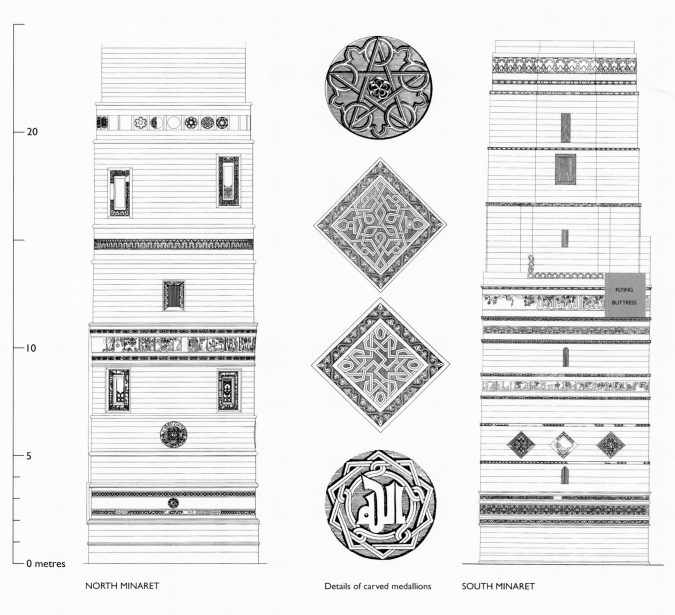

NORTH MINARET

Details of carved medallions

SOUTH MINARET

FIG. 70

The mosque of the caliph al-Hakim, elevations of the northern and southern minarets with details of decoration

ceremonial music, at the same time escalating his religious bigotry and intensifying his puritanical regulations that included the prohibition of Shi'i 'Ashura mourning among other religious rituals. During this later period, he made excessively generous donations and distributed disproportionate gifts. The beginning of this ascetic period of al-Hakim's life corresponds to the construction of the rectangular salients around the original minarets of his mosque, which can be considered a reflection of this new state of mind. This shift of emphasis is also evident in his attitude to the call to prayer itself. Over the years, al-Hakim demonstrated a particular interest in the *adhan*: among the many decrees he issued between the years 395/1005 and 400/1010, several dealt with the timing and formulation of the call to prayer but, as usual, they were later revoked.[24] In his ascetic period, he eliminated the formula that paid tribute to the caliph alongside other reverential rituals.

In a final, bizarre coda to the history of the minarets of the mosque of al-Hakim, Maqrizi reports that during the restoration of the minarets following the earthquake, a small box was found within the walls of the northern minaret, which, upon being opened, revealed a human hand wrapped in cotton and carrying an indecipherable inscription. The hand, it was said, looked as fresh as if it had just been cut off.

ARCHITECTURE

Maqrizi reports that the 'corners', *arkan* (sing. *rukn*), added in 1010 to the minaret, which he mentioned in the singular form, were 100 cubits long. The word *rukn* can mean corner, support, pier and also the side of a rectangle or a cube. The plural form *arkan* thus referred to the four sides of the rectangular towers. Creswell interpreted the 100 cubits as the cumulative measurement of the four sides at the base of the tower, which would be equivalent, according to the cubit of that time, to a length of between 50 and 65.6 metres.[25] The sides of the base of the southern minaret indeed measure 68 metres. The northern cube, however, is larger at the base, but this is not its original size. During the reconstruction of the city fortifications by Badr al-Jamali in the late eleventh century, the mosque of al-Hakim, which was initially outside the walls,

was integrated within their confines and its northern façade merged with the fortification wall, which was extended to enclose the northern minaret. In the course of this construction, the new wall that enclosed the northern minaret was erected plumb, not tapering according to the original design seen at the southern minaret, and in direct abutment with the face of the earlier wall around the minaret. The reason for this additional 'thickening' of the masonry around the tower cannot have been structural: rather, it must have been done to create an aesthetic balance with the mass of the adjoining gate of Bab al-Futuh.

Unlike the rest of the mosque the main façade with its portal and the minarets are made of stone. The dimensions of the latter must have exceeded by far the size of the brick minaret built above the entrance of al-Azhar, and probably all other minarets built hitherto in the double capital of Fustat and Qahira. Their monumentality remained unmatched until the construction of Qalawun's minaret slightly less than three centuries later. The elaborate carved decoration of these minarets is of a quality that has no extant precedent in Islamic Egypt. The original minarets are structurally independent of the rest of the mosque, their staircases being contained within their shafts from ground level. This arrangement was rare in Cairo, where a separate staircase normally led to the roof from where the upper section of the minaret was accessed.

The location of the minarets, projecting from the corners of the façade, was not an innovation, since the mosque of 'Amr at Fustat also had minarets at each of its four corners. They do not, however, project at 45 degrees from the corners, but are weighted towards the side of the entrance. Perhaps this was done to create a stronger visual effect when approaching the mosque from the front, or to maintain existing subsidiary entrances on the north- and south-flanking walls of the mosque. We do not know whether the upper structures of the original minarets were made of stone or brick. Both minarets were decapitated at almost the same level, with only half a metre difference between the two. This may suggest that although the minarets are not identical, they might have shared a common design of superstructure that collapsed in the same manner.

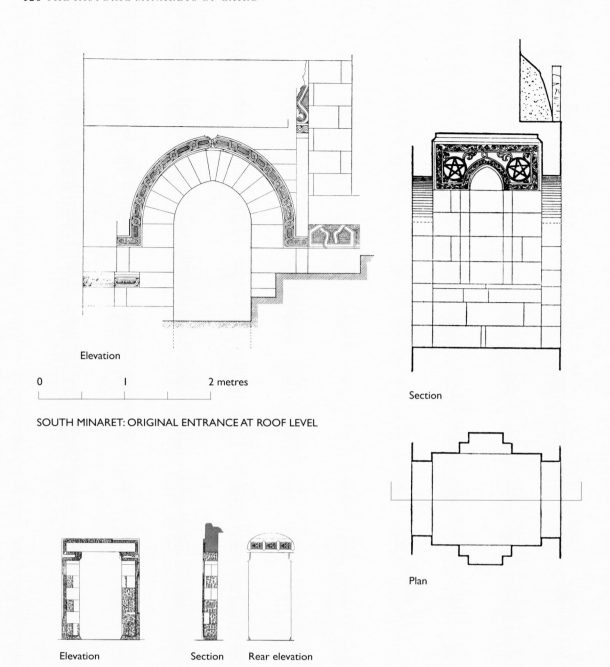

Elevation

0   1   2 metres

SOUTH MINARET: ORIGINAL ENTRANCE AT ROOF LEVEL

Section

Plan

Elevation   Section   Rear elevation

SOUTH MINARET: ORIGINAL ENTRANCE AT GROUND LEVEL

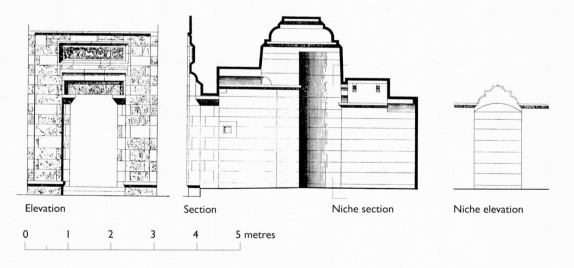

Elevation   Section   Niche section   Niche elevation

0   1   2   3   4   5 metres

NORTH MINARET: ORIGINAL ENTRANCE AT GROUND LEVEL

FIG. 71

The mosque of the caliph al-Hakim, architectural details of the minarets

THE DECORATION OF
THE ORIGINAL MINARETS

The fact that the two minarets have both different shapes and a different decorative programme led Creswell to assume that they were designed by different architects, the one who designed the southern minaret being also responsible for the design of the similarly decorated portal. Their common feature, however, is the distribution of the decoration over the entire shaft from bottom to top. Their projection from the façade wall allowed the display of carvings on all sides, as is the case with the projecting portal. The decoration is interrupted only at the junction with the mosque wall. The decorative programmes of these two minarets are unique: they have no known precedent, nor did they have an impact on later minarets.

The southern minaret is composed of a rectangular shaft, which carries an octagonal tapering section. The total height of the preserved original shaft is 24.2 metres. The design of the rectangular shaft is based on the horizontal division of its surface into eleven bands separated by horizontal mouldings. The surface of these bands alternates between plain and carved, two of them being inscribed with Koranic texts and the foundation date Rajab 393/May 1003, written in beautiful Kufic. Small openings are pierced in the shaft to introduce light into the staircase, without decorative emphasis. The original entrance to the staircase of the southern minaret is through a simple square-headed door framed by a much-damaged arabesque projecting moulding. The reverse side of the lintel has further arabesque decoration executed in three panels. The door leads into a shallow vaulted tunnel passing through the thickness of the wall into the stairwell.

The base of the octagonal section has four rounded buttresses at the corners. The octagonal shaft is sloping and divided into five segments; each receding segment is separated from the previous one by carved horizontal moulding similar to those on the lower rectangular shaft. Except for the uppermost tier, which displays a carved frieze above the moulding, the carving of the mouldings is the only decoration on the octagonal section.

At the level where the octagonal shaft begins, which corresponds to the roof level of the mosque, there is a

doorway leading from the interior of the minaret to the roof. On this side, the door has a fine pointed arch with a cable moulding carved around its head. The door gives onto a small square room within the thickness of the wall of the shaft with pointed arched niches to the left and right. Stone columns that are now missing would originally have flanked these niches. The surround to the hood of the northern niche and the flat stone soffit above are both finely carved in limestone, the soffit in two large blocks. The former bears two roundels with five-pointed stars surrounded by an interlacing moulding, and the latter has a 'rope-pattern' moulding framing an arabesque design within. The companion niche to the south is plain. This room, whatever its date, is quite without parallel in the architecture of Cairo. It may have been reserved for the use of the muezzin, but may equally have had a more esoteric purpose. Because it is open to the staircase on one side and to the roof of the mosque on the other, the room provides a passage to the roof, which is lacking in the northern minaret.

Al-Hakim's masonry cladding around the southern minaret is adorned with a finely carved Koranic text on marble, located about halfway up the wall, executed in a different style from those seen on the interior shaft. The equivalent inscription on the lower cube of the northern minaret was masked by the construction of Badr al-Jamali. At roof level, the remains of some crenellation around the top of the southern cube show the only surviving Fatimid imitation of the intricate pattern of crenels seen at the mosque of Ibn Tulun.

The original northern minaret is slightly shorter than its counterpart, at 23.7 metres, and consists of a tapering cylinder standing on a square base. The cylinder does not slope smoothly, however, as is the case with the Upper Egyptian brick minarets of the Fatimid period,[26] but rather in a segmented form recalling the configuration of a telescope, as noted by Creswell. The shaft of the cylinder is divided into eight segments of diminishing diameter marked by horizontal mouldings. The original entrance to stair-case of the northern minaret is very elaborate and comparable to the high-level 'oratory' of the southern minaret. It is significantly larger than the doorway into the stair of the southern minaret, and also has an inscription panel in floriated Kufic set within a

FIG. 72

Room in the southern minaret (ceiling)

moulding above it.[27] The doorway leads to a remarkably complex space, considering it is only the functional entrance to a minaret used by comparatively few people. The first part of this space, in the thickness of the wall of the minaret, is a shallow vault, while the second is a tall vestibule with a central coffer framed by cavetto cornices. Off the vestibule lies an elaborate deep pointed-arched niche with miniature corbels within it. The staircase is roofed with a rising tunnel vault, which is made of stone. A number of Ancient Egyptian stone blocks were used in the construction of this minaret: such spoils appear regularly in Cairo's Islamic architecture of all periods.

The carved decoration of the northern minaret is based on a combination of horizontal bands with vertical rectangles. An upper horizontal band includes a row of medallions filled with geometric patterns,

arabesques and inscriptions. A lower band is carved with an inscription that dates the minaret to the month of Rajab, but the year is no longer visible. A middle band is carved with arabesques. The space between these bands displays carved vertical rectangles adorned with epigraphic or arabesque frames and stone grilles. Some of these rectangles are blind recesses while others frame openings to introduce light into the staircase.

A striking omission on both shafts is the absence of any trace of a balcony for the muezzin to deliver the call to prayer. This is the case for both the inner minarets and their outer casings. After the construction of the cubes, the only place for the muezzin to stand would have been in the lower part of the upper structure. We may assume that, like the present mabkharas added in 1303, which had a platform with a wooden railing for this purpose, the original upper structures were equipped with a platform for the muezzin. This would be the only place for the delivery of the call to prayer and it is relatively high above the roof of the mosque. Normally in Cairene minarets, there would be a muezzin's platform or a balcony closer to the roof level.

THE RESTORATION BY EMIR BAYBARS AL-JASHNAKIR (1303)

The earthquake that shook Egypt in 1303, destroying the original mabkharas of al-Hakim's minarets, occurred during the reign of al-Nasir Muhammad, who charged various emirs with the restoration of damaged buildings. The emir Baybars al-Jashnakir, who was assigned the minarets of al-Hakim, was also in charge of the restoration of the Lighthouse of Alexandria that was also badly affected. At the mosque of al-Hakim, Baybars replaced the lost tops with the present brick mabkharas, which follow the style of the early Mamluk period. Both are composed of a ribbed helmet above an octagon decorated with muqarnas. They are, however, of different sizes, and show a slightly different arrangement in their respective octagonal sections. Unlike al-Hakim's minarets, which were entirely asymmetrical, this minor difference might be the result of difficulties in coordination between two different teams of masons working simultaneously on each mabkhara. It is far more likely, however, that the difference was intentional and due to location. The northern, larger mabkhara is positioned on the edge of the city wall and therefore may have been intended to be seen from a much greater distance.

Baybars made further changes to the appearance of the minarets, blocking up the space between the inner structures and their enclosing walls and building new entrance doorways to the minarets that projected into the mosque. This was done to provide structural support for his vertical extension of the external walls – the cubes – above the roof level, set back from the crenellations.

The top of the southern cube is decorated with a stucco band displaying an interlace pattern, while the upper part of the northern cube bears a Koranic inscription, also in stucco, which begins on its eastern side. Its style attributes it to Baybars al-Jashnakir's restoration.

Apart from the restorations ordered by Baybars al-Jashnakir in 1303, only one change regarding the minarets occurred in the subsequent history of the mosque of al-Hakim. In 1423, a merchant from the neighbourhood added one more minaret at the southeast wall near the prayer niche; it is no longer there except for the remains of an octagonal masonry stub.

EPIGRAPHY[28]

Northern minaret: lower band
Sura 9:128 followed by 'This is what the slave of God and his friend, al-Mansur Abu 'Ali, the Imam al-Hakim bi-Amr Allah, Commander of the Believers – may the blessings of God be on him and on his pure ancestors – ordered in Rajab of the year...'

Northern minaret:
framing three windows, west, east, and south
Sura 24:35–8

Northern minaret: north-east medallion
Sura 5:55 and fragments of Sura 5:16; Sura 33:43; Sura 57:9

Northern minaret: above the entrance to the staircase
Sura 17:80 (fragment)

Northern minaret: northern upper cube
Inscription added by Baybars al-Jashnakir, Sura 2:255; Sura 7:52

Southern minaret: lower band
Sura 9:18 followed by 'this is what al-Hakim bi-Amr Allah, Commander of the Believers...'

Southern minaret: middle band
Sura 1:73 followed by 'This is what the slave of God and His friend al-Mansur Abu 'Ali, the Imam al-Hakim bi-Amr Allah, Commander of the Believers – may the blessings of God be on him and on his rightly guided ancestors – ordered to be done in the month of Rajab of the year 393.'

Southern minaret: southern cube
Sura 33:56; Sura 9:107; Sura 24:26–28; Sura 62:9.[29]

FIG. 73

General view of the mosque of al-Juyushi after restoration

FIG. 74

The minaret of the mosque of al-Juyushi

THE FORMATION OF THE MINARET IN CAIRO

5. THE MOSQUE OF AL-JUYUSHI (1085)

The mosque of al-Juyushi commands a dramatic location on the Muqattam Hills to the south-east of Cairo.[30] It was built by the Fatimid vizier Badr al-Jamali, who also rebuilt the walls of Qahira, with its magnificent masonry gates, the Bab al-Futuh, Bab al-Nasr and Bab Zuwayla. The name of the mosque derives from Badr al-Jamali's title as commander of the army, *amir al-juyush*. The inscription located above the entrance to the building (directly beneath its minaret) describes it as a *mashhad* or memorial monument.

The mosque is constructed partly of stone and partly of brick masonry: the walls up to the roof level are in stone, while the dome over the sanctuary, the upper sections of the minaret, and small structures on the roof are of brick. These distinctions were, however, invisible since the entire building was plastered. Palm-log beams in the shaft of the minaret are visible on archival photographs. The minaret stands directly above the axial entrance to the building on its north side. A staircase in the north-west corner leads to the roof, from where access to the interior of the minaret is gained. Unlike al-Hakim's minarets, a cantilevered stone staircase attached to the inner walls of the structure runs from roof level to the top of the shaft in a space that is roofed with a brick barrel vault. The minaret consists of a rectangular shaft carrying a second, narrower rectangular storey crowned with a domed structure. This domed structure has a keel-arched profile set above an octagonal drum pierced by arched openings. It is in the same style as, and is proportionally related to, the dome above the prayer hall. At the top of its lower shaft, the minaret of al-Juyushi carries the earliest muqarnas in Cairene architecture, also executed in brick. Creswell suggests that the two surviving tiers of the muqarnoas cornice were originally crowned by a third tier. He also relates the style of this muqarnas to Iranian prototypes, while

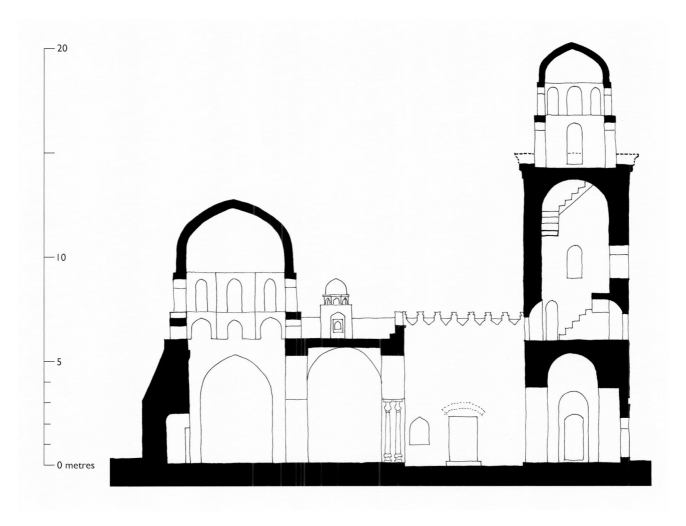

FIG. 75

The mosque of al-Juyushi, north–south section through minaret

attributing, unconvincingly, the architecture of the minaret itself to a Syrian inspiration.

The function of the building has been subject to debate. Farid Shafi'i considered the building to be a watchtower 'disguised as a mausoleum' with no true religious or funerary purpose. He remarked that 'it is difficult to believe that the site on which the monument was built had once been so crowded with people occupying high buildings that calling them to prayer required a high massive minaret'. The minaret, being equally visible from most parts of Cairo, could conveniently have been used to give light signals to observe suspicious gatherings of people in any part

of the city or to warn of the advance of troops coming from Upper Egypt, where Badr al-Jamali succeeded in subduing rebellions. In this period, Egypt was also threatened by a possible attack from Sunni antagonists abroad, which also explains the vizier's care to renew and consolidate the fortifications of the Fatimid precinct Qahira. Being the army commander, Badr al-Jamali was likely to have thought in strategic terms even when founding a mosque, which may furthermore have been intended as his own burial site.

Yusuf Ragib and Oleg Grabar have interpreted the *mashhad* rather as an oratory celebrating Badr al-Jamali's military achievements. However, the

FIG. 76

The minaret of the shrine of Abu 'l-Ghadanfar

function of the building as a Sufi oratory providing seclusion for meditation seems reiterated by the presence on the roof of small domed structures that sit over projecting buttresses to the west and flanks of the building. These look like little kiosks, and are large enough to allow one person to stand within them, but not to prostrate themselves. Each of these structures has a small mihrab or prayer niche and minute openings facing outwards. If the domed structures were meant as shelters for guards, as suggested by Shafi'i, these mihrabs would have no justification in this location. The structures could rather have been cells for meditation. The Muqattam Hill was strongly associated with both pre-Islamic and Muslim sanctuaries, shrines and venues of retreat and meditation. Some cells in the side of the cliff beneath the mosque are still visible. The prior existence, also on the Muqattam Hill, of an oratory with a minaret built by Ibn Tulun on the site of a pre-Islamic watchtower called *tannur fir'awn* or pharaoh's furnace, should also be recalled in this context. This earlier oratory was called the *masjid al-tannur*, the Oratory of the Furnace. Al-Juyushi's mosque seems, thus, to perpetuate a tradition of building oratories on isolated sites in the outskirts of the city combining strategic with pious elements, perhaps for apotropaic purposes. Immediately to the south-west of the main building stand the remains of the base of a Mamluk stone minaret perched on the edge of the cliff, indicating the continuous significance of this site.

6. THE SHRINE OF ABU 'L-GHADANFAR (1157)

This small minaret, standing to a height of 17.5 metres, is the only surviving structure of the original building, which included the *mashhad* or mausoleum of Mu'adh, a descendant of the Prophet and the caliph 'Ali through his son Hasan. Mu'adh died in 907.[31] Sakhawi mentions a madrasa near the mausoleum and the minaret. The door of the mausoleum bears an inscription with the date 552/1157 attributing its construction to the Fatimid emir Abu 'l-Ghadanfar al-Asadi al-Fa'izi.

Although the minaret may not be impressive, it is one of the few Fatimid minarets to have survived and the earliest specimen with a mabkhara top. The octagonal transitional zone of the cupola is pierced on all sides with lobed arches. Stucco carved keel-arches decorate the shaft.[32] The upper structure or mabkhara lacks the muqarnas that are commonly seen on later minarets of the same type, but these may simply have detached over time since the minaret is built in brick and covered with plaster. The staircase starts at ground level.

7. THE AYYUBID MINARET AT THE SHRINE OF AL-HUSAYN (1236–7)

Only one and a half minarets have survived from the Ayyubid period (1171–1250), this stub being the earlier 'half'.[33] It is attached to the venerated shrine of al-Husayn, established under the Fatimids to house the head of the martyr al-Husayn, the Prophet's grandson through his daughter Fatima and the caliph 'Ali. According to one account it was the vizier al-Afdal Shahinshah, the son of Badr al-Jamali, who transferred the relic in 548/1153–4 from a shrine at Askalon built there by his father. Another account attributes the transfer to the vizier al-Salih Tala'i' in order to rescue the relic from the advancing Crusaders and to bury it in the mosque he built in 1161 outside the Bab Zuwayla. The caliph is reported to have decided that the palace precinct was a more appropriate location to house the head of the saint whom the Fatimids considered to be their ancestor.

Maqrizi's account does not tell whether a minaret was attached to the shrine, which was within the confines of the Fatimid Great Palace, in the area of the caliphs' cemetery. In the Ayyubid period a madrasa was attached to the shrine.

The Ayyubid minaret is built of brick, and stands over a doorway that originally led into the shrine known as al-Bab al-Akhdar, the 'Green Door', which probably dates from the Fatimid period. The door is now concealed from view by modern constructions.

The minaret was sponsored in 1235–6 and completed in 1237. The lower of two inscriptions located in two panels set immediately above the centre of the pointed arch of the doorway, identifies the sponsor as Abu 'l-Qasim ibn Yahya known as

Zurzur. The inscription includes the word *al-marhum* before his name, indicating that he was already deceased, and states that his son Muhammad oversaw the completion of the construction during the year 634/1235–6.

The upper inscription repeats the patron's name as al-Hajj Abu 'l-Qasim ibn Yahya ibn Nasir al-Sukkari known as Zurzur and indicates that he ordered by testament (*awsa*) the foundation of this minaret, that his youngest son was the supervisor (*mubashir*) of the construction works and co-sponsor of the foundation, which was completed in Shawwal 636/June 1237. The founder al-Sukkari may have been, as his name indicates, a sugar-maker, and his son might have been in the building craft. The father sponsored the minaret and the son built it. The panel with the later date might have been originally inserted in the upper structure of the minaret and subsequently moved down when the structure was demolished or collapsed. Such detailed epigraphic evidence is unusual on a minaret, and it is probably due to the significance of the shrine. At the same time, the fact that the minaret was sponsored by an individual apparently without any political status is significant. Although commoners are mentioned in the sources as sponsors of religious foundations, epigraphic evidence of this kind of patronage is rare.

The rectangular shaft of the minaret is set back from the plane of the portal beneath it, and is fronted by a freestanding form of crenellation. The design of this crenellation is most unusual; it is carved in stucco with a geometric pattern whose resemblance to fretwork is enhanced by the presence of pierced openings running through its full thickness. The shaft of the minaret itself is further decorated directly above the portal and nowhere else with three blind double-arched stucco niches. The outer frame of the niches has keel-arched hoods with a sunburst design and central medallions. Two lobed roundels with central bosses are placed between these hoods. Below the hoods are recessed lobed niches delicately carved with arabesques.

The inner stucco panel of the central niche is a Comité restoration, while the two flanking panels are original, as can be recognised from the depth of their carving and its complexity. Epigraphic

roundels of a paired design adorn the spandrels of each recessed niche. The central niche has a feature obscured by the later emplacement of the second inscription of the minaret right in front of it. It is a separately framed smaller panel in the same plane as the frame and is also decorated with arabesques. The extremely delicate stucco carving with floral patterns seen here is unparalleled in minaret decoration in Egypt except on the minaret of the madrasa of Sultan al-Nasir Muhammad built almost seventy years later. In the Ayyubid period stucco decoration was particularly refined, elaborating on the Fatimid legacy and adding to it Western Islamic influences.[34] The upper part of the minaret is an unremarkable eighteenth-century addition by the emir 'Abd al-Rahman Katkhuda who also replaced the dome over the tomb of the saint.

EPIGRAPHY

Upper panel
'the virtuous shaykh Abu 'l-Qasim Ibn Yahya Ibn Nasir al-Sukkari (the sugar-maker), known as Zurzur, aspiring to God's favour and hoping for His reward. It was completed by his son Muhammad in the year 633 (1235–6) may God forgive him.'

Lower panel
'In the name of God the Lord of Mercy, the Giver of Mercy, has recommended the foundation of this auspicious minaret above the gate of the memorial [*mashhad*] of the saint al-Husayn aspiring to God's vicinity and raising the beacon [*manar*] of Islam, the pilgrim to the house of God Abu 'l-Qasim ibn Yahya Ibn Nasir al-Sukkari (the sugar-maker) known as Zurzur may God accept [it] from him. The overseer of the construction is his youngest son, who paid the costs of the completion executed according to his father's will, from his own pocket. It was completed in the month of Shawwal of the year 634 (June 1237).'

FIG. 77

The Ayyubid minaret at the shrine of al-Husayn

8. THE MADRASA OF SULTAN AL-SALIH NAJM AL-DIN AYYUB (1245)

This is the only complete minaret to survive from the Ayyubid period. It was erected by Sultan al-Salih Najm al-Din at his madrasa at the Bayn al-Qasrayn street.[35] It is the third extant royal minaret after Ibn Tulun's and al-Hakim's.

Like the minaret at the shrine of al-Husayn, that of Sultan al-Salih Najm al-Din stands over an entrance, in this case a passage that is flanked on both inner and outer faces with pre-Islamic granite columns and capitals and that gives on to a street that separates the two wings of the madrasa. This street, named after the madrasa, *harat al-salihiyya*, is a main thoroughfare. The quarter would have been accessed through a gate located directly under the minaret. Thus, the minaret also served as an urban marker for the whole quarter. A magnificent keel-arched niche framed by receding tiers of muqarnas is positioned above the entrance, and forms the centrepiece of the long façade of the complex on the Bayn al-Qasrayn Street. This niche contains a marble panel inscribed with the foundation inscription of the madrasa, which dates the construction.

The minaret is of a timber frame with an infill of fired brick, and is plastered entirely, with all its decorative detailing executed in plaster. Thanks to its relatively lightweight construction, it has survived the centuries well, keeping its original top despite a pronounced lean of the shaft. The interior is accessible from a timber roof over the east side of the passage and has a wooden staircase attached to the rectangular walls without a central supporting newel.

The minaret is composed of three basic elements, apart from the entrance passage it straddles: a square shaft is decorated with three plain keel-arched panels on each façade, of which the central one is pierced with an opening that lights the staircase within. The octagonal second storey is carved on all sides with keel-arched niches similar in proportions to the lower ones, containing recessed openings with lobed arches that give access to a cantilevered wooden balcony for the muezzin. All the niches were originally decorated with radiating hoods of Fatimid origin. The octagonal

FIG. 78

The Ayyubid minaret at the shrine of al-Husayn,
stucco panel

section of the minaret is surmounted by two tiers of
stucco muqarnas, the upper tier being narrower than
the lower. Each facet of the muqarnas cornice is pierced
by small arched openings, lobed in the lower case and
following the module of the muqarnas pattern in the
upper. The ribbed dome above the muqarnas cornice
has a keel-arch profile.

   The topmost pavilion is of the type commonly
described as the mabkhara, or 'incense-burner',
although, as already mentioned, no parallel exists
between this architectural form and the documented
medieval incense-burners.[36] The conservation works
carried out at the minaret in 1993–5 revealed that
the internal wooden staircase had been used as a
supplementary reinforcement for the structure
by linking it to the main timber skeleton of the
surrounding shaft, perhaps a response to the lean in
the structure that had developed during construction.
The staircase and other wooden elements of the minaret
included carved and painted fragments deriving from
the pre-existing Fatimid palace on the site.

FIG. 79

The minaret of the madrasa of Sultan al-Salih Najm
al-Din Ayyub, rear view

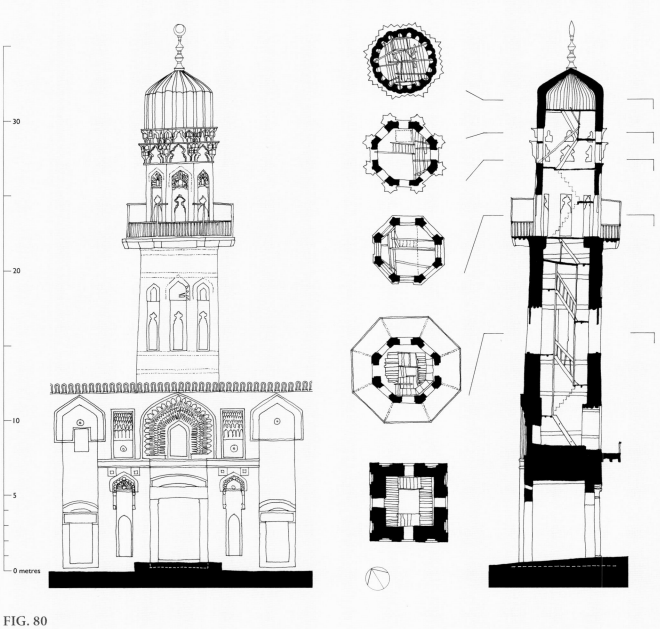

FIG. 80

The minaret of the madrasa of al-Salih Najm al-Din Ayyub, elevation, plans and section

FIG.81

The minaret of the madrasa of al-Salih Najm al-Din Ayyub, street view

TEN

Mamluk Minarets

(1250–1517)

9. THE MADRASA OF SHAJAR AL-DURR
(1250)*

Among the drawings of Pascal Coste, the nineteenth-century French architect who worked for Muhammad 'Ali, published in his book on the Islamic architecture of Cairo, is a view of a now vanished minaret of the mabkhara type located in the cemetery of Sayyida Nafisa.[1] As Coste provides no information concerning the identity of the building, only stylistic analysis and topographical research can assist in its identification. Coste dated his drawing 1822 and noted that Bonaparte's soldiers had demolished the building to which this minaret was originally attached during the French Expedition of 1798–1801.

The minaret appears in Coste's illustration as freestanding, although protruding stubs of masonry at its base indicate that it was once connected to the façade of a building, of which only a great vaulted hall or *iwan* and part of the mihrab wall had survived destruction. At first glance, this minaret recalls that of al-Salih Najm al-Din Ayyub at his madrasa in the Bayn al-Qasrayn, both having almost identical mabkhara tops. The manner of decoration is also reminiscent of the minaret of al-Salih, as well as the minaret at the shrine of al-Husayn. The rectangular shaft of this minaret is not decorated symmetrically, however. One side, over the entrance, displays two tiers of keel-arched panels, four over three. Three lozenges are set above the upper panels, and seven medallions above the lower ones. This arrangement

FIG. 83

The vanished Minaret of Shajar al-Durr in the cemetery of Sayyida Nafisa

PASCAL COSTE

FIG. 82 *(facing page)*

The minaret of the complex of Sultan Qalawun, from the east (see entry 12)

was presumably duplicated on the opposite and rear side of the minaret. The alternate side, which has a northern orientation to judge from the placement of the mihrab seen in the rear of the picture, has a simpler arrangement of three panels over three with rows of four and two medallions above their respective arches. This arrangement is likely to have been duplicated on the southern side. Taken together, the decoration here is denser than at the minarets of al-Salih and al-Husayn.

The lower part of the minaret, contiguous with the façade, includes a portal and is made of stone, whereas the minaret's shaft is built of brick with a timber frame, as is the case at the madrasa of al-Salih. The keel-arched entrance is flanked by a pair of rectangular recesses crowned with muqarnas, recalling the design of the niche and flanking recesses at the madrasa of al-Salih, which occupy a similar position between the apex of the entrance and the minaret. This pattern of keel-arched niches flanked by rectangular recesses with muqarnas was later adopted at the portals of the mosque of al-Zahir Baybars (1266–9). The keel-arched entrance, with a window above it, is framed in turn by a larger keel-arched recess. The drawing suggests that this may have been the entrance to the madrasa rather than to the staircase of the minaret. The absence of staircase windows in the lower part of the shaft suggests that a separate staircase led to the roof of the madrasa and to an entrance to the minaret's interior at roof level. A projecting wooden balcony must have marked the transition from the rectangular to the octagonal shaft. In Coste's drawing the emplacements for the missing timber corbels that would have supported this balcony are clearly visible.

The scale and architectural quality of this minaret suggest that it belonged to a royal monument. The strong parallels between this and the minaret of al-Salih Najm al-Din convincingly date its construction to around the mid-thirteenth century. Shajar al-Durr, al-Salih's widow, who succeeded him on the throne for three months during the year 1250 and then abdicated in favour of her second husband, the Mamluk sultan al-Muʿizz Aybak, is reported to have established a complex comprising a madrasa with her mausoleum, a bathhouse, a palace and a garden located together in the cemetery of Sayyida Nafisa. Today only her domed mausoleum, datable to her rule in 1250,[2] has survived

at the site. However, a minaret is reported by Mubarak to have existed at the mosque of Shajar al-Durr until 1877, when it was torn down to make way for a new mosque. At that time, almost half a century after Coste's visit, the minaret of Shajar al-Durr must have been severely dilapidated. The fact that no other royal monument is reported to have been erected in the cemetery of Sayyida Nafisa around the mid-thirteenth century, which is the date imposed by its style, leaves no alternative but to attribute the minaret depicted by Pascal Coste to the funerary complex of Shajar al-Durr.

10. THE MOSQUE OF SULTAN AL-ZAHIR BAYBARS (1269)

The mosque of Sultan al-Zahir Baybars, one of the largest and most impressive buildings of medieval Cairo, has no surviving minaret.[3] Though it is partly ruined today, its general proportions still convey an idea of the magnificence the mosque must once have displayed. The size of the dome that formerly stood above the prayer hall, matching the scale of the dome of Imam Shafiʿi, would have been particularly striking. This mosque was one of the first Friday mosques to be built by Baybars in Qahira after the Ayyubids had limited the number of Friday mosques to only one per urban agglomeration.[4] This may partly explain its inspiration in the monumental architecture of pre-Ayyubid congregational mosques such as that of Ibn Tulun or al-Hakim. An important innovation in design displayed in this mosque, however, is the presence of three gates, one on the main axis of the building and two smaller ones on the lateral façades.

The historian Ibn Shaddad, a contemporary of al-Zahir Baybars, mentions three minarets above the entrances in his description of this mosque.[5] It is entirely plausible that this monumental mosque had more than one minaret. As a freestanding mosque outside the urban centre of Cairo, a single axial minaret would not have been visible (nor its call to prayer audible) to those dwelling on different sides of the building. Minarets over the side entrances would spread the *adhan* more widely. Evliya Çelebi, who lived in Egypt in the seventeenth century, reiterated

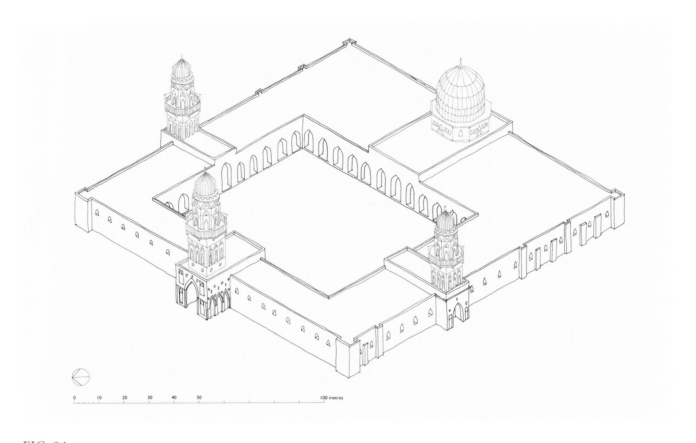

FIG. 84

Isometric reconstruction of the mosque of Sultan Baybars with three minarets

Ibn Shaddad's description, reporting that the mosque of Baybars had three short minarets, without indicating their location.[6] When Bonaparte's troops occupied Cairo, they found the mosque of Baybars long abandoned and deprived of many of its columns. Attracted by its location and sturdy construction, the French turned it into a fortress, which they named Fort Schulkowski after one of their officers who had been killed by the rebellious population of the neighbourhood. Jabarti wrote that the French installed a cannon on the roof of the mosque and used its sole minaret as a watchtower.[7] They also used it as a triangulation point in their survey of Cairo that resulted in the production of the first detailed map of the city. An illustration in the *Description de l'Égypte* shows the stub of this minaret, a rectangular shaft with keel-arched panel decoration similar to that of al-Salih Najm al-Din and early Mamulk minarets,

over the main entrance.[8] Like the surviving examples of this period, it probably had a mabkhara top.

The isometric reconstruction of the mosque seen here shows the building with a minaret located over each of its three entrances: the central minaret being of larger size owing to the larger portal and its location on the main axis of the building. A staircase that leads to the roof of the mosque, and thence to the minarets, is located within the western wall of the building.

11. THE MADRASA OF FATIMA KHATUN (1284)

The funerary madrasa of Fatima Khatun, the wife of Sultan Qalawun, is located in the cemetery of Sayyida Nafisa, and has now been largely destroyed.[9] Of the minaret only a massive rectangular stone shaft has survived, standing at the left-hand side of the entrance to the madrasa. The shaft is similar in style to that of the minaret of Qalawun's complex, which this minaret slightly predates, and has a strongly projecting horizontal moulding running along its top edge. On each of its four sides at high level is a trilobed window opening flanked by embedded colonettes. These are set within pointed-arched recesses with cavetto returns, and stand above projecting sills with a moulding that is similar to that seen at the top of the shaft.

Further architectural information, however, can be derived from photographs that reveal the original appearance of the lost upper portion of the minaret. Above the stone shaft originally stood a two-storeyed plastered brick structure with a simple rectangular base and a slender octagonal pavilion. On each side of the pavilion were tall openings with semicircular arches set within larger recesses of similar design. A cavetto cornice separated this part of the pavilion from a second, much shorter, octagon with a smaller cornice that was pierced by tiny trilobed window

openings. The whole pavilion was originally crowned with a simple globular cap. Instead of muqarnas, pronounced horizontal mouldings are carved at the top of the rectangular shaft.

This form of minaret constructed without any attempt to create a transition between the rectangular section below and the markedly smaller octagonal section above remained rather unusual. It appears again at the nearby minaret of al-Baqli, the northern minaret of al-Nasir Muhammad at the Citadel, and the minaret of Tankizbugha in the northern cemetery.

12. THE COMPLEX OF SULTAN QALAWUN (1284–5)

Like many other features of the complex built by Sultan Qalawun in the Bayn al-Qasrayn, the minaret is unparalleled (figs 82 and 87).[10] Even its location within the complex, separated from the entrance and adjoining the mausoleum rather than the madrasa, is unusual. In this position, the massive tower of the minaret faces the viewer approaching the heart of the city along the Bayn al-Qasrayn coming from the northern gate of Bab al-Futuh. The most striking features of this minaret are its monumentality and the material of its construction – stone. They remained unique in the design of minarets for several subsequent decades. Although the minaret of Qalawun has a rectangular shaft, its staircase is spiral and ascends around a central newel, as had become common with stone minarets since the time of al-Hakim.

The position of the minaret in relation to the street effectively adds a northern façade to the complex, where the inscription band begins before turning the corner onto the east and main façade. The supporting wall beneath the minaret is bare on the northern side, except for delicately carved crenellations at roof level and a small inset rectangular plaque, framed by a moulding on the upper part of the rectangular section. This plaque is inscribed with a text that commemorates the restoration of the upper structure by Qalawun's son, Sultan al-Nasir Muhammad. A similar plaque is positioned above the entrance door to the minaret at roof level on the south. On the eastern and principal

FIG. 85

Nineteenth-century photograph of the complete minaret of Fatima Khatun

FIG. 86

The madrasa of Fatima Khatun today

façade, the base of the minaret is included within the overall architectural ordering of the elevation. It has pointed-arch recesses similar to the rest of the façade, with the difference that they contain blind niches instead of windows and have muqarnas heads. The decoration of the base of the minaret diverges from later practice, which generally did not include this element in the decorative scheme of the façade.

The cornice at the top of the rectangular shaft of the minaret consists of a series of small niches forming a kind of linear, rather flat muqarnas, unlike the common muqarnas used in Cairo at that time. It seems as if the mason who carved this cornice was not familiar with local muqarnas technique. In fact, muqarnas decoration is missing on the façade of this monument, whose composition is reminiscent of Norman architecture. On each of the four sides of the rectangular shaft is a carved horseshoe-arched recess that includes an oculus in its tympanum. As in the decoration of Ibn Tulun's minaret, carried out by Sultan Lajin a few years later, this horseshoe arch, which is a western Islamic feature, points to a possible contribution of Andalusian or North African craftsmen in the design of the structure. These recessed arches have mouldings around their edges and rest on muqarnas-like projecting cornices. They are flanked by separate octagonal marble colonettes with tulip bases and capitals.

The second storey of the minaret is set back from the first, allowing for a muezzin's balcony, and is also rectangular in plan. It has similarly proportioned recesses with horseshoe arches in each of its faces, defined by a projecting moulding. On the west side of the structure, which is least visible from the street, the recess of the arch descends to balcony level to provide a door opening into the staircase. On the remaining three sides, a narrow double-arched window, split by a central colonette, is located at high level above the point of the springing of the horseshoe arch. Unlike the first-storey arches, those at this level have no projecting sills below them. They do, however, have cushion voussoirs, a feature of decorative stonemasonry that appeared first in Cairo at the Fatimid gate of Bab al-Futuh. Immediately above the arches is a row of seven small recessed trilobed arches forming a miniature arcade.

FIG. 87

The minaret of the complex of Sultan Qalawun from the south

The upper, third, storey of the minaret was added by Sultan al-Nasir Muhammad to replace the original structure that had been damaged by the earthquake of 1303. The overseer of the construction was the emir Kahardash al-Mansuri.[11]

As with the storey below, it is set back and surrounded by a wooden platform with a railing for the use of the muezzin; the platform is octagonal in plan with chamfered corbels. The third storey is a brick construction of cylindrical section, with dense stucco decoration in four distinct yet interrelated horizontal zones. The lowest of these forms a sixteen-sided arcade composed of colonettes, including on four sides four trilobed doorways to the interior. The sixteen arches are interlaced to form large loops at their apexes. The stucco 'ground' here is very finely carved in the manner of the adjacent minaret of al-Nasir Muhammad's madrasa, and has a mixture of geometric and vegetal motifs. A foundation inscription, made in raised relief on a ground of vegetal patterns, comprises the third zone above the arcade. The inscription is enclosed by a projecting moulding that also forms four circular loops containing windows with geometric plaster grilles. The final zone is a cornice adorned with vertical flutes that K.A.C. Creswell has compared to an Ancient Egyptian papyrus motif. It is difficult to tell whether this motif, which reappeared later in the minarets of Manjaq and Shaykhu, is indeed of Ancient Egyptian inspiration or if the resemblance is merely a coincidence. The conical cap that crowns the upper cylinder is an Ottoman contribution.

Al-Nasir had one of the inscriptions commemorating his restoration of the final tier of his father's minaret carved in stone above the horseshoe-arched recesses on the first storey rather than on the section he rebuilt. Placed lower down the minaret the inscription is more visible, and carving in stone rather than plaster makes it more durable. The inscription is, however, set in four cartouches rather than a continuous band, a style that recalls the epigraphic cartouches carved in stucco on al-Nasir's adjacent minaret. The depth of carving on the inscription certainly makes it far easier to read from a distance. His second inspiration is located further down below the crenels. All the inscriptions can be seen to be the work of al-Nasir, who seems to have made the most of his father's minaret, which was originally devoid of epigraphy. Qalawun placed his own foundation inscription running in a continuous band on the lower levels of the façade where it could be read

very clearly, using the text as an architectural device to tie together the different elements of his complex.

EPIGRAPHY

First storey
'Basmala, O God renew mercy and gratification for the soul of the martyr al-Malik al-Mansur may God have mercy upon him. The renewal of this minaret has been ordered during the days of his son al-Malik al-Nasir Nasir al-Dunya wa 'l-Din Abu 'l-Fath Muhammad, following the appearance of the revealed signs with the collapse of its summit during the earthquake of the months of the year 703 of the Prophet's Hijra, prayer and peace upon him.'

Panel on the northern façade
'Basmala, Koran 24: 36, the renewal of this minaret was ordered by our Lord the sultan al-Malik al-Nasir Nasir al-Dunya wa 'l-Din Muhammad the son of Qalawun al-Salihi following the appearance of the revealed signs and the collapse of its summit in the months of the year 703 of the *Hijra* of the Prophet.'[12]

Plaque above the door of the south façade of the minaret
'Basmala, the renewal of this minaret was ordered by our Lord the sultan al-Malik al-Nasir Nasir al-Dunya wa 'l-Din Muhammad the son of Qalawun al-Salihi following the appearance of the earthquake and the collapse of its summit in the months of the year 703 of the Hijra of the Prophet.'[13]

Third storey
A fragmentary text which suggests that the inscription here once included the name of al-Nasir Muhammad.[14]

13. THE MINARET OF THE ZAWIYAT AL-HUNUD (1260–90)

Little can be added today to Creswell's analysis of this mysterious minaret,[15] which owes its name to a *zawiya* of a later date associated with a community from India or perhaps Central Asia. It is a fine example

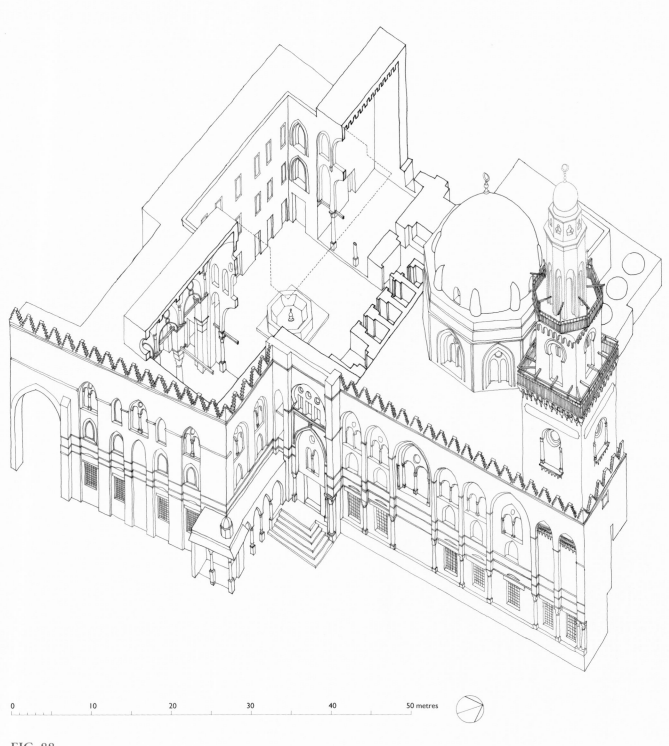

0   10   20   30   40   50 metres

FIG. 88

The minaret of the complex of Sultan Qalawun, axonometric reconstruction of the original upper structure

FIG. 89

The minaret of the Zawiyat al-Hunud with the minaret of Umm al-Sultan Sha'ban behind

of a plastered brick mabkhara-style minaret. The square shaft, which stands above an empty room at ground level, is decorated with blank keel-arched recesses with radiating hoods on each face. This supports, with plain wooden corbels, an octagonal wooden balcony and railing. The second octagonal tier of the minaret has the usual form of the mabkhara pavilion: an arcade of keel-arched recesses with trilobed door openings, a double muqarnas cornice with trilobed window openings, and a ribbed helmet.

Compared with the minaret of al-Salih Najm al-Din, to which it is very similar, the key elements of the second storey – the muqarnas zone and the ribbed cupola – are more elongated here, which suggests it was constructed at a slightly later date. This minaret cannot be compared with those of Fatima Khatun and Qalawun, which are royal constructions made of stone, but rather with the minaret, no longer extant, of the *ribat* of Sulayman al-Rifa'i datable to 1291. On the grounds of this analogy, the minaret of the Zawiyat al-Hunud could be dated anywhere between 1260 and 1290, that is to say between the reigns of al-Zahir Baybars and al-Ashraf Khalil. It is frustrating that primary sources have so far not provided a plausible patron for this handsome minaret whose architecture suggests that it once belonged to a building of some importance.

14. THE *RIBAT* OF SHAYKH SULAYMAN AL-RIFA'I (1291)*

A vanished minaret is recognisable on an anonymous nineteenth-century panoramic photograph taken from the quarter of Bab al-Wazir.[16] This image shows the palace of Emir Alin Aq next to the mosque of Khayrbak at the right and the mosque of Sultan Hasan dominating the background. In the middle of the panorama, the small minaret appears as a rectangular shaft with a damaged mabkhara top. This minaret must have collapsed shortly after the photograph was taken. The context of the panorama allows a reasonably certain identification of its site, which corresponds exactly to the beautifully decorated *ribat* or Sufi chapel of Shaykh Sulayman al-Rifa'i, of which only a fine

FIG. 90

Nineteenth-century photograph of the minaret of Shaykh Sulayman al-Rifa'i

dome and a ruined prayer hall have survived.

The rectangular shaft of the minaret, certainly a plastered brick construction, was decorated on each of the two visible sides with four medallions in the form of sunken rosettes. The octagonal mabkhara pavilion above this had trilobed openings within keel-arched recesses and was crowned by a double muqarnas cornice over which sat the ribbed cupola. The style of the structure is of the early Mamluk period and thus in accordance with the date of the *ribat* 691/1291.

15. THE MAUSOLEUM OF SHAYKH 'ALI AL-BAQLI (1297)

The building to which this minaret belonged was identified by 'Ali Mubarak, according to an inscription on a wooden cenotaph, as the mausoleum of Shaykh 'Ali al-Baqli, who died in 691/1291.[17] The style of the minaret, which is uninscribed, fits this date.

FIG. 93

The minaret of the Madrasa of Sultan al-Nasir Muhammad

FIG. 91

The minaret of the mausoleum of Shaykh 'Ali al-Baqli

FIG. 92

Unknown minaret in the cemetery

DESCRIPTION
DE L'ÉGYPTE

Although a modest construction, the minaret is of art historical interest. Its general configuration recalls the minaret of Fatima Khatun; a rectangular stone shaft is surmounted by a slender brick structure crowned by a bulbous cap. Unlike the minaret of Fatima Khatun, however, the upper structure is hexagonal, not octagonal, and it rests directly on the shaft without a plinth. Each of the six sides is pierced with a keel-arched panel within which are pairs of window openings, the lower of which is trilobed and the upper also keel-arched. The topmost structure has a simple cornice of mouldings and a cavetto. The muqarnas-like cornice atop the rectangular shaft is similar to that of Qalawun's minaret, but heavier.

A picture in the *Description de l'Égypte* shows a similar minaret, no longer extant, in a cemetery, suggesting that the type was more wide-spread than the surviving physical evidence admits.

16. THE MADRASA OF SULTAN AL-NASIR MUHAMMAD (1304)

The narrow façade of the madrasa of Sultan al-Nasir Muhammad stands in a slightly disadvantageous location in the Bayn al-Qasrayn,[18] hidden behind the corner of Qalawun's complex and dominated by its projecting monumental minaret. Seen from the north, it is squeezed between the madrasa of Sultan Barquq and the complex of Qalawun. The close vicinity of these three minarets in relation to one another is remarkable and characteristic of the urbanistic and architectural aesthetic of Mamluk Cairo.

The famous Gothic portal of the madrasa, removed as booty from a church in Acre during the decisive battle against the Crusaders, and praised by Maqrizi as one of the most magnificent doorways in the world, cannot be perceived until one stands right in front of it. It is enhanced, however, by the minaret that stands right above it, crowning it.

This madrasa has a complex building history. It was initially founded by Sultan al-'Adil Katbugha, who ruled briefly from Muharram 694/November–December 1294 to Safar 696/December 1296 during the interregnum preceding al-Nasir Muhammad's second reign, and it was completed by the latter sultan, who celebrated its inauguration in 703/1303, during his second reign. Katbugha built the façade, the mausoleum and the prayer *iwan*, and al-Nasir Muhammad completed the remainder of the building and added the brick minaret in 1304. The minaret is not aligned with the façade of the madrasa, but stands at a slight angle to it, following the Mecca orientation of the prayer hall. This differs from the adjacent minaret of Qalawun, which is aligned to the street rather than to the inner orientation of the building. The decoration of the minaret conforms with the same style of carved stucco as that of the third storey added by this sultan to Qalawun's minaret. Of the minaret we see today, only the square section is original; the octagonal second storey is a later construction. The staircase, as documented by Creswell, is made of timber inserted in the walls without a newel, leaving the interior hollow. Creswell could not locate the original staircase to the roof of the building, which was presumably located in

0   10   20   30   40   50 metres

FIG. 94

Axonometric view of the madrasa of Sultan al-Nasir Muhammad in relation to the complex of Qalawun

one of the destroyed sections of the madrasa. The brick shaft is light enough to be carried by the walls of the passage beneath that separates the madrasa and the mausoleum, as was the case with the minaret of al-Salih Najm al-Din.

The magnificent filigree-like stucco decoration of the shaft is perhaps too delicate for its body. The decoration on the south and west sides of the shaft has been more or less totally eroded, but the remaining north and east sides, although restored, give an excellent impression of its original appearance. The design is composed of blind miniature arcades, keel-arched panels, diamond shapes, medallions and other decorative elements set against a ground of varied arabesques. The heavily clustered muqarnas corbels that support the sixteen-sided platform for the octagonal second storey are very similar to those seen in an analogous location on the minaret of Baybars al-Jashnakir.

There are a total of three inscription bands on the shaft, all broken up into cartouches, according to the available space. The uppermost band, which survives on all sides of the shaft except the eastern, contains the names and titles of the sultan. As at Qalawun's minaret, this inscription starts on the north side of the shaft. The second, much smaller, epigraphic band runs through the recessed keel-arched openings, and survives only on the north and east faces. The lowest inscription band only survives in a cartouche on the north face: that on the east face over the portal and other sides has vanished.

Interestingly, the decoration of the north face does not begin consistently at its eastern edge, as one would expect, but leaves an undecorated space on this side over the lower two-thirds of the total height of the shaft. The reason for this blank space, which is neatly demarcated by a moulding, seems to have been the proximity of the vanished mausoleum dome that once stood very close to the minaret, its octagonal base almost touching it. If the dome was built before the minaret, as textual sources indicate, the craftsman in charge of the decoration would not have been able to reach this section of the shaft and, most importantly, any inscriptions in this location would not have been visible. If he had placed the beginning of the inscription above the portal, in other words on the eastern side of the minaret, it would have been interrupted at

FIG. 95

The fifteenth-century second storey at the minaret of the madrasa of Sultan al-Nasir Muhammad

the point where the minaret and dome met. Only by starting the inscription on the northern side could the text be completed before it came into contact with the dome. It is clear from the relative position of the dome and minaret, and the decorative programme of the latter, that the building had not been planned in its entirety before work commenced.

The style of decoration of the octagonal second storey of the minaret indicates that it must have been added in the mid-fifteenth century, perhaps by Sultan Inal when he cleared the Bayn al-Qasrayn of encroachments and founded a commercial building and a bathhouse a short distance to the north.[19] The decoration of the keel-arched niches of this storey is remarkable for the variety of patterns its hoods display. The blue ceramic discs that are inset into the interstices of the decorative mouldings above and, occasionally, within these niches also appear on Inal's mausoleum dome, and the strapwork moulding is reminiscent of that of his minaret in the northern cemetery.

FIG. 96

The minaret at the funerary complex of Emir Sanjar al-Jawli

The structure at the top of the minaret is made of lath and plaster and dates to the Ottoman period.

EPIGRAPHY

First storey
Upper band beginning on the north side: 'Basmala, O God prolong the days of al-Malik al-Nasir Nasir al-Dunya wa 'l-Din Muhammad the son of the Sultan the martyr al-Malik al-Mansur Sayf al-Dunya…'

Central band
A series of small cartouches, partly damaged, are inscribed in ornate Kufic with the word Allah followed by an attribute.

Lower band, south side only
'Has founded this blessed minaret our Lord…'

17. THE FUNERARY COMPLEX OF EMIR SANJAR AL-JAWLI (1304)

The composition of a minaret standing next to a pair of unequal domes is a remarkable and unique spectacle in medieval Cairo.[20] Perched on a rock that borders the street, the complex, consisting of a madrasa or a *khanqah* with two mausoleums built by Sanjar for himself and his friend and mentor Salar, dominates the view that faces the spectator descending from the Citadel along the processional route through Saliba Street. Seen in the sequence of Mamluk minarets, the minaret of Sanjar's complex is a milestone. It is the earliest extant example of the three-storeyed square-octagonal-circular composition, which was to become henceforth the standard form of Mamluk minarets. Unlike Qalawun's minaret, the wall within the façade beneath it is plain, with no articulation other than a blank inscription band. The crenellation at roof level separates the minaret proper from the façade. The square shaft of this minaret is made of stone, while the octagonal middle section and the cylindrical mabkhara at the top are built in brick.

The square shaft does, however, follow the style of Qalawun's minaret though in a more slender form.

Its four sides are adorned with arched recessed panels of different designs and windows flanked with colonettes resting on a muqarnas frieze. On the rear southern side, the panel has a horseshoe arch with a cushion voussoir and includes an oculus in the tympanum. On the front northern side the panel contains a trilobed double window with an oculus that introduces light into the staircase. The eastern side is pierced with a single window set in a keel-arched panel and the western side, behind the eastern dome, has an arched panel with an oculus. A horizontal moulding runs beneath all these arched panels and windows along all four sides of the shaft. The front has an additional lower window set within a keel-arched panel. As on the minaret of Qalawun, deeply inscribed cartouches, here with Koranic texts, are carved beneath the muqarnas at the upper edge of the square shaft.

The brick second storey forms the elongated octagonal base for the circular mabkhara top. This storey is set back from the square shaft, making room for the muezzin's balcony, which can be seen on old photographs to have had a wooden railing. The present balustrades are recent restorations in pierced stone, perhaps inspired by the remarkable openwork arabesque stone screens inside the building. Each side of the octagon has square recesses framing trilobed doors, topped by radiating keel-arched hoods. Above this is an elaborate muqarnas cornice that flares to provide a balcony around the mabkhara. This consists of a circular pavilion made of piers separated by trilobed door openings, again crowned by an elaborate muqarnas. A ribbed cupola with a domed profile completes the structure.

The minaret of Sanjar also displays some novelties. The staircase within the square shaft has at the summit of its newel a column with an acanthus capital. More visible is the design of the rear elevation of the minaret. Here, at roof level, the shaft contains a portal that emphasises the entrance to the staircase. This has the shape of a trilobed recess and, as in the case of mosque portals, is flanked by a pair of small stone benches (*maksalas*). The minaret of Sanjar shares this feature with the minaret of Bashtak, built thirty-two years later. At the time this monument was erected, the quarter of Qal'at al-Kabsh to its rear was a residential

FIG. 97

Elevation of the façade of the complex of Sanjar al-Jawli

area where Emir Sanjar's palace stood. This may explain the presence of the minaret portal, which would have been visible from the palace. Other architectural indicators confirm the importance of this dual orientation. One is the presence of a handsome secondary portal standing on the street to the south of the complex with a muqarnas vault leading through a rear passage to the prayer hall. The other is the arrangement of the Koranic inscription bands on the minaret and the adjacent domes. While the inscription on the minaret begins on the side of the main façade, thus reflecting the more public function of the minaret, the inscriptions on the funerary domes begin facing the Qal'at al-Kabsh quarter on the rear side.

EPIGRAPHY

Rectangular section
Sura 24:36–8

is crowned with bunches of elaborate stucco muqarnas that are very similar to those on the minaret of the madrasa of Sultan al-Nasir Muhammad. The muqarnas corbels support a balcony with a wooden railing. The surface of the cylindrical second storey is plain except on the lower section where rectangular recesses are crowned with a muqarnas cresting. On the southern side, most visible from the street, this muqarnas spreads horizontally to create a paired element. Above this runs another muqarnas cornice, defining the platform for the mabkhara itself. A further muqarnas ring underlines the ribbed cupola. The ribbing had, until some years ago, traces of green glazed tile decoration, which may once have covered it. At the time when the *khanqah* was built, the use of ceramic external decoration was singular; it became a fashion only in the subsequent decades, notably during the third reign of al-Nasir Muhammad. The green-ribbed cupola at the top of this minaret must thus have been an extra-ordinary spectacle at the time of its construction.

18. THE *KHANQAH* OF SULTAN AL-MUZAFFAR BAYBARS (AL-JASHNAKIR) (1308)

This minaret is a brick construction built above and slightly back from the main entrance to the *khanqah*.[21] Its juxtaposition with the mausoleum dome presents a harmonious composition that strikes the viewer proceeding north to the Bab al-Nasr from al-Jamaliyya, an impression enhanced by the bold projection of the façade of the tomb-chamber onto the street. Internal support for the minaret is provided by the walls of the square vestibule immediately inside the portal. Although this minaret, which has a wooden staircase, belongs structurally to the same category as the brick minarets of the madrasas of al-Salih Najm al-Din and al-Nasir Muhammad, its configuration is noticeably different. The second storey is cylindrical, as is the mabkhara. That makes this minaret the only surviving example with a cylindrical middle section supporting a cylindrical mabkhara top.

The square shaft is articulated with three radiating keel-arched hoods per side, the central hood in each case having a rectangular opening beneath it. The shaft

FIG. 98

The minaret and dome of the khanqah *of Sultan al-Muzaffar Baybars*

FIG. 99

Elevation of the façade of the khanqah *of Sultan al-Muzaffar Baybars*

19. THE MINARET OF PRINCESS (KHAWAND) ZAHRA [?] (FIRST HALF OF THE FOURTEENTH CENTURY)*

A photograph of the Bab al-Wazir area taken by Francis Frith circa 1857 shows a now lost minaret. Although the identity of the minaret is a matter of speculation, the picture leaves no doubt about its location. The minaret stood in Bab al-Wazir Street, between the mosque of Aytimish al-Bajasi, whose distinctive stone dome is visible on the right side of the picture, and the palace of Emir Alin Aq, which appears behind the minaret to the left.

The minaret is very similar in form to the minaret of the *khanqah* of al-Muzaffar Baybars (al-Jashnakir), sharing the design of a cylindrical mabkhara top combined with a cylindrical middle section. There is a difference, however, in the composition; this minaret had only two instead of three storeys. Its ribbed cupola, which rests above a narrow muqarnas cornice, is set directly above the cylindrical shaft without the mediation of a pavilion. The muqarnas corbelling at the upper edge of the square shaft also resembles that of Baybars' minaret, as well as that of the minaret of al-Nasir Muhammad's madrasa.

This minaret can be dated on stylistic grounds to the mid-fourteenth century. It is probably this building that 'Ali Mubarak identified as the 'mosque of Bab al-Wazir' and attributed mistakenly to Qawsun.[22] A text in Ibn Iyas' chronicle offers a clue to the identification of this structure; in his report on the plundering of the residence of Emir Aytimish al-Bajasi, he mentions the presence nearby of a mausoleum dome of a daughter of Sultan al-Nasir Muhammad, Khawand Zahra.[23] The plundered residence was originally the palace built by Alin Aq in the late thirteenth century, as is documented in the foundation document of Aytimish. The mausoleum of Khawand Zahra, located near Aytimish's house, is likely to be the building to which the minaret in Frith's photograph was attached. This attribution is further strengthened by the foundation deed of Emir Khayrbak, which mentions a waterwheel belonging to Khawand Zahra among the boundaries of the Alin Aq palace, which later in the early sixteenth

FIG. 100

Nineteenth-century view of Tabbana Street, including (centre of picture) the minaret of Princess Zahra

century became Khayrbak's residence. The surviving remains of a large Mamluk *iwan* in this location were also perhaps a component of the princess' complex at the site.[24]

No independent biography of Khawand Zahra is known; she is briefly mentioned as one of the daughters of al-Nasir Muhammad. The princess must have founded her mausoleum some time during the first half of the fourteenth century.

20. **THE MADRASA AND *RIBAT* OF EMIR SUNQUR AL-SAʿDI (HASAN SADAQA) (1315–21)**

The minaret, the mausoleum dome and the façade are almost all that survives of the funerary madrasa and hospice founded by Emir Sunqur al-Saʿdi. The minaret stands directly above the portal, juxtaposed with the mausoleum dome.[25] It is a particularly slender brick construction crowned with a remarkable mabkhara structure. The main shaft is square, and decorated with stucco keel-arched niches that include openings to introduce light into the stairwell. The stair is of timber, and runs around the internal walls of the shaft. The second octagonal storey is set back, starting above the wooden platform of the muezzin. Whereas the platform lacks the usual muqarnas that one would expect beneath it, the profile of the mabkhara, in contrast, is striking for the opulence of its nine-tiered cascade of stucco muqarnas divided into two sections beneath the ribbed cupola. The designer obviously concentrated all the decorative intent on the summit of the minaret, thus creating a novel silhouette.

In the nineteenth century the complex was inhabited by Turkish dervishes belonging to the Mevlevi Sufi order, who built a circular hall over the remains of the Mamluk madrasa for their ritual performances of music and dance. They also added a copper finial to the minaret in the shape of the distinctive woollen hat worn by the Sufis of this order, in place of the traditional crescent-shaped finial.

FIG. 101

The minaret of the madrasa of Emir Sunqur al-Saʿdi

21. THE MOSQUE OF SULTAN AL-NASIR MUHAMMAD AT THE CITADEL (1318)

The Citadel had been the residence of the sultans since the end of the Ayyubid period and contained not only a royal mosque and the barracks of the Mamluks to the north, but residential structures including the harem to the south, with the royal palaces positioned between the two.[26] In 1318, Sultan al-Nasir Muhammad built a new mosque in the Citadel to replace an older foundation, and subsequently modified its construction in 1335. The foundation inscription above the western entrance makes reference only to the earlier date.

The mosque of al-Nasir Muhammad is the fourth in Cairo to have been designed with multiple minarets, being preceded by the mosques of 'Amr, al-Hakim and al-Zahir Baybars. Unlike its predecessors, however, its minarets are not positioned symmetrically, but are adapted to the mosque's regal setting within the Citadel. The western portal and its minaret addressed the royal palace complex, while the northern minaret addressed the area of the offices and barracks. A close examination of the masonry of the mosque reveals that the second stage of construction included raising the entire ceiling of the building to a higher level and enlarging the dome in front of the mihrab while maintaining the original external perimeter. The masons made no effort to conceal the traces of the first phase of construction. That the minarets were erected during the first phase of work is indicated by the location of their bases, which are below the raised roof level. This explains what would otherwise be an anomaly in Mamluk architectural practice, according to which the base of the minaret is always located above the roof of the mosque. Moreover, the entrances to both minarets' staircases are likewise situated below the present roof level. The masonry of the main portal suggests that it may have allowed the construction of flanking minarets, in the Seljuk manner; while a substantial buttress on the southern side of the mosque would also allow a minaret to stand on this side of the building.

The western minaret stands to the right of the main entrance and the other at the north-east corner

FIG. 102

The western minaret of the mosque of Sultan al-Nasir Muhammad at the Citadel

FIG. 103

The western minaret of the mosque of Sultan al-Nasir Muhammad at the Citadel, the bulb

patterns of the two minarets are of slightly different configurations.

Both minarets have similar tops. These take the form of a fluted garlic-shaped bulb on a fluted cylinder covered with ceramic glazed tiles and adorned with an epigraphic band in tile mosaic. In the case of the western minaret, the bulb rests directly above the upper balcony. The bulb on the north-eastern minaret, however, is set above a hexagonal pavilion and has a simple row of tiled stepped crenellations at its base. The placement of a cylindrical section above a hexagonal pavilion produces a rather awkward profile, which the crenellations would have masked to a certain extent. The addition of the hexagonal pavilion was obviously intended to increase the height of this minaret, which is taller than the other, probably to make it more visible to those within the northern enclosure of the Citadel. The basic colours used are dark blue and green, with white used for the lettering and dark blue for the ground on the inscription bands. As a large part of the tile cladding has been replaced with modern tiles, it is hard to assess the quality of the original work here. The crenellations on the north-eastern minaret bulb were obviously a 'special order', but there seem to be no tiles made with a curved profile that would have given the many ribs on the two structures a cleaner finish than that achieved by using ordinary flat tiles. The quality of this tile decoration appears quite inferior to that of later tile mosaics used on the drums of the mausoleum domes of Aslam al-Silahdar and Princess Tughay, and may not have been executed by the same craftsmen.

As they were built in stone to such an unprecedented design, the two minarets were obviously too precious to be pulled down in the course of the reconstruction of the mosque in 1335. The glazed tile mosaics displayed on these minarets are of Iranian origin, developed in the Ilkhanid period and also adopted in Anatolia. Michael Meinecke dates the exotic ceramic decoration to the second building phase of 1335, linking it to the arrival of an Iranian craftsman in Cairo, some time between 1322 and 1328, a craftsman who in 1330 built the minarets of Emir Qawsun's mosque, no longer extant, in the style

of the mosque. The two minarets display radically different designs although both are built in stone throughout. The minaret at the main entrance is cylindrical, tapering and carved over all three storeys. The surface of each section is deeply carved in rounded profile with a zigzag motif. The north-eastern minaret has a cylindrical second storey, considerably set back above its square shaft. Both sections are bare of carving except for a narrow muqarnas cornice beneath the muezzin's balconies. The interior of this minaret also exhibits a unique feature: inside the square lower storey, the spiral stair rises within an octagonal rather than a circular envelope. This would have been much harder for the masons to build and has no advantages over a circular interior, so it is hardly surprising that the experiment was never repeated. The muqarnas

FIG. 104

The two minarets of the mosque of Sultan of al-Nasir Muhammad at the Citadel

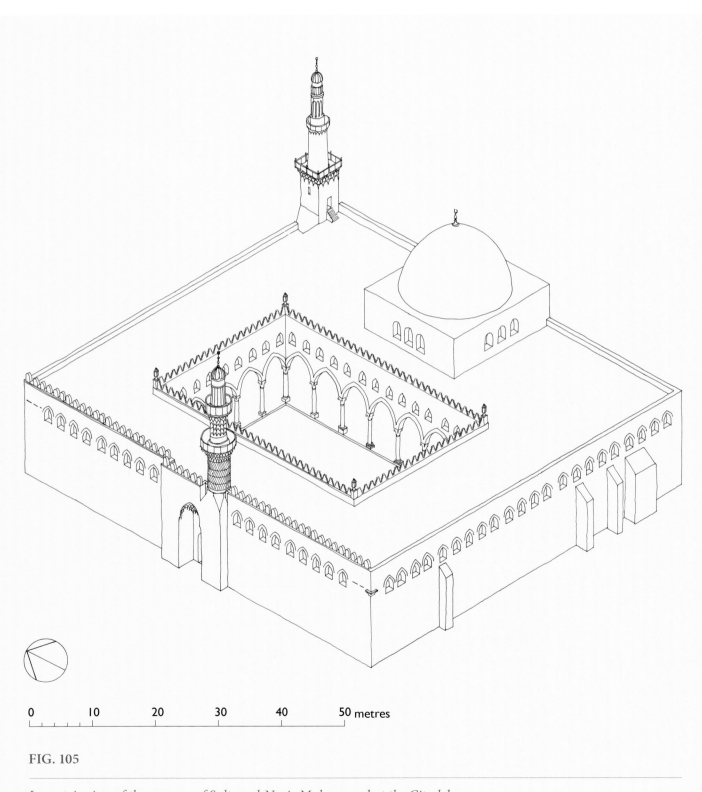

0   10   20   30   40   50 metres

FIG. 105

Isometric view of the mosque of Sultan al-Nasir Muhammad at the Citadel

of contemporary Tabriz.[27] The arrival of this builder, however, postdated the erection of the minarets, which bear no sign of alterations. The Ilkhanid influence therefore should not be linked exclusively with this particular Tabrizi builder. The minaret of the *khanqah* of al-Muzaffar Baybars already provides an example of the use of glazed tiles on its cupola. Other, earlier, examples of Mamluk decoration reflecting Iranian influence can be seen in Cairo, such as the stucco mihrab of al-Nasir's madrasa in the Bayn al-Qasrayn.[28] The fact that a number of later Mamluk monuments were also decorated with tile mosaics in the style of the minarets of al-Nasir's mosque does, nevertheless, indicate, that a specialised workshop dedicated to architectural ceramics must have existed in Cairo for some decades.[29]

The masonry construction of al-Nasir's minarets clearly deviates from Ilkhanid minaret architecture, which is mostly in brick. Another possibility, suggested by Ülkü Bates, that their inspiration may have come from Anatolia, where stone architecture with elaborate carving co-existed with ceramic decoration, deserves consideration. This view seems to be supported by the style of the stone carving of the western minaret. Although this was unprecedented in Cairo, the rounded profile of the deeply carved zigzags was common in Anatolian architecture. In Cairo, it was also adopted on ribbed masonry domes.

The configuration of the north-eastern minaret is neither Anatolian nor Iranian but follows local antecedents. Its square shaft with a muqarnas cornice recalls the minaret of al-Baqli. The combination of square and circular sections was already adopted at the minaret of al-Muzaffar Baybars, albeit executed in brick, with a less slender profile.

The muezzin's balconies of both minarets today have stone balustrades pierced with geometric and arabesque patterns, as does the miniature balcony in the northern wall of the mosque behind which is the staircase of the north-eastern minaret. A drawing of the western minaret by Pascal Coste indicates that the original balustrades were indeed made of stone.[30] These balustrades may have been the earliest of their kind used in minaret architecture: they have a stylistic precedent in the famous pierced stone screens that decorate the funerary complex of Emir Sanjar.

FIG. 106

The northern minaret of the mosque of Sultan al-Nasir Muhammad

EPIGRAPHY

Western bulb
Basmala, Sura 2:255 (only as far as *qayyum*)

North-eastern bulb
Sura 1:1–2

FIG. 107

The minaret of the mosque of Emir Bashtak

22. THE MOSQUE OF EMIR BASHTAK (1336)

The monumentality of the minaret of Bashtak, the quality of its stonemasonry and the assured manner in which so many features new to minaret design are executed make this one of the most impressive minarets in Cairo. Only the minaret and a magnificent portal have survived of the original mosque, which was part of a complex that also included a *khanqah*.[31] Maqrizi wrote that Bashtak, who was one of the mightiest emirs of Sultan al-Nasir Muhammad, built a mosque at Qabuw al-Kirmani between the lake called Birkat al-Fil, or the 'Lake of the Elephant' and the bank of the Khalij or 'Canal of Cairo'. The lake covered the area occupied today by the Hilmiyya quarter to the north of Sayyida Zaynab. The *khanqah* was opposite the mosque and connected to it by a bridge; it overlooked the canal to the west. In urban terms, this arrangement was the earliest example in Cairo of a single matching complex on both sides of a street. Similar layouts were later executed by Emir Shaykhu and Sultan al-Ghawri.

The early mabkhara form of minaret commonly used an octagonal section with keel-arched niches to form the base of the cupola at its summit. At the minaret of Bashtak, the octagonal section with keel-arched niches has been transferred to the first storey of the shaft, while the second storey is circular. This is a significant innovation because it introduces a major feature in the architectural aesthetic of Cairene minarets, which is the smooth transition between the first and the second storeys rather than a sharp break, seen hitherto, between the square and the cylindrical sections of the shaft. This innovation was also to lead ultimately to the design of a minaret shaft with an octagonal plan in all of its sections. The earlier design, with a recessed cylindrical section over a square shaft without transition, was abandoned until the beginning of the next century, when it reappeared at the twin minarets of the *khanqah* of Sultan Faraj ibn Barquq in the northern cemetery.

Although the western minaret of al-Nasir Muhammad's mosque at the Citadel is the first to display a stone shaft covered with carved decoration,

thus setting a new trend, the minaret of Bashtak is the earliest extant example with a 'panelled' octagonal first storey and a carved middle section. Its octagonal section is exquisitely treated with keel-arched recessed panels with radiating hoods connected by mouldings: a delicate arabesque pattern is carved on the spandrels between the arches, and four of them, pierced with trilobed openings that light the stairwell, are connected to graceful miniature balconies supported by muqarnas brackets. Each of the eight hoods of the panels includes in its centre a miniature keel-arched inscribed plaque. The inscriptions consist alternately of the formulas *al-mulk li 'llah* and *al-'izz li 'llah*, meaning respectively 'Power is God's' and 'Glory is God's'.[32] These words, not visible to the naked eye, are obviously expressions of piety in their invocation to God rather than mere decoration. In addition to these niches that give a vertical emphasis to each side of the octagon, horizontal articulation is provided by a projecting moulding that links the balconies, as well as a broad inscription band that runs above the arches, and the muqarnas cornice that supports the upper balcony. This is a design that was to be repeated countless times with subtle variations on the octagonal first storeys of Cairo's Mamluk minarets. The Koranic verse that is found on the inscription band is part of Sura 7 (The Heights) and is particularly appropriate for a minaret since it celebrates the creation of the planets and the passage of night into day. This is the first documented appearance of this verse on a minaret in Cairo.

By contrast, the deeply carved pattern of pointed arches defined by thick rounded profiles seen on the middle section of Bashtak's minaret remains unique in Cairo. This storey also has an inscription band running beneath its muqarnas cornice. Some of the stone panels of the balustrades to the muezzins' balconies, pierced with geometric and arabesque patterns, appear to be original. The posts between the panels of the balustrades are carved with small faceted bulbs, reminiscent of the bulbs on top of the later minarets.

The upper structure seems unusual for its simplicity and rather compact appearance, but it must be remembered that the evolution of the upper bulb was still at an early stage. An investigation of the

FIG. 108

The minaret of the mosque of Emir Bashtak, detail of the carved shaft

FIG. 109

The minaret of the mosque of Emir Bashtak, interior of the bulb

inner walls and the staircase shows that the masonry of the upper structure is continuous with the stone-work below, leaving little doubt that the top storey is original.[33] A cylindrical section, pierced with four narrow and arched openings, culminates in a flaring projection, above which the bulb rises. The projection beneath the bulb is decorated with a line of miniature trefoil crenels, some of which preserve a delicately carved arabesque decoration only visible from through a powerful lens. The rounded bulb is carried by a tapering cylinder. The style of this upper section does not seem to have been repeated, at least according to the evidence of extant structures. It represents a transition between the upper structure of the western minaret of al-Nasir Muhammad at the Citadel and the octagonal pavilion, as represented by the minaret of al-Maridani.

The spiral vault of the staircase within the minaret is also beautifully executed, with a carved moulding running at the base of the vault from the bottom of the structure to its top.

The inscriptions on the minaret of Bashtak do not start on the side of the main façade, as was usual, but on the rear, or eastern, side of the mosque. Moreover, the entrance to the staircase from the roof of the mosque is emphasised by the presence of a portal also facing east (fig. 35). Normally minarets do not have a portal emphasising the door to the staircase; the only precedent is on the minaret of the funerary complex of Sanjar al-Jawli. Here, the portal was meant to add an aesthetic touch to the back of the minaret, which the patron could appreciate from his residence. In the case of Bashtak's minaret, the elaboration of a portal in this position is more difficult to explain. Had the portal been on the west side, it would have been seen from the bridge connecting the *khanqah* with the mosque. However, with the minaret being on the western façade of the mosque, only someone standing on the roof, or perhaps on the ground at a considerable distance to the east, can see the portal. The portal has a recess with a muqarnas crest and is equipped, like mosque portals, with a flanking pair of stone benches or *maksalas*. Moreover, it bears a separate inscription band in a cartouche above the door, indicating that construction began in early Ramadan 736/April–May 1336 and was completed

in late Rajab 737/February–March 1337, that is, within less than a year. It is not clear from the text, which presents some problems of interpretation, whether the date refers to the minaret alone or the mosque as a whole.

Another remakable feature seen on this minaret for the first time is the transitional zone that mediates between the square base and the octagonal shaft of the first storey. The upper four corners of the base are connected to four of the eight facets of the octagonal section through masonry triangles, which are sculpted to form an undulating curved profile. These undulating volutes frame the portal on both its sides and greatly enhance the base of the minaret. This form of transitional zone was later to be adopted in the architecture of stone domes in Cairo, as well as on numerous other minarets.[34]

The remains of two lightly carved sundials can still be recognised on the minaret, one near the entrance to the staircase and another on the upper storey. They were for the use of the muezzin to determine the time for prayer. Sundials are not always carved on minarets; they may also be found in other external parts of the building.

EPIGRAPHY

Cartouche above the door of the staircase
'Basmala, This is what was prepared for his mosque' [*masjidihi*][35] by the lofty, the most noble Bashtak, the royal (officer of) al-Nasir. It was begun at the beginning of the venerated month of Ramadan in the year 736 and completed at the end of the month of Rajab the unique in the year 737.'

First storey
Sura 7:54

Second storey
Sura 2:285

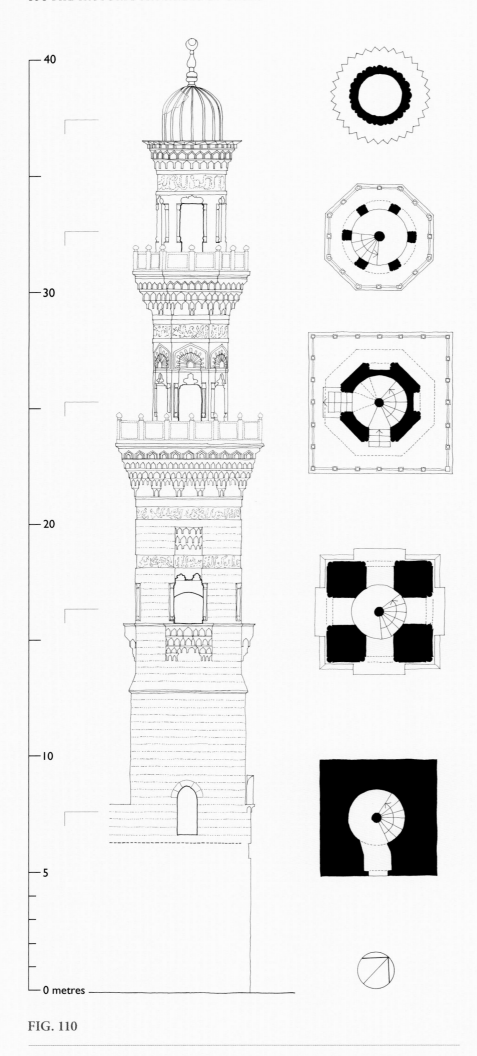

FIG. 110

The minaret of the khanqah *of Emir Qawsun, elevation and plans*

23. THE *KHANQAH* OF EMIR QAWSUN (1336–7)

Like the minaret of Bashtak, the minaret of Qawsun reflects the grandeur of one of the mightiest emirs of Sultan al-Nasir Muhammad's golden age.[36] It stands in the Suyuti cemetery on the south-east side of the Citadel, and was once attached to a funerary *khanqah* with two mausoleum domes. The *khanqah* was inaugurated in 736/1335, and the minaret was completed in the following year. Qawsun later built a Friday mosque in the same area, which, according to Maqrizi, boosted the prestige of this cemetery.

The minaret was not freestanding as it appears today, but was attached to the perimeter wall of the *khanqah*. This is also confirmed by the fact that the entrance to the staircase of the minaret is above the roof level of the building, which is marked by surviving crenellations around the base of its shaft. The inscription bands on the surviving dome and on the supporting wall of the minaret can be seen to stand at the same level from the ground, and both contain verses from the same Sura of the Koran (36). The verses on the minaret are from the beginning of the Sura while those on the dome are from a later part of the text. On these grounds Laila 'Ali Ibrahim has reconstructed the original layout of the complex. It must have been a large building on a scale similar to the later *khanqah* of Faraj ibn Barquq in the northern cemetery, with the minaret positioned at the north-west corner. There is no evidence here to support a speculation that a second matching minaret was ever built on the opposing corner of the *khanqah*.

Besides the inscription from Sura 36 that runs from below the minaret along all the exterior walls of the building, the shaft proper of the minaret bears four other inscription bands. One of them, in the upper part of the square section of the shaft, indicates a date of 737/1336–7, which is a year later than the date given by Maqrizi for the construction of the complex. This discrepancy is not surprising, since the construction of a religious building usually began with the prayer hall, which was used immediately, often before the other ancillary structures were completed. The minaret was normally among the last parts of a mosque to be built.

FIG. 111

The minaret of the khanqah *of Emir Qawsun*

The design of this minaret is a further development of the style of the minaret of Sanjar al-Jawli. The minaret of Qawsun, however, is made of stone throughout, and marks the apogee of this particular style. Its masonry is accomplished and its decoration is deeply carved and of remarkable quality. The inscriptions are of high quality. The square first storey of the minaret is exceptionally tall, but has an elegance derived from the fact that the shaft is chamfered to reduce its width. Above this chamfer are four square recesses with muqarnas hoods within which are paired trilobed openings separated by central freestanding columns. Smaller columns flank the edges of the recesses, which have matching columns placed on each corner of the shaft. The columns of the circular upper section are engaged and embedded in the masonry, whereas those of the rectangular shaft are carved independently, which is a remarkable feature. This feature explains that many of them are missing. Their capitals and bases are, by contrast, carved out of the shaft. The bases are of a standard tulip pattern, the tops are classically inspired acanthus capitals. The recessed openings of this storey are related to projecting miniature balconies supported by muqarnas corbels, and are linked horizontally by a string moulding at balcony level and an inscription band that runs through them. Above the recesses runs a second inscription band, and above that the muqarnas corbelling for the muezzin's balcony.

The use of columns to articulate the corners of a square minaret shaft is seen for the first time on the minaret of Qawsun, but is a feature that was to be repeated on many later Mamluk minarets. The first storey is also unusual in having two inscription bands, which contain the earliest documented appearance of Sura 33 on a minaret in Cairo. The middle section of the minaret displays no such originality on its exterior: it is essentially a copy of the octagonal first storey of Bashtak's minaret, built only a year earlier. Like Bashtak's minaret, it also has one inscription band running below the muqarnas that supports the upper balcony. Inside this section of the shaft, however, the spiral of the staircase winds more tightly than in the rest of the structure.[37] There may have been a structural motivation, to increase the resistance of the minaret to the lateral thrust imposed by earthquakes.

The mabkhara of Qawsun's minaret is only the second stone example to survive intact in Cairo after that added by Sultan Lajin to the minaret of Ibn Tulun. It has large arched openings that give it an airy character, anticipating the later pavilion-type of final stage, crowned with a bulb. Its ribbed cupola has been rightly considered by Christel Kessler to be the architectural model for later ribbed stone domes. The muqarnas at the base of the cupola culminates in a ring of outward-pointing triangles, or spikes, which is also the earliest appearance of this form of decoration. Another epigraphic band runs like a collar below the muqarnas.

At the end of the third decade of the fourteenth century when Qawsun was erecting his *khanqah* and mosque in the cemetery, the master-builder of Sultan al-Nasir Muhammad was a man named Ibn al-Suyufi. It is to him that Maqrizi attributes the construction of the minaret of the madrasa of Aqbugha and the entire mosque of al-Maridani. Whether al-Suyufi erected the minaret of Qawsun as well remains an open question. The emphasis here is on carved stonework rather than the inlaid decoration displayed at the minarets of Aqbugha and al-Maridani. This would suggest that, supposing al-Suyufi's authorship, this decoration was executed by a different team of craftsmen.

During the restoration of the minaret in the 1930s the pierced stone balustrades around the balconies and some stone blocks in the cupola were replaced.

EPIGRAPHY

First storey lower band, facing south and east
Sura 36:13 (partial); Sura 2:262 or 274 or 277 (partial)

First storey upper band
Sura 9:18; Sura 33: 41–4 followed by 'on the date 737'

Second storey
Sura 9:18; Sura 33:45

Mabkhara (top)
Sura 24:36–7

24. THE 'SOUTHERN' MINARET
(1330–1350s)

The 'Southern' minaret, so-called in the absence of information about its patron, is an extraordinary construction that displays ambitious proportions and outstanding masonry.[38] Located in the Suyuti cemetery near the Citadel, the minaret acquired its name because it stands to the immediate south of the minarets of Qawsun and the Sultaniyya mausoleum. It is the only surviving structure of an as yet unidentified building. Although they were erected in a cemetery rather than in an urban context, the three minarets of this group are aligned in a manner that gives grandeur and scale to the road leading south from here through the cemetery. They would have been clearly visible from the royal apartments in the Citadel (fig. 7).

This minaret is unlike any other in Cairo, although its proportions recall the minarets of Bashtak, Qawsun and Aqsunqur. It has a square base, octagonal first storey, circular second storey and octagonal third storey. Whether it originally had a fourth storey is a matter of speculation. Some details of its decoration, such as the treatment of the muqarnas below the miniature balconies of the lower octagonal section, the hoods of the keel-arched panels that are alternately carved and plain, and the muqarnas of the upper balcony, recall the much smaller minaret of Baydar al-Aydumuri (1347) at Jamaliyya. The 'Southern' minaret has a pyramidal transitional zone. Above this, the recessed arches in each facet of the octagon have lost the columns that once flanked their edges: unlike the minaret of Qawsun, the capitals and bases for these columns were not integral to the masonry. Above the arches runs a band of looped mouldings and the muqarnas cornice for the first balcony. There is no inscription band on this section of the minaret, where it would have been more visible than on the upper storeys.

The only decoration of the cylindrical second storey is a deeply carved moulding with a rounded profile that runs like a belt around the shaft and arches over the entrance to the staircase. This moulding is of the same quality of carving as seen in the moulded blind arches of the second storey of the minaret of Bashtak,

FIG. 112

The 'Southern' minaret

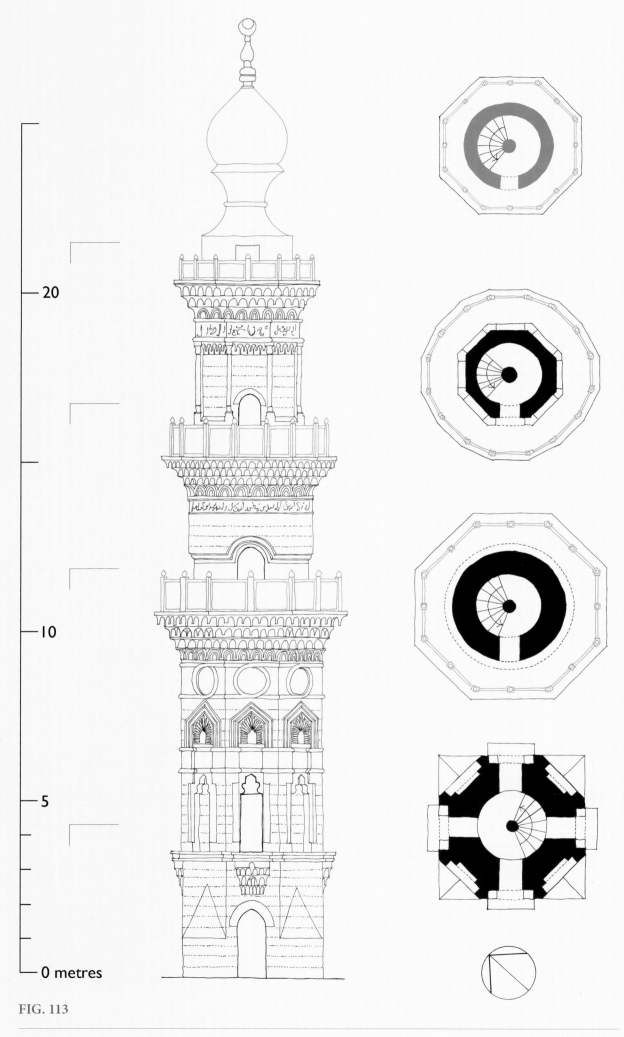

FIG. 113

The 'Southern' minaret, elevation and plans

FIG. 114

The 'Southern' minaret, view of the carving

but here it also delineates a recess in the profile of the shaft. An inscription band, of the highest calligraphic quality of carving, containing the first documented use of Sura 41 on a minaret in Cairo, runs around the upper part of this section, beneath another ring of muqarnas and the second balcony level. This balcony is sixteen-sided in order to relate more smoothly to the circular storey below.

The insertion of an octagonal section at the level of the third storey is atypical, and suggests that it might originally not have been the final stage of the minaret, but that there was a fourth storey in the form of a pavilion or a mabkhara above it. The modern bulb above this storey appears awkward without a pavilion beneath it. The decoration of the third storey is unusual: it retains the vestiges of carved capitals and column bases at each of the eight corners of the octagon that point to the prior existence of freestanding colonettes in these locations. A similar arrangement was adopted earlier at the mabkhara added by Lajin to the minaret of Ibn Tulun. Another epigraphic band is found at the top of this section. The Comité planned to replace the missing colonettes of the minaret, both on this storey and the first, but in the end installed only pierced stone balustrades around the balconies.

Michael Meinecke has attributed this minaret to the vanished mosque that Qawsun is reported to have built next to his *khanqah*.[39] The mosque was founded in 738/1338 and completed in 739/1339. There are, however, pronounced stylistic discrepancies between the 'Southern' minaret and that of Qawsun's *khanqah*. The construction of two such different minarets on two adjoining buildings founded by the same patron, although it cannot be entirely excluded, would have been unusual in Mamluk practice. Bashtak, slightly earlier, and Shaykhu two decades later, each built a Friday mosque facing a *khanqah*, as did Emir Manjaq. Bashtak and Manjaq seem to have built only one minaret apiece; Shaykhu's two minarets are essentially identical. As a patron of outstanding status Qawsun might well have made unconventional choices. His earlier Friday mosque (1330) built near the Birkat al-Fil had two minarets covered with glazed tiles, attributed to the designs of a craftsman from Tabriz.[40]

On the basis of its style and dimensions, the 'Southern' minaret can almost certainly be dated between the mid-1330s and 1350s, late in the reign of Sultan al-Nasir Muhammad or slightly beyond. This period saw the flourishing of masonry construction in Cairo of an unprecedented quality and scale. A very large number of religious funerary buildings were founded by the emirs of that period in this area of the southern cemetery close to the Citadel, many of which have vanished.

EPIGRAPHY

Second storey
Sura 41:30–1

Third storey
Sura 24:35

---

25. THE MINARET OF EMIR AQBUGHA AT THE AZHAR MOSQUE (1339–40)

The oldest surviving minaret at al-Azhar is the minaret attached to the adjacent madrasa built by Emir Aqbugha. Due to the location of the madrasa behind the western wall of the mosque, in between it and the madrasa, the minaret effectively belonged to both buildings. It is surprising that Maqrizi, our primary source for the Mamluk history of Cairo and its architecture, listed this minaret as the second one in Cairo to be built in stone after the minaret of Qalawun. He thus demonstrates a remarkable lack of awareness by disregarding the minarets of the mosques of Ibn Tulun, al-Hakim, al-Nasir Muhammad, Bashtak and Qawsun, and perhaps others that might since have disappeared. The historian's comment, however, suggests that he viewed this minaret as somehow groundbreaking for its time. It is also the only minaret that Maqrizi attributed to a named builder – to Ibn al-Suyufi, the master-builder of Sultan al-Nasir Muhammad.

Both the architecture and the decoration of the base and octagonal first storey of this minaret are remarkable, particularly when seen from a close range (fig. 33). The transitional zone is made of downward-pointing triangles of masonry demarcated by a heavy double

FIG. 115

The minaret of Emir Aqbugha at the Azhar mosque

moulding with rounded profiles. These mouldings connect the bottom of the triangles and run over the entrance door, as well as looping at the centre of the bottom of each of the octagonal facets of the upper shaft. Each loop contains an inset green ceramic or glass paste disc, a form of decoration commonly seen in the mid-fifteenth century. The triangles are inlaid with white and blue-grey marble, a combination of stones also used to decorate three roundels occupying the sides of the base apart from that occupied by the entrance door. These roundels are partially convex, have a radiating design, and are surrounded by a single circular moulding with a rounded profile. The octagonal shaft has keel-arched recesses but no projecting miniature balconies. Instead, the articulation is provided by pairs of octagonal white marble columns that are mounted at each corner of the octagon. These columns have tulip-style marble bases that are not all identical, suggesting the building material has been appropriated from elsewhere. The capitals, however, are part of the masonry of the minaret itself, and are carved as paired pseudo-Corinthian elements that are kinked in plan to adjust to their locations at the corners of the octagon. The masonry on the recessed planes of the shaft is all bichrome, simply striped on most faces. Two facets, however, have an interlocking chevron design. The hoods of the recesses are framed by a single moulding, looping at their apexes. The spandrels between each arch are infilled by a blue-grey marble border and white limestone centre, the latter carved with delicate arabesques. The hoods of the arches have a radiating pattern executed in the same combination of blue-grey and white stone. The foundation inscription of the minaret runs in a band above all this dramatic stonework.

The circular middle section of the shaft displays an overall pattern of lozenges with trefoil edges, made of bichrome inlaid limestone. A Koranic inscription band runs beneath the muqarnas ring of upper balcony that contains the first recorded example of Sura 3 on a minaret in Cairo. The muqarnas, and everything above it, is modern restoration work. The slenderness of the whole shaft suggests that this would have consisted of a pavilion with a bulb similar to that of the minaret of the mosque of al-Maridani,

built by the same architect, rather than the traditional mabkhara. It may have been the earliest ever appearance of this form of upper structure; and the novelty of a slender octagonal pavilion crowned with a pear-shaped bulb over a cornice of muqarnas may have made this minaret stand out in the eyes of Maqrizi. In fact, this device developed at the time minaret shafts were becoming increasingly slender, with a corresponding shift towards stone masonry instead of brick architecture. This also coincides with the prevalence of an octagonal, instead of square, first storey.

A striking feature of this minaret, compared with others built in the same period, is the treatment of its surface. If not the first, then it must be one of the first minarets in Cairo to display bichrome masonry comprehensively.

EPIGRAPHY

First storey lower band
'Basmala, his excellency, the eminent, the lordly, the emir, the illustrious Sayf al-Din Aqbugha al-Awhadi, the majordomo of al-Malik al-Nasir has ordered the construction of this blessed minaret in the year [7]40/1339–40.'[41]

Second storey
Sura 3:191

26. THE MOSQUE OF EMIR ALTINBUGHA AL-MARIDANI (1340)

Although the royal master-builder, *mu'allim* Ibn al-Suyufi, who built the minaret of Aqbugha at al-Azhar, was also the architect of this mosque, this minaret has a different profile and it lacks the bichrome stonework decoration.[42] They may once have shared a common design for their upper structures, but since the loss of the original top of Aqbugha's minaret, this remains uncertain.

The minaret of al-Maridani is the earliest extant minaret with an entirely octagonal shaft, which Creswell has attributed to a Syrian influence. Although it is true that octagonal minarets existed earlier in Iraq and Syria, the appearance of the octagonal shaft on a Cairene minaret should be attributed rather to a gradual local development. The mabkhara of Lajin at Ibn Tulun's minaret had an octagonal section, for example, that was also adopted at the minaret of Sanjar al-Jawli. Over time the mabkhara became increasingly elongated and eventually the first storey also took the shape of an octagonal shaft, as can be seen at the minarets of Bashtak, Aqbugha and at the 'Southern' minaret. It is therefore not surprising that Cairene masons would finally build a minaret with all three storeys octagonal in form, without external influence. Considering the magnitude and significance of Mamluk buildings in Cairo at that time, where, unlike the case in Syria, minarets were added even to relatively minor foundations, a Syrian influence seems unlikely.

The minaret stands at the corner of the mosque on the left side of the plain entrance on Tabbana Street. A close look at the stones of the supporting wall of the minaret shows that the coursing of its masonry differs from that of the rest of the façade of the mosque. This wall, which also conceals part of an inscription band that starts on the right side of the portal and continues to the left around the building, must therefore be a later addition made to reinforce the original base of the minaret.

Although the mosque of al-Maridani is lavishly decorated and densely inscribed in its interior, the minaret is entirely bare of inscriptions and the decoration of its shaft is strikingly sparse in comparison with its immediate predecessors. The first storey has keel-arched recesses with plain hoods, four of which have openings to the stairwell and miniature balconies on muqarnas brackets. A masonry band runs around the recess arches forming a loop above their apex. Each recess includes a carved arch with a delicate lobed profile. The octagonal second storey is completely plain. The faint traces of stripes that can be seen on the masonry throughout seem to be a remnant of later overpainting rather than evidence for bichrome stonework: the covering of dust makes it hard to tell. Restoration works were done at the upper structure of the minaret between 1897 and 1904, along with the balustrades of all the balconies. Fortunately, however, the new work followed traces of the original bulb, part of which was still *in situ* at the time of the restoration.[43]

FIG. 116

The minaret of Emir Altinbugha al-Maridani

The minaret of al-Maridani displays today the earliest extant octagonal pavilion with a bulb. The bulb is not set yet over freestanding columns, but on masonry piers that are circular outwards and rectangular inwards. They are crowned with unusual capitals.

27. THE MADRASA OF EMIR BAYDAR AL-AYDUMURI (1346–7)

This minaret stands adjacent to a small mausoleum dome. They are the only remaining original elements of a funerary madrasa built in the Jamaliyya quarter near the residence of the founder, who is also popularly known as Aydumur al-Bahlawan.[44] The minaret is interesting and handsome despite its small proportions. It displays the high quality of masonry carving that characterised Mamluk architecture of the mid-fourteenth century. The carved decoration of the octagonal first and cylindrical second sections recalls that of the 'Southern' minaret in the Suyuti cemetery. The square base has an undulating transitional zone, following the model of Bashtak's minaret. The middle cylindrical section is deeply carved with a horizontal zigzag pattern with rounded profile, seemingly inspired by al-Nasir Muhammad's western minaret at the Citadel.

In 1896 the Comité dismantled the original upper pavilion when it began to lean, and it was never replaced. The upper pavilion was instead reconstructed in the ruins of the mosque of al-Hakim in 1910, where it stood for many years. Photographs and drawings show it to have had a rather heavy bulb, analogous in appearance to that of the minaret of Bashtak, with an inscription carved around its neck. The bulb was placed on marble columns, some of them re-used from other sources, with tulip capitals. The present whereabouts of the blocks of this pavilion are unknown.[45]

EPIGRAPHY

Lower band
Fragments of invocations

Upper band
Sura 3:190–1

FIG. 117

The minaret of the madrasa of Emir Baydar al-Aydumuri

28. **THE MOSQUE OF EMIR AQSUNQUR** (1347)

The minaret of the mosque of Aqsunqur is one of the most impressive Cairene minarets in shape, proportions and placement. It does not stand at the portal of the mosque, but at its southern corner, projecting into the street in a dominant position facing those coming down the Darb al-Ahmar from the Citadel towards the Bab Zuwayla.[46] Its prominent location in the street perspective earned it the attention of numerous artists and photographers, which in this particular case, proved to be felicitous. Given this striking location it is, perhaps, surprising that the minaret had no inscriptions carved upon it.

The minaret of Aqsunqur currently has three storeys: the lower two circular and the uppermost octagonal. The first storey is strikingly plain, and rises from its square base with a simple transitional zone formed by concave (rather than flat) sloping triangles to the muqarnas ring of the first balcony. Deeply carved vertical ribs with rounded profiles adorn the shaft of the second storey. These are arranged in such a manner that each pair of ribs corresponds to one three-tiered unit in the muqarnas ring of the balcony above.

The circular plan of these two storeys was chronologically preceded by the western minaret of al-Nasir Muhammad at the Citadel and followed by the minaret of Mahmud al-Ustadar (al-Kurdi), although it differs stylistically from both these. However, Aqsunqur's minaret may not have originally looked as it does today. The third storey, which has been subject to restoration, is different from the image of this minaret conveyed in several illustrations made by artists in the nineteenth century.[47] Furthermore, Pascal Coste, Girault de Prangey, David Roberts and Prosper Marilhat all depicted the minaret with four instead of three storeys,[48] its upper pavilion with the bulb being one level higher above an octagonal pavilion. This now lost section is shown as being pierced with arched openings. It should be recalled that the four-storey composition may also have been adopted at the earlier 'Southern' minaret and was definitely used at the later minaret of the funerary

FIG. 118

The minaret of the mosque of Emir Aqsunqur with four storeys

CARLO BOSSOLI (1815–84), COPYING DAVID ROBERTS

FIG. 119

The minaret of the mosque of Emir Aqsunqur with four storeys

AFTER P. COSTE

complex of Sultan al-Ghawri. Minarets with four storeys were also built more frequently in the provinces than in Cairo, perhaps because they were designed to serve as watchtowers and be seen from a greater distance.

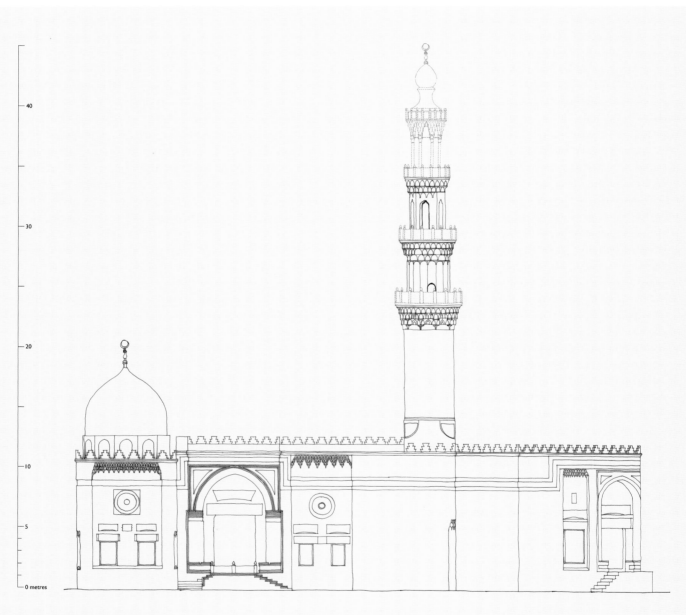

FIG. 120

The minaret of the mosque of Emir Aqsunqur, elevation

FIG. 121

The minaret of the mosque of Emir Aqsunqur

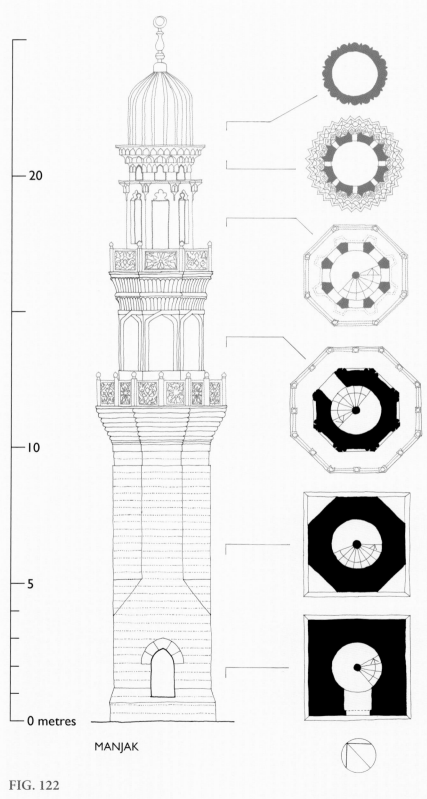

MANJAK

FIG. 122

The minaret of the mosque of Emir Manjaq al-Yusufi, elevation and plans

29. THE MOSQUE OF EMIR MANJAQ AL-YUSUFI (1349–50)

This minaret is located on the northern side of the Citadel on the slope of the spur of the Muqattam Hills known as *al-mahjar* meaning 'the quarry'. It was part of a significant, now largely vanished, religious and funerary complex that included a *khanqah*.[49] Its founder, the wealthy and powerful Emir Manjaq al-Yusufi, served the sons and successors of al-Nasir Muhammad, including Sultan Hasan. Manjaq's complex was begun in 750/1349 and completed the following year, well within his lifespan as he died in 776/1375.

Only the magnificent, half-buried portal leading to the complex, some remains of the walls of the mosque, and the stone minaret have survived. Although the layout of the original structures cannot be determined at this stage, it seems that the buildings were adapted to the sloping topography of the hill on which they stood. This consideration may have resulted in some unusual features such as the minaret being built as a freestanding structure beside the mosque with the entrance to its staircase opening at ground level. The minaret was perhaps erected between the mosque and the *khanqah*.

The minaret of Manjaq is the only extant minaret to combine an entirely octagonal shaft with a mabkhara top. Its architecture is unusual because it has no muqarnas cornices beneath the first two balconies. This common form of decoration is here replaced with linear carvings. The bands of horizontal rounded mouldings beneath the lower balcony are an innovation. The upper balcony stands over a cornice of vertical flutes, similar to a pharaonic papyrus motif, a pattern used earlier on the upper structure of Qalawun's minaret that was added by his son al-Nasir Muhammad. Muqarnas decoration only appears on the mabkhara top. The present mabkhara is a reconstruction made by the Comité, which may have followed the depiction of this minaret by David Roberts in the mid-nineteenth century.[50] The pierced stone balustrades are similarly modern reconstructions, although similar balustrades are shown by Roberts to have existed on the original minaret.

FIG. 123

The minaret of the mosque of Emir Manjaq al-Yusufi

The decoration of the middle section of the minaret has projecting mouldings that form keel-arched panels on each of the eight facets. The first storey, which begins at ground level, is bare of decoration; an empty band that might have been intended for an inscription runs around its upper part. On the lower part of the shaft, beside the arched entrance, is a carved sundial. This position would seem to indicate that the minaret originally faced an open space to its south that allowed the sun to shine on the sundial throughout the day. The transition from the square base to the octagonal shaft above occurs above the apex of the door.

30. **THE MOSQUE AND *KHANQAH* OF EMIR SHAYKHU** (1349, 1355)

One year after the peak of the Black Death, in 750/1349, the Emir Shaykhu built a mosque that also included his mausoleum on the northern side of Saliba Street.[51] This has a stone minaret erected directly above the main portal. Six years later, he founded a large *khanqah* directly across the street with a similar minaret, in a similar position, achieving a composition of remarkable symmetry, with two portals surmounted with minarets. The model for this layout might have been the *khanqah* and mosque of the Emir Bashtak, near Birkat al-Fil, which also faced each other across a street. As only one minaret and one portal survive from this complex, and textual information is lacking, no evidence exists for any further analogy with the layout of Shaykhu's buildings. The portals and double minarets of Shaykhu are positioned at the western tip of the east–west oriented complex, creating the impression of a gate on the Saliba Street leading up to the Citadel. These minarets anticipate the twin minarets of Sultan al-Mu'ayyad Shaykh that were built on the towers of the Bab Zuwayla. The Saliba was a major processional road connecting the Citadel to the southern and western outskirts of the city.

The weight of Shaykhu's minarets is carried by the inner stone vaults of their respective portals, a form of structural support that was commonly applied to brick minarets but is rarer in the case of stone constructions. Stone minarets normally stand on a solid base near the entrance to a building. Both shafts are entirely octagonal in plan, with the exception of cylindrical top storeys, which are pierced with four openings apiece. On the minaret of the mosque the openings at this level have been walled up.

Instead of the traditional muqarnas, a cornice carved with a horizontal linear pattern marks the base of the first balcony and another with a two-tiered sequence of vertical ribs – the 'reed' cornice – marks the second balcony. At the *khanqah* of Shaykhu an Ancient Egyptian stone block, used as a door lintel over the main entrance, also has a cavetto cornice carved with a vertical papyrus motif, which may, however, be coincidental. The design of both the octagonal storeys at Shaykhu's complex almost exactly replicates the architecture (if not the decoration) of the minaret of Manjaq that was being built at the same time.

The surfaces of the first storeys of each minaret are decorated with bichrome stone bands that delineate their recessed keel-arched panels. The stonework framed by these darker bands is carved with a tracery of delicate arabesques: the first time such a treatment is found on a minaret in Cairo over such a large area. The inscription bands that run above these panels contain different Koranic texts, but they are both used here on minarets for the first time. That of the mosque also contains an illegible date. The decoration of the upper octagonal shaft on both minarets consists of a bichrome chevron design formed by inlaid stones. All the balustrades on the balconies are simple timber railings. As is the case with the facing portals of the complex, the two minarets are not identical, showing subtle variations in the patterns of their carving and in the shape of their transitional zones. The transitional zone of the mosque's minaret is pyramidal, for example, while that of the *khanqah*'s minaret consists of downward-pointing triangles of masonry. The two miniature balconies facing the street at first-storey level have different styles of brackets beneath them. Unusually, these balconies only appear on the faces of the shafts addressing the road and not on the other sides, as if to emphasise the primacy of the street in the overall composition.

Muqarnas decorates the upper balconies that surround the bulbs of both of Shaykhu's minarets. The bulbs here are quite sizeable and hollow and

FIG. 124

The minarets of the mosque (left) and khanqah *of Emir Shaykhu*

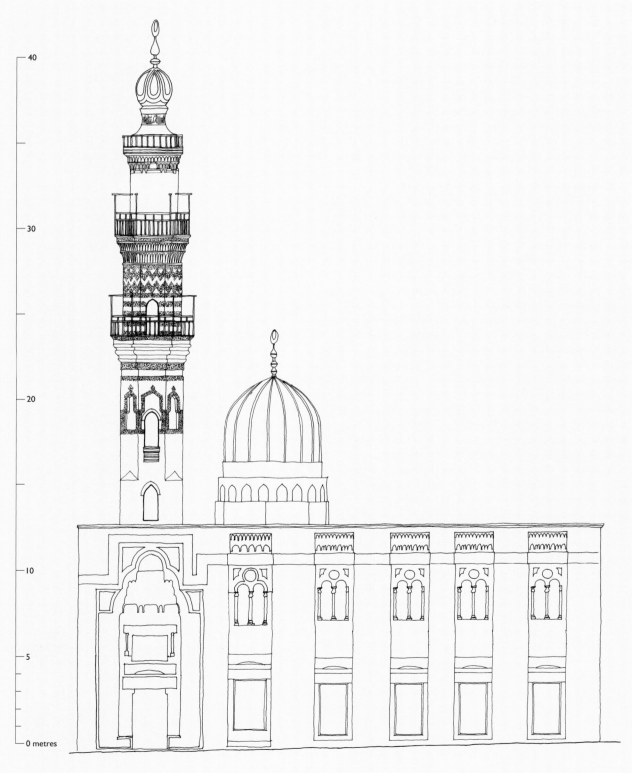

FIG. 125

The minaret of the mosque of Emir Shaykhu, elevation

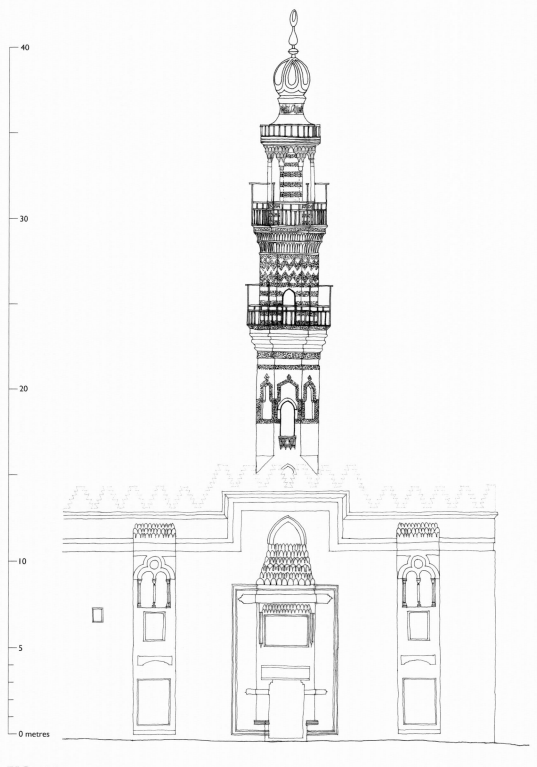

FIG. 126

The minaret of the khanqah *of Emir Shaykhu, elevation*

FIG. 127

The bulb of the khanqah's *minaret*

include openings at their bases. They are carved with an almond-shaped pattern and bear Koranic inscriptions on their necks. Only the bulbs of the minarets of al-Nasir Muhammad at the Citadel, which are quite different in style, provide an earlier parallel to this positioning of an inscription. However, some minarets of the reign of Qaytbay bear traces of inscriptions on the neck of the bulb. It may well also have been the case that the bulbs of numerous other minarets were similarly carved and that it is the accident of survival that has denied us this knowledge. The bulbs set above stone minbars, such as that in the *khanqah* of Faraj ibn Barquq, are treated in a similar manner.

The inscription on the first storey of the minaret

of the *khanqah* is a Sura, rarely used on minarets, which refers to the pilgrimage to Mecca. Shaykhu himself was not reported to have fulfilled the commandment of pilgrimage. However, the unusual foundation inscription of the *khanqah*, located above the main door, refers to the offer of shelter to pilgrims on the premises. The *khanqah* might have functioned, therefore, as a hospice for pilgrims from North Africa on their way to Mecca. The area around Saliba Street, particularly in the vicinity of the mosque of Ibn Tulun, was traditionally inhabited by people from this region.

EPIGRAPHY

The mosque: first storey
Sura 55:1–7

The mosque: the neck of the bulb
Sura 48:1–2 (part of 2)

The khanqah: *first storey*
Sura 22:27–8

The khanqah: *the neck of the bulb*
'In the name of God, the Lord of Mercy, the Giver of Mercy…?'

31. THE MADRASA OF EMIR SARGHITMISH (1356)

The minaret of the madrasa of Emir Sarghitmish is located immediately adjacent to the mosque of Ibn Tulun.[52] This position results in a remarkable architectural vista, in which the minaret plays a significant role. On entering the mosque of Ibn Tulun from the northern door leading to the sanctuary, passing by the courtyard (*ziyada*) that surrounds the mosque, the minaret of Sarghitmish emerges at the end of this side of the *ziyada* on the central axis of the space, as if it had been designed for it. On the exterior, the viewer coming along Saliba Street from the west perceives the madrasa of Sarghitmish as flanked by two minarets, one of them being the minaret of the mosque of Ibn Tulun. The appropriation of the latter

FIG. 128

The minaret of the madrasa of Emir Sarghitmish

within the architectural design of the madrasa could not have been accidental (fig. 13).

The minaret stands immediately to the left of the main entrance to the complex. It has a graceful octagonal shaft in two storeys, decorated with bichrome stonemasonry throughout. As on the minarets of Shaykhu, slightly to the west along Saliba Street, the first storey only has a single miniature balcony overlooking the street rather than one on alternate sides of the shaft. The remaining panels are decorated with an inlaid sunburst motif. The second storey has an inlaid chevron pattern as its decoration. The Comité restored the upper structure of the minaret. A nineteenth-century photograph shows it before restoration with an integral upper pavilion but with wooden railings around the balconies, instead of the present stone balustrades. The top of the bulb over the pavilion has the same almond-shaped carved decoration as seen on the bulbs of the minarets of Shaykhu.

It is noteworthy that the Iranian influence that characterises the profile of the two domes of this complex, over the *qibla iwan* and the mausoleum respectively, had no bearing on the architecture of the minaret. In fact, with the exception of the western minaret at the mosque of al-Nasir Muhammad at the Citadel, Mamluk minarets in Cairo, above all other features in religious architecture, seem to remain faithful to local building traditions.

32. THE SULTANIYYA MAUSOLEUM
(1350s)

The twin bulbous ribbed domes of the mausoleum, popularly called al-Sultaniyya, look as exotic as they are mysterious. No name or date survives to name the founder. The surviving minaret was once connected to the tombs by an enclosure wall, giving the complex a similar arrangement to that of Qawsun's adjacent construction. A convincing attribution of the mausoleum complex to the mother of Sultan Hasan has now been made,[53] which is supported by the description of the site in the foundation deed of the nearby Ottoman mosque of Masih Pasha. This attribution can be further confirmed by the account

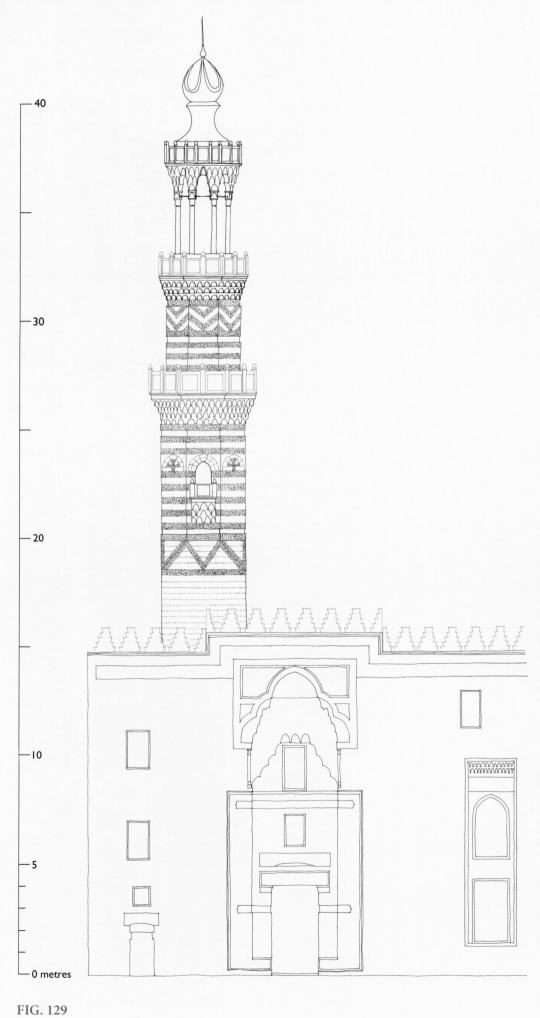

FIG. 129

The minaret of the madrasa of Emir Sarghitmish, elevation

of Evliya Çelebi, who also mentioned a mausoleum of Sultan Hasan's mother in this area. This would date the minaret to the 1350–60s. Sultan Hasan himself, whose mother died when he was a child, is likely to have been the founder of this majestic monument. The minaret follows the same general style as the minarets of the mosque of Sultan Hasan and the madrasa of Princess Tatar al-Hijaziyya, both dating to the mid-fourteenth century. As in the case of the madrasa of Sarghitmish, Iranian models inspired the architecture of the domes, but no foreign inspiration can be detected on the minaret.

The shaft of the minaret of al-Sultaniyya is octagonal and decorated with bichrome masonry like the minarets of Sultan Hasan and Princess Tatar. However, a closer look at the composition of the Sultaniyya minaret reveals that its design is more complex than either of these parallels. The first storey has four simple keel-arched openings on alternate sides corresponding to four projecting miniature balconies supported by muqarnas brackets and linked by a horizontal moulding. Four panels of identical size on the other sides, which may have been open, appear to have been walled up at some point. The decorative stonework takes the form here of bichrome chevrons, small ones below the horizontal moulding and large ones above. The second storey only has a single arched doorway in it, but the other faces of the shaft have blank arches that are framed by the darker stone. The spandrels between all these arches are filled with a very lightly carved tracery of arabesques, similar to that seen on the upper storeys of the minarets of Shaykhu.

An unusual feature of this minaret is the shape of its third storey. It is not an open pavilion, as is the case at the minaret of Sultan Hasan, but rather a faceted shaft that appears at first glance similar to those below it. This would be misleading, however, because it is not octagonal but hexagonal in plan. The only other extant pavilion with a hexagonal shape is at the minaret of al-Baqli. The shaft has arches on each side, three of which are blind, while the three others contain rectangular openings. The question that arises here is whether the hexagonal shaft was intended to be the uppermost structure of the minaret, directly surmounted by a bulb as it appears today after the

FIG. 130

The minaret of the Sultaniyya mausoleum

Comité restoration, which included replacing all the balcony balustrades in stone, or whether the bulb was originally supported by a pavilion, giving the minaret a four-storeyed configuration. This is the same unanswered question that arises in connection with the octagonal third storey at the 'Southern' minaret.

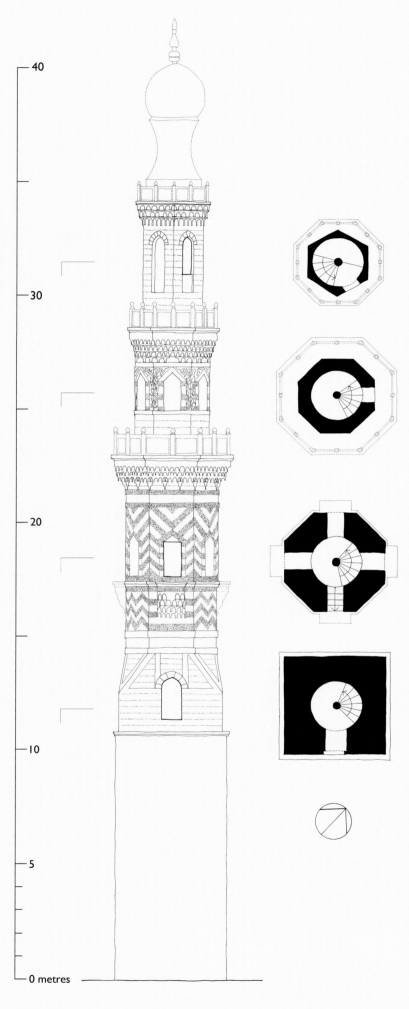

FIG. 131

The minaret of the Sultaniyya mausoleum, south elevation and plans

EPIGRAPHY

First storey lower band
Sura 3:190–1

First storey upper band
Sura 33:41–3

33. THE MOSQUE OF SULTAN HASAN (1356–61)

The mosque of Sultan Hasan stands directly below the residence of the sultans at the Citadel,[54] once overlooking Rumayla, the only public square of Cairo and the venue of gatherings and festivals, alongside the prestigious horse market and the great hippodrome. This grand urban setting called for an exceptional architectural response. The unprecedented number, for a Mamluk mosque, of four planned minarets is just one singular feature of many that contribute to the outstanding character of this monument (see the isometric reconstruction of the complex reproduced here, fig. 135). Two of the three façades of the building were designed to address the Citadel, and both were designed with minarets. A pair of minarets was erected on the main façade to flank the monumental mausoleum dome. Another pair on the northern façade was to crown the gigantic portal, which turns from the façade with an angle of 17 degrees to be better visible from the Citadel.

The portal and the massive buttresses flanking it suggest that it was intended to have twin minarets, following the arrangement of Anatolian monuments such as the Gök madrasa in Sivas, whose portal decoration, as has been suggested by J.M. Rogers, is echoed at Sultan Hasan's. Only one of the minarets of the portal was ever erected and it collapsed shortly after its completion, killing many children in the primary school attached to the complex. Poems were composed to commemorate the tragedy, which was interpreted as an act of God, and a bad omen, rather than the result of a structural deficiency. Indeed, the death of the sultan a month later seemed to confirm what the fall of the minaret had augured, putting an

FIG. 132

The minaret of the mosque of Sultan Hasan, upper pavilion

end to the ambitious scheme of the mosque with four minarets. The monument remained for ever incomplete.

The only surviving original minaret stands at the south-eastern corner of the mausoleum, eighty metres high including its buttress, which makes it the tallest minaret in medieval Cairo. Its octagonal shaft has a conventional design and, following the pattern of the earlier minaret of Sarghitmish that it very much

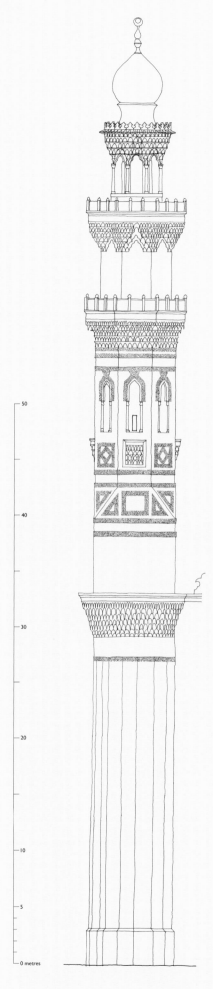

FIG. 133

The southern minaret of the mosque of Sultan Hasan, elevation

resembles in proportion but not in scale, is similarly decorated with bichrome stone bands. Four miniature balconies and plain keel-arched niches adorn the first storey. The second storey is plain, and neither level has an inscription. The upper structure of the minaret was dismantled and reconstructed by the Comité in the last century.[55] Eighteenth- and nineteenth-century illustrations indicate that the top was always there. It consists of eight piers flanked on their external side with marble columns. Following the example of the minaret of Qawsun, the upper muqarnas beneath the bulb culminates in a tier of outward-pointing triangles.

Unlike the buttresses of the portal minarets, which are concealed behind the façade, those of the mausoleum minarets are unique in Mamluk architecture, protruding at the corners in the form of mighty semicircular faceted towers. Notwithstanding the excellence of design and workmanship of this monument, the builders were not very successful in establishing a smooth visual connection between the rounded buttresses and the rectangular bases of the minarets above. Perhaps the gigantic muqarnas cornice that runs along the façade, visually separating the minarets from their buttresses, took precedence in the design. In the sixteenth-century mosque of Mahmud Pasha nearby, which copies Sultan Hasan's rounded buttress, a more aesthetic device was found to connect the minaret with its buttress.

Were the two minarets flanking the mausoleum intended originally to be the same size, as the overall architectural composition would suggest? In their external elevation, the buttresses are of slightly different sizes. The smaller northern buttress could still have physically supported a minaret of the same dimensions as the southern counterpart. Christel Kessler has attributed this asymmetry of the buttresses to the foundations of the pre-existing palace that was demolished to make place for the religious complex of Sultan Hasan. These foundations, reported by

FIG. 134

The southern façade of the mosque of Sultan Hasan with the original minaret

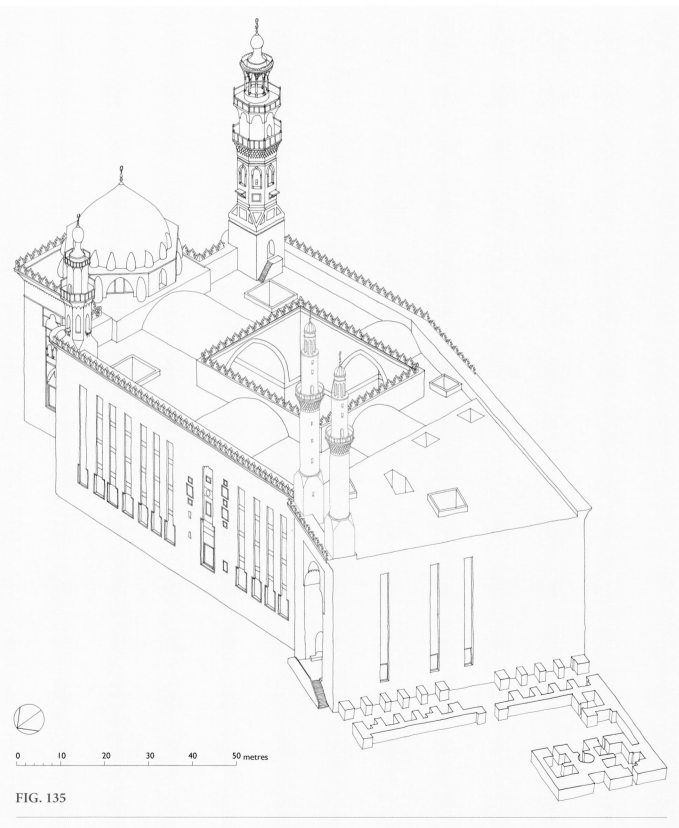

0   10   20   30   40   50 metres

FIG. 135

Isometric reconstruction of the mosque of Sultan Hasan with minarets at the portal

Maqrizi to have been extremely costly, may have led the master-builder to reuse them, which would have limited his options regarding the layout of the mosque. The combination of the constraints of the previous foundations and other layout requirements with the imperative of the Mecca orientation led the master-builder to compromise by reducing the size of the northern minaret buttress. It is not documented whether the northern minaret was of the same shape as the southern one. Only the testimony of the Syrian historian Ibn Kathir (d.1373), who never visited Egypt but described this minaret as having a double-headed structure, suggests that it did not. However, this account is not confirmed by other sources.

Three centuries after the erection of the mosque, on a Friday in 1070/1659, the northern minaret flanking the mausoleum collapsed while the mosque was filled to capacity. It fell outwards from the building, however, and only two people were killed by the falling masonry. The seventeenth-century Moroccan traveller al-ʿAyyashi, reported the collapse of the minaret during his passage through Egypt on his way to Mecca. On his return from the pilgrimage he was astonished to find that the ruined minaret had been replaced by the structure that stands in its place today. Full of admiration for the zeal of the Egyptians and the care they took to restore their buildings, al-ʿAyyashi wrote that a sum of sixty *kis* was spent on the task of collecting the fallen stones for reuse in the reconstruction of the minaret alone, adding 'imagine then the expense of the reconstruction itself!' He also deplored the condition of the monuments in his own country, which no one bothered to maintain. He seems not to have noticed how inferior the new version looked compared with the original (fig. 10).⁵⁶ The bulb of this minaret is set directly above the second storey without the support of a Mamluk-style pavilion. Although the seventeenth-century reconstruction of the northern minaret reveals a certain notion of stylistic continuity that was absent in earlier restorations, a glance at the unequal pair of minarets makes clear that the craftsmen of this period did not master the skill of muqarnas carving as their Mamluk predecessors had done. The muqarnas cornice that crowns the façade, which was also destroyed with the northern minaret, was never restored.

34. THE MADRASA OF PRINCESS TATAR AL-HIJAZIYYA (1360)

Princess Tatar al-Hijaziyya, a daughter of Sultan al-Nasir Muhammad, initially founded on this site a mausoleum for her first husband, the emir Maliktamur, who was assassinated in 1347. She then added the madrasa at a later date; it was completed in 1360.⁵⁷ Philipp Speiser's analysis of the architecture of this complex attributes the minaret to the second phase of construction, which coincides with the reign of her brother Sultan Hasan. The delayed construction of the madrasa and the minaret may be related to the circumstances surrounding her husband's death. Maliktamur apparently died as the innocent victim of treachery, stabbed to death by a group of six emirs acting with the connivance of Sultan al-Muzaffar Hajji, another of the princess's brothers. Maliktamur was a glamorous prince, of legendary beauty, a champion of chivalry, and one of her father al-Nasir Muhammad's most favoured and privileged emirs.⁵⁸ The Koranic inscription placed on the second storey of the minaret may have been selected in connection with his asassination as its content is unique for a minaret. It refers to the Day of Judgement when idolaters, unless they repent, will suffer God's painful punishment.

The minaret follows the style of the period: its octagonal design and bichrome stone decoration recall the minaret of Sultan Hasan, notwithstanding the difference of scale, and that of the Sultaniyya mausoleum. The first storey has three arched openings into the stairwell, and corresponding miniature balconies on projecting muqarnas brackets (the one at the rear of the minaret has been omitted). There is a chevron pattern in its masonry and an inscription band below the muqarnas cornice of the first balcony. The second storey has pointed-arched recesses flanked by colonettes on each panel and a further inscription band above. The minaret's upper pavilion was already missing in 1895, before the minaret was entirely dismantled by the Comité when it threatened to collapse, and no reconstruction of the missing upper part was ever attempted.⁵⁹

FIG. 136

The minaret of the madrasa of Princess Tatar al-Hijaziyya

EPIGRAPHY

First storey
Sura 3:190–1

Second storey
Sura 9:3

35. THE *KHANQAH* OF EMIR TANKIZBUGHA (1362)

This *khanqah* with its founder's domed mausoleum is located on a hill to the south-east side of the northern cemetery. Its austere appearance, once isolated in the desert, well suited its function as a funerary monastery.[60] The stone minaret stands at the entrance of the building, separated from the mausoleum by the courtyard of the complex. Seen from the city to the west, the minaret and the dome form a harmonious composition.

The minaret has a plain square shaft with a simple muqarnas cornice. This carries an elongated octagonal pavilion with double-arched recessed openings crowned with a ribbed cupola. A broad inscription band runs above the openings. Beneath the cupola the muqarnas cornice displays, as on the minarets of Qawsun and Sultan Hasan, a tier of outward-pointing triangles, resembling spikes. A similar muqarnas variant was also adopted on the dome of a second mausoleum built by the same emir in the cemetery to the south of the Citadel. Composed of only two storeys, superimposed without any transition, the configuration of this minaret is archaic, recalling the minarets of Fatima Khatun and al-Baqli, both of which were built much earlier, in the late thirteenth century. It also bears the latest example of a mabkhara top in Cairo.

EPIGRAPHY

Beneath the mabkhara
Sura 24:36–7

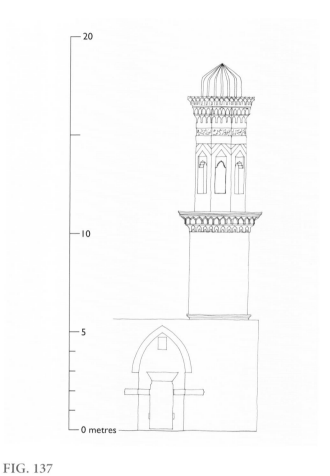

FIG. 137

The minaret of the khanqah *of Emir Tankizbugha, elevation*

FIG. 138

The khanqah *of Emir Tankizbugha, 1950s*

FIG. 139

The minaret of the khanqah *of Emir Tankizbugha: the upper structure*

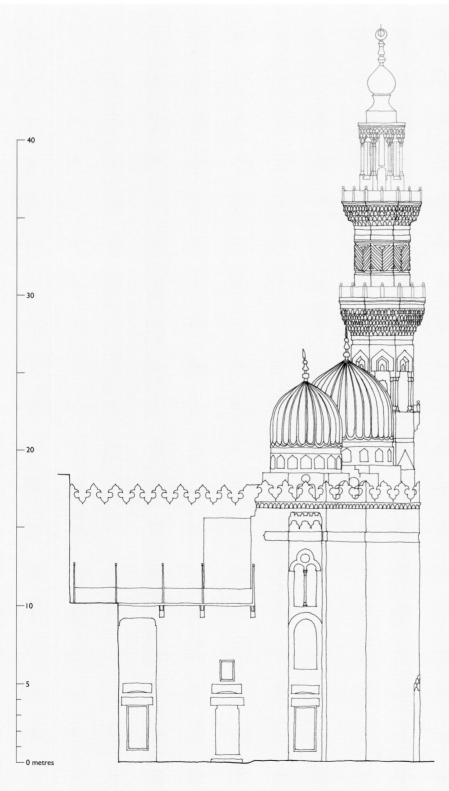

FIG. 140

The minaret of the madrasa of Sultan Sha'ban's mother, elevation from south

36. THE MADRASA OF THE MOTHER OF SULTAN SHA'BAN (1368–9)

The madrasa of Umm al-Sultan Sha'ban (Sultan Sha'ban's mother) is peculiar for the great divergence it shows between the exterior and the interior layout.[61] The main façade gives the illusion that the funerary madrasa overlooks the main street of Tabbana, whereas in fact none of it corresponds to the main part of the madrasa. The unusual portal, the minaret and the two mausoleum domes have been arranged to obtain optimal visibility from the street in accordance with Mamluk urban architectural priorities. For those elements above the parapet line, this was achieved by accentuating the overall height of the façade. The minaret was separated from the portal and pushed further east to be visually connected to the larger of the two funerary domes and to command the view along Tabbana Street.

The decoration of the minaret, which is octagonal throughout, displays a carved pattern rather than the bichrome stonework used in the previous examples. The first storey has the familiar pattern of keel-arched recessed openings and miniature balconies, separated by clusters of three engaged columns at each corner of the shaft. The second storey has the much-favoured carved zigzag pattern, previously seen on many domes and minarets. Both storeys have bare inscription bands. The upper pavilion of the minaret, which collapsed during an earthquake in 1884, was restored in 2003 by the Aga Khan Trust for Culture as a structure with piers and engaged columns. All the balustrades of the balconies are modern replacements.

FIG. 141

The minaret of the madrasa of Sultan Sha'ban's mother

FIG. 142

The minaret of the madrasa of Emir Asanbugha

37. THE MADRASA OF EMIR ASANBUGHA (1370)

The minaret is the only original structure to have survived from the mosque of Emir Asanbugha, the rest having been rebuilt by the Comité.[62] The minaret is a stone construction in three storeys over a base that is, remarkably, a triangle in plan. The normal planimetric progression in Cairene minarets is from a square to an octagon to a circle. Mamluk builders favoured a smooth transition between a square base or a square first storey and a circular top, which was achieved by inserting an octagonal section. The common alternative design is the shaft with a rectangular-circular profile, as can be seen at the minarets of Fatima Khatun, al-Baqli, Baybars al-Jashnakir, Tankizbugha and the northern minaret of al-Nasir Muhammad at the Citadel. In only two cases in the Mamluk architecture of Cairo does a minaret have a triangular base: the minaret of Asanbugha and that of Qanibay al-Muhammadi, built over forty years later. In these examples, the normal central octagonal section of the shaft had to be replaced by a hexagonal one.

The oddity of the triangular base, hardly noticeable from the street, must be attributed to structural rather than aesthetic considerations. After the Mecca-orientation of the mosque had been established along with the main entrance, and a *sabil-maktab* (a charitable water dispensary and Koranic school for orphans) positioned in its traditional location at the corner of the building, there was obviously insufficient space left for the builders to erect a minaret on a standard square base. Instead they adapted the base of the minaret to the available space, which was roughly triangular. This decision led, inexorably, to the hexagonal format of the section above that, providing a smooth transition to the cylindrical top storey.

Despite its anomaly, the minaret of Asanbugha is a masterpiece of architecture and decoration. The triangular base is even celebrated through the choice of undulating volutes to express the transitional zone. The decoration of the hexagonal section is treated conventionally as on an octagonal surface. It is carved with six plain keel-arched recesses flanked by colonettes, three of which contain window-openings connected

to miniature balconies. A continuous projecting moulding links these balconies horizontally. The design of the carved decoration on the cylindrical middle section of the minaret displays a sequence of interlaced cross-shaped ribs connected through upper and lower loops. This is the earliest appearance of such a pattern in Cairo, to be repeated on the minarets of the mosques of Barsbay, Qaraquja al-Hasani and Qanim al-Tajir as well as in stucco on the brick domes of the mausoleums of Umm al-Ashraf (1430s) and Taghribirdi (1440). This design also served as a model for the minarets of the mosque of al-Rifa'i, erected much later, in the early twentieth century.

The quality of the carving of Asanbugha's minaret is remarkable. The octagonal pavilion consists of stone piers carved on the outside in the shape of paired columns. Above the muqarnas cornice is a ring of miniature *fleur-de-lis* crenellations around the base of the bulb, which itself bears, like a necklace, a tier of carved petals around its neck. It has been restored by the Comité.

38. THE MOSQUE OF EMIR ULJAY AL-YUSUFI (1373)

The mosque of Uljay is located at the centre of the Armourers' Market, the Suq al-Silah, at a short distance from Rumayla Square beneath the Citadel.[63] The minaret of the mosque has fine proportions and stands immediately over the main portal at the north end of the façade, in this resembling other minarets like those of the complex of Shaykhu. In this position it is harmoniously juxtaposed with the magnificent spiral-ribbed mausoleum dome on the southern end of the complex, and visible to anyone walking down the street in either direction.

The design of this minaret is similar to that of Asanbugha, especially in the treatment of the transitional zone and the panelled first storey. The second cylindrical storey is not carved, as on the minaret of Asanbugha, but decorated instead with a chevron of bichrome stone, which is hardly visible under the layers of Cairo's dust. The inlaid blocks of this chevron display a curiosity in their shape: they

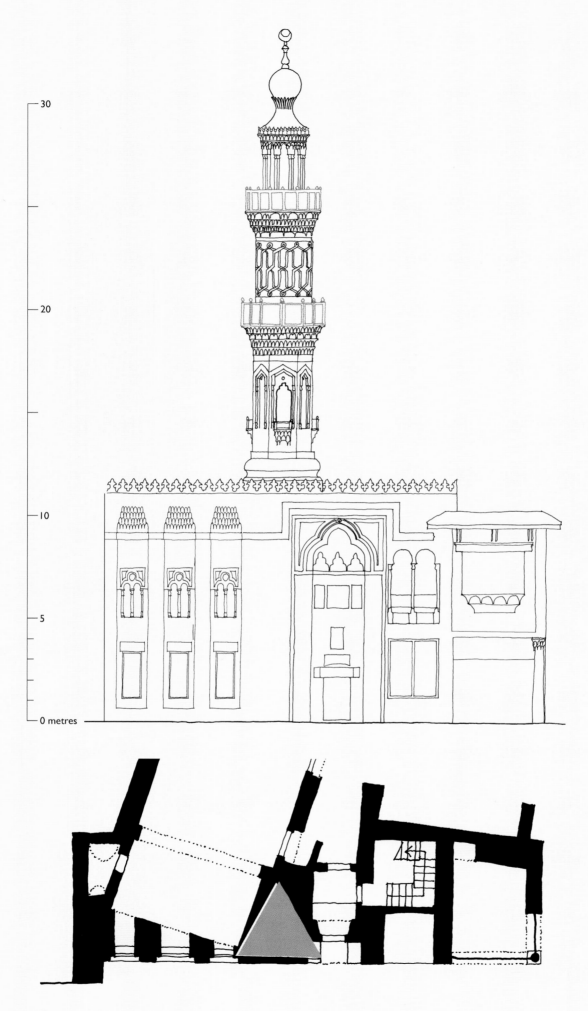

FIG. 143

The madrasa of Emir Asanbugha, elevation and plan

have polylobed rather than straight sides, giving the chevron the appearance of interlocking trefoil elements. As can often be observed on Mamluk minarets, two horizontal sunken bands on the upper part of the first and second storeys look as if they had been intended for inscriptions that were never added. The top of the minaret is crowned by a pavilion of marble columns supporting a muqarnas cornice topped by a ring of miniature crenellations and a bulb that has another device seen at the minaret of Asanbugha – a decorative collar. It has been dismantled and reconstituted by the Comité, who used many of its original stones. Also, the stone balustrades on the balconies of the minaret are modern replacements.

39. THE MOSQUE OF SULTAN BARQUQ (1386)

Barquq built his complex, which comprised a family mausoleum, a madrasa and a *khanqah*, on the Bayn al-Qasrayn immediately to the north of the madrasa of al-Nasir Muhammad.[64] Although he did not sign his work, the master-builder of this monument is known: the *mu'allim* Ahmad Ibn al-Tuluni, a prominent Egyptian contractor, who gave his daughter in marriage to the sultan and eventually acquired the status of a Mamluk emir and court architect.[65] His descendants continued to play a major role in the construction of royal monuments up to the end of the Mamluk period. The architecture of the minaret is felicitous, its proportion and position taking advantage of the prestigious site and contributing at the same time to the majestic spectacle of this major artery of the medieval city.

The minaret adjoins the founder's mausoleum dome on the northernmost edge of the façade, echoing the arrangement of the complex of Sultan Qalawun nearby and its relationship to the street. The octagonal first storey has keel-arched niches and projecting miniature balconies framed with bichrome stonework – a standard feature in this period. What is less usual is the carving of the three engaged columns that flank these niches and adorn the corners on each of the eight facets of the first storey. The middle of the three columns

FIG. 144

The minaret of the mosque of Emir Uljay al-Yusufi

FIG. 145

The minaret of the mosque of Sultan Barquq

FIG. 146

0   10   20   30   40   50 metres

Isometric view of the minaret of Sultan Barquq

FIG. 147

The minaret of the mosque of Emir Jamal al-Din Mahmud (al-Kurdi)

is carved with zigzag pattern, while those flanking it are carved with oblique flutes, in a rope-like pattern. Furthermore, in the otherwise blank panels between each balcony is a sunken rosette, a novelty in this location. The second storey of the minaret is also an octagon. The carving of the shafts of the central sections of minarets had increasingly gained favour in the late fourteenth century. In this minaret, the decoration of the second storey combines inlaid blue-grey marble with carved stone, which is extremely unusual. Its carved intersecting circles, which remained unique in Cairo, are a variation on the theme of intersecting arches connected with upper loops, displayed in the stucco work at the upper storey of Qalawun's minaret next door. Small white marble circles are also set into the blue-grey marble circles as accents. The upper pavilion consists of piers with engaged columns supporting the usual superstructure. The pavilion was restored in 1899, but as nineteenth-century pictures and photographs have often depicted this minaret with the upper pavilion appearing as it does today, the restoration can be seen to emulate the original design.[66] The minaret has no inscriptions of any kind upon it, and the balustrades to the balconies are modern.

40. THE MINARET OF THE MADRASA OF EMIR MAHMUD AL-USTADAR (AL-KURDI) (1395)

This is one of the few examples of an entirely circular minaret to be constructed after the northern minaret of al-Hakim and the western minaret of al-Nasir Muhammad at the Citadel. Unlike its predecessors, however, this minaret is a brick construction. It stands right above the portal. The first storey is plain, the second fluted. The upper pavilion is the only one of this style to be preserved on a brick shaft. All other brick minarets have their bulbs set directly above the second storey, without a pavilion, which makes it difficult to guess whether this was the original configuration or the result of restoration work. The minaret of Khayrbak was depicted in the nineteenth century with such a

pavilion. This pavilion stands on a circular stone base and has stone columns. It supports a brick bulb that has an unusually high cylindrical neck. The handrails of the muezzins' balconies are all made of timber.

41. THE MAMLUK MINARET AT THE AQMAR MOSQUE (1397 or 1412)

FIG. 148

The Mamluk minaret at the Aqmar mosque

No original minaret has survived at the mosque of the Fatimid vizier Ma'mun al-Bata'ihi, known as the al-Aqmar mosque, built in 1125.[67] The mosque was heavily restored at the end of the fourteenth century, and a minaret was added to it by the Emir Yalbugha al-Salimi in 1397.[68] Maqrizi further reports that Yalbugha's minaret had to be pulled down in 1412 when it started to lean. Either it was partially dismantled, leaving the present first storey *in situ*, or this first storey structure was part of the reconstruction of 1412. The minaret must have been damaged again at a later date, perhaps in the Ottoman period, which made the addition of the present second storey above the wooden balcony necessary. It was subsequently restored by the Comité in 1907.[69]

The cylindrical shaft of the first storey is made of plastered brick and recalls the minaret of Mahmud al-Ustadar built in the same period. A fine stucco frieze beneath the muqarnas has raised and pierced circular bosses of stucco. This type of stucco work is of Iranian origin and exceptional in Cairo, where it appears elsewhere only on the mihrab of the madrasa of al-Nasir Muhammad. However, at this date it was an archaism.

FIG. 150

The minarets of the khanqah *of Sultan Faraj ibn Barquq*

FIG. 149

Nineteenth-century view of the stub of the minaret of Emir Sudun min Zada

42. THE MOSQUE OF EMIR SUDUN MIN ZADA (1401)*

The ruins of this funerary mosque-madrasa with a courtyard plan were razed in the 1960s.[70] A nineteenth-century photograph shows its minaret standing next to a bulbous wooden dome. The minaret appears to have been very similar in design to the earlier minaret of the madrasa of Sultan Sha'ban's mother. It was octagonal, with keel-arched recessed panels on its first storey and a carved zigzag pattern in the middle section. The upper octagonal pavilion is missing on the picture, and a simple bulb rests above the second balcony level.

43. THE *KHANQAH* OF SULTAN FARAJ IBN BARQUQ (1411)

The funeral complex of Sultan Faraj ibn Barquq in the northern cemetery, with a *khanqah* and a double mausoleum, is one of the most outstanding constructions of medieval Cairo.[71] Symmetry is one of its most remarkable features. The complex includes two identical domes as well as two identical minarets. They are arranged so as to display twin minarets on the western façade, twin domes at the corners of the east façade, and a combination of the two elements on the northern and southern façades. The minarets also strongly reinforce the main axis of the building through the mihrab, which has a smaller dome above it.

The horizontality of the façade with twin minarets facing the city is unique. Unlike the minarets of the mosque of al-Hakim, which project at the corners of the building, or the minarets conceived to crown the portal at the mosque of Sultan Hasan, the minarets of the complex of Sultan Faraj are distanced from the corners, which are instead occupied by *sabil-maktab*s. In the complex of Faraj, and probably as a result of its freestanding position, all principal elements have been doubled, including the *sabil-maktab*s which occupy the north-west and the south-west corners.[72]

The profile of the minarets, with their cylindrical second storeys set above square shafts without a transition, recalls the north-eastern minaret of the mosque of al-Nasir Muhammad at the Citadel. It is also the first time after almost a century had elapsed that this configuration was repeated: the later minarets of the madrasa of Sultan Barsbay and Emir Qanibay al-Sharkasi follow the same pattern. This profile may additionally have been adopted at the truncated minaret of the funerary *khanqah* of Barsbay further south in the same cemetery, which also displays a square first storey.

The square section of the shaft of both minarets is pierced on each side with a lobed opening set inside a rectangular recess with a muqarnas hood. These relate to miniature balconies on projecting muqarnas corbels, here given an unusual degree of prominence by the use of a moulding to frame them. The second storeys are carved with the same interlacing pattern

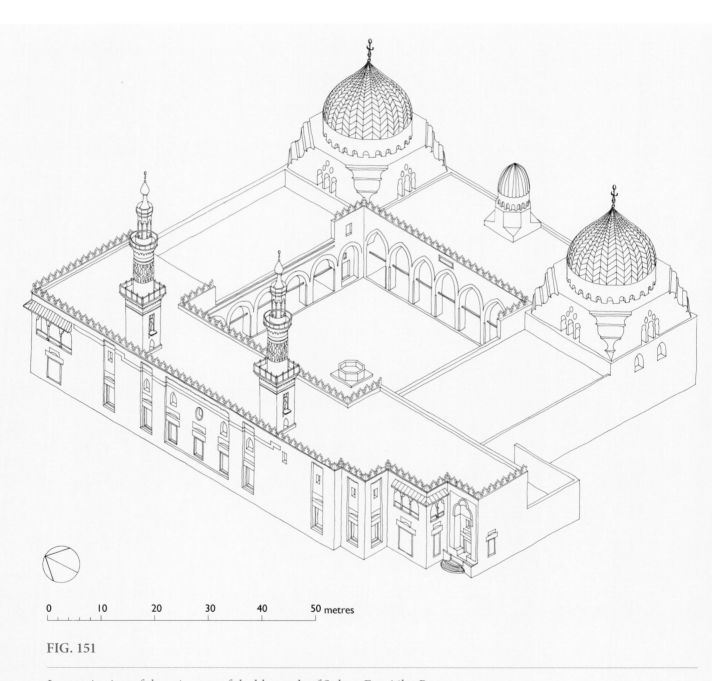

0   10   20   30   40   50 metres

FIG. 151

Isometric view of the minarets of the khanqah *of Sultan Faraj ibn Barquq*

Nineteenth-century illustrations and photographs reveal that the bulbs and stone balustrades of the balconies have all been replaced in modern times. The latter were made of wood before restoration, which may have been the original timber or Ottoman substitutions.

EPIGRAPHY

The northern minaret
Sura 62:9

The southern minaret
Sura 3:18

44. THE MOSQUE OF EMIR QANIBAY AL-MUHAMMADI (1413)

The only remarkable feature of this minaret is its triangular base supporting a hexagonal first and an octagonal second storey.[74] The builder of this minaret was not as successful, however, as his predecessor, who designed the minaret of Asanbugha, in achieving a harmonious construction. The reason for using a triangular base must have been the limited space available. As in the previous case, the base of the minaret has an undulating transitional zone and trilobed arched recesses flanked by colonettes adorning three sides of the first storey. These extend vertically to the base of the muqarnas cornice, cutting through the inscription band on this tier. The zigzag carving of the second storey duplicates the design of the adjacent dome, thus creating a decorative link between the two, which compensates for the awkward juxtaposition of their bases. The bulb is set directly above the second balcony, without a pavilion.

EPIGRAPHY

First storey
Sura 39:73

Second storey
Sura 24:35

FIG. 152

The minaret of the mosque of Emir Qanibay al-Muhammadi

seen on the minaret of Asanbugha, and have rather shallow carved inscriptions above. The verses of these inscriptions provide the only point of difference between the two minarets. The upper structures are modern.[73]

45. THE MOSQUE OF SULTAN AL-MU'AYYAD SHAYKH (1419–20)

The minarets of the mosque of Sultan al-Mu'ayyad Shaykh are the most prominently located of all the minarets in Cairo. Standing like a pair of sentinels on the twin towers of the Bab Zuwayla, built by the Fatimid vizier Badr al-Jamali in the late eleventh century, they seem to confirm the city's epithet, *al-mahrusa*, the 'Well-Protected'.[75] Surmounting the gate, they faced the processions entering the heart of the city along its main artery from the south, which had witnessed an expansion in Mamluk times far beyond the boundaries of the Fatimid city of Qahira. Historians report, however, that the location of al-Mu'ayyad's mosque was chosen not for aesthetic reasons or considerations of status, as one might think, but because of his personal experience as a prisoner in one of the worst jails of medieval Cairo, located next to the gate. He made a vow that if he came out of it alive he would build a mosque on the site: it was a vow that he fulfilled.

These were not the first paired minarets to be built across a street in Cairo: the minarets of the mosque and *khanqah* of the Emir Shaykhu at Saliba Street may have inspired the idea. The towers of the Bab Zuwayla offered themselves as appropriate physical props, and accentuated the overall height of the minarets. Grafting the two new minarets onto the existing towers, however, did not make things any easier for the builder, who had to construct square bases within the towers themselves to support the added load. According to Maqrizi, the minaret that was above the western tower, next to the mosque (*'ala badanat Bab Zuwayla allati tali al-jami'*), began to lean and was pulled down in June 1418. This minaret bears the date of Rajab 822/July 1419, the reconstructed eastern minaret is dated a year later;[76] which means that it took a year to construct each minaret.

When he finally succeeded in erecting his two, magnificent, identical minarets, which at that time were painted with gold and lapis lazuli,[77] the architect, Muhammad ibn al-Qazzaz, found his achievement worthy of a signature. The twin minarets are both signed and dated on two separate inscriptions, one on their base, above their respective entrances. These signatures, besides the one at the portal of the palace of Qawsun, are the only examples thus far known of an architect's signature on any building in Mamluk Cairo and the only ones to be found on minarets.[78] Muhammad ibn al-Qazzaz's inscriptions refer only to his construction of the minarets, and it is not known whether he made any contribution to the building of the rest of the mosque of al-Mu'ayyad. Maqrizi names Baha' al-Din Muhammad ibn al-Burji as supervisor of the construction works of the mosque. He was a high-ranking bureaucrat, who held for a while the office of market inspector, and died at the age of seventy-two in 824/1421,[79] one year after the minarets were completed. The supervisor of building construction, who could also be an emir of lower rank, was responsible for the management of the project but not necessarily for design, which would remain the competence of specialised master-builders such as Ibn al-Qazzaz. The poems cited by Maqrizi lamenting the deficiencies of the minaret that had to be rebuilt blame al-Burji for it by making puns about his name, al-Burji being an attribute of *burj* meaning 'tower'.

The minarets of the mosque of al-Mu'ayyad are remarkable for their positioning, their slenderness and their elegance in profile. Their carved decoration, however, though well executed, has little novelty. The first storey has a typical arrangement of keel-arched recessed niches with radiating hoods with mouldings around them, clusters of three columns at the corners of each facet, and miniature balconies supported on muqarnas brackets. The spandrels between the arched hoods are carved with a light tracery of arabesques, and a sunken rosette framed by a projecting moulding occupies the space on the shaft between each miniature balcony. There are two inscription bands located above and below the zone of niches and balconies. The second storey has a zigzag pattern of decoration that had been earlier applied to the minarets of Umm al-Sultan Sha'ban and Qanibay al-Muhammadi. A third inscription band runs directly above this. The original upper structures of the minarets were damaged in the earthquake in 1863, and they were replaced in 1892 with more slender pavilions supported by marble columns.[80] The mosque also had a third minaret, mentioned in the foundation deed and by the

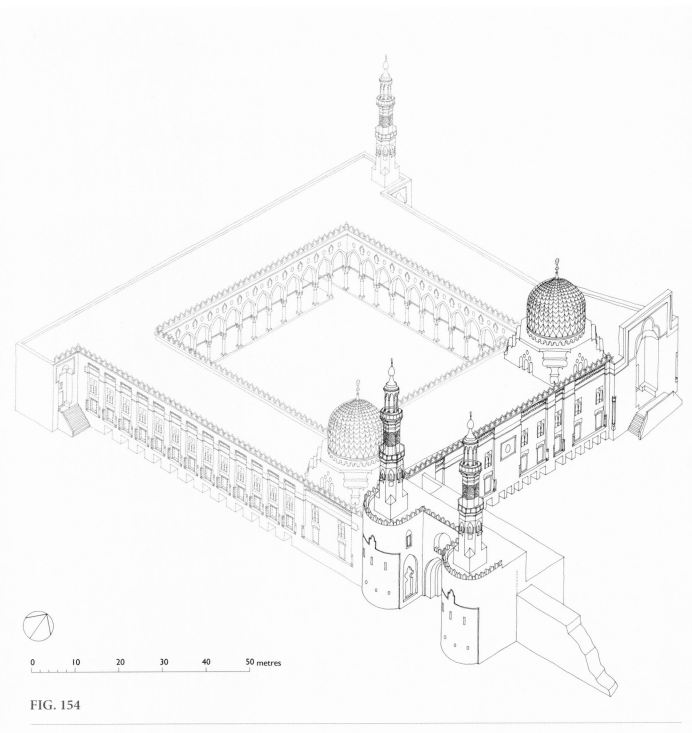

0   10   20   30   40   50 metres

FIG. 154

Isometric view of the mosque of Sultan al-Mu'ayyad Shaykh with the vanished third minaret and second dome

FIG. 155

Signature of Ibn al-Qazzaz on the eastern minaret

chroniclers, which stood near a secondary northern portal. It was apparently different from the other two, since the historian Jawhari described it as lavishly decorated, bejewelled and without parallel.[81] This minaret, which was described by Maqrizi as the smallest, began to lean in 1427, so that Sultan Barsbay ordered its demolition and reconstruction.[82]

EPIGRAPHY[83]

Eastern minaret: above the entrance to the staircase
'Our Lord the Sultan, the Possessor, the Sovereign al-Mu'ayyad Abu 'l-Nasr Shaykh has ordered the foundation of these two minarets [*manaratayn*], which the servant longing for God Muhammad ibn al-Qazzaz has executed [*naffadha*[84]], and the completion was in Sha'ban the glorious of the year 823 [August 1420].'

FIG. 156

Signature of Ibn al-Qazzaz on the western minaret

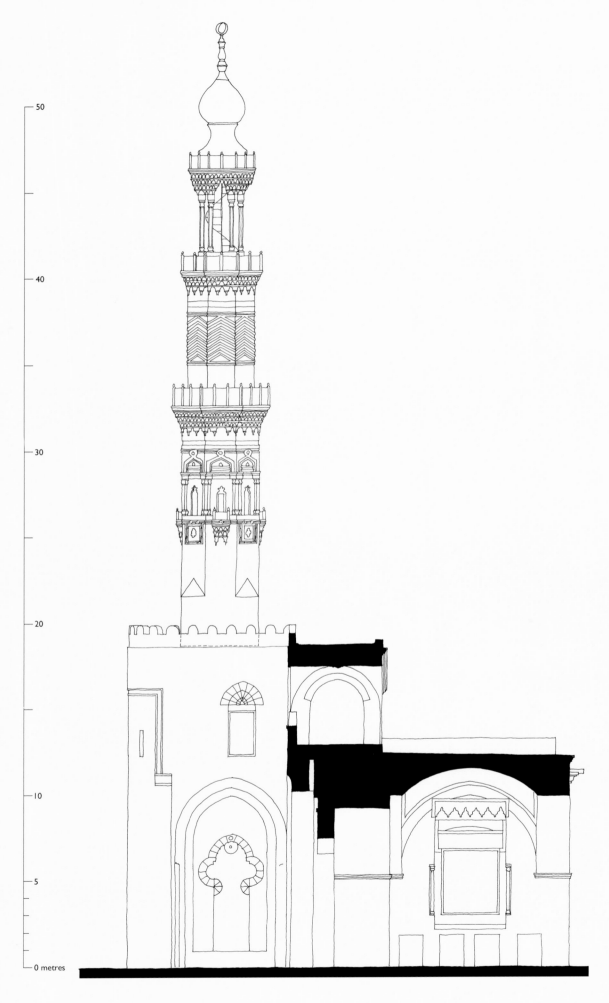

FIG. 157

The minaret of the mosque of Sultan al-Mu'ayyad Shaykh, sectional elevation

Eastern minaret: first storey lower band
Sura 24:36–7

Eastern minaret: first storey upper band
Sura 2:255

Eastern minaret: second storey
Sura 24:36–7

Western minaret: above the entrance to the staircase
'The servant longing for God Muhammad ibn
al-Qazzaz has made this blessed minaret [*mi'dhana*]
and this was completed at the beginning of Rajab
of the year 822 [July 1419].'

Western minaret: first storey
Lower band: Sura 24:36–7; upper band: Sura 2:255
(the inscriptions of the first storey are the same,
the upper ones differ.)

Western minaret: second storey
Sura 33:41–2

46. THE MOSQUE OF QADI 'ABD AL-BASIT (1420)

This mosque has two façades with two portals;
the main eastern one conceals the mihrab wall and
includes the *sabil-maktab* at its northern corner.[85]
The minaret is not attached to the main façade, but
stands rather near the northern side-portal. Seen
from the courtyard of the mosque the minaret stands
exactly above its north-west corner, thus connecting
the slender octagonal shaft with the inner architecture
of the mosque to which it adds a vertical accent. It was
not usual to position the minaret in relation to the
interior rather than the exterior plan of a mosque.

The minaret looks very like the twin minarets of
the mosque of al-Mu'ayyad at the Bab Zuwayla and it
is likely that the same master-builder, Ibn al-Qazzaz,
was responsible for its construction.[86] The niches of the
first storey, however, have trilobed hoods, rather than
keel-arches with a radiating motif, and no inscriptions.
The second storey has an identical chevron carving

FIG. 158

The minaret of the mosque of Qadi 'Abd al-Basit

FIG. 159

The minaret of the mosque of Sultan Barsbay

and inscription band above. The upper pavilion and stone balustrades are modern restorations.

Qadi ʿAbd al-Basit made the pilgrimage to Mecca and was furthermore the official in charge of the yearly dispatch of the Kaaba covering to Mecca (*nazir al-kiswa*), a tradition the Mamluk sultans considered their exclusive privilege. The foundation inscriptions of the mosque mention this prestigious office among ʿAbd al-Basit's responsibilities. To underline the significance of ʿAbd al-Basit's role, the inscription on the minaret comes from the Sura 22, 'Pilgrimage'.

EPIGRAPHY

Second storey
Sura 22:27–8

47. THE MOSQUE OF SULTAN BARSBAY (1425)

The complex of Barsbay is located on the main artery of Qahira, some distance to the south of the cluster of monuments at Bayn al-Qasrayn.[87] The minaret is positioned immediately to the right of the main portal, and is juxtaposed with a stone mausoleum dome that occupies the northern corner of the façade. Both the square base of the minaret and that of the dome are set at an angle to the façade wall, however, following the inner, Mecca-oriented, alignment of the sanctuary.

The minaret of Barsbay is a copy, with some minor differences in treatment, of the twin minarets of the *khanqah* of Sultan Faraj ibn Barquq. Although there are two inscriptions on the minaret of Barsbay, one on each storey, even the upper inscription replicates the text carved on the second storey of the northern minaret of Sultan Faraj ibn Barquq.

EPIGRAPHY

First storey
Sura 62:9–10

Second storey
Sura 33:41–3

48. THE MOSQUE OF EMIR JANIBAK AL-ASHRAFI (1427)

The funerary mosque of Emir Janibak is a handsome building, located on the main route south of Qahira beyond Bab Zuwayla.[88] The mosque is lavishly furnished and decorated, and includes a mausoleum dome of carved stone at the southern end of the façade. The minaret is a more modest construction that stands to the right of the entrance portal. It is built of plastered brick with a hexagonal first storey, which is rare. We have seen hexagonal first storeys at the minarets of Asanbugha and Qanibay al-Muhammadi, combined in both cases with a triangular base. At the minaret of Janibak the first storey is hexagonal from the roof level, however, without a base. Instead, three short pointed buttresses reinforce the shaft on every second facet. The niches of the first storey have pointed arches instead of the more common keel-arched niches, but are decorated, however, in the conventional manner with radiating hoods. The niches are surrounded and linked together at their bases by a continuous broad projecting moulding, and have a damaged inscription band running above them. The cylindrical second storey has a very sharp taper up to its muqarnas cornice. It is uncertain whether the upper bulb was originally set directly above the cylindrical shaft as it is now, or whether the current bulb replaces an upper pavilion of the type seen on the minaret of Mahmud al-Ustadar (al-Kurdi).

EPIGRAPHY

First storey
Sura 33:41–4

49. THE MOSQUE OF EMIR FAYRUZ (1427)

The minaret of this mosque is positioned directly on the line of the main façade, without the customary setback with crenellations passing in front of its base.[89] Trefoil crenellations are in this case actually carved into the base of the minaret to achieve the visual

FIG. 160

The minaret of the mosque of Emir Janibak al-Ashrafi

FIG. 161

The minaret of the mosque of Emir Fayruz

FIG. 162

The minaret of the mosque of Shaykh 'Ali al-'Imari

continuity of this feature at the top of the façade. The minaret has two octagonal sections, the first of stone and the second of brick, separated by a muqarnas ring beneath the muezzin's balcony. The transitional zone is delineated with projecting rounded mouldings and the first storey has keel-arched recesses with radiating hoods, supported by clusters of three columns at each corner of the shaft. Four of the recesses are open to the stairwell and are connected with miniature balconies with muqarnas brackets. Between these, the shaft is decorated with sunken rosettes of a radiating pattern. The second storey has no decoration and is topped by a plain moulded cornice, above which the upper bulb rests without a pavilion. The minaret has neither balustrades nor inscriptions.

50. THE MOSQUE OF SHAYKH 'ALI AL-'IMARI (1428–30)

The minaret is all that remains of the mosque attributed in the recent edition of the Index of the Islamic Monuments of Cairo to Qadi Amin al-Din al-'Imari al-Harrani and dated 832/1429–30.[90]

The minaret is a handsome, octagonal construction built in the style of the early fifteenth century. The first storey, set over an undulating transitional zone, deploys the usual vocabulary of keel-arches, triple-columns and miniature balconies. The second storey is decorated with the then popular zigzag pattern, and the pavilion that would have rested above this is missing. The muqarnas on this minaret, however, looks unlike any other in Egypt, employing pendant structures that are elaborately carved with a kind of miniaturised muqarnas themselves. These elements are also visible on the brackets supporting miniature balconies and the cornice of the first storey: they do not appear on the muqarnas cornice of the second storey. Such hanging muqarnas elements had been common in Ottoman architecture since the early fifteenth century, as can be seen, for example, at the portal of the Green Mosque in Bursa, and later in Istanbul, where they adorn a number of minarets and portals. The stone balustrades on the minaret are modern replacements, and there are no inscriptions.

FIG. 163

The minaret of Shaykh 'Ali al-'Imari, muqarnas detail

FIG. 164

The muqarnas portal at the Green Mosque in Bursa

FIG. 165

The minaret of the mosque of Shaykh Muhammad al-Ghamri

DAVID ROBERTS

51. THE MOSQUE OF SHAYKH MUHAMMAD AL-GHAMRI (1441–2)*

One minaret that no longer stands today was beautifully illustrated by the Scottish artist David Roberts in the mid-nineteenth century. It belonged to the mosque of a Sufi shaykh, Muhammad al-Ghamri.[91] The founder, who died in 849/1445, was a very humble man, who originated in the town of Miniyat Ghamr (Mit Ghamr) in the Delta and led an ascetic life, earning his living as a craftsman. However, the significance and prestige he acquired during his life as a mystic shaykh, gathering a large number of disciples around him, allowed him to found several mosques in the provinces and in the capital, including this one, once located in Marjush Street in the north-west part of historic Qahira. Reports state that the mosque was founded in 843/1440 as a congregational mosque, in response to an apparently urgent need for a sanctuary in this quarter. Shaykh al-Ghamri died prior to its completion: a local merchant sponsored the construction of the minaret, which was probably erected after his death. 'Ali Mubarak writes that, according to an inscription, the Shaykh's son Abu 'l-'Abbas oversaw the final stages of the mosque's construction.

The watercolour sketch made by Roberts on site shows the minaret dominating the street, thus emphasising the presence of the mosque in the quarter. Its design recalls the later minaret of the Emir Bardabak, which also has a plain middle section. It appears to have been made of stone, including its elaborate upper pavilion. This would not be surprising since Shaykh al-Ghamri also sponsored a mosque in the city of al-Mahalla al-Kubra, where he had a community of disciples.

Although it appears in good condition in the drawing by Roberts, the building had decayed by the end of the century to such an extent that the Comité had to demolish it in 1884 to prevent its collapse. Van Berchem saw among the stone debris of the dismantled minaret magnificent inscriptions in Kufic of an archaic style reminiscent of Fatimid monuments. He rightly wondered about this find. It is indeed remarkable that a provincial shaykh would found a mosque with a stone minaret of such quality. The appearance of the minaret, and the fact that it attracted the attention of Roberts, attests to the princely architecture of this building. Moreover, a magnificent wooden minbar donated in 1456 to the mosque can be seen today at the mosque of Sultan Barsbay in the cemetery.

52. THE MOSQUE OF EMIR QARAQUJA AL-HASANI (1441–2)

The minaret of the mosque of Qaraquja al-Hasani is freestanding, accessible today only via a wooden bridge from the roof of the mosque.[92] This is also how it was in 1892 when the Comité inspected it. Although the foundation deed describes the complex in detail, as consisting of two buildings with the mosque and shops on the eastern side and the *sabil*, an oratory and dependencies on the opposite side of the street, it does not mention the detached minaret on the northern side. The mosque and the detached minaret are all that survives of this complex so that it is not possible to establish with certainty the reason for the unusual location of the latter. The square base of the minaret does not show any traces of an adjoining structure. The reason for detaching the minaret from the mosque may have been the lack of space in the façade wall for its support. The façade included three shops, and next to them a waterwheel and an apartment unit.

The minaret is built of stone. The transitional zone is articulated with strapwork mouldings. The first storey is of the common type, but with a tracery of arabesques carved on the spandrels between the hoods of the niches on each facet of the shaft. A sunken uninscribed band runs above this. The decoration of the middle section is remarkable: it displays interlaced geometric X-patterns in raised relief set against carved recesses to enhance the relief effect. The X-pattern is the same as already used at the minarets of Asanbugha, Faraj ibn Barquq and Barsbay, with a second inscription set above. A similar pattern is applied in stucco on the contemporary brick domes of Emir Taghribirdi and Umm al-Ashraf.

A bulb sits directly above the second storey, and there are no balustrades. The wooden bridge we see today connecting the roof of the mosque with the minaret may be modern, but the minaret's entrance, which faces the mosque, indicates that there must always have been a bridge there. The remains of a stone corbel in the upper part of the mosque's wall facing the minaret may have been part of an original masonry bridge.

FIG. 166

The minaret of the mosque of Emir Qaraquja al-Hasani

FIG. 167

The minaret of the mosque of Qanibay al-Jarkasi

FIG. 168

The minaret of the mosque of Qanibay
al-Jarkasi, elevation

EPIGRAPHY

First storey
Sura 7:54

Second storey
Sura 2:255

53. THE MOSQUE OF EMIR QANIBAY AL-JARKASI (1441–2)

Although the minaret seems to be the most fragile structure in a building, sometimes it survived its mosque, as is the case here. The present mosque is a modern reconstruction. The founder of this mosque, Qanibay al-Jarkasi, was one of the most prominent emirs of Sultan Jaqmaq. The sultan, who did not build his own funerary complex, was buried there alongside a brother.[93]

The minaret is made of stone with a conservative design. The combination of a square first storey with a cylindrical second one had been revived in the early fifteenth century with the minarets of Sultan Faraj, and is repeated here. The zigzag carving found on the cylindrical section, above which was placed an inscription band, already had a long tradition at that time on domes and minarets. The upper structure and balustrades of the minaret are missing.

The positioning of this minaret is noteworthy. Although the mosque was erected alongside the great hippodrome beneath the Citadel on its south-western side, its façade with the main entrance and the minaret did not overlook the hippodrome but a small street to the rear. The architect could have followed the example of the royal monuments of Qalawun, Barsbay and al-Ghawri in the city and placed the façade along the more important street, on the side of the hippodrome side. Doing so would have required some architectural gymnastics, and so a simpler solution with the main façade and the minaret on the western side street was adopted. The minaret is thus not visible from the hippodrome, addressing instead the inhabitants of the quarter behind.

EPIGRAPHY

Second storey
Sura 2:255

54. THE MOSQUE OF EMIR TAGHRIBIRDI (1444)

This small funerary mosque manages to pack all the traditional elements of a Mamluk mosque – dome, minaret, portal and *sabil-maktab* – into a very small area and still make the resulting whole somehow harmonious. The minaret does not stand close to the mausoleum dome, but immediately to the left of the main portal. It has a square first storey and a cylindrical second, a common configuration in this period. The brick dome is carved with the same pattern that was originally created for minarets and that decorates the minaret of Qaraquja. The decoration of the second storey of the minaret displays a geometric star pattern that had just been applied for the first time as carved decoration on the domes of Sultan Barsbay's funerary complex in the northern cemetery. The stone balustrades and the pavilion with bulb set over the second storey are modern restorations: the balustrades were formerly in timber. A sunken inscription band can be seen on the lower shaft, but it is empty.

55. THE MOSQUES OF QADI YAHYA ZAYN AL-DIN ON THE KHALIJ AND AT BULAQ (1444 and 1448)

A total of three mosques in Cairo are attributed to Qadi Yahya Zayn al-Din, all of them with stone minarets. Two of these, built during the reign of Sultan Jaqmaq, are discussed here and the third in a separate entry.

The earliest of the minarets, dated 848/1444, is located at a mosque near what was once the Khalij, or Canal of Cairo, on what is currently al-Azhar Street.[94] The location of the minaret is on the extreme north-east corner of the building with the portal

immediately to its right. In this position the minaret would have dominated the street approached from the north. The original octagonal first storey of this minaret is inscribed but conventional in its design. Substantial restorations by the Comité at the mosque in 1896 included the entire second storey and superstructure of the minaret.[95] Their decoration with blue tiles was obviously inspired by the minaret of Sultan al-Ghawri at the Azhar mosque, which is an anachronism. Ignoring Mamluk practice, the restorers executed the muqarnas beneath the balconies of the upper storeys, using the same pattern as below.

The minaret of Qadi Yahya's mosque in Bulaq, built in 852–3/1448–9, is also placed directly to the left of the main portal.[96] Only the first storey survives, but this is of more architectural interest than its earlier counterpart because of the unusual treatment of the cornice at the base of the first balcony. Instead of the usual muqarnas ring, the octagonal shaft flares at the top into a concave cornice with a carved lozenge pattern on its underside that even extends vertically onto the edge of the balcony above. This device, which appears here for the first time, was imitated decades later at the minarets of Sultan Qaytbay at Qal'at al-Kabsh and at Rawda, and at the minaret of Yashbak attached to the shrine of Imam al-Layth. This decoration has been carved in stucco. An inscription band is located immediately below the flaring cornice, and the remainder of the shaft is decorated with keel-arched niches, miniature balconies, and decorative strapwork mouldings. Unusually, the inscription is placed in a series of cartouches on each face of the shaft rather than being carved continuously around it.

EPIGRAPHY

The minaret of the mosque along the Khalij
Sura 24:36–7

The minaret at Bulaq
Illegible, may not be Koranic

FIG. 169

The minaret of the mosque of Emir Taghribirdi

FIG. 170

The minaret of the mosque of Qadi Yahya on the Khalij

FIG. 171

The remains of the minaret of Qadi Yahya at Bulaq

FIG. 172

The minaret of the madrasa of Sultan Jaqmaq)

56. THE MADRASA OF SULTAN JAQMAQ (1451)

Sultan Jaqmaq (r.1438–53) was a learned and pious man, who was also described as an austere, even puritanical, character. He collected books, but was no aesthete and no patron of art or architecture. He deliberately abstained from building a funerary monument for himself and preferred instead to concentrate his endeavour on infrastructure projects and the restoration of monuments in need of repair. The madrasa he founded in 1451 is not a great architectural achievement.[97] It does, however, possess a minaret that stands at the north-east corner of the building. This does not follow the façade alignment, but the inner Mecca-orientation of the mosque. The shaft has two octagonal storeys. Only the first storey is made of stone, the upper section is in brick. The present bulb, which has no pavilion, is made of wood and the balconies have wooden railings.

Although the lower shaft is made of stone, the entire decoration of the minaret, including the muqarnas cornices, is executed in stucco, a combination that characterises a few other minarets of the mid-fifteenth century. The decorative pattern of the second octagonal storey of the minaret is unique, forming vertical bands with a rounded profile that interlock on the sides and at the apex to frame a series of eight niches. Similar bands frame the hoods of the keel-arched niches on the lower storey. The muqarnas cornices beneath the two balconies are elaborate.

Another mosque attributed to this sultan stands close to Sayyida Zaynab and is known as the mosque of Lajin al-Sayfi.[98] It has a simple octagonal first storey with a muqarnas cornice at its summit and a short Ottoman second storey with a conical cap.

57. THE MOSQUE OF SULTAN JAQMAQ AT DAYR AL-NAHAS (1438–53)*

Another mosque attributed to Jaqmaq stood at Dayr al-Nahas to the north of Fustat and opposite the southern tip of the Nilometer of the island of Rawda.

FIG. 173

The vanished minaret of the mosque of Sultan Jaqmaq at Dayr al-Nahas

This has now disappeared but its appearance is preserved in archival photographs.[99] The suburban location of the mosque, known also by the name of Shaykh Muhammad al-Makhfi, who was buried inside its premises, suggests that Jaqmaq sponsored this foundation to honour a holy man. The date of the mosque is unknown.

It is difficult to tell whether the octagonal first storey of the minaret was made of stone or brick, but the muqarnas cornice above it and the cylindrical second storey were certainly made of the latter material. The minaret had applied plaster decoration to the first conventional storey, and the second storey is plain, with a second muqarnas cornice. A bulb sits directly above this level.

58. THE MINARET AT THE MOSQUE OF AL-RUWAY'I (1440s–1450s)

Whereas the present mosque of al-Ruway'i is Ottoman and insignificant in terms of its architecture, the minaret is a plastered brick shaft built and decorated in the style of the mid-fifteenth century. The dating of this minaret remains problematic, however. According to 'Ali Mubarak the mosque was built by a chief merchant of this name in the early sixteenth century.[100] This is contradicted by archival sources, which identify Ruway'i as a very important coffee merchant at the turn of the seventeenth century.[101]

As has been mentioned earlier, the Ottoman conquest introduced a rupture in the architecture of the Cairene minaret by replacing the Mamluk three-storied sculptured shaft with a squat pencil-shaped structure. Almost a century after the last documented Mamluk minaret was erected by Khayrbak, it may have been difficult to find a builder who worked in the Mamluk style, although the mosque of Burdayni built in 1629 was a successful return to the Mamluk style. It is, finally, to the style of the Ruway'i's minaret itself that we must return in order to settle the question of its date. The minaret has an octagonal first and a cylindrical second storey surmounted by a bulb without a pavilion. The fine stucco muqarnas, now partly disfigured, is also clearly of Mamluk style. The use of stucco was completely abandoned in the Cairene architecture of the Ottoman period. Moreover, the structure of the muqarnas of this minaret does not have any parallel in the architecture of the time. Creswell convincingly compares the moulding used in the transitional zone between the base and the first storey to that of the minaret of Qaraquja al-Hasani, built in 1441–2.

One may argue that al-Ruway'i might have recruited a craftsman from the provinces where Mamluk-style brick minarets continued to be built until the nineteenth century. This interpretation is not supported by the style of the minaret, which, although unpretentious, is not provincial.

It is more than likely, therefore, that al-Ruway'i reused, re-endowed and gave his name to an unknown Mamluk mosque. In the fifteenth century, a great

FIG. 174

The minaret of the mosque of al-Ruway'i

number of scholars, Sufi shaykhs and commoners were authorised to build Friday mosques, multiplying the number of mosques in the city to an unprecedented extent. This minaret is of the quality one may associate with such a patron. The quarter around it was part of the western suburb of the medieval city, north of the Azbakiyya lake, and is poorly documented.

59. THE MINARET AT THE MOSQUE OF EMIR ARGHUN AL-ISMAʿILI (1450s)

Although the foundation date of the mosque of Emir Arghun al-Ismaʿili, 748/1347, poses no problem,[102] the style of its present minaret does not fit into this period of masterly achievement in masonry construction and decoration. It rather seems that the original minaret was replaced at some point during the century that followed its construction by the present unpretentious structure. Stylistic and technical comparisons assign this structure to the reign of Sultan Jaqmaq.

The minaret consists of an octagonal first storey made of stone and a cylindrical middle section made of brick. The muqarnas at the summit of the stone section is made of stucco. The original upper structure is missing. Both the minarets of Sultan Jaqmaq, the one attached to his madrasa and the demolished one at his mosque at Dayr al-Nahas, were built with a similar combination of a stone octagonal first storey surmounted by a brick cylindrical second storey, with the muqarnas between them made of stucco. This combination suggests a dating of this minaret to the mid-fifteenth century. Further arguments for this dating are the coarse stone masonry of the octagonal first storey, which contrasts with the fine muqarnas portal of the same mosque, the treatment of the upper muqarnas cornice of the brick section, which recalls the cornices of the contemporary minarets of the madrasa of Sultan Jaqmaq and the mosque al-ʿAlaya, and the similarity between the transitional zone of this minaret and that of the minaret added to the mosque of Emir Husayn in the 1460s.

FIG. 175

The minaret at the mosque of Emir Arghun al-Ismaʿili

FIG. 176

The funerary complex of Sultan Inal

60. THE FUNERARY COMPLEX OF SULTAN INAL (1451)

One glance at the façade of this complex in the northern cemetery suffices to reveal an irregularity in its composition, which is confirmed by literary sources and surviving inscriptions that give different dates for the completion of this building.[103] In 1451, while still an emir, Inal built a domed mausoleum for himself, as stated by an inscription band on its façade. When his career advanced, he expanded his funerary complex. In 1453, after he became sultan, he added a large *khanqah*, and in 1456 a Friday mosque was completed.

The architecture of the minaret indicates that it was erected prior to the construction of the Friday mosque; its octagonal first storey starts far below the roof of the mosque. Its base, however, stands at the same height as that of the mausoleum dome, suggesting that they were erected at the same time, which would be in 1451. Prior to the addition of a Friday mosque in 1456, the mausoleum would have had, in all likelihood, a prayer hall attached to it. Such funerary buildings, even when their mosques were simple oratories for Sufi gatherings, were generally equipped with a minaret. The complex of Emir Azdumur, for example, which similarly consisted of an oratory with Sufi functions and a mausoleum, also included a minaret. In comparison with the impoverished contemporary minarets of Sultan Jaqmaq, the minaret of Inal is a fine stone construction, densely carved down to its square base. It thus anticipates the plethora of decoration on the minarets of the reign of Sultan Qaytbay. The carved decoration is among the most refined of the fifteenth century.

The engaged carved columns with muqarnas capitals at the corners of the minaret's base indicate that it was once freestanding on three of its sides, perhaps projecting at a corner of its parent structure. Proceeding vertically, we come to the level of the roof of the initial building with an entrance to the stairwell of the minaret, located below the transitional zone. The other faces of the square base at this height are decorated with magnificent large square panels of interlocking geometric designs in raised relief,

flanked at the corners of the shaft by embedded columns carved with spiral fluting and with tulip capitals and bases. Above this lies the transitional zone, with additional, smaller, square geometrically decorated panels on its vertical surfaces. Strapwork mouldings define the edges of this zone, and the downward-pointing triangles of masonry at the corners are also decorated with a triangle containing a carved fleur-de-lis.

The octagonal first storey emulates the model created at the minaret of the madrasa of Sultan Barquq with engaged triple columns of different designs at the corners of each facet. The hoods of the keel-arched recesses supported by these columns are not identical, however: they display alternately two patterns, one with radiating ribs that extend to form a ribbed voussoir around the arch, and the other with ribs curling to form a lobed voussoir. A similar pattern was used to decorate the hood of the mihrab in the mosque that was added to the complex. The niches have four miniature balconies on muqarnas brackets as is normal, but unusually have further recessed panels of arabesque carving on alternate facets that take the form of vertical cartouches. Smaller panels of decoration sit between the balconies themselves, and the whole composition is 'tied' together by fine double mouldings with loops. Above the niches is a delicate inscription band that runs below the muqarnas cornice of the first balcony.

The decoration of the second storey consists of a carved zigzag pattern with an inscription band above it. Although the use of the chevron or zigzag was already common on the central sections of minarets, it is treated here in a novel manner. Each unit of the zigzag is carved on a projecting triangle of masonry that forms a three-dimensional profile accentuating the contrast of light and shade. The recessed vertical grooves in the masonry are capped with delicately carved fan-shaped ogival arches. This design was repeated on a few other minarets. The appearance of the pavilion above the second storey of the minaret is hard to interpret. At first glance, the space between the piers appears to have been walled up on two separate occasions. The first of these had blocking walls built in four openings displaying a surface carved with a chevron, which is an unusual feature. Four further

plain walls were constructed later within the remaining openings. The pavilion has a fine cornice of muqarnas above it, culminating in a ring of spikes pointing outwards. Above this sits the bulb that is constructed from a stone lower section and a brick top, probably a repair. Seen within the stylistic development of Cairene minarets, the minaret of Sultan Inal is one of the most innovative examples that set the aesthetic standard up to the end of the Mamluk period.

EPIGRAPHY

First storey
Sura 3:190–1

Second storey
Sura 2:255

61. THE MOSQUE OF QADI YAHYA AT HABBANIYYA (1452–3)

FIG. 177

The minaret of the mosque of Qadi Yahya at Habbaniyya today

The minaret at the mosque of Qadi Yahya at Habbaniyya was built in 856/1452–3.[104] Today, only the first octagonal storey, made of stone, stands immediately to the right of the main portal of the complex. It is a conventional but elegant construction with two inscription bands, one at the base and the other beneath the muqarnas ring. An archival photograph shows the second storey of the minaret to have been cylindrical, and made of timber lath and plaster. Its proportions suggest that it was original.

EPIGRAPHY

Lower band
Sura 3:190

Upper band
Sura 3:191–2

62. THE MINARET AT THE MOSQUE OF EMIR HUSAYN (1462)*

The original minaret of the mosque of Emir Husayn (1319) is reported by the chronicler Ibn Iyas to have collapsed after a heavy storm in 866/1462.[105] It must have been replaced shortly afterwards to judge from the style of the later structure. The minaret was reconstructed in stone in its original location, which according to Maqrizi was directly above the portal of the mosque. Both minaret and portal have fallen victim to recent demolition.

The archival photographs of the minaret that remain show that it had a transitional zone with concave triangles of masonry, as on the minaret of Aqsunqur. The articulation of its lower octagonal section was accomplished with keel-arched niches in the usual manner, but here they have muqarnas hoods, which is surely unique. Heavy mouldings framed the hoods of the niches, executed in a style that recalls the minaret of Sultan Jaqmaq. The first storey of the minaret was carved in a raised zigzag pattern similar to that of the minaret of Sultan Inal, built a few years earlier, similarly in stone. The same design was applied in stucco on the brick minarets of al-Khatiri and al-'Alaya, both dating to the end of the Mamluk period. The cylindrical upper storey seen on the photograph was an Ottoman addition. Both minaret and portal were dismantled in 1984, and the blocks removed to an unknown location. There has been no subsequent project to rebuild them *in situ*.

FIG. 179

The vanished minaret at the mosque of Emir Husayn

FIG. 181

The minaret of the mosque of Emir Tanam Rasas

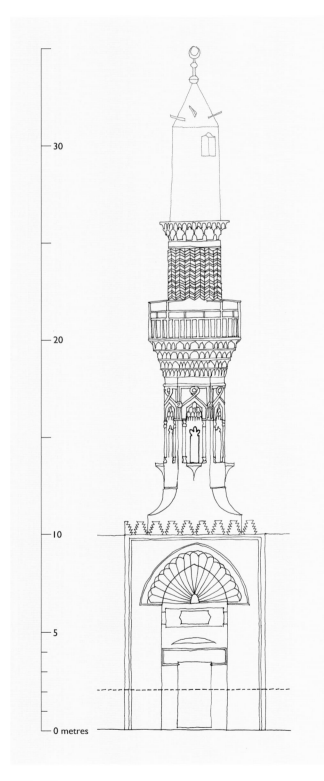

FIG. 180

The vanished minaret at the mosque of Emir Husayn, elevation

63. **THE MOSQUE OF EMIR TANAM RASAS** (before 1463)

This mosque, popularly known by the name Tamim al-Rasafi, should be attributed to Emir Tanam Rasas, who was killed at a young age in 867/1463, and who was reported to have founded a mosque in this area.[106] The minaret is a stone construction with a graceful profile; its upper structure has been restored. The carved decoration is of high quality. The treatment of the transitional zone and first storey is almost 'classic' by this stage in the development of minaret architecture. The zigzag pattern carved on the cylindrical second storey also perpetuates a design that had become a 'standard' amidst the great variety of patterns used in this period. The minaret has an inscription band on each storey.

EPIGRAPHY

First storey
Sura 33:41–2

Second storey
Sura 3:190–1

64. **THE MOSQUE OF SHAYKH MADYAN** (1465)*

This mosque was sponsored by the wife of Sultan Jaqmaq, who revered the mystic Sufi Shaykh Madyan. It was a richly endowed and once lavishly decorated building, as can still be recognised today.[107] The stone construction of the minaret, now demolished, testifies to the high prestige that Madyan enjoyed, as was the case with his colleague and friend Muhammad al-Ghamri. The minaret stood near the portal of the mosque at a bend in the façade. As it was not aligned with the section of the façade that contains the main portal, it had a rather uncomfortable relationship with the latter. The keel-arched niches of its octagonal first storey had alternating plain and decorated hoods, but the design was otherwise conventional. The original

FIG. 182

The vanished minaret of Shaykh Madyan

upper structure was replaced in the Ottoman period with a conical cap.

This minaret happens to be mentioned in the biography of the founder, where it was directly associated with his miraculous powers. The Sufi historian Sha'rani reported that, after the minaret was erected, it began to lean, so scaring the inhabitants of the quarter that the call went out to pull it down. Shaykh Madyan, however, found a better solution: he climbed to the roof of the mosque, and, leaning

his back on the shaft of the minaret, began to push it until it regained its upright position, which it maintained thereafter. [108] Unfortunately, the recent apparently motiveless demolition of the minaret could not be prevented.

65. THE MOSQUE OF EMIR QANIM AL-TAJIR (1466)*

A nineteenth-century drawing by Prisse d'Avennes illustrates the minaret of a now lost mosque that he calls 'Al-Kalmy', without further indications. On the eighteenth-century map of Cairo in the *Description de l'Égypte*, the mosque of 'al-Qalmy' was located near the mosque of Ibn Tulun. This corresponds in its position to the mosque of 'al-Tagher' on the plan of Grand Bey of 1874. The foundation deed of the mosque of Emir Qanim al-Sharkasi al-Tajir, also mentioned by 'Ali Mubarak, is dated 871/1466. The minaret of the mosque seen in the drawing by Prisse was made of stone with an octagonal first storey and cylindrical second. The first storey had a standard articulation of keel-arched niches and balconies with an inscription band above it. The second storey was carved with the same interlocking lozenge pattern of decoration used at the minaret of Asanbugha and some others. The upper structure was already missing by that time. According to Van Berchem, the mosque had to be demolished by the Comité, and today a modern construction stands on the site.[109]

66. THE MOSQUE OF EMIR MUGHULBAY TAZ (1466)

The square base, octagonal first storey and circular second storey survive of this minaret that stands above the entrance portal of its mosque on the same orientation as the street it faces. Although a number of minarets erected in the last quarter of the fifteenth century display similarly dense and accomplished carved decoration, the minaret of Mughulbay Taz deserves special attention because it predates them

Imp. par Lemercier & Cⁱᵉ

FIG. 183

The vanished minaret of the mosque of Emir Qanim al-Tajir

GIRAULT DE PRANGEY, PRISSE D'AVENNES

FIG. 184

The minaret of the mosque of Emir Mughulbay Taz

FIG. 185

The minaret of the mosque of Emir Bardabak al-Ashrafi

all, and also because it was built before the reign of Qaytbay, which saw the full flourishing of this style of carving.

As we have seen, the minaret of the funerary complex of Sultan Inal, erected a decade earlier, was already entirely covered with carved decoration from the base to the top. The minaret of Mughulbay Taz, however, introduces the use of arabesque in the middle section of the minaret, where so far geometrical patterns had prevailed. The pattern applied here is basically similar to that carved on the mausoleum dome of Jawhar al-Qanqaba'i dated 1440, near the Azhar mosque. Yet in the minaret of Mughulbay Taz the design is treated in a new and more refined manner, making it appear as if it was composed of two super-imposed networks of arabesques, one with a plain surface and the other split by a groove in its middle to add further contrast in light and shadow. The same mason may have carved the undated mausoleum dome built by Qaytbay for his son prior to the foundation of his own mausoleum in 1474.[110] The arabesques on the first storey of the minaret of Mughulbay Taz were to inspire the decoration of two other minarets of the same period: the mosques of Timraz al-Ahmadi (1477) and Janim al-Bahlawan (1478). This style of 'grooved carving' was new in Cairo, but it was applied much earlier in Anatolia in the Seljuk period and became a characteristic feature of architectural decoration in Cairo up to the end of the fifteenth century.

Apart from the new form of arabesque carving seen on the second storey of this minaret, there is also a surviving inscription band and the first row of blocks of a muqarnas cornice, between which further shallowly carved arabesques can be detected. The first storey has an arcade of niches with polylobed hoods, separated by clusters of three columns with chevron carved decoration used in both vertical and horizontal directions. The hoods interlock gracefully with the underside of the muqarnas cornice that crowns this storey. The recessed panels, where they are not connected to the stairwell with windows, have further arabesque carving. Below the arcade, miniature balconies alternate with square panels containing partly sunk rosettes, all framed by strap-work mouldings. Another inscription band runs

immediately below this, in a rather unusual position, forming a kind of collar above the transitional zone. The transitional zone itself is delineated by further mouldings and has every facet of its structure carved with decorative panels. In the style of the minaret of Sultan Inal, the base of the minaret has a large square geometric carved panel with an arabesque border and a pair of columns carved with chevrons embedded at the two flanking corners. This only occurs on the side facing the street, and thus privileges this façade above the others.

The inscription of the minaret is the only one known to refer to the foundation of the mosque to which it is attached. Another inscription from the wooden ceiling of the mosque, moved to the Islamic Museum, dates the mosque to 871/1466.[111]

EPIGRAPHY

First storey
'This construction of this auspicious and blessed mosque has been ordered through the grace of God and his universal generosity in the venerated month of Ramadan…. [reference to the Prophet] on his companions, O Lord of the worlds. This was completed in… [missing].'[112]

Second storey
Identical text

67. THE MOSQUE OF EMIR BARDABAK AL-ASHRAFI (after 1468)

The founder of this mosque, Bardabak al-Ashrafi, also called *al-faranji*, meaning 'the European', was the son-in-law of Sultan Inal. He was a converted Cypriot, who was brought to Cairo as a prisoner of war. He found favour with the sultan, who later married him to his daughter, appointed him as second secretary, and granted him the authority to become one of the mightiest men in the state. His prestige did not, however, outlast the lifespan of his patron: Bardabak was assassinated in 1464 under Sultan Khushqadam.[113] He is credited with the foundation of several mosques,

FIG. 186

The minaret of the mosque of Sultan Qaytbay in the cemetery

of which only the one to which the minaret in question belongs survives. The mosque, which stands close to the main street of historic Cairo, was completed by one of his sons in 872/1468, the year of Qaytbay's accession to the throne.[114]

As to be expected, the European origin of the founder is not reflected in the architecture. Neither is the decorative style that later characterised the minarets of Qaytbay's reign perceptible in the minaret of Bardabak. The minaret stands directly over the portal of the mosque and is made up of a square base, an octagonal first storey, a circular second storey; the bulb is placed directly over the last without its pavilion. The first storey is octagonal and, in contrast to most contemporary minarets, the cylindrical second storey is plain. Following the example of the minaret of Sultan Inal, the base is accentuated by mouldings and the triple engaged columns at the corners are also carved. There is an inscription at the top of this storey.

EPIGRAPHY

First storey
Invocations (*du'a*)

68. THE MOSQUE OF SULTAN QAYTBAY IN THE CEMETERY (1474)

The minaret of Sultan al-Ashraf Qaytbay at his funerary mosque in the cemetery is one of the most accomplished of the Mamluk period in terms of its proportion and decoration. The profile of the mosque has a jewel-like gracefulness, yet the dome and the minaret are not juxtaposed, as is traditionally the case in the cemetery. Instead, the minaret stands at the north-west corner of the complex on the opposite side of the dome that occupies the south-east corner. The two structures harmonise by balancing each rather than by their juxtaposition. Nowhere is this more apparent than in the view of the front of the building when seen from the north, as it was presented in numerous nineteenth-century drawings and photographs. This view is, to a great extent, obstructed today.

The aesthetic appeal of the minaret lies in its elegant proportion and the quality of its masonry and carving rather than in any specific innovative feature. The square base has colonettes with chevron carving embedded at each corner, and the lower octagonal section has a conventional arrangement of elements. The geometrical star motif carved on the circular middle section of the minaret is not the earliest of its kind. The minaret of Taghribirdi already shows a network of geometrical stars, albeit in a different design. The star motif also has a secondary, lower level of carving in the form of rosettes. The ring moulding around the centre of the neck of the crowning bulb is also an original detail. In the nineteenth century, the upper pavilion was slightly different in appearance as the space between the eight piers was partly walled up. This feature, shown on a detailed and precise lithograph by Ludwig Libay dated 1857,[115] might have been part of the original design, as is the case at the minaret of Qaytbay attached to the Azhar mosque, but was removed by later restorers who also installed new pierced stone balustrades. One inscription band is located on the first storey above the level of the arcade, and contains the first documented use of Sura 62 on a minaret. Two other bands are found on the second storey: the lower of the two is unfinished, and provides an interesting glimpse of the technique used to set out such an epigraphic band.

At the turn of the fifteenth to the sixteenth centuries, a muezzin spent long hours inside the minaret contemplating the panorama of bustling Cairo to the west, and the cemetery to the east and north, and meditating. Wherever the shaft of the minaret received enough light from the door and window openings, this muezzin would carve inscriptions in a fine *naskhi* script on its inner walls. He also carved further inscriptions on the exterior walls of the minaret and the base of the dome. He signed himself several times, adding the title *al-mu'adhdhin* to his name, followed by dates. His name can be read as Muhammad al-Nasabi or al-Nashani – the position of the dots does not allow a conclusive reading. The earliest date he gives is 885/1480 and the latest 911/1505. As already mentioned, muezzins, at least those working in major mosques, were usually educated and often recruited

FIG. 187

View of the cemetery from the minaret of the mosque of Sultan Qaytbay with his mausoleum dome

from among members of the Sufi community attached to a particular foundation. They are likely to have learned the art of calligraphy. This muezzin may also have been trained as an epigraphic sculptor, as the quality of his carvings suggests. Many of these graffiti are Koranic, urging believers to remember God and to mention his name; others contain Sufi homilies or epigrams, and several of them mention death.

GRAFFITI

There are four kinds of humiliation: to be poor, to be ill, to have debts [a word here was tampered with].

Perfection is in four [things]: intelligence, good character, high morals, and restraint.

I wonder about he who sheds tears at the loss of others, and does not shed tears of blood about himself, I wonder about he who sees the deficiencies of others while God has struck his eyes with blindness. May God forgive the writer and the reader [of this] and our brothers the muezzins; may He forgive their sins. O God forgive them on the Day of Judgement.

Do not fear your enemies, for God is Powerful against them.

Know people, you will find there should be no confidence.

He who is modest will be appreciated; he who is greedy will be humiliated.

I have found more support in long suffering than in (my fellow) men.

God is my love and my succour.

He has created everything and He knows everything.

Life is an hour let it be one of devotion.

All good is in remembering God, do not fail to remember God, remember God often.
God have mercy upon us; You are most Merciful.

FIGS 188, 189 & 190

The minaret of the mosque of Sultan Qaytbay in the cemetery, graffiti by a muezzin

FIG. 191

The minaret of the mosque of Sultan Qaytbay at Qal'at al-Kabsh

The Mercy of God who is Merciful be upon he who carved [this].

God's mercy be upon the writer and reader of this.

Everything is doomed to vanish.

There is no escape from destiny, no rest in this world, no rescue from Death.

Death, which you try to escape, will catch you.

Death spares neither father nor son.

Death is the greatest moralist.

Death must be.

EPIGRAPHY

First storey
Sura 62:9–11

Second storey lower band
Sura 33:40–1

Second storey upper band
Sura 3:190–1

69. THE MOSQUE OF SULTAN QAYTBAY AT QAL'AT AL-KABSH (1475)

The minaret of Qaytbay at his madrasa in the quarter of Qal'at al-Kabsh is well placed at the corner of this freestanding monument.[116] It differs in several notable respects from the minaret built by Qaytbay earlier at his complex in the cemetery. Its profile shows one major anomaly: the elimination of a first octagonal storey, with the first balcony being located right above the square base of the minaret. The first balcony lacks the traditional muqarnas corbels beneath it; instead, it stands above a flaring octagonal cornice carved with a diamond pattern similar to that already applied

in the same location on the minaret of the mosque of Qadi Yahya at Bulaq. Although other minarets, such as those at the mosques of Qadi Yahya at Bulaq, Qaytbay at Rawda and the minaret of Emir Yashbak Min Mahdi at the shrine of Imam al-Layth, also lack muqarnas cornices at their first level, their lower shafts have not been dwarfed in the manner that is apparent here. With the contraction of the first storey, the profile of this minaret lost the harmony of its proportions. This short-coming is compensated for, however, by the superb carved decoration, displaying in the cylindrical section a geometric star pattern, recalling forms of wooden inlaid marquetry, combined with arabesque infills. Above the cylindrical section is a pavilion, of the type with piers rather than columns that displays an unusual combination of arch-types in its structure. A bold muqarnas cornice leads to a ring of 'spikes' above which sits the bulb. This has a rare inscription band around its neck: the only inscription in fact to be found on this minaret. It is, however, fragmentary and illegible. All the pierced stone balustrades are replacements.

70. THE MOSQUE OF EMIR TIMRAZ AL-AHMADI (1477)

The stone minaret of the mosque of the Emir Timraz, located close to the former route of the Khalij near the mosque of Sayyida Zaynab, is remarkable for a number of reasons.[117] It rises at the same level as the adjacent mausoleum dome – untypically, this is below the rest of the façade, which includes the portal. This irregularity suggests that the mosque was not built at the same time as the mausoleum and that the minaret and the mausoleum were erected together. The plain base of the minaret interrupts the crenellation of the portal, which is visibly higher than that of the mausoleum on the other side of the minaret. At the mosque of Fayruz, where the minaret stands in a similar relationship to the façade, an attempt was made to continue this line by carving the crenellations into the shaft of the minaret. In this case, the different levels of the façade did not allow such a solution.

FIG. 192

The minaret of the mosque of Emir Timraz al-Ahmadi

An important innovation displayed by this minaret is in the treatment of the transitional zone above the rectangular base. This has been raised up to the level of the miniature balconies on the octagonal first storey. The transitional zone is thus downplayed, though it is still expressed architecturally as undulating volutes, and the first storey is effectively compressed. The third development seen here is decorative rather than architectural. The intricate decoration of the central section of the minaret takes on the theme introduced at the minaret of Mughulbay Taz but elaborates the design and refines the carving. Instead of plain trilobed frames superimposed on the network of arabesques, a zigzag of plain trilobed arches interacts with a network of arabesques drawn with grooved lines.

Apart from these features, the minaret has a fairly standard articulation of its first storey, and a pavilion supported by octagonal marble columns and bulb above. The minaret is not inscribed, and the pierced stone balustrades on the balconies are replacements. The juxtaposition of the major architectural elements of the complex – the portal, the minaret and the mausoleum dome – have been less successful in this case than in other contemporary mosques.

71. THE MOSQUE OF EMIR JANIM AL-BAHLAWAN (1478)

The decoration of the minaret and the façade are remarkable features at this mosque, located on the main artery of the historic city to the south of the Bab Zuwayla. The original minaret, however, which was badly damaged, was pulled down at the beginning of the twentieth century and reconstructed by the Comité under the direction of Herz Pasha, who also published a study of this mosque.[118] Herz reported that the minaret was rebuilt using the original stones and loose blocks that were found in the premises; these included fragments of the bulb that could be thus restored according to its original profile.

The minaret stands immediately to the left of the entrance, slightly set back from the line of the façade. As with the minaret of Timraz al-Ahmadi,

FIG. 193

The minaret of the mosque of Emir Timraz al-Ahmadi, detail

the transitional zone is merged with the octagonal section of the first storey at the level of the miniature balconies. In this case, however, its finely carved triangles of masonry have shallow pyramidal projections that further accentuate this element. The muqarnas cornice at the top of the first storey is delicately pierced with arabesque patterns, which was an innovation of this period.

Noteworthy also is the carved pattern of the minaret's second storey, which is among the finest of that century. As on the dome of Qaytbay's mausoleum, the carved design here is double-layered, displaying a geometric pattern, in the shape of a sequence of trilobed arches, filled with arabesques. The arcade represents a further elaboration of the theme initiated at the minaret of Mughulbay Taz and further developed at the minaret of Timraz al-Ahmadi. Here, the plain lines of the trilobed arches display knots, a pattern which was common in metalwork and was later applied to the carved decoration of the dome of the emir Khayrbak built in 1502. The horizontal band above this section is carved with arabesques instead of an inscription. The individual units of the muqarnas cornice of this storey display a variety of decorative patterns. This treatment is also extended to the muqarnas of the upper pavilion that supports the final bulb of the minaret. The carved decoration is lavish and a clear testimony of *horror vacui*; to

FIG. 194

The minaret of Emir Janim al-Bahlawan

FIG. 195

The minaret of the mosque of Emir Janim al-Bahlawan, detail

what extent this reflects the patron's or the Comité's creativity is difficult to tell.

EPIGRAPHY

First storey
Sura 3:190–1

72. THE MINARET OF EMIR YASHBAK MIN MAHDI AT THE SHRINE OF IMAM AL-LAYTH (1479)

The stone minaret that the emir Yashbak min Mahdi, the Great Secretary of Sultan Qaytbay, added to the shrine of Imam al-Layth is a freestanding construction located on the south-west side of the mosque, above a public passage connecting it to the street.[119] However, the minaret seems to have been once attached to another structure belonging to the mosque, perhaps a fountain or dwellings that are no longer extant. This is suggested by the entrance to the staircase of the minaret, which faces the mosque above the passage. This entrance, today inaccessible except by a ladder, must originally have been reached from the roof of a building nearby connected to the mosque.

The carving that decorates this minaret is

noticeably shallower throughout than that of its contemporaries, but it has novel architectural and decorative treatments that give it quality. The first storey is octagonal and has a low-level inscription band, with a foundation text, that runs immediately above the transitional zone formed by pyramidal masonry blocks. The shaft is plain, without keel-arched niches or miniature balconies. Instead, four narrow semicircular arched staircase windows alternate with delicately carved arabesque medallions with trefoil tops and bottoms. This is an unusual form of decoration to be seen on the shaft of a minaret, and it is more commonly found in bookbindings. A carved frieze running along the facets of the octagonal section displays a pseudo-Kufic pattern of the type found on some contemporary metal vessels. At the top of the first storey, instead of an inscription, a decorative band displays a miniature arcade combined with an intricate knotted moulding. In the place of the traditional muqarnas corbels supporting the first balcony, the octagonal section of the shaft flares beneath the balcony, displaying a two-tiered concave band carved with two different arabesque patterns. This double-cornice device recalls the minarets of Emir Shaykhu, but there the concave bands are carved with vertical ribs. Here, the underside of both cornices is carved with an interlocking arabesque pattern.

The cylindrical second storey is carved in high relief with a geometrical star pattern. The raised geometrical lines are cut along their length to produce contrasting underlines of shadow and light that emphasise the design. The stars and hexagons are also filled with arabesques. Immediately above this carved area is another inscription band with a Koranic text. A more conventional cornice of muqarnas starts above this, and creates a circular platform for the upper structure that is now missing. The balcony of the first storey has a timber railing.

EPIGRAPHY

First storey
'The foundation of this blessed minaret was ordered by his excellency, the most noble, the lofty, the lordly, the great emir, the sovereign, the well-served, the holy warrior, the defender, the protector of frontiers, the

FIG. 197

*The minaret of the mosque of Qadi Abu Bakr
ibn Muzhir*

assisted by God, the provider, the magnanimous, the
steadfast, the master, the succour Sayf al-Din Yashbak
min Mahdi, (executive secretary) of al-Malik al-Ashraf
[Qaytbay], may his victory be glorified, in four…'
(884/1479). [120]

Second storey
Sura 2:255

73. THE MOSQUE OF QADI ABU BAKR IBN MUZHIR (1480)

The minaret of the mosque of Abu Bakr ibn Muzhir
is set flush with the main façade,[121] and stands
immediately to the right of the main portal on what
is now the corner of the building. It is clear, however,
that a major part of the façade to the right of the
minaret, which would have matched that to the left
in height, is no longer there. This would have altered
the architectural configuration. As at the mosque
of Timraz al-Ahmadi, no attempt is made to conceal
the base of the minaret behind a line of crenellations.
Also following earlier examples, the transitional zone,
which is here articulated by a double moulding with
loops, merges with the octagonal first storey of the
shaft, with its corner triangles set between the four
miniature balconies. The hoods of the keel-arched
niches are integrated in the muqarnas cornice, being
set between its lower niches to unite the two decorative
elements.

Although it may be said that relatively little change
takes place in the architecture of the minaret during
the reign of Sultan Qaytbay, there is not a single
repetition in the pattern of carved decoration that
adorns the middle cylindrical section of minarets
constructed at that time. The patterns of the muqarnas
also varied markedly from one structure to another.
In the decoration of its second storey, the minaret
of Abu Bakr shares the same design scheme with a
number of other minarets erected during the reign
of Sultan Qaytbay. Within this group, it belongs to
a sub-category of minarets displaying a geometrical
composition carved on their cylindrical middle
sections. These are the minarets at the mosques

FIG. 198

The mosque of Emir Qijmas al-Ishaqi, elevation

of Qaytbay in the cemetery, at Qal'at al-Kabsh and al-Azhar, and the mosques of Khushqadam al-Ahmadi and Azbak al-Yusufi. The later minaret of Khayrbak, which also has geometrical decoration, differs in being made of brick decorated with stucco rather than stone. The curvilinear geometrical star pattern seen on the minaret of Abu Bakr has an earlier parallel on the mausoleum dome of the Emir Janibak in the funerary complex of Sultan Barsbay, built in the 1430s.[122] It can also be seen in a wooden version on the minbar or pulpit made for the mosque of Shaykh Muhammad al-Ghamri, which is now in the mosque of Barsbay.

The pavilion and upper bulb of the minaret are Comité replacements, as are the pierced stone balustrades at balcony levels. The minaret has no inscription.

74. THE MOSQUE OF EMIR QIJMAS AL-ISHAQI (1481)

The mosque of Qijmas al-Ishaqi is built on a tight triangular plot where the road forks on the slope of the Darb al-Ahmar.[123] The minaret and the adjacent dome are sparsely decorated when compared with the remainder of the façade. Was this an aesthetic decision by the builder to let the profiles of the minaret and the dome impress the viewer without recourse to any of the very elaborate and varied surface finishes seen on the remainder of the façade and inside the mosque? Or had the money run out by the time the two last elements, the minaret and dome, were built? An argument for the latter hypothesis can be seen in the transitional zones of both structures. The dome has a well-finished stone transitional zone but was completed in plastered brick, while the minaret has strapwork mouldings defining the edges of the transitional zone but nowhere else on its shaft. The transitional zone is integrated in the octagonal first storey at the level of the miniature balconies, following the system established on the minarets of Timraz al-Ahmadi, Janim al-Bahlawan and Abu Bakr ibn Muzhir. The first storey has an otherwise traditional arrangement of niches and muqarnas, and the second circular storey is entirely plain. The

FIG. 199

The minaret of the mosque of Qijmas al-Ishaqi

pavilion, bulb and balustrades are all additions of the Comité.[124] Given the general tendency of the period to leave no surface undecorated, the bare minaret of Qijmas is a remarkable exception.

FIG. 200

The minaret of Shaykh Abu 'l-'Ila

75. THE MOSQUE OF SHAYKH ABU 'L-'ILA (c.1485–6)

The mystic shaykh Abu 'Ali, popularly called Abu 'l-'Ila, lived in a *zawiya* by the shore of the Nile at Bulaq in the fifteenth century. The life of Shaykh Abu 'l-'Ila is described in his biography as most wondrous, full of miracles and metamorphoses, alchemy and other fantastic deeds that read like a fairy tale. The funerary mosque that bears his name was built for him by one of his disciples, a merchant called Nur al-Din 'Ali ibn al-Qanish, from the town of Burullus.[125] The construction of the mosque predates the death of the shaykh in 1486. The mosque was heavily restored in the years 1915–20. The dome and the minaret maintained their original features although the minaret was dismantled and rebuilt using the same stone blocks but with a new upper structure.

Architecturally, the minaret of Abu 'l-'Ila resembles many others of the Qaytbay period; its decoration, however, is unusual. The transitional zone is in the 'normal' position below the area occupied by the projecting miniature balconies. The keel-arched recesses of the octagonal first storey have the usual cluster of three colonettes separating them, but their hoods are decorated with arabesques, which are repeated in the spandrels between them. A plethora of mouldings gives definition to the different elements that make up the shaft. Below each of the two balconies carved arabesques fill the space between the hanging muqarnas triangles. The decoration of the circular second storey is unique; instead of carving it is executed in bichrome inlaid stone displaying a geometric pattern of rectangular loops linked diagonally in a zigzag composition. Below the muqarnas cornice of the upper balcony is an area of carved arabesque above a frieze carved with a series of trilobed arches filled with arabesques; this frieze is reminiscent of the one that runs around the first storey of the minaret of Yashbak at the shrine of Imam al-Layth. The pavilion, bulb, and pierced stone balustrades are all Comité replacements.

This minaret deserves special attention, however, because of its inscriptions. These quote eighteen verses from *Surat al-Mulk*, or 'Sovereignty' of the Koran

(Sura 67). This Sura is inscribed on the minaret in different places, with a heavier concentration of texts on the lower, more visible, part of the shaft. Unusually, the texts are also inscribed using different scripts. Four square panels with geometric Kufic are set in the transitional zone, two epigraphic bands in the usual *thuluth* script run around the lower and the upper parts of the octagonal first storey and a further four square panels sit between its small balconies. A final band is located at the top of the circular second storey of the minaret.

The text of *Surat al-Mulk*, is loaded with mystic lyricism and symbolism. It deals with the miracle of creation and the beauty of the universe, stresses the contrast between the divine scheme and the human perception of it. It warns unbelievers with powerful descriptions of Hell and promises resurrection to the righteous. The choice of this text, which belongs to the late Meccan Suras, was probably not haphazard, as it is the only time this text is ever used in architectural epigraphy in medieval Cairo. Indeed, this Sura has great significance in Sufism. The traveller Ibn Battuta, who visited Cairo in the first half of the fourteenth century, reported that it had a special place in the rituals of Sufis in Cairo. According to a tradition, reading the *Surat al-Mulk* is equivalent to worship on *Laylat al-Qadr*, the 'Night of the Power'. That night, the 27th of the holy month of Ramadan, is described in Sura 97 in the Koran as 'a night of peace, better than a thousand months', when the doors of Heaven are open and the angels come down to fulfil man's hopes. Endowed with this inscription, the minaret stands as a link between the community of the mosque of Abu 'l-'Ila and Heaven itself.

The text inscribed on the minaret is exclusively from Sura 67, which is composed of thirty verses, eighteen of which, from the beginning of the Sura, are carved on the shaft. The text fills three horizontal bands on the shaft, starting from the top, and continues further in the square panels in the lower part of the shaft between the miniature balconies, ending on the south-west panel. These inscribed panels are unique, and they show just how keen the patron must have been to inscribe as much as possible of the Sura on the minaret: more than the three horizontal bands could contain, so that eventually it became necessary to

add these extra four panels. The text continues on the north-west panel and ends abruptly on the south-west panel in the middle of verse 18. Apparently it was not possible to determine with precision how much space the inscription would require; the rectangular panels themselves may have been inscribed at the last moment.

The square epigraphic panels in geometric Kufic script, set on the base of the minaret, represent the only documented use of geometric Kufic on a minaret in Cairo. It is possible that the text formed a continuation of Sura 67, though this would not justify a change in script from *thuluth* to Kufic. Unfortunately, the panels can no longer be read because when the minaret was dismantled and reconstructed by the Comité, the stone blocks were mixed up and the panels wrongly reassembled. Because these verses of Sura 67 occur only once in Cairo on this minaret, and are a major feature of its design, a translation is provided below.

EPIGRAPHY

Second storey
Sura 67:1–3. 'In the name of God, the Lord of Mercy, the Giver of Mercy. "Exalted is He who holds all control in His hands; who has power over all things; who created death and life to test you [people] and reveal which of you does best – He is the Mighty, the Forgiving; who created the seven heavens, one above the other."'

First storey upper band
Sura 67:3–8. 'You will not see any flaw in what the Lord of Mercy creates. Look again! Can you see any flaw? Look again! Your sight will turn back to you weak and defeated. We have adorned the lowest heaven with lamps and made them [missiles] for stoning devils for whom We have also prepared the torment of a blazing fire. For those who defy their Lord We have prepared the torment of Hell: an evil destination. They will hear it drawing its breath when they are thrown in it. It blazes forth almost bursting with rage. Its keepers will ask every group that is thrown in "Did no one come to warn you?"'

First storey lower band
Sura 67:8–14. 'They will reply, "Yes, one came to

warn us, but we did not believe him." We said, "God has revealed nothing: you are greatly misguided". They will say, "If only we had listened, or reasoned, we would not be with the inhabitants of the blazing fire", and they will confess their sins. Away with the inhabitants of the blazing fire! But there is forgiveness and a great reward for those who fear their Lord though they cannot see Him. Whether you keep your words secret or state them openly, He knows the contents of every heart. How could He who created not know His own creation…'

First storey rectangular panels
Sura 67:14–18. 'when He is the Most Subtle, the All aware? It is he who has made the earth manageable for you – travel its regions; eat His provision – and to Him you will be resurrected. Are you sure that He who is in Heaven will not make the earth swallow you up with a violent shudder? Are you sure that He who is in Heaven will not send you a whirlwind to pelt you with stones? You will come to know what my My warning means. Those who went before them disbelieved…'

76. THE MOSQUE OF EMIR KHUSHQADAM AL-AHMADI (1486)

Khushqadam converted a fourteenth-century residence into his mosque and added to it a minaret aligned with the street.[126] It is difficult to judge how this minaret was originally related to any other elements of the façade created by Khushqadam, since these have largely disappeared. The minaret, however, stands to the top of its second storey and is another remarkable example of the craft of carving from the time of Sultan Qaytbay.

The square base of the minaret is articulated with plain engaged columns on each of the corners, in the tradition established by Sultan Inal at his complex. The transitional zone, like many others from this decade, merges with the octagonal first storey with its corner triangles set between the miniature balconies articulated by a double moulding segmented by loops. The corner triangles are carved with pyramidal

FIG. 201

The minaret of the mosque of Emir Khushqadam al-Ahmadi

projections in the manner of Janim al-Bahlawan's minaret and framed by a double moulding with loops. A similar moulding runs around the hoods of the keel-arched niches, forming a pentagonal loop above each of their apexes. A complex geometric pattern adorns the circular shaft of the second storey. Its pierced stone balustrades are modern replacements.

77. THE MOSQUE OF SULTAN QAYTBAY AT RAWDA (1491)

The mosque of Qaytbay on the island of Rawda was designed by the royal master-builder, the *mu'allim* al-Badri Hasan ibn al-Tuluni, a descendant of the master-builder who constructed the complex of Sultan Barquq in the Bayn al-Qasrayn.[127] Ibn Iyas reports that al-Badri lived on the island, which explains why he acted as a co-sponsor of the foundation by endowing it with a monthly religious festival that used to attract a large audience. People came by boat from the mainland to listen to Koran recitations, sitting in tents illuminated with a multitude of lanterns. The event was called 'Badriyya' after the sponsor, and on this occasion, the stately minaret must also have been brightly illuminated.

The mosque stands out among its contemporaries for the profile of its minaret and its interior stucco decoration, which was exceptional at that time – only the dome of Yashbak in the northern suburb of Cairo is decorated with stucco carvings. The octagonal first storey culminates in a flaring cornice instead of the usual muqarnas. The second storey, which is cylindrical, is plain except for a double moulding at its upper part beneath a concave band. It is only the third storey, which is also cylindrical and plain, that bears a muqarnas cornice. Judging from its present configuration, this minaret may have been built initially with another storey: it is difficult to imagine that the bulb rested directly over the balcony without the traditional pavilion beneath it. Other minarets of that time, like those of Bardabak and Qijmas al-Ishaqi, have their second storeys bare of decoration, in contrast to main-stream practice. Both the mosque and the minaret were heavily damaged by a gunpowder explosion in 1801 and subsequently restored on more than one occasion.

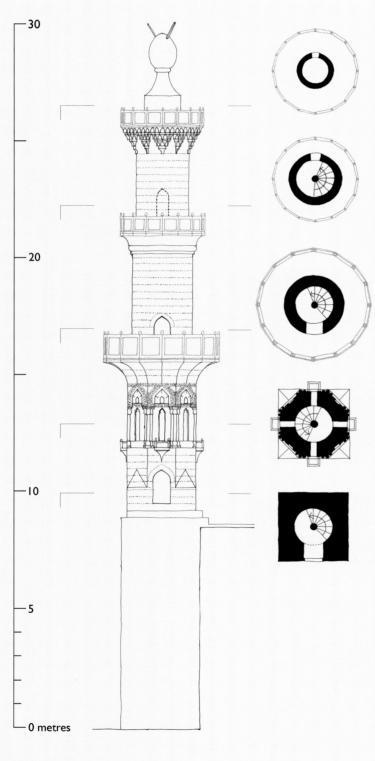

FIG. 202

*The minaret of the mosque of Sultan Qaytbay at Rawda,
elevation and plans*

FIG. 203

The minaret of the mosque of Sultan Qaytbay at Rawda

FIG. 204

The minaret of the mosque of Sultan Qaytbay at the Azhar mosque

78. THE MINARET OF THE MOSQUE OF SULTAN QAYTBAY AT THE AZHAR MOSQUE (1495)

The minaret added to the mosque of al-Azhar by Sultan Qaytbay was part of a substantial programme of restoration he undertook there, which included the addition of two new portals. The works were completed in Jumada I 900/February 1495.[128] An Anatolian merchant called Mustafa ibn Mahmud ibn Rustam was placed in charge of the construction works. The minaret stands to the north of the inner portal into the courtyard of the mosque, rebuilt by order of Qaytbay. Its profile is graceful, and closer inspection from the roof reveals exquisite workmanship (fig. 34).

The octagonal section is entirely covered with a variety of carved patterns, leaving no space bare of decoration. The keel-arched hoods of the niches on each facet have different designs: radiating ribs with seven or fifteen lobes. Further differentiation is made in the triple-colonettes to each side of the niches: the central column is carved with interlocking bands, those framing the window to the stairwell have horizontal chevrons and those on the other flanks have vertical chevrons. Each keel-arched hood is surrounded by strapwork mouldings that form a pentagonal loop at its apex, similar to but smaller than the pentagons seen at the minaret of Khushqadam al-Ahmadi. A blue-grey marble is used for small inserts in the knots formed by these strapwork mouldings. The same marble is used for inlaid borders above and below the inscription band that crowns the first storey, which documents the sultan's sponsorship of this minaret. The muqarnas cornice beneath the first balcony level is carved and pierced with arabesque motifs.

The first storey also bears a lower inscription band in ornate Kufic script, which is rare on Mamluk minarets. There was a revival of the Kufic script during the reign of Qaytbay, which appears in the inlaid marble decoration of some mosques and also on metal vessels. As mentioned earlier, a pseudo-Kufic frieze adorns the minaret of Yashbak at the shrine of Imam al-Layth. The second storey of the minaret, which is also octagonal, has a central, broad band of carving that takes the form of a braid. Inlaid marble is also used

FIG. 205

The minaret of Sultan Qaytbay at the Azhar mosque, detail of the zone of transition

here. Blue-grey marble is set in the interstices and at the edges of the central band. The leitmotiv of the carved decoration of this minaret is the horizontal braided band. It fills the middle section and is also carved on a pair of carved ribbons above and below it; another pair of ribbons, parallel to these, are carved with chevrons. The overall decoration of this storey is horizontally designed to girdle the shaft. The muqarnas cornice at the top of the second storey is much more sober than its counterpart below, displaying only a minimal carved decoration. The upper pavilion is a cylindrical construction with four arched openings flanked by engaged columns rather than an octagonal pavilion with eight piers, or a pavilion supported by marble columns. The bulb has an inscription carved around its neck, like Qaytbay's mosque at Qal'at al-Kabsh and the earlier precedents of the minarets of Shaykhu and Tatar al-Hijaziyya.

The pierced stone balustrades at the level of the first balcony appear to be original, owing to the refinement of their carving, which alternates geometric and arabesque patterns in each panel. The remainder of the balustrades are of inferior quality and likely to be replacements.

One more feature of this minaret deserves mention. The entrance to the staircase at the roof level of the mosque is, uniquely, surmounted by an inscribed

cartouche with the Koranic quotation 'Enter it in Peace and Faith', referring to Paradise. The staircase itself is roofed with a spiral barrel vault. The shaft of the second storey contains a double-helix stair, as at the contemporary minaret of Azbak al-Yusufi, that is accessed through two separate entrances at balcony level.

EPIGRAPHY

First storey
'Basmala, our lord and master dominant over us, the sovereign, al-Malik al-Ashraf Abu 'l-Nasr Qaytbay, may his victory be glorified, sultan of Islam and the Muslims, slayer of the infidels and idolaters, the Sultan al-Malik al-Ashraf Qaytbay has ordered the construction of this blessed minaret.'[129]

Bulb
Fragments of an inscription, illegible.

79. THE MOSQUE OF EMIR AZBAK AL-YUSUFI (1495)

The mosque of Azbak al-Yusufi stands just to the west of Saliba Street not far from the mosque of Sarghitmish.[130] The minaret is placed flush with the façade to the immediate right of the main portal, following the orientation of the street. The design of the first storey of the minaret is similar to that of the minaret of Mughalbay Taz, located a short distance away. The surface of the transitional zone is carved with arabesques delineated with mouldings that define the profile of this entire section. The carving of the octagonal first storey is conventional and exquisite. Its upper and lower inscription band refer to the foundation of the minaret, discussed below. The pattern carved on the second-storey cylindrical shaft is similar, but not identical, to that seen on the minaret of the madrasa of Sultan Qaytbay at Qal'at al-Kabsh. It is a deeply carved geometric intricate pattern of interlocking crosses set on the diagonal, reminiscent of woodwork. An inscription band completes the decoration of the shaft.

FIG. 206

The minaret of the mosque of Emir Azbak al-Yusufi

The most remarkable structural feature of the minaret of Azbak, however, can only be seen within its shaft. This is the double-helix staircase that runs from the first to the second balcony levels. As this and the minaret of Qaytbay at the Azhar mosque were completed in the same month, it can be assumed that the same Anatolian master-builder, Ibn Rustam, who built the minaret of Qaytbay, was also responsible for the double staircase in this one. The staircases have elegant stone semicircular vaults marked at the springings with profiled mouldings.

Both the mosque itself, which displays a striking density of historical and Koranic inscriptions on its walls and furnishings, and the minaret are inscribed. The latter has two epigraphic bands: the upper band is Koranic and the lower, more visible, band bears a foundation inscription with the full titles of the emir and a date, which corresponds to February 1495. Compared with the other dating inscriptions inside the mosque, this indicates that the minaret was erected at the same time as the rest of the construction. It is curious, however, that of all the historical inscriptions in this mosque, this is the only one to refer to Azbak's pilgrimage, which he performed twelve years before the foundation of the mosque, in 887/January–February 1483, and to include his title *hajj*.[131] After the minarets of Bashtak and Mughulbay Taz, this is the only Mamluk minaret not added to a pre-existing mosque to bear a foundation inscription. Unlike the inscription of the minaret of Bashtak, which is set in a cartouche above the entrance to its staircase and is visible only from the roof of the mosque, the text of Azbak occupies a prominent position on the shaft of the minaret. Azbak was obviously particularly keen to thoroughly document his pious foundation with exact dates for all elements of the monument.[132]

EPIGRAPHY

First storey upper and lower bands
'His excellency the noble, the eminent, the lofty, the lordly, the authority, Sayf al-Din the bountiful, the supporter, the methodical, the magnanimous, the holy warrior, the defender, the pilgrim to the holy shrine of Mecca, the visitor of the tomb of the Messenger of God, upon him the blessing and salvation, the

fasting, the praying, the worshipper, the God-fearing, the pious, the great emir, the revered, the masterful, the bountiful, Sayf al-Din Azbak al-Yusufi chief of the guards of al-Malik al-Ashraf, has ordered the construction of this auspicious minaret, dated Jumada the first 900 of the Hijra.'[133]

Second storey

33:41–2

80. THE MOSQUE OF SHAYKH BADR AL-DIN AL-WANA'I (1496)

The foundation deed of the mosque of Badr al-Din al-Wana'i, situated near the cemetery of Sayyida Nafisa, is dated 902/1496.[134] The founder, who is buried there, has no documented biography. The minaret is made of stone, with an octagonal first and a circular second storey. The first storey seems more massive than was common at that time, but has the usual arrangement of keel-arched niches, engaged columns, and miniature balconies. The niches of the octagonal section are framed by a course of inlaid stones that form a loop at their apex. The sunken band beneath the first balcony has no inscription. The cylindrical second storey is plain. The muqarnas beneath the balconies is the only decoration to be carved on the shaft. The impression that the profile of the minaret is pronouncedly tapered is increased by the partial walling up of the top pavilion which was originally supported by eight rather short piers with engaged external columns. The present bulb is made of wood, and the railings of the balconies, though missing, were probably also made of timber.

81. THE MOSQUE OF AL-'ALAYA (late fifteenth century)

Although the Index assigns this building to the seventeenth century, its minaret looks like a fine example of late Mamluk craftsmanship.[135] A surviving endowment deed mentions the mosque of al-'Alaya

FIG. 207

The minaret of the mosque of Shaykh Badr al-Din al-Wana'i

as being the foundation of Qilij Arslan Sultan of al-'Alaya.[136] 'Alaya, or Alanya, is the name of the Anatolian port city founded by the Seljuk Sultan of Rum, 'Ala' al-Din Kaykubad, in the early thirteenth century.[137] In 1427, the Qaraman ruler handed the city over to the Mamluk sultan al-Ashraf Barsbay. When the Ottomans captured 'Alaya in 1471, it was governed by a descendant of the Seljuk dynasty, Qilij Arslan, son of Lutfi Bey. A son of Qilij Arslan lived in Egypt and died there in 913/1507. The information given in the sources dates this minaret to the late Mamluk period, some time before 1507, and is complemented by the style of the minaret, which does not in any way reveal the Anatolian origin of the patron.

The minaret of al-'Alaya is built of brick with stucco decoration. The octagonal first storey bears the conventional decorative features of the period, which include the moulding running along the sides of the transitional zone. The most remarkable feature of the minaret, however, is the spiky profile of the second storey, resulting from its zigzag profile articulated with brickwork, aleady documented in a series of minarets of the late Mamluk period following the example of the minaret of Sultan Inal. The muqarnas of the second storey and the pavilion above are both missing.

82. THE MINARET AT THE MOSQUE OF EMIR AL-KHATIRI (second half of the fifteenth century)*

The mosque of al-Khatiri was founded in Bulaq by Emir 'Ilzz al-Din Aydumur al-Khatiri in 737/1336.[138] Nothing of the original building, once located on the Nile shore at Bulaq, has survived. Maqrizi praised the mosque of al-Khatiri for its beauty and the lavishness of its decoration. The minaret, which was destroyed in the 1960s, shown on the archival photograph reproduced here could not have been, for stylistic reasons, the original one built by al-Khatiri. Its brick shaft was decorated in the spiky style displayed on the previous minaret of al-'Alaya. The overall style of the minaret attributes it to the second half of the fifteenth century. The upper muqarnas could be a restoration of the Ottoman period.

FIG. 208

The minaret of the mosque of al-'Alaya

FIG. 209

The minaret of the mosque of Emir al-Khatiri

83. THE MOSQUE OF SULTAN AL-ʿADIL TUMANBAY (1501)*

Sultan al-ʿAdil Tumanbay ruled for only four months, from January to April 1501. He nevertheless built a large religious complex, which included a mosque with his mausoleum alongside residential and commercial structures, along the caravan road at the edge of the northern cemetery.[139] Today, only a lonely dome has survived within the military barracks on the road to Heliopolis: Ibrahim Pasha, the son of Muhammad ʿAli, demolished the complex to build a paper factory on the site. His nephew ʿAbbas I, who planned to rebuild it, died before implementing his scheme.

A nineteenth-century watercolour by Owen Jones shows the remains of the mosque with a carved masonry dome and a minaret built in the late Mamluk style.[140] The minaret seems to have been located at the corner of the complex, adjacent to the main portal, and was built flush with the façade. It had an octagonal first storey decorated with arched recessed panels, and an entirely plain circular second storey. The circular third storey was articulated with eight lobed openings, but the upper structure of the minaret is missing in the drawing.

84. THE FUNERARY COMPLEX OF EMIR AZDUMUR (1502)

The funerary complex to which the minaret of Azdumur was attached was located near the aqueduct of Sultan al-Ghawri below the Citadel.[141] The complex disappeared a long time ago, leaving only some ruins behind, and a handsome minaret. The soldiers of Napoleon's expedition used the place as a military base and its minaret as a watchtower. The foundation deed dated 908/1502 describes the complex as a small funerary complex with a stone-domed mausoleum attached to a non-congregational mosque. The mosque, where six Sufis and their shaykh were appointed to hold their gatherings and pray for the dead, was also a kind of mausoleum, being built above a crypt for burial.[142] The minaret seems to have been added as the late Mamluk period. The square base of the shaft has engaged corner columns, and the transitional zone has here been shifted up to correspond with the level of the miniature balconies. The octagonal first storey conforms to the norms of the period. Both the second storey and the upper pavilion are circular and plain. The pavilion is defined by piers with engaged colonettes rather than columns, and the muqarnas below the bulb culminates in a remarkable crown of spikes pointing outwards. The pierced stone balustrades are replacements.

85. THE MOSQUE OF SULTAN AL-GHAWRI (1502–4)

When the historian al-Jabarti reported the demolition of the mosque of Sultan Janbalat, located near the Bab al-Nasr, by Napoleon's troops, he described it as having a double-headed minaret.[143] Janbalat, who ruled briefly in 1500, would have been the first known patron to launch this new design in Cairo, unless we believe Ibn Kathir, who called the northern minaret of Sultan Hasan double-headed. A recent study of the minarets of the Delta provinces[144] has complicated the history of the multiple-headed minaret by convincingly dating the rectangular double-headed minaret of Shaykh Shaykh Abu 'l-'Abbas al-Ghamri to 1499, which predates the mosque of Janbalat. It is difficult to believe that a mosque founded by or for a provincial shaykh would initiate a design that would be later adopted in Cairo. This raises the unanswered questions as to when and where exactly the double-headed upper structure appeared for the first time in the evolution of the minaret.

Sultan al-Ghawri founded his funerary complex only a year after Janbalat built his mosque. It has a spectacular minaret of monumental proportions with an upper storey originally made of four bulbs covered with dark blue tiles.[145] Pascal Coste carefully documented the top of the minaret in the nineteenth century, in appreciation of its great architectural significance. The present arrangement of five bulbs is an inaccurate modern reconstruction, which must have copied the top of the minaret of Abu 'l-Dhahab

FIG. 210

Nineteenth-century view of the mosque of Sultan al-'Adil Tumanbay

OWEN JONES

an afterthought. It stands on a separate base near the ruins of the mosque to which it is connected through a passage carried by an arch giving access from the roof to the entrance of the minaret's staircase.

The minaret is made of stone and combines an elegant silhouette with a simple design. Its shaft is bare of carving as is the case with the minarets of Qijmas al-Ishaqi, Bardabak and a few others, contrasting with the majority of the richly carved minarets of

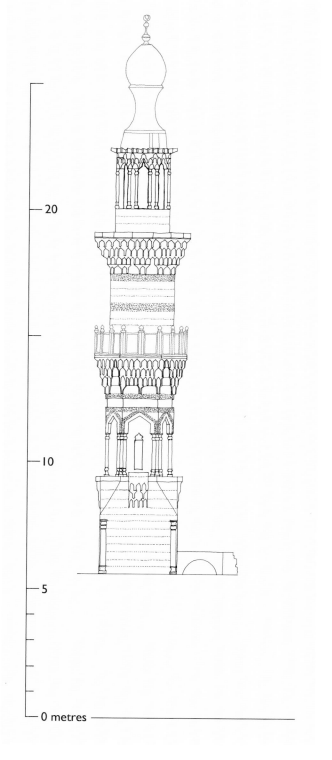

FIG. 211

The minaret of the funerary complex of Emir Azdumur

FIG. 212

The minaret of the funerary complex of Azdumur, elevation

FIG. 213

The minaret of the mosque of Sultan al-Ghawri today, elevation

FIG. 214

The minaret of the mosque of Sultan al-Ghawri

FIG. 215

The minaret of the mosque of Sultan al-Ghawri
PASCAL COSTE

nearby, which itself, with five bulbs, was most likely inspired by the theme of al-Ghawri's quadruple top! Perhaps because of the inexperience of the builder in dealing with such a complex and novel upper structure of four bulbs, each supported by a rectangular pavilion, the minaret of al-Ghawri's mausoleum was not erected without difficulty. Two years after its construction, a deficiency appeared in the masonry that made it necessary to dismantle the minaret and rebuild it. According to Ibn Iyas, the top of the minaret leaned under the heavy weight of the four bulbs, which were rebuilt in brick. This suggests that the initial construction was of stone.

The location of the minaret, projecting onto the street at the south-east corner of the mosque, diverges from that of other royal minarets along the same street. It might be compared, however, with the minaret of Qalawun, which projects at the northern corner of the complex to dominate the street in the perspective of the viewer coming from the north. In al-Ghawri's complex, the minaret addresses the viewer coming from the south, emerging into sight shortly after one passes through the gate of Bab Zuwayla. The minaret was originally balanced by an equally monumental dome, similarly covered with blue tiles, positioned on the opposite side of the street. Taken together, the two superstructures effectively framed the street, including it within the design of the complex. Although separated by the street, the minaret and the dome were harmonised with each other, as a lithograph by Girault de Prangey and Prisse d'Avennes demonstrates.

Unlike the rectangular minarets of Qanibay al-Rammah, and unlike any other minaret of this period, the minaret of al-Ghawri consists of four storeys. It is the first minaret in Cairo to have an entirely square plan at all levels. The fact that it stands on a square base emphasises the verticality of the shaft. Only the minarets of Sultan Hasan have visible and articulated buttresses. Otherwise, the support of the minaret was usually concealed in the thickness of the façade wall.

The original four-headed top storey was covered with glazed lapis blue tiles, as was the third storey. This matched the treatment of the mausoleum dome across the street. The drawing by Coste shows that the centres of the tiles were pierced to allow a nail fixing to the wall behind. An inscription band in painted ceramic

FIG. 216

The minaret of the mosque of Sultan al-Ghawri, original upper structure

PASCAL COSTE

runs along the upper part of the third storey, and similar inscribed bands adorn the square pavilions that support the bulbs. These were probably of the same type of underglaze painted ceramics that appeared in architectural decoration during the reign of Qaytbay. Monochrome tiles continued to be used through the early sixteenth century, as can be seen at the dome of Sulayman Pasha in the Citadel, dated 1528. Besides its tile covering, the dome of al-Ghawri also had an inscription band, executed in underglaze painting, at its base.[146] Coste's drawing of the minaret also shows another feature that cannot be seen today on the top of the second storey: an inscription band. It is unlikely that Coste would have been mistaken in his survey, so one must conclude that this inscription also vanished in a later rebuilding of the upper part of the minaret. The disappearance of these elements has left the minaret today without any inscriptions.

The surviving original sections of the shaft are executed in bichrome masonry throughout, which represents a return to the fourteenth-century style of decoration on minarets. The second storey has a round window on each side, framed by an inlaid interlaced band that has white marble discs set into its cardinal points. Only the minaret of Qalawun provides a precedent for this, and it is of a wholly different architectural character. The first storey displays a blind niche with a pointed stilted arch flanked by columns on each side, with openings to the stairwell and miniature balconies. The inlaid hood around the arch is also decorated at its apex with a disc of inlaid white marble as seen on the second storey. The balustrades of the principal and miniature balconies are all made of timber.

86. THE MOSQUES OF EMIR QANIBAY QARA BELOW THE CITADEL (AT RUMAYLA) AND AT NASIRIYYA (1503, 1506)

During the reign of al-Ghawri, three minarets (including his own) were built with a square section throughout, all made of stone. The two minarets of the mosques of Qanibay Qara, built respectively at Rumayla Square beneath the Citadel and in the quarter of Nasiriyya, are very similar in terms of their design and decoration.[147] It is a pity that both minarets are not the original structures.

Although they share the same design, the minarets of the two mosques of Qanibay are located differently in the context of their respective mosques. The minaret at Nasiriyya occupies a corner of the building while that of the mosque at Rumayla is placed between the portal of the mosque and the entrance to a passage that once led to residential structures. In this location it is separated from the mausoleum dome by the bulk of the mosque. The latter is a careful Comité reconstruction of the 1930s; the present minaret at the mosque of Nasiriyya is a less successful reconstruction that replaces the original, which collapsed in the 1980s.

Both minarets are composed of three storeys and have double-headed tops. With the exception of the muqarnas beneath the balconies, their shafts display no carving. The decoration is rather subtle and confined to bichrome striped masonry and arched recesses. At first-storey level there is one pointed arch on each side, exactly copying the style introduced at the minaret of al-Ghawri. On the second storey is a novel arrangement of three small pointed arches on each side, pierced with openings to introduce light into the stairwells. The upper storey consists respectively of two square pavilions with an arch on each side, crowned by a bulb above a muqarnas cornice. Photographs show that the minaret at Nasiriyya had wooden railings along its balconies, and a drawing by Pascal Coste indicates that this was also the case with the minaret at Rumayla before it was rebuilt with stone balustrades. Both minarets are anepigraphic.

The architect of these towers had a distinct aim, to address the viewer from a distance by emphasising the silhouette of the minaret with the unusual double-headed rectangular shaft rather than displaying a heavily ornamented surface. With this in mind, the positioning of the double pavilions varies at each minaret. At Rumayla they are set parallel to the main façade to be better appreciated from the open square in front of the building, and at Nasiriyya they are at right angles to the façade to allow them to be seen by those

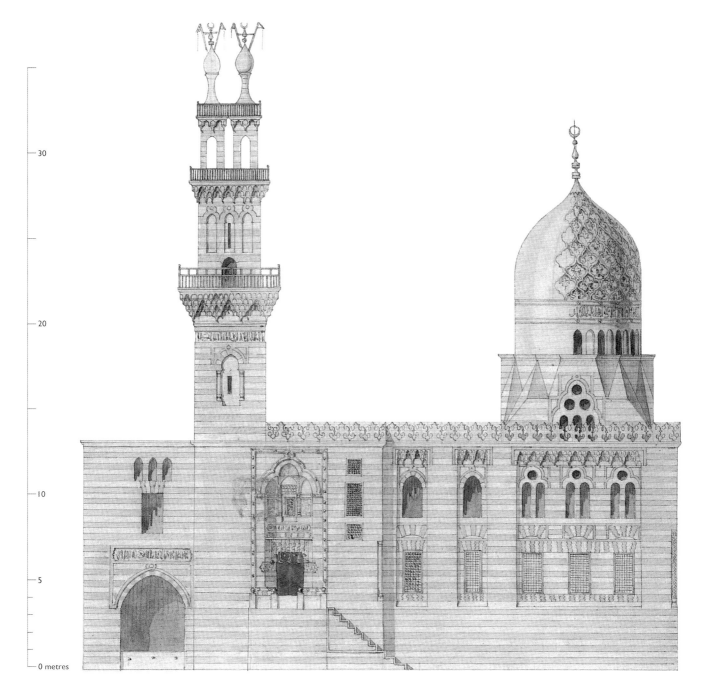

FIG. 217

The minaret of the mosque of Emir Qanibay Qara below the Citadel, elevation

FIG. 218

The minaret of the mosque of Emir Qanibay Qara below the Citadel

FIG. 219

The original minaret of the mosque of Emir Qanibay Qara at Nasiriyya

walking in both directions along the street. This may also be the reason that the Rumayla minaret is set back behind the crenellations of the main façade and the Nasiriyya minaret is set flush with the façade.

87. THE MOSQUE OF EMIR QURQUMAS (1507)

The stone minaret at the funerary complex of Emir Qurqumas in the northern cemetery (fig. 220),[148] built in 1507, ignores the developing pattern of square-shafted minarets in favour of a return to the style created at the minaret of the adjacent complex of Sultan Inal. It is the last extant stone minaret to be built in the 'classic' Mamluk manner. Its position, to the immediate right of the portal facing north, and the position of the funerary dome, seem to be deliberate imitations of the layout of Qaytbay's funerary mosque further south.

The shaft of the minaret of Emir Qurqumas is lavishly carved: even below the transitional zone is a wide band of decorative carving. On the first storey, one inscription band sits immediately above the transitional zone, while another epigraphic band, that is double the normal height, occupies the top of the shaft of this storey. Between the two exuberant carved decoration covers the keel-arches, niches, columns and panels of this section. The second storey also has two inscription bands. While the upper band is set back from the plane of the cylindrical shaft and is bordered by profiled mouldings, the lower inscription is carved directly onto the shaft's surface without a border, as if added in an afterthought.

The most remarkable feature of the minaret of Qurqumas, however, is the unique and interesting pattern that occupies the centre of the second storey. This design departs from the star or arabesque motifs seen on the minarets built during the reign of Qaytbay and presents a further development of the poly-faceted articulation with 'spiky' decoration of some minarets discussed earlier. Here, the shaft combines the star-shaped or spiked plan with a new carving pattern that displays rows of lozenges instead of lines of zigzag. These lozenges are based on the zigzag pattern,

FIG. 221

The minaret of the mosque of Emir Qurqumas

FIG. 220

The minaret of the mosque of Sultan al-Ghawri at 'Arab Yasar

however, with two zigzag lines opposed to each other, in a mirror arrangement, making two triangles meet to form a lozenge.

The pavilion at the top of the minaret is supported by octagonal marble columns and, unusually, has polylobed arches. The neck of the bulb above has a ring at its centre like that on the bulb of the minaret of Qaytbay – possibly a result of restorers using the latter as a model. The pierced stone balustrades are modern replacements.

EPIGRAPHY

First storey upper band
33:41–2

First storey lower band
Sura 2:164

Second storey upper band
Sura 2:255

Second storey lower band
Sura 18:108–9

88. THE MOSQUE OF SULTAN AL-GHAWRI AT 'ARAB YASAR (1510)

The mosque Sultan al-Ghawri erected in 915/1510 in the quarter of 'Arab Yasar on the eastern border of the old hippodrome, facing the Suyuti cemetery, is not a great architectural achievement, nor does it bear royal attributes. It is, however, interesting on other grounds, notably its tiny minaret. Rather than standing above the roof of the mosque, as is normally the case, the minaret rises from the street level, flanking the south-east corner, and projecting forward from it like a corner tower. Because the mosque stands on sloping ground, and the minaret is on the shorter side, its octagonal first storey corresponds to the full height of the building and the elaborate muqarnas of the first balcony level adjoins the crenellations of the façade. This first storey has decoration that is what one might consider a vestigial form of the keel-arched recesses seen on more regular minarets. It has colonettes embedded at the edge of each facet, between which are keel-arches defined by a raised square moulding. This moulding loops at the apex of each arch, and the loop used to be filled with a blue ceramic disc. Only the plain cylindrical second storey rises above the roof of the mosque. The crowning bulb rests above the second muqarnas cornice without the support of a pavilion, which may, however, have once existed. Unusually, this muqarnas cornice has a polylobed perimeter at its top, also seen on the minaret of the mosque of Abu 'l-'Ila.

FIG. 222

*The minaret of the mosque of Sultan al-Ghawri
at the Azhar mosque*

89. THE MINARET OF SULTAN AL-GHAWRI AT THE AZHAR MOSQUE (1511)

The minaret added by Sultan al-Ghawri to the mosque of al-Azhar was built on the site of an earlier ruined minaret,[149] which was removed. This is documented in a foundation deed without, however, any further information regarding the identity of the former minaret being supplied. The previous minaret is likely to have been attached to the madrasa built in 1309–10 by Emir Taybars against the western wall of the mosque. The endowment or *waqf* deed of this minaret is dated 916/1511,[150] which is probably the date of the completion of the work. The document includes an extraordinarily detailed description of the minaret, using technical terms that do not occur elsewhere. According to the document, the minaret was built in the course of a large-scale reconstruction of residential and commercial buildings contiguous to the Azhar.

The main concern of the designer of al-Ghawri's minaret was originality and monumentality. His vast stone minaret at al-Azhar combines exceptional height with an unusual profile that comprises an octagonal first, a twelve-faceted second and a rectangular third storey. This combination of geometries results in a rather heavy elevation, without the receding storeys that are so characteristic of Cairene minarets. The use of the double upper pavilion makes the minaret appear as wide in this storey as in the section below. The pavilions are pierced with stilted arched openings on each side, and have bands of arabesque carved decoration around their tops. They are crowned individually with a narrow muqarnas cornice and support twin bulbs above.

Colour, instead of carving, dominates the second storey in the form of glazed blue ceramic 'arrows' inserted in the masonry in a geometrical arrangement. These lapis blue ceramic elements must have been produced in the same workshop that al-Ghawri established to produced the glazed tiles of the same colour that once decorated his mausoleum dome and the upper section of the minaret attached to his madrasa. Bands of geometric carved decoration border the area occupied by the inlaid tile pattern. The second storey of the minaret also contains a double staircase

FIG. 223

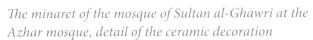

The minaret of the mosque of Sultan al-Ghawri at the Azhar mosque, detail of the ceramic decoration

FIG. 224

The minaret of the mosque of Sultan al-Ghawri at the Azhar mosque, stone carving

described in the *waqf* deed as accessible from two doors and built 'one above the other', a device also used in the adjacent minaret of Qaytbay and the minarets of Azbak al-Yusufi and Khayrbak.

The first storey of the minaret is more conventionally treated. Each facet has a keel-arched niche with hoods of a radiating pattern. These are separated by the usual clusters of three columns carved with chevrons and other geometric patterns. Other interstitial spaces are filled with carved arabesque decoration. The quality of the carving contrasts sharply with that of the minarets of Qaytbay's reign in the last quarter of the fifteenth century; it is shallow and lacks the contrast

effect created by the multilevelled carving, which the decorators of the previous generation artfully accomplished at the minarets of Timraz al-Ahmadi, Mughulbay Taz and Janim al-Bahlawan. It seems as if these craftsmen had suddenly left Cairo or abandoned their craft, without having disseminated their skills.

A foundation inscription is included in a band on the lower part of the shaft, and a second inscription band celebrates the patron on the upper part. As is usual, a separate staircase leads to the roof of the mosque from where the staircase of the minaret is accessible. This is beautifully vaulted, as in the case of the minaret of Qaytbay nearby.

Although *waqf* documents almost never include descriptions of minarets, the *waqf* deed of this minaret is of great interest. It indicates that the railings of the balconies were all made of turned wood originally, and not of the pierced stone used in the recent reconstruction. This evidence is confirmed by nineteenth-century photographs. The muqarnas beneath the miniature balconies and below the first sixteen-sided balcony is called 'Egyptian style' (*misri*). It is described as fashioned with 'eight-shaped', 'twelve-shaped' and 'sixteen-shaped' patterns on five tiers.[151] The muqarnas beneath the second balcony is described as 'Damascene "sixteenish"' (*muqarnas shami sitta 'ashari*). It is interesting that in Mamluk architectural terminology, styles are often defined in geographical or regional terms. There was also an Aleppine and a local or *baladi* style of muqarnas.[152] The foundation deed also mentions that the twin bulbs of al-Ghawri's minaret were each crowned with brass crescents and included three poles for the suspension of lanterns.

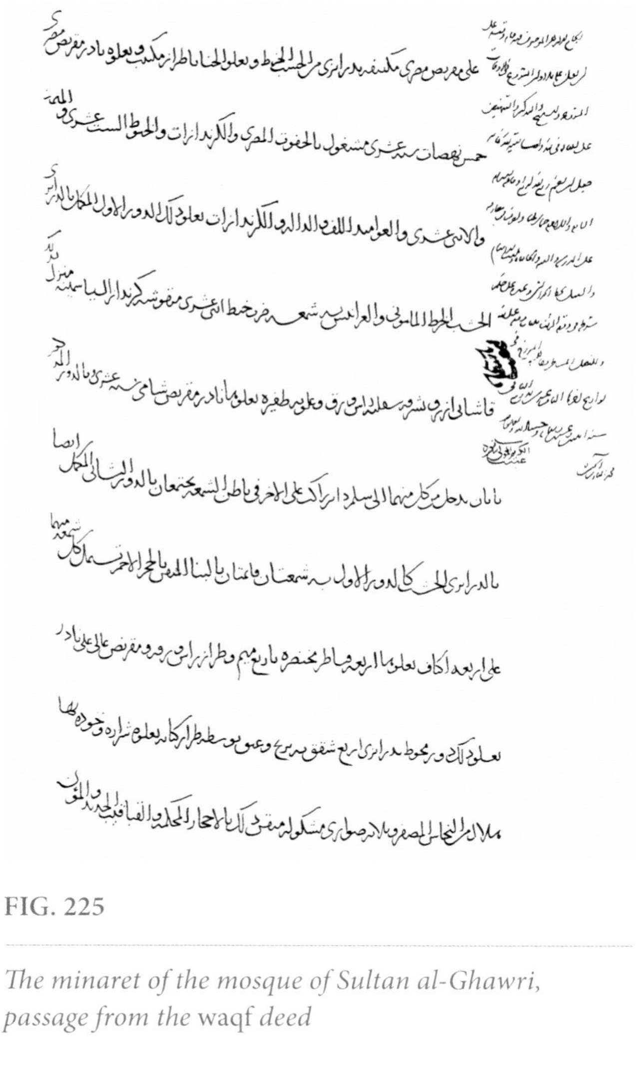

EPIGRAPHY

Base
Foundation inscription mostly abraded

First storey lower band
'Basmala, our lord and master, the reviver of justice in the worlds, father of the poor and the humble, the provider for widows and the dispossessed ... commander of the faithful, guardian of the territory of religion, the Sultan al-Malik al-Ashraf Qansuh al-Ghawri has ordered the construction of this blessed minaret.'[153]

First storey upper band
'Basmala, O God support Islam and ... the best among those who ruled in his time, the Sultan al-Ashraf Abu 'l-Nasr Qansuh al-Ghawri, may his victory be glorified.'[154]

FIG. 225

The minaret of the mosque of Sultan al-Ghawri, passage from the waqf *deed*

90. THE MADRASA OF EMIR KHAYRBAK (1502–20)

The Mamluk emir Khayrbak had been the governor of Aleppo during the reign of Sultan al-Ghawri.[155] As a reward for his betrayal of the sultan and collaboration with the Ottoman conquerors, as well as for the sake of continuity, Sultan Selim appointed him the first governor of Egypt under Ottoman rule.

Although his funerary madrasa adjoining his residence at Tabbana is entirely Mamluk in style,[156] its history reflects the founder's career passing from Mamluk to Ottoman regimes. An inscription dates the domed mausoleum to 908/1502–3. The foundation deed of the madrasa is dated three years after the Ottoman conquest, 927/1520–1. The contemporary chronicler Ibn Iyas mentioned that Khayrbak ordered the burial of the emir Taqtabay in his 'madrasa' in 926/1520, slightly earlier than the date of its endowment deed. This indicates that the madrasa was founded before the deed was drawn up, which was not unusual. It was most likely founded after the Ottoman conquest, which explains why it did not have initially the status of a Friday mosque as was common in late Mamluk princely foundations but not so in Ottoman practice, where a clear-cut separation existed between the madrasa and the Friday mosque. A pulpit or minbar, liturgically necessary for the Friday sermon, was endowed ten years later than the foundation deed, suggesting that eventually, after the death of Khayrbak, the madrasa acquired the status of a Friday mosque. Unfortunately, the foundation document does not mention the minaret, so that it is not known whether it was erected simultaneously with the mausoleum or later after the madrasa was endowed.

Unlike the adjacent masonry dome, the minaret is a brick construction with plastered decoration. It stands above a small vaulted chamber reached through a vestibule connected to the main domed mausoleum. The chamber is at the north-west corner of the main domed mausoleum, sharing the same façade, with two windows overlooking the street. According to the endowment deed, it was a funerary chamber and includes the crypt for burial, where members of Khayrbak's family were interred. The small chamber is built entirely of stone and roofed with a shallow dome supported by pendentives and four round arches at the summit of its four walls. The dome displays concentric stone courses carved with a whirling rosette in the centre surrounded by an inscription band. Another Koranic inscription band runs along the four walls of the room. This vaulting system is analogous to that of the madrasa and other buildings of the reign of Sultan al-Ghawri. It is also structurally adequate for carrying the brick minaret above, which could have been planned to occupy this location from the outset.

The staircase of the minaret is accessible from the roof, through a separate staircase inside the madrasa. This may be an argument for dating the minaret as late as the madrasa, that is, 1520. However, the attachment of a minaret to a funerary complex without the functions of a madrasa was common. Although the madrasa

FIG. 226

The minaret of the madrasa of Emir Khayrbak

was endowed at a later date, the building adjacent to the mausoleum where it was housed may have been built contemporaneously, to be used for Sufi gatherings, as was common in funerary complexes. This space may, at a later date, have been dedicated to fulfil the functions of a madrasa. The axis of the madrasa diverges by a substantial angle from *qibla* orientation, and even from the mihrab axis of the adjacent mausoleum. Perhaps this is a further proof

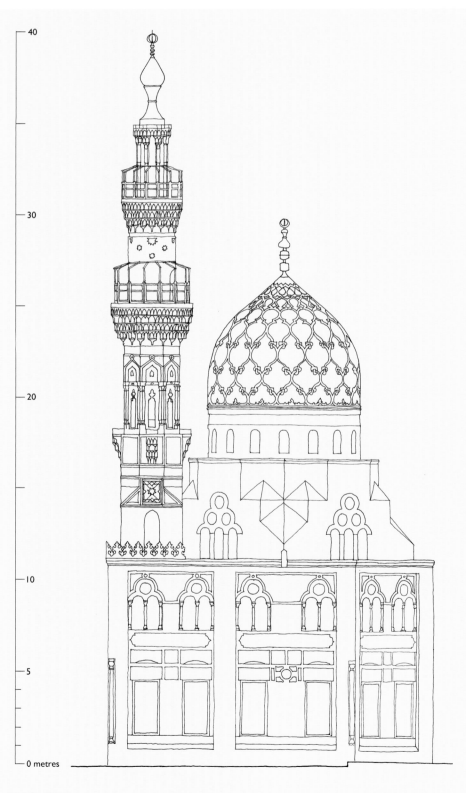

FIG. 227

The minaret of the madrasa of Emir Khayrbak, elevation

that the building did not initially fulfil the function of a madrasa. Unfortunately, there is no historical inscription in the madrasa to clarify the matter.

The construction of the minaret of Khayrbak may not be outstanding, but its position and proportion, especially in relation to the mausoleum dome, are felicitous. It forms an aesthetic, indeed photogenic, composition that strikes the passer-by descending from the Citadel to the city. It was one of the most frequently represented of all Cairo's monuments in the nineteenth century. The builder must have been inspired by the nearby minaret of Aqsunqur, which dominates the street view at a distance and is often seen in the background of Khayrbak's dome and minaret. Together, these monuments form a handsome urban composition that could not escape attention.

As a brick construction, the minaret was decorated with stucco. The octagonal first storey has a conventional arrangement of keel-arches and miniature balconies, and the circular second storey is covered with a geometric pattern of stars. The balconies have wooden railings and the bulb at the top was made of timber lath and plaster. The staircase is made of timber and brick. The staircase from the base of the minaret to the first balcony level is a double-helix staircase with two entrances, while the second storey has only a single spiral stair. This is unlike the double-helix stairs at the minarets of Azbak al-Yusufi, and Qaytbay and al-Ghawri at al-Azhar, which occupy the second storey of the construction rather than the first. There are no inscriptions on this minaret, which was the last genuine Mamluk minaret to be built in Cairo. Subsequent Ottoman governors adopted the pencil-shaped minaret, as did other founders, even when the main building was in a Mamluk or 'fusion' style.

FIG. 228

Vault supporting the minaret of the madrasa of Emir Khayrbak

FIG. 229

The minaret of the mosque of Sulayman Pasha

ELEVEN

Minarets under Ottoman Rule

91. THE MOSQUE OF SULAYMAN PASHA (1528)

The earliest mosque built in Cairo after the Ottoman conquest was that of the governor, Sulayman Pasha, within the Citadel. It served a simultaneously founded quarter for the Janissary corps of the Ottoman army. The plan of the mosque is Ottoman, as is the style of its minaret. However, their respective decoration is mostly Mamluk.

The stone minaret remained for more than two centuries, alongside that of Mahmud Pasha, one of the most elegant Ottoman minarets in Cairo. Unlike all subsequent minarets, which are shorter and with only one balcony, the minaret of the mosque of Sulayman Pasha has two balconies on muqarnas rings displaying, in the Mamluk tradition, two different muqarnas patterns. The balconies have wooden railings. Another Mamluk legacy from the late Mamluk period is the use of glazed tiles on the pointed cap of the minaret and on the domes of the mosque and the primary school. These tiles must have been produced in the ceramic workshop established by Sultan Qansuh al-Ghawri for the decoration of the dome and minaret of his funerary complex and his minaret at the Azhar mosque. Similar tiles were also applied on the cap of the later minaret of Shahin al-Khalwati.

Three rings of blind arches adorn the shaft beneath the cap and the two balconies, a device that will be repeated at the Sulaymaniyya in Istanbul, where arched panels beneath the cap are filled with blue ceramic

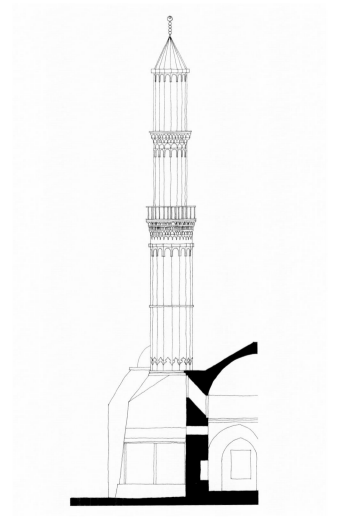

FIG. 230

The minaret of Sulayman Pasha, elevation

FIG. 231

The mosque of Shaykh Shahin al-Khalwati

tiles. Two rings of horizontal moulding decorate the shaft beneath the first balcony.

The integration of a minaret into an Ottoman mosque façade has always required architectural dexterity, which is here totally lacking. The mosque lacks a façade concept and the base of the minaret is clumsy and awkwardly placed near the unpretentious entrance. However, the heavy minaret base allowed the builder to erect a relatively tall shaft that exceeds the 2:1 ratio in relation to the vertical walls.

Sulayman Pasha built another small mosque in Bulaq; its minaret has a cylindrical shaft with two balconies on elaborate muqarnas and an Ottoman conical cap.[1] These two minarets at the Citadel and Bulaq were the first and last Ottoman minarets in Cairo with two balconies.

92. THE MOSQUE OF SHAYKH SHAHIN AL-KHALWATI (1538)

This sanctuary perched on the Muqattam Hills and almost inaccessible was established by the Sufi shaykh Shahin al-Khalwati, as a *zawiya* for retreat and meditation.[2] Shahin, who died in 901/1495–6, had been a soldier of Sultan Qaytbay before he chose the mystic path and asked the sultan for permission to withdraw from his service to dedicate his life to Sufism. He then travelled to Tabriz for initiation into the Khalwati order, which he eventually introduced to Egypt. The Khalwatiyya, whose name derives from *khalwa* meaning 'retreat' was a Sufi order that originated in Azerbayjan. This accounts for the secluded site. The order flourished in the Ottoman Empire and in Egypt after the conquest.

Whereas two other foundations of contemporary Khalwati shaykhs were conceived as *zawiya*s without minaret, it is surprising that this isolated sanctuary should have one. Under Ottoman rule, the Egyptian custom of attaching minarets indiscriminately to all kinds of religious foundations was not maintained. An inscription in this building dated 945/1538 reveals indeed that, four decades after Shahin's death, in spite of its remoteness from urban life, the foundation was turned into a Friday mosque by his son and successor.

It was probably at this date that the minaret was added to the mosque.

The minaret was the second Ottoman-style construction following the minaret of Sulayman Pasha. Its stone shaft is similarly faceted and with two balconies, which have lost their original railing. The remains of tiles on the minaret's cap also recall the minaret of Sulayman Pasha.

93. THE MOSQUE OF MAHMUD PASHA (1568)

Unlike all other Ottoman governors before Muhammad 'Ali, who returned to Istanbul after the end of their short tenure, Mahmud Pasha planned to remain in Cairo.[3] This explains why he attached a mausoleum for himself to his mosque overlooking Rumayla Square beneath the Citadel. The external design of his mosque was inspired by the mosque of Sultan Hasan, and, similarly, the domed mausoleum was erected behind the prayer hall of the mosque. The architect also copied the device of the protruding cylindrical buttress at the corner but, surprisingly, he did better by uniting it with the minaret shaft in a more harmonious manner. He did so by eliminating the rectangular base of the minaret, thus incorporating the whole buttress-and-shaft construction in one tall cylindrical structure. The corner of the roof with its crenels has been extended to turn around the minaret to form a balcony enhanced by a muqarnas frieze beneath it. Another balcony with different muqarnas patterns is attached to the upper part of the shaft.

To further enhance the height and the unity of the shaft with its buttress, the buttress and the shaft have been similarly carved with vertical mouldings that give them a faceted appearance. Horizontal and vertical mouldings meet in the middle and upper part of the buttress and the lower and upper parts of the shaft. The upper section above the second balcony is plain.

The architecture of this minaret is the most original of the entire Ottoman period in Cairo.

FIG. 232

The minaret of the mosque of Mahmud Pasha

94. **THE MOSQUE OF SINAN PASHA** (1571)

Although the mosque of the Ottoman governor Sinan Pasha in Bulaq is a most remarkable building, notably because of its stately stone dome, the minaret is rather disappointing.[4]

Seen in conjunction with the dome, of about 15 metres in diameter, the minaret seems to break the rule of harmony between dome and minaret established in Mamluk architecture. Although the relation of its height to the rectangular walls of the mosque does follow the proportional rule of 2:1 applied in Cairo's minaret architecture, the apex of the dome is almost as high as the summit of the minaret below the cap. This configuration disturbs the mosque's profile; the minaret should have been taller. A close look at its masonry suggests that this may not be the original minaret built by Sinan Pasha. The shaft is made of stone up to the balcony, the upper level is a construction of plastered timber. The stonework is visibly inferior to that of the mosque, especially the muqarnas of its balcony when compared to the muqarnas cornice above the three entrances of the sanctuary; it is rather reminiscent of the ugly muqarnas at the reconstructed minaret at the mosque of Ulmas, with which it may be contemporary'.[5]

FIG. 233

The mosque of Sinan Pasha

FIG. 234

The minaret of the mosque of Sinan Pasha

95. THE MOSQUE OF MALIKA SAFIYYA
(1610)

Although the minaret of this mosque has no remarkable architectural feature, the imperial associations of the mosque to which it belongs and its Ottoman layout make it worth an individual entry. The mosque was originally founded by a black eunuch, 'Uthman Agha, who had been attached to the imperial harem of Sultan Murad III.[6] Like many of his colleagues in charge of the supervision of the pious endowments of the Haramayn, Mecca and Medina, he seems to have planned his retirement in Cairo. He planned the foundation of a mosque with his mausoleum in this quarter, where many other Ottoman black eunuchs were already settled. As a result of intrigues in the imperial harem, however, he was executed before construction work began, and his endowment was invalidated by the sultan's widow, Queen Safiyya, who re-endowed the mosque in her own name and probably ordered a new design for it that would reflect her status. The mosque was erected over a platform that was unique in Cairo but common in Istanbul, accessible through an unusual rounded flight of steps. Its plan with a dome on a hexagonal canopy must have come from Istanbul. The construction modules, however, betray only Egyptian workmanship, which also applies to the very ordinary minaret. It stands at the junction of the sanctuary with its courtyard, in the middle of the lateral, undecorated southern façade of the building.

96. THE MOSQUE OF AL-BURDAYNI
(1629)

The Mamluk style of al-Burdayni's minaret stands out among its contemporaries in Ottoman Cairo. Karim al-Din ibn Ahmad al-Burdayni's biography is not so far documented; his inscribed name indicates that he adhered to the Shafi'i rite and might have been a scholar.[7]

Al-Burdayni erected his mosque in the close vicinity of the slightly earlier Ottoman mosque of Malika Safiyya. Designed entirely in the late Mamluk

FIG. 235

The minaret of the mosque of Malika Safiyya

FIG. 236

The minaret of the mosque of al-Burdayni

style, outside as inside, the little mosque stands in sharp contrast to its Ottoman neighbour, perhaps deliberately. Whereas the mosque of Malika Safiyya is elevated on a platform and dominates the quarter with a domed structure and a symmetrical layout, al-Burdayni's mosque is integrated into its street. Also unlike the queen's mosque, it is lavishly decorated in the Mamluk style – in homage to local traditions?

The minaret of al-Burdayni is inscribed with the illegible founder's name followed by 'al-Shafiʻi' and the date 1038/1629. The inscription inside the mosque identifies the founder as Shaykh al-Burdayni and dates the foundation to 1025/1616. Minarets were usually among the last structures to be added to the construction of a mosque; however, the gap of thirteen years between the foundation of this mosque and the construction of its minaret is unusual. It may be explained by the Mamluk style of the minaret, which was unusual at the time. More than a century after the last Mamluk minaret was erected, it may have been difficult to build and decorate a shaft in this style. By that time, the techniques and modules that set Mamluk architectural proportions, and that were forwarded through apprenticeship or from father to son, were forgotten. The involvement of a builder from the province, where the Mamluk minaret tradition continued, can be excluded on the grounds that provincial minarets were brick constructions without inscriptions. If there were Ottoman regulations prohibiting the construction of Mamluk-style minarets, al-Burdayni may have had to find a way to exempt his own from this rule, which could be another explanation for the long delay between the construction of the mosque and its minaret.

The mosque is richly decorated with carved stone, polychrome marble mosaics and painted wood, to the point of almost exceeding the lavishness of late Mamluk mosques. The minaret has an octagonal first storey with a balcony on a muqarnas; the carved cylindrical middle section is surmounted by a second balcony on a muqarnas of different design. The parapets of the balconies are made of pierced stone and both their muqarnas corbels are of good quality. The upper bulb rises directly above the second balcony without the intermediary of the traditional octagonal pavilion. Ottoman security regulations might have prevented

the builder from adding a pavilion.

This minaret is the only one in Ottoman Cairo to bear an inscription. It is in the Mamluk format of a band at the top of the octagonal shaft and includes the name of the sponsor and the construction date. An upper band beneath the second balcony that would normally be inscribed is carved instead with a decorative pattern. In contrast to Mamluk practice, the minaret is supported by a wall that is shorter than the façade so that its base is below the roof level.

The minaret of al-Burdayni marks the earliest Mamluk revival in Ottoman Egypt. It is unfortunate that no information is available so far about the patron and the circumstances that led him to build a mosque in a style that powerfully evoked Mamluk architecture in the close vicinity of an Ottoman royal foundation and in a quarter that was predominantly inhabited by Ottoman dignitaries. Whether this nostalgia was merely aesthetic or motivated by more profound concerns is not possible to tell with any certainty. It should be recalled, however, that this quarter came to be known around that time as Dawudiyya, referring to Dawud Agha, a black eunuch of the Ottoman imperial harem who had begun, around 1601,[8] to carry out substantial urban transformations in this area and elsewhere in Cairo. The eastern part of Habbaniyya was favoured by the community of imperial black eunuchs who had retired in Egypt, where they supervised the endowments of Mecca and Medina. They enjoyed a prominent status, also acting as sponsors of charitable foundations. It may be speculating too far to suggest that the style of al-Burdayni's minaret is linked to the Ottoman transformations this neighbourhood was under-going. The presence of an inscription band that associates the founder with the Shafiʻi rite is also noteworthy; this was the legal school favoured by the Egyptian population whereas the Ottomans adhered to Hafanism. A political motivation for the Mamluk features of the mosque would imply a 'conceptualisation' of architectural style by its association with political ideology, for which there is no strong evidence in this period. However, the Ottomans, by imposing their minaret style in Cairo, may have already opened such an architectural debate.

FIG. 237

The minaret of the mosque of 'Abidin Bey

EPIGRAPHY

'This blessed minaret was founded by the humble servant [...] the Shafiʿi may God forgive him and his parents in the year 1038.'[9]

97. THE MOSQUE OF ʿABIDIN BEY (1631)

Shortly after al-Burdayni's Mamluk-style minaret was erected, the emir ʿAbidin Bey built a mosque with a remarkable Ottoman minaret. The minaret is all that survived from this mosque, which was entirely rebuilt in 1920.[10] The mosque of ʿAbidin, also called *jamiʿ al-fath*, was built in 1628. ʿAli Mubarak, who refers to its tall minaret, does not give a date. *Waqf* documents attest that Emir ʿAbidin Bey, who was emir of the Pilgrimage Caravan (*amir al-hajj*) developed the quarter that today bears his name between 1619 and 1631.[11] Evliya Çelebi, who wrote in 1672–80, dedicated special attention to this minaret, praising its architecture and decoration in euphoric terms.[12] He described the minaret as a faceted shaft, built in the Istanbul style, its beauty unparalleled not only in Cairo but on earth! He went on to compare it to the decorative palms (*nahil*) that were paraded in sultanic festivals, and to praise its balcony as a cup with rotating stars. Finally, he blessed its architect for the refinement of his work. Evliya Çelebi's praise is justified; this is one of the most elegant minarets of the period because of its proportions, and the vertical mouldings that intersect increasingly tightly as they rise along the shaft to finally display an elaborate network at the summit.

98. THE MINARET AT THE MOSQUE OF EMIR ULMAS (1713)

In comparison with the attractive mosque to which it is attached, built in 1330 by the powerful and wealthy Emir Ulmas, the quality of this minaret is evidently inferior. The muqarnas below its single gallery is a failure, the masonry work is mediocre, the shaft is bare of decoration and the upper bulb lacks

FIG. 238

The minaret at the mosque of Emir Ulmas

FIG. 239

The minaret of the mosque of al-Kurdi

a supporting pavilion. There is an inscription band running around the lower part of the octagonal section where the name Ulmas can be identified, but the rest of the text is illegible. An Ottoman chronicle reported that the original minaret of Ulmas collapsed in the year 1125/1713 and was immediately rebuilt, re-using the same stones.[13] This may well explain the illegibility of the inscription.

99. THE MOSQUE OF AL-KURDI (1732)

The mosque to which this minaret belongs was dedicated to a shaykh called al-Kurdi, whose identity is not clear. Many shaykhs had the *nisba* al-Kurdi as part of their name to indicate a direct or remote Kurdish origin or perhaps other affiliations. This one, whose first name is unknown, is a mystery.

The minaret is an intriguing case.[14] Although the date of its mosque is 1732, its style does not bear much resemblance either to the reconstructed minaret of the mosque of Ulmas a decade earlier or to the minarets built by 'Abd al-Rahman Katkhuda two decades later. In particular, the structure of its muqarnas differs from its contemporaries. However, the keel-arched panels of the octagonal section are adorned with a moulding that is typical of the façade decoration of the period. The design of the minaret is in Mamluk revival style. Like the minaret of al-Burdayni, it lacks the pavilion beneath the bulb.

100. THE MINARETS OF EMIR 'ABD AL-RAHMAN KATKHUDA (1750s)

'Abd al-Rahman Katkhuda, commander of the Janissary corps, was a major sponsor of pious foundations in Cairo and an ambitious and refined patron of architecture. He restored almost all major shrines in the Egyptian capital and embellished them with lavish façades in a style of his own creation. In the course of this embellishment he added a number of new minarets to the mosques he repaired. At the Azhar mosque he added three minarets, of which

FIG. 241

*The southern minaret of 'Abd al-Rahman Katkhuda
at the Azhar mosque*

one has disappeared. The remaining two minarets
are almost identical, hardly differing from his other
minarets or from the many other stereotyped and
unpretentious minarets of this period. Their only new
feature is the pierced or openwork muqarnas, which
was a revival of a style introduced during the reign
of the Mamluk sultan Qaytbay. The muqarnas beneath
the balconies of Qaytbay's minaret and his portal at the
Azhar mosque display this openwork. 'Abd al-Rahman
Katkhuda must have had at his disposal creative stone
carvers but no great architects. His master mason may
have been 'Ali Shaltut, who signed his name in the
portal of the mosque of Shaykh al-Mutahhir at Bayn
al-Qasrayn, which 'Abd al-Rahman renovated in 1754
and equipped with a new minaret.

FIG. 240

*The northern minaret of 'Abd al-Rahman Katkhuda
at the Azhar mosque*

FIG. 242

The minaret of the mosque of Muhammad Bey Abu 'l-Dhahab

101. **THE MOSQUE OF MUHAMMAD BEY ABU 'L-DHAHAB** (1774)

This monumental minaret attached to the mosque located opposite the Azhar mosque is unique in Cairo's architecture of the Ottoman period. Its shaft is entirely rectangular with three storeys. Quite distinct from the modest minarets of 'Abd al-Rahman Katkhuda, erected slightly earlier, its proportions are monumental. Thus, although the architecture of this mosque is very similar to that of the mosque of Sinan Pasha in Bulaq, built two hundred years earlier, the proportional relationship between the minaret and the mosque is more successful here. Clearly, Muhammad Bey Abu 'l-Dhabab had been able to form a new school of builders.

Although it is quite visible from the street which includes the main façade with the portal, the minaret has not been erected on this side but, rather, at the south-west corner of the mosque, from where it dominates the street of al-Azhar. There, in the late fifteenth century, Sultan Qaytbay had built a magnificent caravanserai, and two decades earlier, prior to the mosque of Abu 'l-Dhahab, 'Abd al-Rahman Katkhuda had added a minaret and a spectacular side portal to the Azhar mosque.

The upper structure is unusual, composed of five sculptures similar to jars that have lost their upper bulbs. The design of this minaret is obviously a close imitation of the minaret of Sultan al-Ghawri located a few steps away, with the difference that the former was originally crowned with only four bulbs. Unlike Mamluk minarets, however, this one emerges visibly below the roof level of the mosque. Its decoration is restrained.

There may well have been a political meaning for the revival of Mamluk minaret architecture in this building. Abu 'l-Dhahab belonged to the clan of the emir 'Ali Bey al-Kabir, who rebelled against Ottoman central rule and tried to emancipate Egypt and Syria under his authority. Abu 'l-Dhahab, who first joined 'Ali Bey's rebellion, later turned against his master, and endeavoured to gain power for himself. His minaret revives the memory of al-Ghawri, who fell in the battlefield fighting the Ottoman conquerors, and whose minaret stands in the vicinity.

FIG. 243

The minaret of the mosque of Hasan Pasha Tahir

102. THE MOSQUE OF HASAN PASHA TAHIR (1809)

The mosque and mausoleum founded by the two Albanian brothers Hasan Tahir and 'Abidin Bey is the only noteworthy monument built during the period of transition that immediately followed Muhammad 'Ali's accession to power.[15] It is also one of the rare funerary buildings to commemorate an Ottoman governor. The two emirs who founded it were the brothers of Muhammad Pasha Tahir, who ruled briefly after the capture and eviction of the governor Khusraw Pasha by a coalition of an Albanian corps led by Muhammad 'Ali and Mamluk troops. The brothers were reported to have been Muhammad 'Ali's nephews. Muhammad Tahir was eventually assassinated and buried in this quarter near a shrine called Maqam al-Arbai'in, which his brothers restored. Hasan Pasha and 'Abidin Bey continued to hold influential positions in Muhammad 'Ali's government. Hasan was the head of the Albanian corps and a major political force until his death in 1818. He was buried elsewhere, near the mosque of Sayyida Zaynab.

Unlike Muhammad 'Ali's architecture in the following decades, which broke with Egyptian architectural tradition, this monument is revivalist, predating the Mamluk revival that followed in the late nineteenth century, which was strongly influenced by Europeans.

The mosque of Hasan Pasha Tahir is an arcaded building with a skylight and an elaborately carved façade. The mausoleum on the left-hand side of the entrance has an exceptionally fine funerary dome. The tall minaret, nicely juxtaposed with the mausoleum dome, is the fourth in Cairo to be built in the Mamluk style after al-Burdayni's, al-Kurdi's and Abu 'l-Dhahab's. It is a remarkable structure following the classical pattern of a three-storeyed shaft with two balconies with stone parapets on muqarnas. The upper storey deviates from the Mamluk tradition; it is a plain cylinder crowned with a bulb on a thin ring of muqarnas. The first octagonal storey is carved with Mamluk keel-arched niches and the middle section is carved with moulding in Ottoman style.

FIG. 244

The minaret of the mosque of Sulayman Agha al-Silahdar

103. THE MOSQUE OF SULAYMAN AGHA AL-SILAHDAR (1837–9)

This mosque is the only Ottoman sanctuary on Bayn al-Qasrayn Street, the main artery of historic Cairo. Its façade, with a bowed *sabil* and a slender minaret, combines Ottoman architectural with Cairene urban aesthetics of street alignment.[16]

The cylindrical masonry minaret with an elongated conical top is an elegant structure, which, like Muhammad 'Ali's minarets, does without the Ottoman baroque decoration of the period. The plain cylindrical shaft displays fine masonry rather than the usual vertical mouldings. Only horizontal moulded bands underline the base, the balcony and the summit of the shaft.

The felicitous proportions and the bold simplicity of this minaret suggest that it might be the work of the architect of Muhammad 'Ali's minarets. This architect may also have built the minaret of the shrine of Fatima al-Nabawiyya founded by 'Abbas Pasha I (1848–54), which has been recently demolished to make place for a new mosque (fig. 40).

104. THE MOSQUE OF MUHAMMAD 'ALI PASHA (1830–48)

Against the background of the Muqattam Hill the slender tall minarets point to the highest spot of historic Cairo. Because of its prestigious location and high visibility, the mosque of Muhammad 'Ali became a landmark of the city of Cairo, though it is the least Cairene of all mosques.[17]

It is paradoxical that a revival of Ottoman architecture took place in Cairo at a time when Ottoman centralised authority in Egypt was in deepest decline. Until the close of the eighteenth century, religious architecture in Cairo had merged Mamluk with Ottoman elements. This changed radically with Muhammad 'Ali's patronage. Aspiring to create a modern Egypt under his aegis, which he conceived only after a radical break with local tradition, Muhammad 'Ali was determined to eliminate once and for all Mamluk power structures and their outward manifestation. His ambition to emancipate himself from the Ottoman sultan aimed to eclipse the sultan's authority on the international scene and at the same time to establish a new Ottoman power in Egypt. The architecture of his mosque is a clear statement of his policy, and this may perhaps explain why it had no impact on subsequent architecture.

Muhammad 'Ali's mosque at the Citadel, erected on the site of the palace that for centuries had been the residence of the Mamluk sultans, is purely Ottoman in architecture and decoration, without the slightest trace of local tradition. Most significantly, by building two minarets, Muhammad 'Ali was obviously defying Ottoman authority, which reserved the right to double or multiple minarets as the prerogative of the sultan and the royal family. These double minarets therefore make a political statement.

Hasan 'Abd al-Wahhab found a document related to the construction of the mosque mentioning the name of an Armenian named Hakakian, possibly Yusuf Hakakian, who was one of the students sent by Muhammad 'Ali to study in France. He eventually became head of the Polytechnic School. Most of the craftsmen involved were Egyptians, except those who worked on the window grilles and the lead covering of the dome and the minaret caps.

Nor did the architecture of the mosque reflect the contemporary trend in Istanbul. At that time, imperial mosques were single-dome structures lit by dense fenestration, without a courtyard but with an elaborate loge for the sultan. Already by the eighteenth century the minarets were no longer what they used to be. The mosque of Muhammad 'Ali, with its quatrefoil plan and the rectilinear profile of its minarets, thus represented a revival of Ottoman architecture, long before revivalism appeared in Istanbul itself. Although the minarets of Muhammad 'Ali are the only ones of Ottoman Cairo that could stand comparison with their counterparts in Istanbul, and may even surpass some of them, their design was archaic by then modern Turkish standards. Their classical simplicity contrasts with the fanciness and 'baroquerie' of contemporary Istanbul minarets, with their curved bases, balconies and caps. However, unlike the Turkish minarets of the sixteenth and seventeenth centuries, Muhammad 'Ali's

FIG. 246

The minarets of the mosque of Muhammad ʿAli Pasha

FIG. 245

The mosque of Muhammad ʿAli Pasha, elevation

have no muqarnas but horizontal mouldings underline the base and the balconies instead. Their shafts are elegantly fluted.

The construction of these shafts, eighty-three metres high, standing on a rectangular base of only three metres on a side, was a tour de force. They were the first to surpass the height of Sultan Hasan's minaret. Most of all, the integration of the minarets into the building was achieved in a particularly elegant manner, with their rectangular buttresses forming salient corners at the western wall and their bases corresponding to the bases of the domes and half-domes of the mosque. This creates a continuous and clear-cut horizontal line between the rectangular and the spherical forms of the mosque. Interestingly also, the eastern corners of the sanctuary opposite the minarets are salient and they bear a pair of unusual domed turrets, which are repeated at the four corners of the main dome.

The shafts are octagonal all the way, carved with thin flutes up to the first balcony, with eight rectangular panels up to the second and plain at the top. The only contemporary Ottoman feature is the disturbing use of garlands below the cap.

The minarets of the mosque of Muhammad ʿAli were the work of an avant-garde architect who was a good structural engineer and a talented designer, capable of conveying a new image to a classical Ottoman pattern, while avoiding late Ottoman Baroque features. The same architect is likely to have built the elegant minaret of the mosque of Sulayman Agha al-Silahdar. Because the mosque of Muhammad ʿAli was for many years under construction, during which the mosque of Sulayman Agha al-Silahdar was erected, it is not clear which minaret was erected first.

105. THE MOSQUE OF AL-HAJJ JUMʿA IBRAHIM (1868–9)

The main interest of the minaret attached to this mosque near the cemetery of Sayyida Nafisa is the unique inscription panel inserted in the portal above which the minaret stands. It dates the building and identifies the founder as the master (*muʿallim*) Jumʿa

FIG. 247

The minaret of the mosque of al-Hajj Jum'a Ibrahim

FIG. 248

The mosque of al-Hajj Jum'a Ibrahim, foundation inscription

Ibrahim al-Hajj, the chief architect (or engineer) of Egypt, *ra'is al-muhandisin bi-misr*. The date of the minaret corresponds to the reign of Khedive Isma'il (1863–79). Its style, however, is very conventional and were it not for the inscription, it could be dated a century earlier, to the period of 'Abd al-Rahman Katkhuda. The early nineteenth century saw the minarets of Muhammad 'Ali and Sulayman Agha al-Silahdar, which belong to a very different category.

The title *ra'is al-muhandisin* cannot be identified as the head of a guild. There was in the nineteenth century a guild (*ta'ifa*) of builders and related crafts, who were called *banna'in*, *mi'mariyya*, not *muhandisin* (sing. *muhandis*) and their chief was called shaykh not *ra'is* as is the case here.[18] The title associated with Master Jum'a sounds more exalted, and may refer to an administrative function. In this case, the minaret may not even be Jum'a's own design.

106. THE MINARET OF KHEDIVE ISMA'IL AT THE SHRINE OF AL-HUSAYN (1878)

Because of its significance as a shrine dedicated to al-Husayn, this building has been continuously restored and modified and its endowment enlarged at all periods ever since its foundation in Fatimid times. Its present layout and the pencil-shaped minaret go back to the works executed during the reign of Khedive Isma'il.[19] The minaret was completed in 1295/1878, more than a decade later than the main building. 'Ali Mubarak, who wrote a detailed account of these works in his colossal book the *Khitat Tawfiqiyya*, was at that time in charge of the administration of the *awqaf* or pious foundations, and heavily involved in the design and reconstruction of the mosque. He reported that he left this post before completion of works, and, as a result, his design was not fully implemented. The design of the minaret might well be based on his drawings. Mubarak is known to have been a vehement advocate of adopting modern western ideas in Cairene residential architecture and urbanism, which he viewed as inferior. His modernist views are also expressed in the façade of the shrine, which is neo-Gothic!

The minaret's buttress is integrated in the façade's design, which could be interpreted as a memento of 'Ali Mubarak's studies in France.[20] At that time, Eugène Emmanuel Viollet-Le-Duc was propagating the neo-Gothic style and ideas were even circulating that Gothic architecture had been influenced by Islamic patterns. Whether or not 'Ali Mubarak was familiar with these ideas, is difficult to tell. On purely aesthetic grounds, the combination here of the pencil-like shaft with Gothic decoration is rather harmonious. The minaret might thus well be an attempt to combine old with new and Eastern with Western motifs.

The first storey is carved with a series of tightly contiguous flutes that intersect at the top and the bottom, following the model of Turkish minarets, in particular the minarets of the mosque of Sultan Ahmad in Istanbul. The second section displays mouldings forming a series of neo-Gothic blind arches, and the top storey is surprisingly carved with the pattern of the late Mamluk minaret of Qurqumas! Equally surprising in this context are the muqarnas rings of different designs beneath the two balconies. The wooden cap is elongated as those of the minarets of Muhammad 'Ali and Sulayman Agha al-Silahdar and the minaret of the mosque of Fatima al-Nabawiyya, which is no longer extant.

107. THE MOSQUE OF AL-RIFA'I
(1869–1911)

By the end of the nineteenth century, Mamluk revivalism took on a new momentum under the influence of European architects and artists imbued with Orientalism combined with contemporary ideas of heritage conservation, all eager to rescue and revive Egypt's medieval heritage after centuries of Ottoman hegemony. The mosque of al-Rifa'i is a good example of this movement. Although replete with European aesthetics and urban concepts, it was designed to embody an Egyptian national style in contrast to Muhammad 'Ali's architecture.[21]

The eclecticism of the architecture, combined with excellent craftsmanship in some of the decoration, justifies the status of this monument as a major tourist attraction.

FIG. 249

The minaret of Khedive Isma'il at the shrine of al-Husayn

The mosque was founded in 1869 by Khushyar Hanim, the mother of Khedive Isma'il (1863–79) on the site of the shrine of two Sufi saints of the Rifa'i order that was incorporated into it. Exploiting the sanctity of the site, the mosque was to include a mausoleum for the royal family, thus celebrating the dynastic succession (following the laws of primogeniture), which Isma'il had managed to acquire from the Ottoman sultan. It somehow echoed the mausoleum of the great saint Imam Shafi'i, which included the tombs of members of the Ayyubid royal family.

The project took much longer than anticipated, and was not completed until 1911 during the reign of Khedive 'Abbas Hilmi (1892–1914). During these four decades many changes took place in the design and construction of the mosque. Naturally, the minarets were among the last elements to be added to the construction.

The original design of the mosque was by Husayn Fahmi Pasha, a member of the royal family, and the initial construction was supervised by the chief eunuch of the harem, Khalil Agha. Following Khedive Isma'il's abdication in 1879, the works were interrupted and five years later the patroness died. The works finally resumed a quarter of a century later, in 1905, by order of Khedive 'Abbas Hilmi, who was a great promoter of the Mamluk architectural revival. Eventually, the chief architect of the Comité, the Austro-Hungarian Herz Pasha, was assigned the task, to which also an Italian architect and 'Ali Mubarak, at that time Minister of Public Works, contributed. Herz reported that he maintained the façades largely as they were designed, and to some extent already erected, by his predecessor, but he remodelled the interior of the mosque, and designed its decoration. Considering that the initial design of the minarets by Husayn Fahmi was only rudimentary,[22] the architecture of the present structures has to be attributed to Herz and his team.

Designed following the urban vision that Haussmann had realised shortly before in Paris, to emphasise the vista of the newly pierced Muhammad 'Ali avenue at its junction with the Citadel square beneath the mosque of Muhammad 'Ali and to match the mosque of Sultan Hasan, the positioning of the mosque dictated its monumentality. Moreover, Husayn Fahmi's keenness to match the grandeur of the mosque of Sultan Hasan added to the complexity and boldness

of this undertaking. The urban context also imposed the priority of the southern façade where the minarets and a dome emphasise the main entrance. This arrangement was detrimental to the architecture of the minarets, which appear squeezed on this relatively narrow street side and dwarfed by the colossal façade of Sultan Hasan's mosque across it. The eastern façade overlooking the Citadel square or the western façade facing an open place would have more effectively emphasised the twin minarets.

Unlike Sultan Hasan's extant minaret, which was designed to match the dimensions of the mosque, the Rifa'i minarets fall short of this standard. Like that of Sultan Hasan, they are supported by a pair of protruding semicircular and nicely fluted buttresses that would have suited, more impressive super-structures. The ratio of the minaret and the mosque's walls is not 2:1 as usual, but nearly 1:1. Particularly maladroit is their association with the small dome that awkwardly crowns the portal vault between them. Husayn Pasha's draft, however, shows that he designed the façade with the apex of the dome below the first minaret balcony, whereas Herz designed it with the apex of the dome visibly above it.[23] Herz may have had little choice, for the sake of structural stability. Indeed, in his report he severely criticised his predecessor for his obsession with the mosque of Sultan Hasan, which led him to emulate Mamluk architecture without having sufficient knowledge of it, and for the lack of solidity of his construction that was too hastily executed.

The decoration of the shafts is an imitation of the design that was carved for the first time on the very graceful minaret of the mosque of Asanbugha, and later adopted on other minarets and on domes. A reason for the choice of this specific minaret as a model may have been its date (1370), a decade after Sultan Hasan's mosque, thus integrating the style of the Rifa'i mosque into the architectural ensemble created here.

FIG. 250

The minarets of the mosque of al-Rifa'i

Colonnes

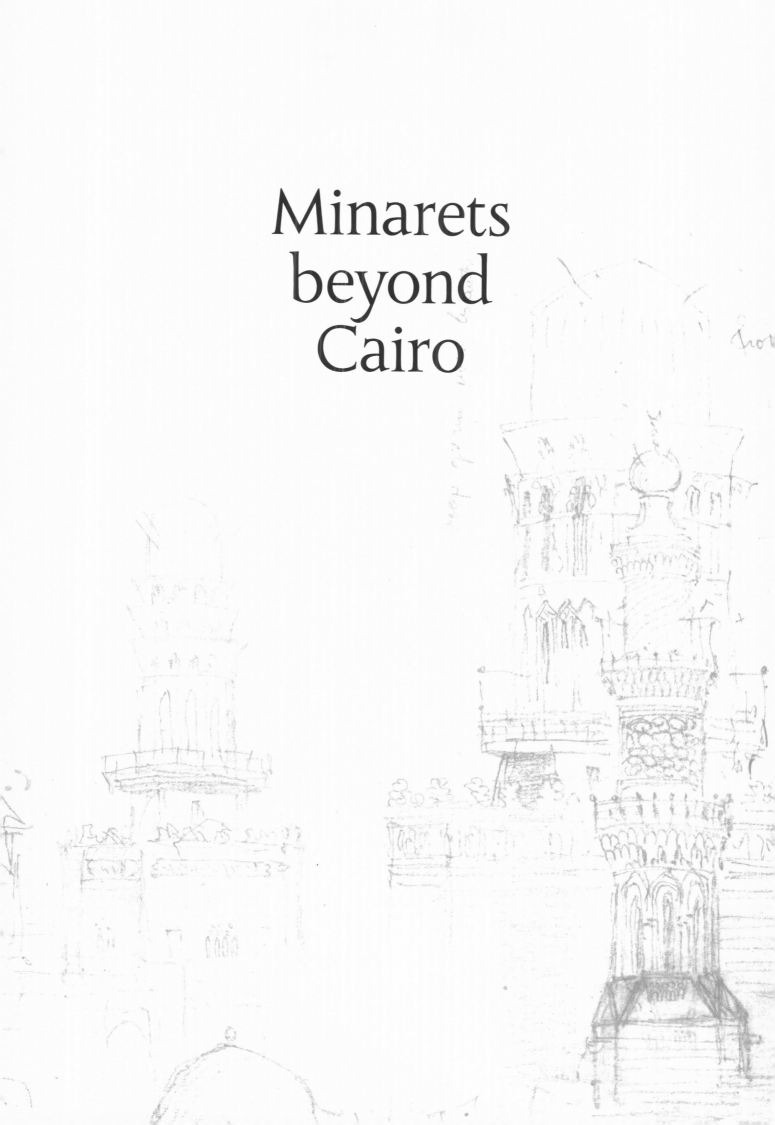

Minarets beyond Cairo

TWELVE

Provincial Minarets in Egypt

Not many historic minarets survive today outside Cairo.[1] Unlike the minarets of the capital, provincial minaret architecture is marked by a strikingly persistent continuity that makes their dating on stylistic grounds impossible. On the basis of the physical evidence, and pictorial and archival documentation, it appears that provincial minarets, from the Fatimid period, and perhaps even earlier, to the late Ottoman period, had one thing in common: they were made of fired brick, as were the vast majority of the provincial mosques themselves. In the oases, sun-dried mud bricks are used. Horizontal timber lacing is usually combined with the brick to add flexibility to the construction. The characteristic technique of architectural decoration used in provincial architecture, most particularly in Lower Egypt, was unknown in Cairo. This technique, which consisted of geometric brickwork with white mortar joints applied on façades and portals, is best displayed on the traditional houses of Rosetta. It is not clear to what extent it was applied on minarets as well. Provincial minarets generally have their stairs within them, beginning at ground level. Only the minarets of Alexandria, which stand above a porch, required access from a separate staircase leading to the roof.

The pre-Mamluk minarets of Upper Egypt have some elements in common with the northern minaret of the mosque of al-Hakim in Cairo, such as a tapering profile and a plan that shifts from a square to a circle moving up the shaft. During the Mamluk period, a simplified brick version of the Cairene minaret was established in the provinces and remained common

until modern times. Regional variations also exist: northern Egyptian minarets, for example, have upper sections that take the shape of a fluted pole, culminating in a bulb. The minarets of al-Mahalla, discussed further below, form an independent group that perpetuates the mabkhara style exemplified at the minaret of Qawsun rather than the minaret with the bulb.

UPPER EGYPT AND THE OASES

The Fatimid minarets of Upper Egypt, one of which has collapsed since the construction of the Aswan Dam, have rectangular bases carrying a cylindrical tapering second storey crowned with a domed structure. The minaret of the mosque known as *al-mashhad al-bahari* (the Northern Oratory) near Aswan is built in fired brick over a base of granite. It also has an inscription running below balcony level, executed in two lines in a crude Kufic script using bricks set vertically, horizontally and obliquely. The inscription refers to the minaret by the name of *manara*, and states that it was sponsored by 'Ubayd ibn Muhammad ibn Ahmad ibn Salama. Its construction is attributed to a man called Hatim al-Banna (the mason) and his son. The upper structure of the minaret, set above a wooden balcony, is a simple domed cube pierced on four sides by arched windows. The minaret of the mosque known as *al-mashhad al-qibli* (the Southern Oratory, now vanished) or the mosque of Bilal was similar in design to its northern counterpart but had

FIG. 251 *(page 310)*

The minaret of the mosque of al-Mujahidin in Asyut
DAVID ROBERTS

FIG. 252

The minaret called al-Tabia in Aswan

a more elaborate and elongated upper structure, which consisted of an octagonal pierced pavilion, in three stages set one above the other. The transitional zone below the domical structure had concave sides, a pattern that is frequent in the contemporary mausoleum domes of Aswan and has no parallel in Cairo.[2] The remains of another contemporary minaret stands near the cemetery of Aswan. Simply known as *al-tabia* (the Fort), this minaret had already lost its upper storey by the beginning of the twentieth century.[3] The lower storey is set on a rectangular base, and consequently is oval rather than circular in plan. Although it, too, was inscribed using a pattern of bricks below its original balcony level, its inscriptions could not be deciphered. All three minarets were built with their own internal staircases starting at ground level. An unknown minaret in Aswan and another one depicted by Ebers in an Upper Egyptian village suggest that this style might have been more widespread than it appears today (figs 253 and 254). The latter is very similar to that of the Umriya mosque in Edfu, attributed by J. Bloom to this group of eleventh-century minarets.[4] Like the vanished minaret of *al-mashhad al-qibli*, it displays concave sides at the transitional zone below the upper structure.

Moving to the north of Aswan, a minaret founded by the Fatimid vizier Badr al-Jamali stands at the Great Mosque of Esna. This is made of fired brick and is dated in an inscription to 474/1081 (fig. 255).[5] The whole of this minaret was probably originally intended to be plastered, but the base has today been stripped. Its rectangular shaft, which is relatively taller than those of the Aswan minarets, ends with four domed posts at its corners, recalling the kiosks on the roof of the mosque of al-Juyushi. This section is articulated by pointed arched openings that increase in size, but decrease in number, as they ascend the shaft. The uppermost arch does not frame a window as on the lower tiers, but creates a niche, which is related in its vertical proportion to arched chamfers at each corner of the shaft. Unlike Cairene parallels where a balcony invariably marks the transition between the lower and the upper recessive sections of the shaft, the timber balcony in this case projects directly from the tapering cylindrical shaft about two-thirds of the way up and is supported by simple projecting brick corbels, as with

FIG. 253

A minaret in Aswan

G. EBERS

FIG. 254

View of a minaret in an Upper Egyptian village

G. EBERS

FIG. 255

The minaret of Badr al-Jamali at the Great Mosque in Esna

the other minarets of Aswan. The minaret's double-tier upper pavilion is similar to that of *al-mashhad al-bahari*, with concave sides at the transitional zone surmounted by a domical structure, which has a hexagonal, rather than octagonal, pierced base.

The minaret of the mosque of Shaykh Abu 'l-Hajjaj in the town of Luxor is built of mudbrick and sits directly above a section of the Ancient Egyptian temple. Stylistically it can be attributed to the Fatimid period, predating the mosque associated with the shaykh, who died in the thirteenth century. Like the examples from Aswan and Esna, this minaret combines a rectangular shaft ending with four corner posts with a cylindrical tapering upper section crowned by a cupola pierced on four sides with windows. The upper structure beneath the cupola is less articulated than that of the minaret of Esna.

Although the chronology of most of the minarets of Upper Egypt is uncertain, Creswell and other architectural historians have dated them by analogy with the minaret of the mosque of Esna and with the minaret of the mosque of al-Juyushi in Cairo, both built by the vizier Badr al-Jamali, to the Fatimid period, attributing their foundation to this same vizier.[6] They all have the same rectangular-cylincrical compostion of the southern minaret of al-Hakim in Cairo.

Related to these Upper Egyptian minarets in form is the minaret of the mosque at the town of al-Qasr in the Oasis of Dakhla in the Western Desert (fig. 257). This structure has been dated to the Ayyubid period, not an unreasonable claim judging by its style. Like that of Abu 'l-Hajjaj, the minaret is made of mud brick and has two sections: a circular tapering shaft standing above a faceted first storey that is decorated with keel-arched recesses. Between the two sections

FIG. 256

The minaret of the mosque of Abu 'l-Hajjaj in Luxor

was a projecting timber balcony for the muezzin, as is indicated by the remaining wooden beams. A similar balcony existed below the pointed summit. Besides the keel-arched niches, no decoration survives. The shaft bears very few openings, four at the summit and a door at the level of the first balcony. Similar minarets, though of an even more simplified design, can be found at the Oasis of Siwa. These are extremely difficult to date.

During the Mamluk period, Upper Egyptian minarets were adapted to the Cairene style, but made of fired brick with their decoration executed in plaster. A simple cylindrical section pierced with arched

FIG. 257

The minaret of the mosque of al-Qasr in Dakhla

FIG. 258

A minaret in Girga, *coloured lithograph*
K.L. LIBAY

openings usually replaced the upper octagonal pavilion of the minaret. Above this, a balcony on a muqarnas cornice supported the bulb and finial on the end of a cylinder. The minaret of the mosque of al-Mujahidin in Asyut as it was depicted by David Roberts (fig. 251) seems to have been one of the most beautiful provincial minarets in all of Egypt.[7] The Ottoman conquest did nothing to disturb that tradition of building Mamluk minarets in the provinces. Even in the town of Girga, which served the Ottomans as the provincial capital of Upper Egypt, minarets were invariably constructed in the traditional Egyptian style (fig. 258).

In the town of Bahnasa in the Fayyum province, the Mamluk minaret at the mosque of Zayn al-ʿAbidin stands today miraculously as a defiant survival against all apparent odds, isolated on its buttress without its

mosque. This minaret is very similar to the fifteenth-century brick minarets of Cairo (figs 259 and 260). Another minaret in the same town belonging to the now destroyed mosque called 'Maʾallak' by the Comité, founded by Hajj Mustafa and dated to 1681, demonstrates the persistence of the Mamluk style to that late date. It has now vanished but was noted and photographed by the Comité in 1896.[8] It was a plastered brick shaft that stood directly over the stone portal of the mosque (fig. 261). A lithograph by K.L. Libay in 1863 shows that the minaret of the mosque of Asalbay, Sultan Qaytbay's wife, in the town of Fayyum was also in the Cairene style. The overseer of its construction was the prominent Sufi Shaykh ʿAbd al-Qadir al-Dashtuti, who built a mosque for himself in Cairo.[9]

FIG. 259

The minaret of the mosque of Zayn al-'Abidin in Bahnasa

FIG. 260

The minaret of the mosque of Zayn al-'Abidin in Bahnasa, detail

FIG. 261

The vanished minaret of the mosque of 'al-Ma'allak' in Bahnasa

FIG. 262

The Minaret of the Mosque of Asalbay in Fayyum, *coloured lithograph*

K.L. LIBAY

FIG. 263

The minaret of the mosque of al-'Attarin in Alexandria

DESCRIPTION DE L'ÉGYPTE

FIG. 264

The mosque of al-Shurbaji

PASCAL COSTE

ALEXANDRIA, FUWA AND ROSETTA

A significant variation in the location of the minaret can be seen in Alexandria. Here, minarets were built directly above a porch attached to a mosque, supported by the façade wall of the building on one side and a pair of piers or columns on the other.[10] The earliest evidence for this type of structure is found in the *Description de l'Égypte*, which contains an elevation of the ʿAttarin mosque, a Fatimid foundation that had been restored by Sultan Shaʿban in 1371 (fig. 263).[11] It shows the minaret to have been a three-storey octagonal structure, in the Cairene Mamluk style, but built on a square base projecting from the central axis of the building. This provided the main entrance with a covered porch: perhaps the preference for porches was dictated by the wetter climate of Alexandria, but this in itself would require no more than a single storey shelter to be effective. The upper structure of the minaret of the ʿAttarin mosque, which is now a modern construction, displayed a slender fluted cylinder crowned with a bulb, rather than an open pavilion. The *Description* shows a similar minaret, no longer extant, at the fort of Sultan Qaytbay, erected on the site of the ancient Lighthouse of Alexandria.[12] No Mamluk minaret has survived in Alexandria, but there is one minaret of the Ottoman period, the mosque of al-Tarbana, built in 1685. This has a porch that stands on re-used antique column capitals and shafts. The octagonal shaft, articulated by simple keel-arched panels and square mouldings, has a transition of very flat muqarnas to the balcony. All that stands above the balcony is a very elongated fluted cylinder and bulb. Pascal Coste depicted the mosque of Shurbaji (1758) (fig. 264) when it still had its minaret, which looked very similar to the extant minaret at the Tarbana mosque.[13] When the mosque of Nabi Danyal, one of the most important mosques in the city, was rebuilt in the early nineteenth century its minaret also adopted the same configuration.[14]

The coastal town of Rosetta and the inland town of Fuwa, located on the Rosetta branch of the Nile, were of particular importance during the Ottoman period, and many buildings of this date survive there. The minarets of their mosques share many features

FIG. 265

The minaret of the mosque of al-Tarbana in Alexandria

FIG. 266

The minaret of the mosque of al-Qana'i in Fuwa

FIG. 267

The minaret of the mosque of Abu 'l-Makarim in Fuwa

with the Alexandrian model, but they do not stand above projecting porches. Almost all the minarets in this part of the country have balcony handrails made of timber and a plastered structure that is painted white. In some cases, notably in horizontal bands beneath the balconies, bichrome decoration of black and red brickwork with white mortar joints is applied as a contrast with the white plaster, as is the case at the monumental minaret of the mosque of al-Qana'i in

FIG. 269

The minaret of the mosque of Zaghlul in Rosetta

FIG. 268

The minaret of the mosque of Daʿi ʾl-Dar in Fuwa

Fuwa dating to 1720. The minaret of the mosques of Abu ʾl-Makarim (1850) and Daʿi ʾl-Dar (1864) in the same town are shorter but in the same tradition.[15]

The sixteenth-century mosque of Zaghlul in Rosetta is a monumental four-storeyed faceted shaft with three wooden balconies. The later minarets of the mosque of Dumaqsis (1720) and the mosque of al-ʿAbbasi erected in the nineteenth century are further evidence of the stylistic continuity also in this town.

FIG. 270

The minaret of the mosque of Dumaqsis in Rosetta

FIG. 271

The mosque of al-'Abbasi in Rosetta

FIG. 272

The minaret of the shrine of Shaykh Dasuqi in Dasuq

G. EBERS

FIG. 273

The minaret of the mosque of Shaykh Abn 'l-'Abbas al-Harithi in Mahalla

AL-MAHALLA AND SAMANNUD

No Mamluk minaret survived in Damietta, but the Mamluk style survived in later minaret architecture. A brick version of Cairene minarets was crowned with an upper bulb supported by a cylindrical shaft.[16] The preference for this kind of treatment may simply be due to the fact that cylinders of brick were far easier to build than the reverse-curve complex structures seen in Cairo. A nineteenth-century illustration of the shrine of Shaykh Dasuqi in the town of Dasuq, which was rebuilt by Sultan Qaytbay, also shows a Mamluk-style minaret (fig. 272).[17]

The town of al-Mahalla al-Kubra, however, has the most interesting group of pre-modern minarets

to be found outside of Cairo.[18] There, unlike anywhere else in the Egyptian provinces, the Cairene minaret with a mabkhara top was adopted and maintained throughout the Ottoman period, centuries after this style had been abandoned in the capital. The Mamluk minaret of the mosque of al-Mutawalli, also called al-Tarini, was built before 1410 when its founder Shaykh Ahmad ibn 'Ali al-Tarini died (fig. 275).[19] It has a massive rectangular shaft, an octagonal receding second storey, and a top in the shape of a mabkhara. Its elaborate octagonal sectin is decorated in Cairene style.The slender octagonal minaret of the mosque of ibn Kutayla, also called al-Hanafi, was built at a later date by the scholar Muhammad ibn Kutayla, who died in 1482.[20] It is a smaller version of the previous one, with two receding tiers above muqarnas corbelling

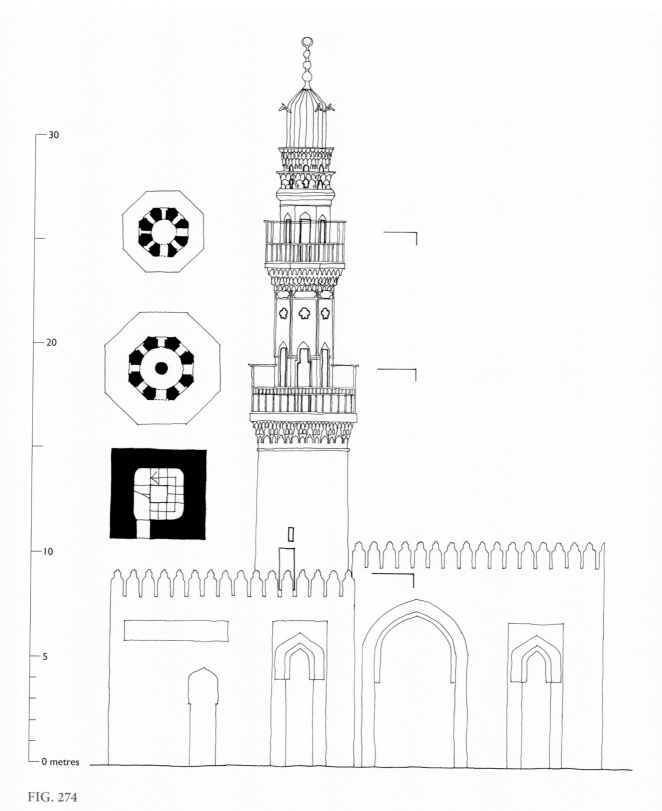

FIG. 274

The minaret of the mosque of Shaykh Abu'l-'Abbas al-Harithi in al-Mahalla, elevation and plans

FIG. 275

The minaret of the mosque of al-Mutawalli al-Tarini in Malhalla

FIG. 276

The minaret of the mosque of Ibn Kutayla (al-Hanafi) in al-Mahalla

FIG. 277

The minaret of Shaykh ʿAbd Allah ʿAsi in al-Mahalla

and a mabkhara top. The mosque built by Shaykh Abu ʾl-ʿAbbas al-Harithi bulit in 1538 has another handsome and monumental minaret that was completed some time after 1544.[21] Its octagonal section is pierced on the upper part of each facet with a rosette-shaped opening. The minaret of the mosque of ʿAbd Allah ʿAsi, erected in 1722, demonstrates the continuity of the tradition of the mabkhara well into the Ottoman period, but this time in combination with an octagonal shaft throughout, as can be seen at the minaret of the emir Manjaq in Cairo.[22] All the

minarets of this area have their staircases accessible at ground level, and the railings of their balconies are made of wood. None of them is inscribed. It has to be added, however, that all the historic minarets of al-Mahalla have been recently pulled down and reconstructed in concrete.

The stub that survived from the minaret of the mosque known as the Mosque of Repentance, *jamiʿ al-tawba,* founded by Shaykh Abu ʾl-ʿAbbas al-Ghamri in the 1490s, should also be mentioned here. Its significance does not lie in any specific

FIG. 278

The stub of the minaret of the mosque of Shaykh al-Ghamri (al-Tawba) in al-Mahalla

FIG. 279

The minaret of the mosque of Shaykh Muhammad al-Ghamri in Mit Ghamr

FIG. 281

*The minaret of the mosque of Shaykh al-'Adawi
in Samannud*

FIG. 280

*The minaret of the mosque of al-Mutawalli
in Samannud*

aesthetic features but rather in its stone construction, which makes it exceptional among Egyptian provincial minarets, since they were normally built in brick. Only the first storey of this minaret is original. The execution of numerous details such as mouldings, window openings, engaged columns, and muqarnas matches the style of contemporary Cairene minarets, and strongly suggests that a craftsman from the capital, perhaps a disciple of the shaykh, was responsible for the construction of this minaret. The present bulb that is placed immediately above the first storey is modern.

The founder of the Mosque of Repentance, Abu 'l-'Abbas, was the son of Shaykh Muhammad al-Ghamri, who also built a mosque with a fine minaret in Cairo,[23] and is reported to have founded a large number of other mosques in various towns in Egypt. He must have had a special interest in minarets, as is evident from the remarkable minaret of another mosque he founded in the town of Mit Ghamr (Miniyat Ghamr). This minaret has a rectangular shaft with a double-bulb at the summit, which seems to predate all the documented double-headed minarets of Cairo. If indeed the double-bulb appeared in the province first and was later transferred to Cairo, this would be an extraordinary occurrence in the history of Egyptian provincial architecture, reversing the common rule of metropolitan–provincial artistic relations. This would imply a remarkably high status for the founder, and perhaps of Sufi shaykhs in this period altogether.

Not far from al-Mahalla, in the town of Samannud, stands another group of three monumental brick minarets that are clearly related in style to the minarets of al-Mahalla although they are undated and believed to be of the early Ottoman period. These minarets have massive rectangular shafts, accessible by staircases at ground level, surmounted by receding octagonal storeys decorated with interlacing mouldings. The minaret of al-Mutawalli, which may have been built in the first half of the sixteenth century, has a mabkhara upper structure. The mabkhara top, however, was not as consistently maintained in Samannud as it was in al-Mahalla. The undated minaret of Sidi Salama that belongs to a very early mosque restored in 1737, for example, is similar to the previous one but is topped with a bulb that has spiral plaster ribbing. The bulb

FIG. 282

The minaret of the mosque of Shaykh al-'Adawi in Samannud, detail

FIG. 283

*The minaret of the mosque of Shaykh Salama
in Samannud*

may be of a later date than the rectangular shaft,
whose sheer monumentality suggests a fifteenth- or
sixteenth-century date for the original construction.
The funerary mosque of al-'Adawi, built in 1718, has a
slender shaft with pronouncedly projecting muqarnas
corbelling.[24] It is also built adjacent to the tomb, which
has a high drum and a bulbous ribbed dome. This style
of dome on a high drum is first seen in Cairo in the
1350s at the mosque of Sarghitmish and the Sultaniyya
mausoleum, and must have been of Iranian origin.[25]
The style was not perpetuated in the capital, however,
but seems to have been exported to the provinces, in
the same way as the mabkhara minaret top. There,
it flourished until the nineteenth century.

FIG. 284

The minaret of Sultan Qaytbay at the mosque of the Prophet in Medina

THIRTEEN

The Minaret of Sultan Qaytbay at the Mosque of the Prophet in Medina

The Mamluks, at the height of their power, controlled from Cairo an empire that extended from Libya in the west, Sudan and Arabia in the south, and Syria in the east to Anatolia in the north. Their architectural patronage was significant in all the urban centres within their territory, notably at Damascus, Aleppo, Tripoli, Gaza, Jerusalem and the Holy Cities of Mecca and Medina.[1]

However, because of the long and continuous architectural history of Cairo even before the Mamluk period, and because of the special and almost exclusive relationship between the Mamluk ruling aristocracy and their capital, the transfer of architectural knowledge between Cairo and other Mamluk cities, including those in the Egyptian provinces, was remarkably minimal.[2] Instead, regional traditions tended to prevail and to evolve autonomously. Whereas Syrian craftsmen contributed occasionally, in particular in the early Mamluk period, to Cairo's architectural decoration, Cairene craftsmen were rarely sent to work outside the capital. As a result, in spite of its aesthetic significance, the Cairene minaret was not reproduced in Syria. Even when Sultan Qaytbay restored the Umayyad mosque of Damascus after a devastating fire in 1479 that necessitated the reconstruction of the south-west minaret, the architecture and decoration of the new minaret were in Damascene style.[3]

However, the connection between the Mamluk capital and the Holy Cities was different from that with Syria. The Mamluk sultans jealously held the privilege of being guardians and sponsors of these shrines (called the Haramayn or 'Two Sanctuaries'), along with the inhabitants of their cities. They took care of the pilgrimage infrastructure, which included the organisation of the caravans from Egypt and Syria as well as hydraulic installations and fortifications on the roads to Mecca and Medina, and they endowed charitable foundations for scholars and sojourners (*mujawirun*) in the shrines themselves. They also held the exclusive privilege of sending the textile coverings for the Kaaba and other shrines. In Mecca and Medina the Mamluks could display their piety to worshippers from the whole Muslim world. Mamluk sultans, such as al-Zahir Baybars,[4] al-Nasir Muhammad and al-Ashraf Qaytbay, used to send builders and building materials either from Egypt or Syria, along with overseers, to execute all major construction works at the holy shrines.

As almost every historic structure has now vanished from the precincts of the Holy Places in Mecca and Medina, we are almost entirely dependent on literary and archival sources to document Mamluk architecture there. In the course of the continuous maintenance works by the Mamluk sultans at the Prophet's mosque of Medina, the pre-existing minarets were restored and reconstructed. The first reconstruction of the Prophet's mosque by the caliph al-Walid in 707–9 had minarets attached to its four corners. One of them, the north-eastern, which had eventually to be demolished because it overlooked a residence nearby.[5] When Ibn Jubayr visited Medina in 1184 during the reign of Salah al-Din, he saw three minarets, one at the south-east corner, which he describes as in the shape of a *sawma'a*, and two small ones that he described as 'two towers' (*burjayn*) at the opposite northern corners.[6]

It is not clear from this terminology what the stylistic difference between the *sawma'a* and the towers was. However, coming from North Africa, where this term referred to minarets that were normally rectangular, he may have meant a tall rectangular shaft. As for the pair of smaller towers, they may have been squat structures. It is obvious that the south-eastern minaret was taller than and distinct from the two others.

Samhudi reports that two northern minarets were built after Ibn Jubayr's visit, to replace the old one and restore the original layout with four-corner minarets. He attributes the reconstruction of the missing south-western minaret to Sultan al-Nasir Muhammad in 706/1306–7;[7] this was executed by Kafur al-Hariri, the chief of the eunuchs in charge of the shrine.[8] However, in 729/1328–9 Sultan al-Nasir Muhammad ordered the addition of two arcades at the southern end of the mosque,[9] which must have implied the replacement of the minaret built by Kafur – otherwise the minaret would no longer have occupied the south-western corner of the mosque but would have remained further north in its western wall. The minaret we see today at the south-west corner of what remains of the medieval mosque has a rectangular first storey crowned with a muqarnas cornice. The upper section is a cylindrical shaft set back behind the balcony, as is the case at the northern minaret of al-Nasir Muhammad's mosque at the Citadel in Cairo. The undulating corbels supporting its upper balcony and the cap that tops it are of late Ottoman style.

The most impressive survival of Mamluk building activity in the Hijaz, however, is the minaret of Sultan Qaytbay built at the Prophet's mosque in 1486. This minaret was the most important minaret of the shrine, standing beside the dome over the Prophet's tomb, at the south-east corner of the sanctuary. It was rebuilt twice by Qaytbay.

Already in 878/1474 Qaytbay dispatched Egyptian craftsmen to restore the mosque, which had fallen into disrepair; no works on any minarets are mentioned on this occasion.[10] A few years later, in 886/1481, lightning struck the south-eastern or 'the Principal Minaret' and caused a fire that devastated the mosque. The minaret had to be reconstructed alongside other substantial restorations.[11] Samhudi and the contemporary historian Ibn Iyas report that Sultan Qaytbay sent

FIG. 285

The old south-west minaret at the mosque of the Prophet in Medina

a team of craftsmen from Egypt to execute the works that were completed in 887/1482.[12] The supervisor of the construction was Shams al-Din Muhammad ibn al-Zaman (d.1492), a merchant from Damascus, who worked for the sultan not only in Medina, but in Mecca, Jerusalem and Cairo as well. He restored the mausoleum of Imam Shafi'i and founded a mosque in Bulaq.[13] Shortly after completion of the works at the Prophet's mosque, the minaret began to lean and the dome showed cracks. This was reported to Qaytbay, with the comment that the damage was due to the use of inadequate materials. The sultan, furious with the supervisor (Ibn al-Zaman) appointed in his place a prominent emir, Shahin al-Jamali, to undertake new repairs.[14] The minaret was eventually pulled down and reconstructed on deeper foundations that reached down below the water table. Samhudi adds: 'its construction in black stone is accomplished and extremely fine; nothing like it has been seen before in Medina.'[15] The minaret is indeed made of basalt.

This minaret, standing at the south-east corner of the Prophet's mosque, was called 'the Principal Minaret', or *al-mi'dhana al-ra'isiyya*, because its muezzin was the first to perform the call to prayer, to be followed by muezzins standing on the other minarets. When lightning struck the minaret in 1482, the muezzin was just on the verge of starting the call to prayer, while the other muezzins of the town were waiting to follow suit. The name and prominence of this minaret strongly suggest that it was also the tallest of the four corner minarets of the shrine. The present structure rises to the impressive height of 59.76 metres from the ground, being significantly larger than all other Qaytbay-period minarets. Its basalt is today plastered and painted white. Samhudi's text indicates that the entrance to the staircase of the minaret was at ground level and accessible from four steps within the mosque.[16]

The minaret has four storeys: a rectangular base with octagonal and faceted sections above, surmounted by a mabkhara top. Its decoration is in the Cairene tradition. The rectangular base is ornamented with four miniature balconies that project on muqarnas corbels. These have recessed keel-arched panels above them with flanking engaged colonettes. Around and above the panels, the surface of the shaft is defined by thick interlaced mouldings in relief which

link each face across the corners. Corner columns embedded in the shaft go some way to lightening its appearance. A traditional muqarnas cornice leads to the rectangular balcony above the shaft that has a modern pierced stone balustrade. The decoration of the octagonal tier above this is unusual, being carved with a horizontal zigzag motif instead of the keel-arched niches with miniature balconies that are typically found in this position. A further muqarnas cornice defines the transition to the section above, which is faceted in sixteen parts and is plain, with the exception of an upper horizontal moulding. Over the topmost pavilion, the ribbed mabkhara cupola supports a little rectangular lantern, which has no parallel in Cairo and which is may be a modern intervention.

Seen in the context of Cairene architecture, however, the minaret of Qaytbay in Medina differs from its contemporaries: it is anachronistic. The latest minaret with a mabkhara top that is documented in Cairo, the minaret of the funerary complex of Tankizbugha built in 1362, has an unusual composition with two storeys and bears no resemblance to the Medina minaret. The closest formal relationship with a Cairene model can rather be seen at the minaret of the *khanqah* of the emir Qawsun, built almost one and a half centuries earlier, in 1336–7. Compared with the minaret of Qawsun, the Medina minaret has, above the octagonal section, an additional faceted storey supporting the mabkhara structure. The muqarnas cornices are significantly less refined and complex than those on contemporary minarets in Cairo. It is difficult to tell to what extent Ibn al-Zaman or Shahin al-Jamali were involved in the undeniably archaic design of this minaret. It is also unclear whether Shahin copied the previous minaret of Ibn al-Zaman or made stylistic changes to the new structure. Nor is it known whether Ibn al-Zaman's minaret copied the previous minaret that had burned down. The fact that the new construction was in basalt, which may not have been the case previously, may also have entailed formal modifications. It should be recalled, too, that reconstructions at this time were normally made in the contemporary style, and not, as in a modern restoration, with faithfulness to the style of the old structure.

The style of the minaret of Qaytbay at Medina does, in fact, conform to the design of minarets in the town of al-Mahalla al-Kubra, discussed in the previous chapter. Here, the mabkhara upper structure was maintained as late as the eighteenth century. However, the builders of al-Mahalla had no experience of stonemasonry, as they built exclusively in brick. It is therefore very unlikely that they would have played any role in the construction of the basalt minaret at Medina. Could the reverse have been true? Might the continuity of the mabkhara form of minaret in al-Mahalla have been inspired by the minaret of Medina as a case of architectural mimesis motivated by piety? Al-Mahalla was a major religious centre in the late Mamluk and Ottoman periods, being endowed with numerous mosques and shrines founded by, or dedicated to, local shaykhs and saints. Such an interpretation, however, does not accord with medieval Islamic practice, that did not normally associate a particular architectural style with religious meanings.

To interpret the archaism of this minaret's style, one should perhaps recall the appearance of the mosque at that time, with a minaret located at each of the four corners of the building. The one on the opposite south corner, erected during the early reign of al-Nasir Muhammad, is likely to have had a mabkhara as its upper structure, as was common at that time in Cairo. The two other minarets at the opposite northern corners of the mosque and no longer extant, may well have also been rebuilt or restored during the Mamluk period in the course of continuous maintenance works. According to Samhudi, the northern minarets were similar ('ala hay'at) to the Principal, except for the height. These pre-existing minarets might have inspired a sense of stylistic homogeneity that led to the choice of an archaic style for the Principal Minaret. Stylistic consistency or homogeneity, however, had never been a matter of major concern for the builders and restorers of that period. The minaret of al-Ghawri at al-Azhar, for example, follows the style of its own time rather than that of the earlier minarets of Aqbugha and Qaytbay that stand only a few metres away. The archaic style of Qaytbay's minaret in Medina remains, therefore, open to interpretation.

GLOSSARY

ablaq: striped (masonry)

adhan: call to prayer

basmala: the opening formula 'bism Allah al-Rahman al-Rahim' = 'In the name of God, the Lord of Mercy, the Giver of Mercy', mentioned at the head of suras in the Koran and commonly spoken by Muslims at the beginning of an activity.

Bayn al-Qasrayn: main avenue of the historic Fatimid centre of Cairo

hijra: literally migration, refers to the beginning of the Islamic calendar with the Prophet's migration from Mecca to Medina

iwan: open hall in a mosque or a palace facing a central space

jami': abbreviation of masjid jami' – congregational mosque, where the Friday sermon is held

khanqah: monastery for Sufis

khutba: the Friday sermon in the mosque

mabkhara: literally incense-burner, used by art historians to describe a type of upper structure of minarets

maddhab: rite or legal school. The four madhhabs of Sunni Islamic law are the Hanafi, Shafi'i, Hanbali and Maliki

madrasa: Islamic college

maksala: masonry bench, usually a pair, flanking the entrance of a building

maktab: charitable primary school for boys (today called kuttab).

masjid: a mosque or oratory

mi'dhana: literally place to announce the prayer,

meaning minaret

mihrab: prayer niche in a mosque, to mark the Mecca orientation

minbar: pulpit

mu'allim: literally teacher, but commonly used in the past and present as a the title of a master craftsman.

muhtasib: market inspector

muqarnas: an architectural decorative device in the form of a three-dimensional composition of small niches arranged in a geometrical order usually to mark transitions

qadi: judge

qibla: the Mecca orientation

ribat: a type of monastery or a dwelling compound in a religious complex

sabil: water-house to provide water to the thirsty on a charitable basis

sabil-maktab: a structure created in the Mamluk period, attached to a building of freestanding with a water-house on ground level and a primary school on the upper floor

shahada: the Muslim tenet of faith 'There is no deity but God, Muhammad is the prophet of God'

sura: chapter of the Koran

shaykh: man of a religious profession, holy man

waqf: endowment, private or charitable, a kind of trust on a perpetual basis, used to upkeep and administer religious foundations

zawiya: a Sufi foundation that may or may not have boarding facilities, often associated with a specific shaykh

ENDNOTES

INTRODUCTION

1 Maqrizi, *Khitat*, II, p. 328.
2 Ibn al-Hajj, II, p. 241.
3 Samhudi, p. 526.

ONE

1 Maqrizi, *Khitat*, II, pp. 269–73; al-Shayzari, pp. 111–13; al-Zarkashi, pp. 364–8; Ibn al-Hajj, II, pp. 240–63; al-Qurashi, pp. 267–9; Th. W. Juynboll, 'Adhan', *EI 2nd edn*; al-Sa'id, *al-Adhan;* Layla Ali Ibrahim, 'The *adhan*: The call to prayer', in *The Minarets of Cairo* (Cairo, 1985), pp. 187–9; Amin, *Awqaf*, pp. 189–91; King, 'On the role of the muezzin'.
2 Amin, *Awqaf*, pp. 189f.
3 Maqrizi, *Khitat*, II, p. 212.
4 Ibn Battuta, p. 54.
5 Maqrizi, *Khitat*, I, p. 317.
6 Maqrizi, *Khitat*, I, pp. 390, 492.
7 Lane, p. 78.
8 Robert Dankoff, *An Ottoman Mentality: The World of Evliya Celebi* (Leiden and Boston, 2006), p. 115.
9 Evliya Çelebi, p. 207.
10 Maqrizi, *Khitat*, I, p. 317.
11 Maqrizi, *Suluk*, II, p. 740.
12 Maqrizi, *Khitat*, II, p. 270.
13 Al-Sa'id, p. 50.
14 Suyuti, *Husn*, II, pp. 250f.
15 Al-Sa'id, p. 71.
16 Al-Sa'id, p. 74.
17 Mubarak, IV, p. 17.
18 Maqrizi, *Khitat*, II, p. 270.
19 Ibn Hajar, *Inba'*, III, p. 403.
20 Ibn al-Ukhuwwa, pp. 267f; Ibn al-Hajj, II, pp. 242, 247f.
21 Ibn al-Hajj, II, p. 241.
22 Ibn al-Hajj, II, p. 247.
23 Mubarak, IV, p. 57.
24 Al-Sa'id, p. 83.
25 Amin, *Awqaf*, p. 191; al-Sa'id, ch. 9.
26 Ibn Khallikan, p. 270.
27 Because diacritical marks are missing from his signature, there are a variety of possible readings of his name.

TWO

1 Maqrizi, *Khitat*, I, p. 230.
2 Maqrizi, *Itti'az*, II, p. 287.
3 Van Berchem, p. 101.
4 Kahle, *Der Leuchtturm*; idem, *Manarat al-iskandariyya*; Sa'd, pp. 590f., 1062f.
5 Ibn Khaldun, *Ta'rif*, p. 308.
6 Le Mascrier, p. 157.
7 Evliya Çelebi, p. 289.
8 The madrasa of al-Zahir Baybars is no longer there.
9 Maqrizi, *Khitat*, II, p. 276.
10 Jabarti, III, p.190.
11 Ibn Iyas, IV, p. 276.

12 Breydenbach, p. 47.
13 Fabri, pp. 528f.
14 Ibn Jubayr, p. 123.
15 Jabarti, IV, p. 30.
16 Ministry of Waqf, no 952.
17 Ibn Tulun, I, pp. 36, 41, 108.
18 Jabarti, II, pp. 102, 189.
19 Jomard, p. 583 (II/2).
20 Qalqashandi, XIV, p. 399; Bloom, *Minaret*, p. 37.
21 Shafi'i, '*Imara*, p. 576.
22 Maqrizi, *Khitat*, I, pp. 155f.
23 Lane, p. 476.
24 Evliya Çelebi, p. 131.
25 Maqrizi, *Khitat*, I, p. 477.
26 Maqrizi, *Suluk*, IV, pp. 713.
27 Al-Jawhari (al-Sayrafi), *Nuzha*, III, pp. 73f.
28 Maqrizi, *Suluk*, IV, pp. 713f.
29 Maqrizi, *Suluk*, IV, p. 716.

THREE

1 See entry no. 1 for the Mosque of 'Amr.
2 Ibn Iyas, V, p. 188.
3 al-Kindi, p. 61; Ibn 'Abd al-Hakam, pp. 178f; this is repeated in later accounts.
4 Abu Salih, p. 54.
5 Ibn Duqmaq, IV, p. 63.
6 al-Zahiri, p. 31.
7 Little, p. 398, n. 69.
8 Maqrizi, *Khitat*, II, p. 455.
9 Creswell, *MAE*, I, p. 274.
10 Maqrizi, *Khitat*, II, pp. 447, 450.
11 Maqrizi, *Khitat*, II, p. 456.
12 Abu Salih, p. 58.
13 J. Bloom assumes that the mosque was initially built without a minaret, arguing that vicinity to the palace would have allowed the muezzin to overlook the caliph's domestic life. However, the position of a minaret that was not likely to have been monumental, considering the size of the mosque, is unlikely to have allowed the muezzin to look deep into the palace's interior located on the rear side of the mosque. *Arts of the City Victorious*, p. 134; O'Kane's review of this book, *CAA Online Review*.
14 Ibn Iyas, I/1 p. 416.
15 Maqrizi, *Khitat*, II, p. 318.
16 Maqrizi, *Khitat*, II, p. 297.
17 Mackenzie, p. 129.
18 Ibn Hajar, *Inba'*, III, p. 87.
19 In the seventeenth century the Turkish traveller Evliya Çelebi wrote that the madrasa of the Ayyubid sultan al-Malik al-Kamil had a disposition of minaret and dome similar to that of its immediate neighbour, the later mosque of Sultan al-Zahir Barquq, although the style of the minaret was different.

This information is not confirmed, however, and we do not know whether Evliya Çelebi was referring to a later

addition since only ruins have survived of this building. Evliya Çelebi, p. 209; Creswell, *MAE*, II, p. 80.
20 Maqrizi, *Khitat*, II, p. 367.
21 Evliya Çelebi, p. 117.
22 Both are madrasas according to their inscriptions and foundation deeds but are popularly known as *takiyya*s.
23 Maqrizi, *Khitat*, II, p. 307; Evliya Çelebi, p. 117.
24 Thiersch, *Leuchtturm*; Behrens-Abouseif, 'Lighthouse'.
25 Creswell, 'Evolution'.
26 *Description de l'Egypte, Antiquités*, V, pl. 43.
27 Ibn Battuta, p. 9.
28 Abd al-Latif al-Baghdadi, *Relation*, p. 183.
29 Ibn Iyas, IV, p. 196.
30 Creswell, 'Evolution', p. 10.
31 Maqrizi, *Khitat*, II, p. 281.
32 See below, Chapter 6.
33 Jabarti, III, p. 159; Evliya Çelebi, pp. 118.
34 See below Part 3 on the provincial minarets.
35 Ibn Kathir, XIV, p. 277; 'Abd al-Wahhab, *Masajid*, p. 285.
36 Maqrizi, *Khitat*, II, p. 329.
37 One of the minarets of the Umayyad mosque in Damascus was called *al-'arus*.
38 See entry no. 58.
39 This mosque, which has lately been demolished and replaced by a new building, was founded by 'Abbas Pasha I (1848–54).

FOUR

1 Samhudi, p. 530.
2 Maqrizi, *Khitat*, II, pp. 318, 451.
3 Ibn Iyas, I, p. 416; Creswell, *MAE*, I, pl. 101b.
4 See entry no. 45.

FIVE

1 Samhudi, p. 633.
2 See entry no. 62.
3 Maqrizi, *Khitat*, II, p.316.
4 Maqrizi, *Khitat*, II, pp. 229f.
5 Ibn Iyas, II, pp. 248, 291; Ibn Taghribirdi, *Hawadith*, p. 16f.
6 Ibn Iyas, III, p. 226f.
7 There are two cartouches, one on each side of the portal; it is not clear whether they refer to a single long name or a pair of names. This signature must be referring to the extraordinary construction of the portal rather than its rather more normal decoration, as assumed by 'Abd al-Wahhab, 'Tawqi'at', p. 555.
8 Maqrizi, *Khitat*, II, p. 384.
9 Creswell, *MAE*, II, p. 238.
10 I am grateful to Bernard O'Kane for drawing my attention to this.
11 Dogan Kuban, *Sinan's Art and Selimiye* (Istanbul 1997), p. 155; Godfrey Goodwin,

A History of Ottoman Architecture (London 1987), pp. 99, 268.
12 See entry no. 78.

SIX

1   Ettinghausen, 'Hilal', *Encyclopaedia of Islam.*
2   Maqrizi, *Khitat*, i, pp. 476, 478.
3   Ibn 'Uthman, p. 20.
4   'Abd al-Ghani, p. 212; Jabarti, i, p. 25.
5   See bibliography.
6   Maqrizi, *Khitat*, ii, p. 267.
7   This element, which is not on display, was shown to me at the Islamic Museum in Cairo in 1983.
8   Ibn Tulun uses the term *sanawbara* for a certain type of lamp. ii, pp. 69 and 75.
9   Goettlicher, *Materialien*, deals with this topic in antiquity.
10 Lane-Poole, p. 138.
11 It is reported, for example, that the pulpit from which the imam-caliph al-Hakim preached on Fridays was adorned with a domed pavilion curtained like a litter and perfumed with incense before his arrival. Maqrizi, *Khitat*, ii, p. 281.
12 Hampikian, 'Restoration of the al-Salihiyya'.
13 Ormos, p. 237, figs. 101,102.
14 Karnouk, p. 125.
15 Maqrizi, *Khitat*, ii, p. 281.
16 Ormos, p. 261.
17 Speiser, p. 151, pl. 44.
18 It seems that the construction of this spectacular minaret led to the change of the village's name to refer to it.
19 Little, p. 398, n. 69. See also O'Kane, 'Taj al-Din 'Alishah: the Reconstruction and Influence of His Mosque at Tabriz' (in press).
20 Ibn Taghribirdi, *Nujum*, x, p. 102; Creswell, *Chronology*, pp. 96f; Van Berchem, pp. 736f.
21 Ibn Taghribirdi, *Manhal*, vi, p. 394.
22 Precedents for such spiral decoration can be found in Roman, Byzantine and Coptic architecture.
23 D.N. Wilber, *The Architecture of Islamic Iran, the Ilkhanid Period* (Westport, CT 1969), pp. 143, fig. 91.
24 See E. Atil, *The Age of Sultan Süleyman the Magnificent* (Washington and New York 1987), p. 86, fig. 39b.
25 G. Goodwin, *A History of Ottoman Architecture* (London 1971), pp. 99, 139, 151.
26 Maqrizi, *Khitat*, ii, p. 307; Evliya Çelebi, p. 126.
27 Kessler, *Domes*, figs. 12, 13.
28 Of a later date than the mosque which was built in 1336.
29 See entry 61.
30 Maqrizi, *Khitat*, ii, pp. 101, 105.
31 This dome (Index no. 106), popularly known by the name Khadija Umm al-Ashraf or Khadija al-Ashraf's mother,

is anonymous, and was probably part of the funerary complex of Sultan al-Ashraf Barsbay.
32 Kessler, *Domes*, pl. 9.
33 Kessler, *Domes*, p. 4.
34 Behrens-Abouseif, 'The 'Abd al-Rahman Katkhuda style in 18th-century Cairo', *Annales Islamologiques* 26 (1992), pp. 117–26.
35 See entry no. 89.

SEVEN

1   Maqrizi, *Khitat*, ii, p. 248; Ibn Duqmaq, iv, p. 63; Wiet, *Corpus*, pp. 4–8.
2   Wiet, *Corpus*, pp. 126–8; Van Berchem, pp. 51f.
3   Van Berchem, pp. 47, 48, 188.
4   Van Berchem, p. 100f; 'Abd al-Wahhab, *Masajid*, pp. 199f.
5   Van Berchem, p. 599.
6   Van Berchem, p. 70; Wiet, *Corpus*, p. 186.
7   Van Berchem, pp. 131f.
8   Van Berchem p. 53.
9   See Hoyland; Dodd and Khairallah.
10 Ibn Khallikan, i, pp. 270f.
11 The verses are cited in numerical order in the translation of Abdel Haleem. The reading is based on fieldwork and on O'Kane et al.

EIGHT

1   For details of this and the earlier views, see Warner, *The True Description of Cairo.*
2   *Description de l'Égypte (État Moderne)*, i, pls. 29 (Ibn Tulun), 28 (al-Hakim), 65.1 far right (Fatima Khatun), 74 (al-Nasir Muhammad), 32–4, 37, 38 (Sultan Hasan), and 25 (Sinan Pasha).
3   *Description de l'Égypte, État Moderne*, i, pl. 27.6.
4   Ibid., pls. 1 and 8.
5   *Im Banne der Sphinx* (exhibition catalogue, Mainz 1994), p. 182, fig. 2.
6   Pascal Coste, *Toutes les Egypte*, p. 114.
7   Ecole nationale supérieure des Beaux-Arts (ENSBA), Paris, inv. 1995.
8   See bibliography.
9   The views in Prisse d'Avennes' publication of the minarets of Qanibay al-Rammah at al-Nasiriyya, the mosque of al-Burdayni, the madrasa of al-Ghawri, and the complex of Khayrbak are all taken from Girault de Prangey's work. See bibliography.
10 Bourgoin, i, pls. 2–5 (al-Nasir Muhammad); pls. 7 and 8 (Aqsunqur) and pls. 9 and 10 (Qawsun?).
11 Ibid., pls. 11–15.
12 See J. Raby, *Venice, Dürer, and the Oriental Mode*, Hans Huth Memorial Studies 1, London 1982, for references to the work of artists such as Gentile Bellini and Carpaccio.
13 David Roberts' work appeared in many

editions, the two most important being *The Holy Land, Syria, Idumea, Arabia, Egypt and Nubia*, 6 vols (London 1842–9), and *Egypt and Nubia*, 3 vols (London 1846–9).
14 Roberts, *The Holy Land*, vi, pl. 226. See also Ormos, pls. 69–71 for the comparison.
15 Roberts, *The Holy Land*, iii, pl. 13.
16 See Caroline Williams, 'Jean-Léon Gérôme: A Case Study of an Orientalist Painter', in S.J. Webber and M.R. Lynd (eds), *Fantasy or Ethnography? Irony and Collusion in Subaltern Representation*, Papers in Comparative Studies 8 (Ohio State University 1993–4), pp. 117–48.
17 Private Collection (whereabouts unknown), 90.5 x 65.4 cm.
18 See Ken Jacobsen, *Odalisques and Arabesques: Orientalist Photography 1839–1925* (London 2007), for an excellent survey.
19 The archive is in the care of the Supreme Council for Antiquities and is hitherto unpublished. For details see Mayer, pp. 157–60.
20 Viewable online at http://creswell.ashmolean.org.
21 Creswell, *MAE*, ii, pls. 123–6.
22 For the world's fairs, see Z. Çelik, *Displaying the Orient: Architecture of Islam at Nineteenth-Century World's Fair* (Berkeley, Los Angeles and Oxford 1992), p. 63.
23 *L'Esposizione Universale di Vienna del 1873 Illustrata* (Milan 1873), p. 19.
24 De Gleon, p. 7.
25 See the images contained in *The Dream City: A Portfolio of Views from the World's Columbian Exposition*, i (Chicago 1893). The street was designed by Max Herz: see Ormos, pp. 458–63.
26 Designed by F.H. Coventry and printed in Cairo in 1935 by Ateliers Kalfer, size 100 x 70 cm. Coventry was a graphic designer from New Zealand, invited to Egypt by the government to design a series of promotional posters.

NINE

1   Index 319; Ibn 'Abd al-Hakam, pp. 178f; Ibn Muyassar, p. 85; Maqrizi, *Khitat*, ii, pp. 246–56, iv/1, 8–37; Ibn Duqmaq, iv, pp. 59–71; Qalqashandi, iii, pp. 338f; Wiet, *Corpus*, pp. 4–8; Ahmad 'Amr, p. 46; Creswell, *EMA*, ii, pp. 200ff.
2   These mosques did not at that time have the status of Friday mosques.
3   Maqrizi, *Itti'az*, iii, p. 176.
4   Evliya Çelebi, p. 109.
5   Index 220, Maqrizi, *Khitat*, ii, pp. 265–9; Ibn Duqmaq, iv, p. 123; Ahmad; Ibn Tulun; Creswell, *EMA*, ii, pp. 348ff; Swelim, 'The Minaret'.
6   Ibn Jubayr, p. 26.
7   Raymond, André, *Artisans et Commerçants*

au Caire au XVIIIe Siècle, 2 vols (Damascus 1984), I, p. 321.

8 Ibn Uthman, p. 20.
9 Evliya Çelebi, p. 111.
10 Muqaddasi, p. 199.
11 Naser e Khosrou (Najmabadi and Weber transl.), p. 96.
12 Index 97; Maqrizi, *Khitat*, II, pp. 275f.
13 Each of these minarets have separate catalogue entries: see nos. 25, 78 and 89.
14 Jalabi, p. 152.
15 Jabarti, II, p. 93.
16 Jabarti, III, p. 51.
17 Index 15; Maqrizi, *Khitat*, II, pp. 277–82; Creswell, *MAE*, I, pp. 85–101; Wiet, *Corpus*, pp. 126–8; Van Berchem, p. 51f; Flury, pp. 8–26, 43–50; Bloom, 'Al-Hakim', p. 21f.
18 Maqrizi, *Itti'az*, I, pp. 267, 272, 279, 283.
19 Maqrizi, *Itti'az*, II, pp. 44, 45; idem *Khitat*, II, pp. 282f.; also Ibn Duqmaq, IV, pp. 78f., indicate the foundation date as Safar 393.
20 Maqrizi, *Itti'az*, II, p. 58.
21 Maqrizi, *Khitat*, II, pp. 282f.
22 Bloom, 'al-Hakim', p. 26.
23 Maqrizi, *Itti'az*, II, pp. 4f., 59.
24 Maqrizi, *Itti'az*, II, pp. 52, 78, 82, 86, 96, 110.
25 Creswell calls the minarets 'northern' and 'western'; our description refers to them as 'northern' and 'southern'.
26 See Chapter 12.
27 Creswell, *MAE*, I, pls. 23A and D.
28 Wiet, *Corpus*, pp. 126f; Bloom, 'al-Hakim', pp. 34f.
29 Creswell citing a reading by Flury, *MAE*, I, p. 87.
30 Index 304; Creswell, *MAE*, I, pp. 155ff; Wiet, *Corpus*, pp. 128f; Grabar, 'Commemorative Studies'; Ragib, 'Oratoire'; Shafi'i, 'The Mashhad al-Juyushi'.
31 Index 3; Sakhawi, *Tuhfa*, p. 99; Mubarak, II, p. 83, V, pp. 120–1; Creswell, *MAE*, I, p. 274.
32 Creswell, *MAE*, I, pl. 96B.
33 Index 28; Maqrizi, *Khitat*, I, p. 427; Creswell, *MAE*, II, p. 83; Van Berchem, p. 101; 'Abd al-Wahhab, *Masajid*, pp. 76–93; Mackenzie, pp. 112–13.
34 Shafi'i, 'West Islamic Influences'.
35 Index 38; Creswell, *MAE*, II, p. 97; Mackenzie, pp. 123f; for detailed descriptions of the construction, see N. Hampikian, 'Restoration of the al-Salihiyya'; 'Al-Salihiyya Complex through Time'; 'The Minaret of the Salihiyya Madrasa'.
36 See Chapter 6 on the structure of the mabkhara.

TEN

1 Coste, pl. LXII; Mubarak, III, p. 82, 120; *Toutes les Egyptes*, p.105; Behrens-Abouseif, 'The Lost Minaret'.
2 Index 169.
3 Index 1; Behrens-Abouseif, *Cairo of the*

Mamluks, p. 124.
4 Towards the end of the Ayyubid period, however, with the expansion of the city, additional congregational mosques were founded in the suburbs to meet the needs of the population. MacKenzie, p. 139.
5 Ibn Shaddad, p. 346.
6 Evliya Çelebi, p. 119.
7 Jabarti, III, p. 33.
8 *Description de l'Égypte (Etat Moderne)*, I, pl. 65
9 Index 274; Creswell, *MAE*, II, pp. 180f.
10 Index 43; Creswell, *MAE*, II, pp. 194f; Van Berchem, pp. 131–3.
11 Ibn Hajar, *Durar*, III, p. 356.
12 O'Kane et al., no 43.15
13 Van Berchem, pp. 243f.
14 'Abd al-Wahhab, *Masajid*, p. 117.
15 Index 237; Creswell, *MAE*, II, p. 140.
16 Index 245; Creswell, *MAE*, II, pp. 249; Behrens-Abouseif, *Cairo of the Mamluks*, p. 143.
17 Index 156; Mubarak, IV, p. 66; Van Berchem, p. 652; Creswell, *Chronology*, p. 84.
18 Index 44; Creswell, *MAE*, II, pp. 237f; Van Berchem, pp. 152–5.
19 Ibn Taghribirdi, *Nujum*, XVI, p. 114.
20 Index 221; Creswell, 'Minaret'; *MAE*, II, p. 246.
21 Index 32; Creswell, *MAE*, II, pp. 252f.
22 Mubarak, IV, p. 64.
23 Ibn Iyas I/2, p. 560; Maqrizi, *Suluk* II, p. 840; *waqf* document of Khayrbak 'Dar al-Watha'iq al-Qawmiyya' no. 292/44, dated 927/1521.
24 Warner, *Monuments*, p. 149, no. (374).
25 Index 263; Creswell, *MAE*, II, p. 269.
26 Index 143; Bates, pp. 39, 45 n. 5; Meinecke, 'Fayencemosaikdekorationen', pp. 97–107; Behrens-Abouseif, *Cairo of the Mamluks*, pp. 173ff.
27 See Chapter 3 on the impact of the Tabrizi builder.
28 Rogers, 'Mamluk-Mongol', p. 387.
29 This subject has been documented by Meinecke in his study 'Fayencemosaik-dekorationen'. Behrens-Abouseif, *Cairo of the Mamluks*, pp. 176, fig. 117.
30 Behrens-Abouseif, *Cairo of the Mamluks*, pp. 176, fig. 117.
31 Index 205.
32 O'Kane et al., no. 205.
33 Hasan 'Abd al-Wahhab attributed this upper structure to a restoration done in 1861 by a princess of the Muhammad 'Ali family.
34 Ali Ibrahim, 'Transitional Zone', p. 15.
35 'Abd al-Wahhab, *Masajid* p. 145, misreads *limasjidihi* (for his mosque) as *li-nafsihi* (for himself).
36 Index 290; Maqrizi, *Khitat*, II, p. 325; Ali Ibrahim, 'The Hanqah of Qawsun'; Kessler, *Domes*, pp. 4, 5, 15; Meinecke, *Architektur*, II, p. 170.
37 It is not a double-staircase as written by 'Abd al-Wahhab, *Masajid*, p. 56.

38 Index 293; Meinecke, *Architektur*, I, p. 84, II, p. 179.
39 This opinion has also been adopted by Abu 'l-'Amayim in his article on this subject, 'al-Mi'dhana'.
40 Maqrizi, *Khitat*, II, p. 307.
41 O'Kane et al., no. 97.124.
42 Index 120; Maqrizi, *Khitat*, II, p. 384; Creswell, 'Minaret', p. 19.
43 For the reconstruction, see Ormos, I, p. 135 and pl. 47.
44 Index 22; Meinecke, *Architektur*, II, p. 208. Today the building is popularly called the *zawiya* of Aydumur al-Bahlawan.
45 Matters are further confused by the presence in the Comité archives of two separate drawings purporting to show the same minaret top in reconstructed states. Ormos, pp. 202, 236.
46 Index 123.
47 For the reconstruction, see Ormos, I, p. 148.
48 A drawing by Marilhat looking down the Darb al-Ahmar dated to 1831–2, now in the Searight Collection of the Victoria & Albert Museum (Prints and Drawings Department), clearly shows the minaret in its original condition. The painting by Carlo Bossoli (1815–84) showing the Tabbana quarter seen from east is a copy of David Roberts' picture. *Bonhams Catalogue*, December 2007, London, p. 74 No 99.
49 Index 138.
50 Roberts, *Egypt and Nubia*, pl. 97.
51 Index 147 (mosque), 152 (*khanqah*); Mubarak, V, p. 36; Behrens-Abouseif, *Cairo of the Mamluks*, pp. 191ff.
52 Index 218.
53 Index 288 (minaret), 289 (mausoleum); F. Makar, 'Farida, Al-Sultaniyya' (unpublished MA thesis, American University in Cairo); Waqf of Masih Pasha, Ministry of Waqf, no. 2836; Evliya Çelebi, p. 230.
54 Index 133; Maqrizi, *Khitat*, II, pp. 316ff; Rogers, 'Seljuk Influences'; Kessler, 'Imperious Reasons'; Behrens-Abouseif, *Cairo of the Mamluks*, pp. 205f.
55 Ormos' statement that both minarets were entirely dismantled and reconstructed is not correct. I, p. 216.
56 Jalabi, p. 187; Warthilani, copying the text of al-'Ayyashi, pp. 265f; Jabarti, I, p. 150; II, p. 107.
57 Index 36; Maqrizi, *Khitat*, II, pp. 71, 382; Speiser, pp. 139–71, 73; Meinecke, *Architektur*, II, p. 210, 231.
58 Ibn Taghribirdi, *Manhal*, XI, pp. 2689f.
59 Ormos, vol.1, p. 207.
60 Index 85; Van Berchem, pp. 273f.
61 Index 125.
62 Index 185.
63 Index 131.
64 Index 187.
65 'Abd al-Wahhab, *Masajid*, p. 194;

Behrens-Abouseif, 'Muhandis', pp. 297f.

66 For the reconstruction see Ormos, I, p. 126 and pl. 33.

67 Index 33.

68 Index 33; Maqrizi, *Khitat*, II, p. 290.

69 For the repairs see Ormos, I, p. 142.

70 Ihsanoglu et al., fig. 83, p. 136; Warner, *Monuments*, p. 109; Warner, 'Detecting the Past', pp. 314–17.

71 Index 149.

72 The south-west *sabil-maktab* is not at the corner proper, but projects near the portal, forming a corner of its own.

73 For the reconstruction of the southern minaret, dating to between 1886 and 1900, see Ormos, I, p. 132 and pls. 50–3.

74 Index 151.

75 Index 190 (mosque of al-Mu'ayyad) and 199 (Bab Zuwayla); Van Berchem, pp. 339ff; 'Abd al-Wahhab, 'Tawqi'at', pp. 52f.

76 This reading of Maqrizi's text corrects the previous interpretation in Behrens-Abouseif, *Cairo of the Mamluks*, p. 241, which identifies the minaret that had to be rebuilt as the eastern one.

77 Al-Jawahri al-Sayrafi, *Nuzha*, II, p. 366.

78 There was, however, another signature on an Egyptian minaret near Aswan dating perhaps from the Fatimid period, which has been deciphered by Hasan al-Hawari. See Chapter 12. Another signed minaret is of a much later date, 1686, at the mosque of Emir Hammad in the town of Mit Ghamr. See 'Abd al-Wahhab, 'Tawqi'at', p. 554.

79 Maqrizi, *Suluk*, IV, p. 11, 12, 366; Ibn Taghribirdi, *Manhal*, X, pp. 29f.

80 For the new design dating to 1891, see Ormos, I, pl. 17 and pp. 115–16.

81 Al-Jawahri al-Sayrafi, *Nuzha* , II, p. 366.

82 Maqrizi, *Suluk*, IV, p. 744.

83 The inscriptions of the first storey are the same, the upper ones differ.

84 The *naffadha* (has executed) has not been identified neither by Van Berchem nor by 'Abd al-Wahhab. O'Kane et al. read it as *bi-'amal*, no. 190.7

85 Index 60.

86 Van Berchem, pp. 344ff.

87 Index 175.

88 Index 119; Mubarak, IV, pp. 73f; Van Berchem, pp. 360f; 'Abd al-Wahhab, *Masajid*, pp. 218; Meinecke, *Architektur*, II, p. 344.

89 Index 192.

90 Index 50, *Dalil al-athar*, p. 123

91 Maqrizi, *Khitat*, II, 331; Sakhawi, *Daw'*, VIII, pp. 238ff; Sha'rani, II, pp. 87f; Mubarak, V, pp. 60f; Van Berchem, pp. 581f; Garcin, p. 163; Meinecke, *Architektur*, II, p. 359.

92 Meinecke, *Architektur*, II, p. 363; Warner, *Monuments*, p. 125; Ibrahim, 'Qaraquja'.

93 Ibn Taghribirdi, *Nujum*, XV, p. 453; Ibn Iyas, II, pp. 391; Van Berchem, pp. 381f.

94 Index 182. Warner, *Monuments*, Map Sheet 27 for the original street pattern in this area, now much modified.

95 For the design, see Ormos, I, pl. 80.

96 Index 344.

97 Sakhawi, *Daw'*, III, p. 71ff; Van Berchem, pp. 392f; Creswell, *Chronology*, p. 133.

98 Van Berchem, p. 391; Meinecke, *Architektur*, II, p. 370.

99 Index 317; Mubarak, V, p. 110; Creswell, *Chronology*, p. 133; Warner, 'Detecting the Past', p. 299.

100 Index 55; Mubarak, IV, p. 120; Creswell, *Brief Chronology*, p. 135.

101 N. Hanna, *Making Big Money in 1600* (New York 1997), p. 136.

102 Maqrizi, *Khitat* II, p. 327; Mubarak, IV, pp. 54f; Van Berchem, pp. 198f; Creswell, *Chronology*, p. 104; Meinecke, *Architektur*, II, p. 209. 'Ali Mubarak wrote that the mosque had no mausoleum, which is true, and no minaret, which is obviously wrong.

103 Index 158.

104 Index 204.

105 Ibn Iyas, II, p. 392; Karim, pp. 175f.

106 Sakhawi, *Daw'*, III, p. 43; Meinecke, *Architektur* II, p. 389.

107 Jawhari, *Inba'*, pp. 465f.

108 Sha'rani, II, p. 101; Garcin, figs. 1, 2.

109 Index 464; Van Berchem, pp. 425f; Meinecke, *Architektur*, II, p. 392; Warner, 'Detecting the Past', pp. 306–7; idem, *Monuments*, p. 158.

110 Index 207; Kessler, *Domes*, pl. 33.

111 Creswell, *Chronology*, p. 137.

112 O'Kane et al., no. 2071–2.

113 Ibn Taghribirdi, *Hawadith*, pp. 209, 339, 577f; idem, *Nujum*, XVI, pp. 335f.

114 Meinecke, *Architektur*, II, p. 390.

115 Libay, *Reisebilder*, the plate is not numbered.

116 Index 223; see Ormos, I, pl. 125 for Comité drawings showing a design dating to 1901 for the reconstruction of the minaret.

117 Index 216; Ibn Iyas, III, p. 70; Mubarak, IV, p. 70; Van Berchem, pp. 428f; Meinecke, *Architektur* II, p. 401.

118 Index 129; Herz, 'Ganem El-Bahlawaouan'; Meinecke, *Architektur* II, p. 464.

119 Index 286; 'Abd al-Wahhab, *Masajid*, p. 199.

120 O'Kane et al., no. 286.4.

121 Index 49.

122 Kessler, *Domes*, pl. 26.

123 Index 114.

124 For the reconstruction, see Ormos, I, p. 143 and pl. 61.

125 Index 340; Sha'rani, II, p. 101; 'Abd al-Wahhab, *Masajid*, pp. 276 ff; Mubarak, IV, p. 52.

126 Index 153.

127 Ibn Iyas, III, p. 283; Sakhawi, *Daw'*, IV, p. 208; 'Abd al-Wahhab, *Masajid*, pp. 273ff.

128 Ibn Iyas, III, pp. 124, 306; Sakhawi, *Daw'*, VI, p. 209; Van Berchem, p. 674f; Wiet, *Matériaux*, pp. 121; 'Abd al-Wahhab, *Masajid*, pp. 55f.

129 Van Berchem, pp. 47f; O'Kane et al., no. 97.44.

130 Index 211.

131 Ibn Iyas, III, p. 193.

132 Behrens-Abouseif, *Cairo of the Mamluks*, pp. 292f.

133 O'Kane et al., no. 211.29.

134 Index 163; Dar al-Watha'iq al-Qawmiyya no. 221 (35); Mubarak, IV, p. 65.

135 Index 348.

136 Ibn Iyas, IV, p. 126; Ministry of Waqf no. 974. My thanks to Nelly Hanna for drawing my attention to this document.

137 'Alanya', *Encyclopaedia of Islam,* 2nd edn.

138 Maqrizi, *Khitat*, II, p. 312; Creswell, *Chronology*, p. 98.

139 Index 2.

140 Searight Collection, now in the Prints and Drawings Department, Victoria & Albert Museum; Prisse d'Avennes, p. 143.

141 Index 174.

142 Ramadan, 'Munsha'āt al-amir Azdumur'; Dar al-Watha'iq al-Qawmiyya, no. 234/55 (37); Jabarti, III, p. 360; Mubarak, V, p. 4.

143 Jabarti, III, p. 159.

144 Majdi 'Abd al-Jawwad 'Ilwan 'Uthman, *al-Ma'adhin al-baqiya bi 'l-dilta.*

145 Index 189; Ibn Iyas, IV, pp. 58, 84; *Toutes les Egypte*, p. 129; Behrens-Abouseif, *Cairo of the Mamluks*, pp. 297f.

146 Prisse d'Avennes, p. 145, describes the inscription band; see also Prost, pp. 11f., pl. IV/2; Kessler, *Domes*, pl. 46; Jenkins, p. 112.

147 Index 136 (Rumayla) and 254 (Nasriyya).

148 Index 170.

149 Ibn Iyas, V, p. 94; Van Berchem, p. 48.

150 This document was offered for sale in London in October 2002, see Sotheby's catalogue *Arts of the Islamic World*, no. 18, p. 27.

151 Many of these terms do not figure in Amin and 'Ali Ibrahim's book *Architectural Terms.*

152 Amin and Ali Ibrahim, p. 113.

153 Van Berchem, p. 48; O'Kane et al., no. 97.47.

154 O'Kane et al., no. 97.46.

155 Ibn Iyas, IV, p. 38, V, pp. 341, 430; Mubarak, IV, p. 110; Van Berchem, pp. 565ff; Meinecke, *Architektur*, II, p. 540.

156 Index 248.

ELEVEN

1 Behrens-Abouseif, *Egypt's Adjustment*, p. 226, pl. 18.

2 Sha'rani, II, p. 184; Van Berchem, pp. 604f; Mahir, IV, pp. 293–5; Behrens-Abouseif, 'Sufi Architecture', 103–14.

3 Behrens-Abouseif, *Egypt's Adjustment*, p. 260.

4 *The Mosques of Egypt*, II, p. 107; Swelim, 'Sinan Pasha'.

5 Entry no. 98.
6 Index 330; Mubarak, pp. 39–41; Williams, pp. 459, 462f; 'Abd al-Wahhab, *Masajid*, pp. 308f; Behrens-Abouseif, *Egypt's Adjustment*, pp. 172f., 253ff.
7 Index 201; Mubarak, IV, p. 65, IX, p.1; *The Mosques of Egypt*, II, pp. 127, 193f; *Dalil al-Athar*, p. 195; Van Berchem's reading of the mosque's date 1105/1694 is wrong, pp. 612f.
8 Behrens-Abouseif, *Egypt's Adjustment*, pp. 172f.
9 Van Berchem's reading.
10 Index 587; Mubarak, V, p. 46; *The Mosques of Egypt*, II, p. 127; 'Abd al-Wahhab, *Masajid*, pp. 372–5.
11 Ministry of Waqf, nos. 989, 991, 992; Behrens-Abouseif, *Egypt's Adjustment*, pp. 169f.
12 Evliya Çelebi, p. 125
13 Index 130; Jalabi, p. 611.
14 Index 610; *Dalil*, p. 237; Mubarak, III, p. 93, V, p. 93.
15 Jabarti, IV, p. 296; Mubarak, IV, p. 87; 'Abd al-Wahhab, p. 357f; Crecelius et al. (eds), *Tarikh*, n. 3, pp. 101f.
16 Mubarak, V, p. 15; 'Abd al-Wahhab, *Masajid*, pp. 360ff.
17 Mubarak, V, pp. 77ff; Wiet, *Beaux- Arts*, pp. 265ff; 'Abd al-Wahhab, *Masajid*, pp. 376–88; Al-Asad, 'The mosque of Muhammad Ali'; Coste; *Toutes les Egyptes*, pp. 111–13.
18 Mubarak, I, pp, 90f; Evliya Çelebi, p. 194; Gabriel Baer, *Egyptian Guilds in Modern Time* (Jerusalem 1964), pp. 43, 44, 147.
19 Mubarak, IV, pp. 88f.
20 Volait, pp. 64f., 70f.
21 Mubarak, IV, pp. 114–9; Herz, *el-Rifa'i*; 'Abd al-Wahhab, *Masajid*, pp. 363–71; Al-Asad, 'The mosque of al-Rifa'i'; Volait, pp. 73, 173–9.
22 Al-Asad, 'The mosque of al-Rifa'i', fig. 14.
23 Herz, *el-Rifa'i*, pl. V.

TWELVE

1 Creswell, *MAE*, I, pp. 146–55, pls, 122, 123; 'Abd al-Wahhab, 'Tarz al-'imara', p. 15f; Shafi'i, *'Imara*, pp. 573–80; Hawari; Bloom,

'Five Minarets'.
2 Creswell, *MAE*, I, pp. 131ff.
3 Creswell, *MAE*, I, pl. 122A.
4 See Bloom, *City Victorious*, pp. 84, 87, fig. 55.
5 Creswell, *MAE*, I, p. 147.
6 Bloom contests the attribution to Badr al-Jamali, using mainly the argument of their being made of brick, ('Five Minarets', p. 167), and suggests instead local provincial patrons. This argument disregards, however, the fact that all medieval provincial architecture was in brick.
7 'Abd al-Wahhab, 'Tarz al-'imara', pl. 6.
8 Comité Bulletin 13, 1896, pp. 142–4 and pl. 10.
9 Ibn Iyas, III, p. 392, IV, p. 97, V, pp. 215, 267f; Van Berchem, pp. 557f.
10 Behrens-Abouseif, 'Note sur l'architecture', p. 106.
11 Nuwayri, *Kitab al-ilmam,* (ed.) A.S. Attiya, 4 vols (Haydarabad 1970), IV, p. 44.
12 *Description de l'Égypte (Etat Moderne)*, II, pl. 85.
13 Coste, pl. LXVI.
14 This mosque has often been depicted and photographed. A good representation is in F. Libay's album.
15 'Azab, p. 57.
16 'Abd al-Wahhab, 'Tarz al-'imara', pl. 10, *The Mosques of Egypt*, II, pl. 217.
17 Ebers, I, p. 85.
18 For the historical documentation of the minarets of Mahalla and Mit Ghamr, I have used the very well-documented MA thesis of Majdi 'Abd al-Jawwad 'Ilwan 'Uthman, *al-Ma'adhin al-baqiya bi 'l-dilta*.
19 Ibn Hajar, *Inba'*, VI, pp. 243f; Sakhawi, *Daw'*, II, pp. 45f; Mubarak, IX, p. 35; 'Abd al-Wahhab, 'Tarz al-'imara', p. 24; 'Uthman, pp. 15ff.
20 Sakhawi, *Daw'*, VIII, p. 248; 'Uthman, pp. 24f.
21 'Uthman, pp. 37f; the author bases the date on archive documents.
22 'Abd al-Wahhab, 'Tarz al-'imara', fig. 15.
23 Sakhawi, *Daw'*, II, pp. 161f; Sha'rani, II, pp. 121f; Ibn al-'Imad, VIII, pp. 25f; 'Uthman, pp. 29f.
24 'Uthman, pp. 67, 77.
25 'Abd al-Wahhab, 'Tarz al-'imara', figs. 11, 12.

THIRTEEN

1 For the Mamluk architecture of Greater Syria, see: M.H. Burgoyne, *Mamluk Jerusalem* (Jerusalem 1987); Meinecke's *Mamlukische Architektur*, which deals largely with Syria; Hayat Salam-Liebich, *The Architecture of Mamluk City of Tripoli* (Cambridge MA 1983); Archie G. Walls, *Geometry and Architecture in Islamic Jerusalem: A Study of the Ashrafiyya* (London 1990); Mohamed-Moain Sadek, *Die Mamlukische Architektur der Stadt Gaza* (Berlin 1991).
2 For the relationship between the metropolitan and the provincial style see Behrens-Abouseif, *Cairo of the Mamluks*, ch. 9.
3 Behrens-Abouseif, 'The Fire of 884/1479 at the Umayyad Mosque in Damascus and an Account of Its Restoration', *Mamluk Studies Review*, 8/1(2004), 279–296, p. 285.
4 Meinecke, *Architektur*, II, pp. 8f.
5 Samhudi, pp. 526ff; J. Sauvaget, *La Mosquée ommayade de Médine* (Paris 1947); Creswell, I, pp. 97ff, 142ff; Creswell and Allan, pp. 15ff; Finster, pp. 131ff; Bloom, *Minaret*, ch. 3; Lam'i, *Almadina Al Munawwara*; (Beirut, 1981), pp. 86, 119; Behrens-Abouseif, 'Qaytbay's Madrasahs in the Holy Cities and the Evolution of Haram Architecture', *Mamluk Studies Review*, 3 (1999), pp. 129–41.
6 Ibn Jubayr, p. 173.
7 Samhudi, p. 528.
8 Ibn Hajar, *Durar*, III, p. 347; Meinecke, *Architektur*, II, p. 98.
9 Samhudi, p. 605.
10 Samhudi, pp. 618f.
11 Ibn Iyas, III, pp. 188ff; Samhudi, pp. 633ff; Meinecke, *Architektur*, II, pp. 424f.
12 Samhudi, pp. 618, 627–33.
13 Sakhawi, *Daw'*, VIII, pp. 703f.
14 Samhudi, pp. 527, 646; Meinecke, *Architektur*, II, pp. 429f; Ibn Iyas, III, pp. 10, 100, 158 182, 252, 387; IV, pp. 165, 402; On Shahin al-Jamali, see Sakhawi, *Daw'*, IV, pp. 293f.
15 Samhudi, p. 646.
16 Samhudi, p. 641.

BIBLIOGRAPHY

PRIMARY SOURCES INCLUDING PRE-EIGHTEENTH CENTURY ACCOUNTS

'Abd al-Laṭīf al-Baghdādī, *Kitāb al-ifāda wa 'l-i'tibār fī umūr al-mushāhada wa 'l-ḥawādith al-mu'āyana bi-arḍ miṣr (Relation de l'Égypte)*, ed. Sylvestre de Sacy (Paris 1810).

Abu Salih, *The Churches and Monasteries of Egypt and Some Neighbouring Countries attributed to Abu Salih the Armenian*, ed. and trans. B.T.A. Evetts (Oxford 1895).

Breydenbach, Bernhard von, *Les Saintes Péregrinations* (Cairo 1904).

Evliya Çelebi, *Seyahâtnamesi*, 10.Kitap, eds, S.A. Kahrama, Y. Dağli, R. Dankoff (Istanbul, 2007).

Fabri, Félix, *Le Voyage en Égypte*, 3 vols (Cairo 1975).

al-Ghazzī, Najm al-Dīn, *al-Kawākib al-sā'ira bi a'yān al-mi'a al-'āshira*, ed. Jibrā'īl S. Jabbūr, 3 vols (Beirut 1979).

Ibn 'Abd al-Ḥakam, *Futūḥ Miṣr wa 'l-Maghrib*, ed. 'Abd al-Mun'im 'Amir (Cairo n.d.).

Ibn Baṭṭūṭa, *Tuḥfat al-nuẓẓār fī gharā'ib al-amṣār wa 'ajā'ib al-asfār* (Cairo 1958).

Ibn Duqmāq, *Kitāb al-intiṣār li wāsiṭaṭ 'iqd al-amṣār* (Bulaq 1314/1897–8).

Ibn Ḥajar al-'Asqalānī, *al-Durar al-kāmina fī a'yān al-mi'a al-thāmina*, 5 vols (Cairo 1966).

——, *Inbā' al-ghumr bi-abnā' al-'umr*, 9 vols (Beirut 1986).

Ibn al Ḥājj, al-'Abdarī al-Fāsī, *al-Madkhal*, 4 vols (Cairo 1929).

Ibn al-'Imād, *Shadharāt al-dhahab fī akhbār man dhahab*, 8 vols (Beirut n.d.).

Ibn Iyās, *Badā'i' al-zuhūr fī waqā'i' al-duhūr*, ed. M. Muṣṭafā (Wiesbaden and Cairo 1961–75).

Ibn Kathīr, *al-Bidāya wa 'l-nihāya*, 14 vols (Beirut 1966).

Ibn Khaldūn, 'Abd al-Raḥmān, *al-Ta'rīf bi-ibn Khaldūn wa riḥlatihi gharban wa sharqan* (Beirut and Cairo 1979).

Ibn Khallikān, Abū 'l-'Abbās Aḥmad, *Wafayāt al-a'yān wa anbā' abnā' al-zamān*, 2 vols (Cairo 1310/1892–3).

Ibn Muyassar, Tāj al-Dīn Muḥammad, *Akhbār Miṣr*, ed. Ayman Fu'ād Sayyid, (Textes arabes et etudes islamiques, XVII), Institut Français d'Archéologie Orientale (Cairo 1981).

Ibn Shaddād, *Tārīkh al-Malik al-Ẓāhir*, ed. Aḥmad Ḥuṭayṭ (Beirut 1983).

Ibn Taghrībirdī, *Ḥawādith al-duhūr fī madā 'l-ayyām wa 'l-shuhūr*, ed. W. Popper (Berkeley 1931).

——, *al-Nujūm al-zāhira fī mulūk Miṣr wa 'l-Qāhira*, 16 vols (Cairo 1963–71).

——, *al-Manhal al-ṣāfī wa 'l-mustawfā ba'd al-wāfī* (Cairo 1956–2005).

Ibn Ṭūlūn, Shams al-Dīn Muḥammad, *Mufākahat al-khillān fī'ḥawādith al-zamān*, ed. Muḥammad Muṣṭafā,

2 vols (Cairo 1962–4).

Ibn al-Ukhuwwa, Muḥammad ibn Aḥmad al-Qurashī, *Kitāb ma'ālim al-qurbā fī aḥkām al-ḥisba*, ed. M. M. Sha'bān and S. Aḥmad 'Īsā al-Muṭī'ī (Cairo 1976).

Ibn 'Uthmān, Muwaffaq al-Dīn, *Murshid al-zuwwār ilā qubūr al-abrār (al-musammā al-durr al-munaẓẓam fī ziyārat al-jabal al-muqaṭṭam*, ed. Muḥammad F. Abū Bakr (Beirut 1995).

al-Jabartī, 'Abd al-Raḥmān, *'Ajā'ib al-āthār fī 'l-tarājim wa 'l-akhbār*, 4 vols (Bulaq 1297/1879–80).

al-Jalabī, Aḥmad 'Abd al-Ghanī, *Awḍaḥ al-ishārāt fī man walā miṣr al-qāhira min al-wuzarā' wa 'l-bāshāt*, ed. Fu'ād Muḥammad al-Māwī (Cairo 1977).

al-Jawharī (al-Ṣayrafī) 'Alī ibn Dāwūd, *Nuzhat al-nufūs wa 'l-abdān fī tawārīkh al-zamān*, 3 vols (Cairo 1970–3).

——, *Inbā' al-ḥaṣr bi- abnā' al-'aṣr*, ed. Ḥasan al-Ḥabashī (Cairo 1970).

al-Kindī, Muḥmmad ibn Yūsuf, *Wulāt Miṣr*, ed. Ḥusayn Naṣṣār (Beirut 1959).

al-Maqrīzī, Taqiyy al-Dīn Aḥmad, *Kitāb al-mawā'iẓ wa 'l-I'tibār bi dhikr al-khiṭaṭ wa 'l-āthār*, 2 vols (Bulaq 1306/1888–9).

——, Taqiyy al-Dīn Aḥmad, *Kitāb al-sulūk li-ma'rifat duwal al-mulūk*, ed. M. Ziyāda and S. 'Āshshūr (Cairo 1970–3).

——, Taqiyy al-Dīn Aḥmad, *Itti'āẓ al-ḥunafā' bi akhbār al-a'imma al-fāṭimiyyīn al-khulafā'*, ed. Jamāl al-Dīn al-Shayyāl, 3 vols (Cairo 1967–73).

Mubārak, 'Alī, *al-Khiṭaṭ al-jadīda al-tawfīqiyya li-Miṣr wa 'l-Qāhira*, 20 vols (Cairo 1306/1888–9).

al-Muqaddasī, Shams-Dīn Abū 'Abd Allāh, *Aḥsan al-taqāsīm fī ma'rifat al-aqālīm*, ed. M.J. De Goeie (Leiden 1906).

al-Qalqashandī, Abū 'l-'Abbās Aḥmad ibn 'Alī, *Ṣubḥ al-a'shāā fī ṣinā'at al-inshā*, 14 vols (Cairo 1932–8).

The Qur'an, trans. M.A.S. Abdel Haleem (Oxford 2008).

al-Rajabī, Khalīl ibn Aḥmad, *Tārīkh al-wazīr Muḥammad 'Alī Bāshā*, ed. Danyāl Krisiliūs (Daniel Crecelius) et al. (Cairo 1997).

al-Sakhāwī, Muḥammad ibn 'Abd al-Raḥmān, *al-Ḍaw' al-lāmi' li-ahl al-qarn al-tāsi'*, 12 vols (Cairo 1896).

al-Sakhāwī, Nūr al-Dīn, *Tuḥfat al-aḥbāb wa bughyat al-ṭullāb* (Cairo 1937).

al-Samhūdī, Nūr al-Dīn 'Alī Aḥmad, *Wafā' al-wafā*, ed. M.M. 'Abd al-Majīd, 2 vols (Mecca n.d.).

al-Sha'rānī, 'Abd al-Wahhāb, *al-Ṭabaqāt al-kubrā al-musammāh bi-lawāqiḥ al-anwār fī ṭabaqāt al-akhyār*, 2 vols (Cairo 1954).

al-Shayzarī, 'Abd al-Raḥmān ibn Naṣr, *Nihāyat al-rutba fī ṭalab al-ḥisba* (Cairo 1946).

al-Suyūṭī, Jalāl al-Dīn 'Abd al-Raḥmān, *Ḥusn al-muhāḍara fī tārīkh Miṣr wa 'l-Qāhira*, 2 vols (Cairo 1968).

al-Warthīlānī, Ḥusayn ibn Muḥammad,

Nuzhat al-anẓār fī faḍl 'ilm al-tārīkh wa 'l-akhbār (Beirut 1974).

al-Ẓāhirī, Khalīl ibn Shāhīn, *Zubdat kashf al-mamālik*, ed. Paul Ravaisse (Paris 1893, repr. Frankfurt 1993).

al-Zarkashī, Muḥammad ibn 'Abd Allāh, *I'lām al-sājid bi aḥkām al-masājid* (Cairo 1384/1964–6).

STUDIES AND LATER TRAVEL ACCOUNTS

'Abd al-Wahhāb, Ḥasan, *Tārīkh al-masājid al-athariyya* (Cairo 1946).

'Abd al-Wahhāb, Ḥasan, 'Tawqī'āt al-Ṣunnā' 'alā āthār Miṣr al-islāmiyya', *Bulletin de l'Institut d'Egypte*, XXXVI (1953–4), pp. 553–8.

'Abd al-Wahhāb, Ḥasan, 'al-Āthār al-manqūla wa 'l-muntaḥala fī 'l-'imāra 'l-islāmiyya', *Bulletin de l'Institut d'Egypte*, XXXVIII/1 (1955–6), pp. 243–3.

'Abd al-Wahhāb, Ḥasan, 'Ṭarz al-'imāra al-islāmiyya fī rīf Miṣr', *Bulletin de l'Institut d'Egypte*, XXXVIII/2 (1956–7), pp. 5–18.

Abū 'l-'Amāyim, Muḥammad, 'al-Mi'dhana al-qibliyya wa mā ḥawlahā min al-āthār khārij bāb al-qarāfa bi 'l-Qāhira', *Annales Islamologiques*, XXXIV/2 (2000), pp. 45–89.

Aḥmad, Yūsuf, *Jāmi' sayyidnā 'Amr ibn al-'Āṣ* (Cairo 1917).

——, *Jāmi' Ibn Ṭūlūn* (Cairo 1917).

Ali Ibrahim, Laila, 'The Transitional Zone of Domes in Cairene Architecture', *Kunst des Orients*, x 1/2 (1975), pp. 5–23.

——, Laila, 'The Great Hanqah of the Emir Qawsun in Cairo', with two appendices by J. M. Rogers, *Mitteilungen des Deutschen Archäologischen Instituts, Abteilung Kairo*, 30, 1 (1974), pp. 37–64.

Amīn, Muḥammad Muḥ., *al-Awqāf wa 'l-ḥayāt al-ijtimā'iyya fī Miṣr (648–923/1250–1517)* (Cairo 1980).

Amin, Muhammad Muh. and Laila Ali Ibrahim, *Architectural Terms in Mamluk Documents (648–923H/1250–1517)* (Cairo 1990).

Al-Asad, Muhammad, 'The Mosque of Muhammad Ali in Cairo', *Muqarnas*, 9 (1992), pp. 39–55.

——, 'The Mosque of al-Rifa'i in Cairo', *Muqarnas*, 10 (1993), pp. 108–24.

Asil, Miguel, 'The Pharos of Alexandria' (Summary of an essay in Spanish), *Proceedings of the British Academy*, XIX (1933).

'Azab, Khālid Muḥammad, *Fuwa, madīnat al-masājid wa 'amā'iruhā al-dīniyya wa 'l-madaniyya* (Cairo 1989).

Bakhoum, Dina, 'Umm al-Sultan Sha'ban before and after Creswell', in Bernard O'Kane (ed.), *Creswell Photographs Re-examined*, pp. 99–120.

Bates, Ülkü, 'Evolution of Tile Revetment

in Ottoman Cairo', in *First International Congress on Turkish Tiles and Ceramics* (Istanbul 1989), pp. 39–58.

Behrens-Abouseif, Doris, 'The Lost Minaret of Shajarat ad-Durr at her Complex in the Cemetery of Sayyida Nafisa', *Mitteilungen des Deutschen Archäologischen Instituts Abteilung Kairo*, 39 (1983), pp. 1–16.

——, *The Minarets of Cairo* (Cairo 1985, repr. 1987).

——, *Egypt's Adjustment to Ottoman Rule: Institutions, Waqf and Architecture in Cairo (16th & 17th centuries)* (Cologne/New York 1994).

——, 'Muhandis, Shadd, Mu'allim: Note on the Building Craft in the Mamluk Period', *Der Islam*, LXXII/2 (1995), pp. 293–309.

——, 'Notes sur l'architecture musulmane d'Alexandrie', in Christian Décobert and Jean-Yves Empereur (eds), *Alexandrie Médiévale 1* (Cairo 1998), pp. 101–14.

——, 'The Islamic History of the Lighthouse of Alexandria', *Muqarnas*, 23 (2006), pp. 1–14.

——, *Cairo of the Mamluks: A History of the Architecture and its Culture* (London 2007).

——, with L. Fernandes, 'Sufi Architecture in Early Ottoman Cairo', *Annales Islamologiques*, XX (1984), pp. 103–14.

Bierman, Irene A., *Writing Signs: The Fatimid Public Text* (Berkeley 1998).

—— (ed.), *Writing Identity in Medieval Cairo*, UCLA Near East Center Colloquium Series (Los Angeles 1995).

Bloom, Jonathan, 'The Mosque of al-Hakim in Cairo', *Muqarnas*, 1 (1983), pp. 15–36.

——, 'Five Minarets in Upper Egypt', *Journal of the Society of Architectural Historians*, 43/2 (May 1984), pp. 162–7.

——, *The Minaret: Symbol of Islam* (Oxford 1989).

——, *Arts of the City Victorious: Islamic Art and Architecture in Fatimid North Africa and Egypt* (London 2007).

Bourgoin, J., 'Précis de l'Art Arabe et Matériaux pour servir à l'Histoire, à la Théorie et la Technique des Arts de l'Orient Musulman', (Paris 1892).

Bulletin du Comité de Conservation des Monuments de l'Art Arabe : Procès Verbaux et Rapports (Cairo 1882–1953).

Colloque international sur l'histoire du Caire (Cairo 1972).

Coste, Pascal, *Architecture arabe des monuments du Caire* (Paris 1839).

Creswell, K.A.C., *A Brief Chronology of the Muhammadan Monuments of Egypt to A.D. 1517* (Cairo 1919).

——, 'The Evolution of the Minaret with Special Reference to Egypt I–III', *Burlington Magazine*, XLVIII (1926), pp. 134–40, 252–8, 290–8.

——, *Early Muslim Architecture: Umayyads, Early ʿAbbāsids and Ṭūlūnids*, 2 vols (Oxford 1932–40).

——, *MAE: Muslim Architecture of Egypt*, 2 vols (Oxford 1952–9, repr. New York 1978).

—— and James Allan, *A Short Account of Early Muslim Architecture* (Aldershot 1989).

Dalīl al-āthār al-islāmiyya bi-madīnat al-Qāhira (Survey of the Islamic Monuments of Cairo), ed. Jāb Allāh ʿAlī Jāb Allāh, Ministry of Culture (Cairo 2000).

Description de l'Égypte par les Savants de l'Expedition Française (Etat Moderne) (Paris 1812).

Diez, Ernst, 'Manāra', in *Encyclopaedia of Islam*, 1st edn (Leiden and London 1913–36).

Dodd, E.C. and S. Khairallah, *The Image of the Word: A Study of Kuranic Verses in Islamic Architecture*, 2 vols (Beirut 1981).

Ebers, Georg, *Aegypten in Bild und Wort*, 2 vols (Leipzig 1880).

Ettinghausen, Richard, 'Hilāl', in *Encyclopaedia of Islam*, 2nd edn. (Leiden 1960).

——, 'Arabic Epigraphy: Communication or Symbolic Affirmation?', in J. Bacharach and D.K. Kouymijian (eds), *Studies in Honor of George Miles* (Beirut 1974), pp. 297–317.

Finster, Barbara, 'Die Mosaiken der Umayyadenmoschee von Damaskus, *Kunst des Orient*, 7(1970–1), pp. 80–141.

Flury, Samuel, *Die Ornamente der Hakim- und Ashar-Moschee* (Heidelberg 1912).

Frith, Francis, *Egypt, Sinai and Palestine* (London n.d.).

Garcin, Jean-Claude, 'L'Insertion sociale de Shaʿrani dans le milieu Cairote', in *Colloque international sur l'histoire du Caire*, pp. 159–68.

De Gleon, Delort, *La Rue du Caire à l'Exposition Universelle de 1889* (Paris 1889).

De Prangey, Girault and Joseph Philibert, *Monuments Arabes d'Egypte, de Syrie et d'Asie Mineure : Dessinés et Mesurés de 1842 à 1845* (Paris 1846).

Goettlicher, Arvid, *Materialien fuer ein Corpus der Schiffsmodelle im Altertum* (Mainz 1978).

Gottheil, J.H., 'The Origin and History of the Minaret', *Journal of the American Oriental Society*, XIII (1909–10), pp. 132–54.

Grabar, Oleg, 'The Earliest Islamic Commemorative Structures', *Ars Orientalis*, 6 (1967), pp. 6–47.

Hampikian, N., 'Restoration of the al-Salihiyya Madrasa Minaret in Cairo', in *Erhalten historisch bedeutsamer Bauwerke*, 14 (1996), pp. 175–80.

——, 'Al-Salihiyya Complex through Time', *Abhandlungen des Deutschen Archäologischen Instituts Kairo, Islamische Reihe*, 9 (Heidelberg 2004).

——, 'The Minaret of the Salihiyya Madrasa', in W. Mayer and P. Speiser (eds), *A Future for the Past: Restorations in Islamic Cairo 1973–2004*, pp. 129–38.

——, 'Recent Discoveries Concerning the Fatimid Palaces Uncovered during the Conservation Works of the al-Salihiyya Complex', in M. Barrucand (ed.), *L'Egypte*

Fatimide, son art et son histoire (Paris 1999), pp. 649–757.

Hillenbrand, R., 'Manāra, Manār', *Encyclopaedia of Islam*, 2nd edn (Leiden 1991).

Howard, I.K.A., 'The Development of the *Adhān* and *Iqāma* of the *Ṣalāt* in Early Islam', *Journal of Semitic Studies*, XXVI/1 (1981), pp. 219–28.

El-Hawary, Hassan Mohammad, 'Trois Minarets Fatimides à la Frontière Nubienne', *Bulletin de l'Institut d'Egypte*, XVII (1934–5), pp. 141–53.

Hay, Robert, *Illustrations of Cairo* (London 1840).

Herz, Max, *La Mosquée el-Rifaʿi au Caire* (Cairo 1912).

Herz, Max, *La Mosquée de Ganem El-Bahlaouan au Caire* (Cairo 1908).

Hoyland, Robert (with a contribution by Venetia Porter), 'Epigraphy', in *Encyclopaedia of the Qurʾan*, vol. 2 (Leiden/Boston 2002), pp. 25b–41a.

Ibrāhīm, ʿAbd al-Latīf, 'Wathīqat al-amīr Qarāqūjā al-Ḥasanī', *Majallat Kuliyyat al-Ādāb, Jāmiʿat al-Qāhira*, 18/2 (December 1956), pp. 183–205.

Ihsanoğlu, Ekmeleddin, et al., *Egypt as viewed in the 19th Century* (Istanbul 2001).

Jenkins, Marylin, 'Mamluk Underglaze-Painted Pottery: Foundations for Future Study', *Muqarnas*, 2 (1984), pp. 95–114.

Jomard, M., 'Description de la Ville et de la Citadelle du Kaire, Explication du Plan de la Ville du Kaire et de la Citadelle', in *Description de l'Égypte (Etat Moderne)*, XVIII/2 (Paris 1812), pp. 113–288.

Juynboll, Th. W., 'Adhān', in *Encyclopaedia of Islam*, 2nd edn (Leiden 1986).

Kahle, Paul, *Der Leuchtturm von Alexandria* (Stuttgart 1930).

——, *Manārat al-Iskandariyya al-qadīma fī khayāl al-ẓill al-miṣrī* (Stuttgart 1928).

Karim, Chahinda, 'The Mamluk Mosque of Amir Husayn: A Reconstruction', in Bernard O'Kane (ed.), *Creswell Photographs Re-examined*, pp. 163–85.

Karnouk, Gloria, 'Form and Ornament of the Cairene Baḥrī Minbar', *Annales Islamologiques*, XVII (1981), pp. 113–41.

Kessler, Christel, 'Funerary Architecture within the City', *Colloque International sur l'Histoire du Caire (1969)* (Cairo 1972), pp. 257–67.

——, *The Carved Masonry Domes of Mediaeval Cairo* (Cairo/London 1976).

——, 'The "Imperious Reasons" that Flawed the Minaret-flanked Setting of Sultan Ḥasan's Mausoleum in Cairo', in *Damaszener Mitteilungen*, XI (1999), pp. 307–16.

King, David A., 'On the role of the Muezzin and the Muwaqqit in Medieval Islamic Society', in F.J. Ragep and S.P. Ragep (eds), *Tradition, Transmission, Transformation: Proceedings of Two Conferences on*

Premodern Science Held at the University of Oklahoma (Leiden 1996), pp. 285–346.

Kriss, Rudolf, *Volksglaube im Bereich des Islam* (Wiesbaden 1960).

Lamᶜī, Muṣṭafā Ṣāliḥ, *al-Madīna al-munawwara, taṭawwuruhā al-ᶜimrānī wa turāthuhā al-miᶜmārī* (Beirut 1981).

Lane, E.W., *An Account of the Manners and Customs of Modern Egyptians* (London 1895, repr. The Hague, London and Cairo 1978).

Lane-Poole, S., *The Story of Cairo* (London 1906).

Libay, Karl Ludwig, *Aegypten, Reisebilder aus dem Orient* (Wien 1857, Dušan Magdolen, repr. and ed., Prague 2006).

Little, Donald P., 'Notes on Aytamiš, a Mongol Mamluk', in *Die islamische Welt zwischen Mittelalter und Neuzeit: Festschrift für Hans Robert Roemer zum 65. Geburtstag* (Beirut 1979), pp. 387–401.

Mackenzie, Neil D., *Ayyubid Cairo: A Topographical Study* (Cairo 1992).

Mahmud, Ahmad, *The Mosque of ᶜAmr Ibn al-ᶜAs* (Cairo 1917).

Makar, Farida, 'Al-Sultaniyya' (MA thesis, American University in Cairo,1972).

Abbé Le Mascrier, *Description de l'Égypte (...) composée sur les mémoires de M. De Maillet* (Paris 1735).

Mayer, Wolfgang, 'Conservation of the Photographic Archive of the Comité de Conservation des Monuments de l'Art Arabe', in W. Mayer and Philipp Speiser (eds), *A Future for the Past: Restoration in Islamic Cairo 1973–2004* (Mainz 2007), pp. 157–60.

Mayer W. and Speiser P. (eds), *A Future for the Past: Restorations in Islamic Cairo 1973–2004* (Mainz 2007).

Meinecke, Michael, 'Die Mamlukischen Faiencemosaikdekorationen: Eine Werkstätte aus Täbriz in Kairo (1330–55)', *Kunst des Orients*, XI (1976–7), pp. 85–143.

——, *Mamlukische Architektur in Ägypten und Syrien*, 2 vols (Mainz 1993).

Migeon, Gaston, *Le Caire, le Nile et Memphis* (Paris 1906).

The Mosques of Egypt, Ministry of Waqf, 2 vols (Cairo 1949).

Naser e-Khosrou, *Safarname: Ein Reisebericht aus dem Orient des 11, Jahrhunderts*, trans. Seyfeddin Najmabadi and Siegfried Weber (Munich 1993).

O'Kane, Bernard (ed.), *Creswell Photographs Re-examined: New Perspectives on Islamic Architecture* (Cairo 2009).

—— et al., *Documentation of the Inscriptions in the Historic Zone in Cairo*, The Egyptian Antiquities Project of the American Research Center in Egypt (ARCE) under USAID Grant N. 263-0000-G-00-3089-00.

Ormos, István, *Max Herz Pasha (1856–1919): His Life and Career*, 2 vols, Institut Français d'Archéologie Orientale (Cairo 2009).

Pascale Coste: Toutes les Egypte, exhibition catalogue (Marseille 1998).

Pauty, Edmond, 'Le Plan de la Mosquée As Salih Talayi au Caire', *Bulletin de la Société Royale de Geographie d'Egypte* (1931), pp. 277–368.

Prisse d'Avennes, *L'Art arabe d'après les monuments du Kaire: Depuis le VIIe siècle jusqu'à la fin du XVIIIe*, 3 vols (Paris 1869–77).

Prost, Claude M., 'Les Revêtements céramiques dans les monuments musulmans de l'Egypte', Mémoires publiés par les Membres de l'Institut Français d'Archéologie Orientale du Caire (Cairo 1916).

Ragib, Y., 'Un oratoire fatimide au sommet du Muqattam', *Studia Islamica*, 65 (1987), pp. 51–68.

Ramaḍān, Ḥusayn Muṣṭafā Ḥusayn, 'Munshaʾat Azdumur min ᶜAlī Bāy, dirāsa athariyya wathāʾiqiyya', *Majallat Kulliyat al-Āthār*, 5 (1991), pp. 179–235.

Roberts, David, *The Holy Land: Syria, Idumea, Arabia, Egypt and Nubia*, 6 vols (London 1842–9).

Roberts, David, *Egypt and Nubia*, 3 vols (London 1846–9).

Rogers, J. M., 'Seljuk Influence in the Monuments of Cairo', *Kunst des Orients*, VII (1970–1), pp. 40–68.

——, 'Evidence for Mamluk-Mongol Relations', in *Colloque international sur l'histoire du Caire (1969)* (1972), pp. 385–403.

Saʿd, Fārūq, *Khayāl al-ẓill al-ᶜarabī* (Beirut 1993).

al-Saʿīd, Labīb, *al-Adhān waʾl Muʾadhdhinūn* (Cairo 1970).

Sanders, Paula, 'Writing Identity in Medieval Cairo', in Irene A. Bierman (ed.), *Writing Identity in Medieval Cairo*, pp. 23–79.

Schacht, Joseph, 'Ein Archaischer Minaret-typ in Ägypten und Anatolien', *Ars Islamica*, V (1938), pp. 46–54.

Shāfiᶜī, Farīd, 'Miʾdhanat masjid ibn Ṭūlūn – raʾy fī takwīnihā al-miᶜmārī', *Majallat Kulliyat al-Ādāb, Jāmiᶜat al-Qāhira*, XIV/1 (1952) pp. 167–82.

——, 'West Islamic Influences on Architecture in Egypt', *Majallat Kulliyat al-Ādāb, Jāmiᶜ at al-Qāhira*, XVI/1 (1954), pp. 1–49.

——, 'The Mashhad al-Juyushi: Archeological Notes and Studies', *Studies in Islamic Art and Architecture in Honour of Professor K.A.C. Creswell* (Cairo 1965).

——, *al-ᶜImāra 'l-ᶜarabiyya fī miṣr al-islāmiyya (358-21/639-969)* (Cairo 1970).

Speiser, Philipp, *Die Geschichte der Erhaltung arabischer Baudenkmäler in Ägypten* (Heidelberg 2001).

Swelim, Tarek, 'An Interpretation of the Mosque of Sinan Pasha in Cairo', *Muqarnas*, 10 (1993), 98–107.

——, 'The Minaret of Ibn Tulun Reconsidered', in Doris Behrens-Abouseif (ed.), *The Cairo Heritage: Essays in Honor of Laila Ali Ibrahim* (Cairo/New York 2000), pp. 77–92.

Thiersch, Hermann, *Pharos, Antike, Islam und Occident; ein Beitrag zur Architekturgeschichte* (Leipzig 1909).

ᶜUthmān, Majdī ᶜAbd al-Jawwād ᶜIlwān, 'al-Maᶜādhin al-bāqiya bi 'l-diltā ḥattā niyāhat al-ᶜaṣr al-ᶜuthmānī' (MA thesis, University of Tanta, 2008).

Van Berchem, Max, *Materiaux pour un Corpus Inscriptionum Arabicarum* (Cairo 1894).

Volait, Mercedes, *Architectes et Architectures de l'Egypte Moderne 1830–1950 : Genèse et Essor d'une Expertise Locale* (Paris 2005).

Warner, Nicholas, *The Monuments of Historic Cairo: A Map and Descriptive Catalogue* (Cairo and New York 2005).

——, *The True Description of Cairo: A Sixteenth Century Venetian View*, 3 vols (Oxford 2006).

Wiet, Gaston, *Matériaux pour un Corpus Inscriptionum Arabicarum*, Part 1, Egypte, II (Cairo 1929–30).

——, 'Sultan Hasan', *La Revue du Caire* (June 1938), pp. 86–109.

——, *Muhammed Ali et les Beaux Arts* (Cairo 1946).

Williams, John Alden, 'The Monuments of Ottoman Cairo', in *Colloque international sur l'Histoire du Caire* (Cairo 1969), pp. 453–66.

INDEX